Strategic Performance Management

A managerial and behavioural approach

André de Waal

palgrave
macmillan

© André de Waal 2007

First published 2007 by
PALGRAVE MACMILLAN
Houndmills, Basingstoke, Hampshire RG21 6XS and
175 Fifth Avenue, New York, N.Y. 10010
Companies and representatives throughout the world

PALGRAVE MACMILLAN is the global academic imprint of the Palgrave Macmillan division of St. Martin's Press, LLC and of Palgrave Macmillan Ltd. Macmillan® is a registered trademark in the United States, United Kingdom and other countries. Palgrave is a registered trademark in the European Union and other countries.

ISBN-13: 978-1-4039-9884-2
ISBN-10: 1-4039-9884-1

This book is printed on paper suitable for recycling and made from fully managed and sustained forest sources. Logging, pulping and manufacturing processes are expected to conform to the environmental regulations of the country of origin.

A catalogue record for this book is available from the British Library.

A catalog record for this book is available from the Library of Congress.

10   9   8   7   6   5   4   3   2
16 15 14 13 12 11 10 09 08

Printed and bound in China

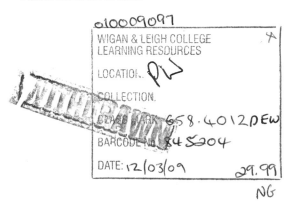

Contents

Figures

Tables

Acronyms and abbreviations

BPM	business performance management
BSC	balanced scorecard
CPM	corporate performance management
CPO	chief performance officer
CSF	critical success factor
DSS	decision support system
EBIT	earnings before interest and taxes
EFQM	European Foundation for Quality Management
EIS	executive information system
EPM	enterprise performance management
ERP	enterprise resource planning
EVA™	economic value added
FTE	full time equivalent
HRM	human resources management
IAS/FRS	international accounting standards/financial reporting
ICT	information and communication technology
KPI	key performance indicator
MIS	management information system
NPM	new public management
OLAP	online analytical processing
PAM	performance alignment model
PMA	performance management analysis
RIW	Returner in the Workplace
ROI	return on investment
SME	small and medium-sized enterprises
STAP	strategy, action and protection
TQM	total quality management
XML	EXtensible Mark-up Language
XMLR	EXtensible Business Report Language

A tale of two farmers

On a fine day, Farmer John was crossing Farmer Pete's field when he saw this gorgeous red and white cow. "That one I must have," he thought.

He rang at the door of Farmer Pete's house, and said: "Dear Pete, I would like to buy that red and white cow of yours. How much is she?"

Farmer Pete thought for a while, and replied: "This cow, Daisy, is indeed a fine animal so she's worth a lot of money. I'm selling her for 1500 euros."

"Dear me! That is a lot of money," Farmer John said, clearly surprised. "Let me think about it."

A week later, Farmer John returned to Pete's doorstep, and said: "I must say, Pete, I have given it some thought, and I have decided I want to buy Daisy after all."

"Great," Farmer Pete responded, "but as you might expect, the price has gone up. She now costs 1750 euros."

Farmer John was not too happy with the price increase but, determined as he was, agreed to pay the new price. He took out his wallet and handed over the money to Farmer Pete.

A week later, Farmer Pete called on Farmer John. "Say, John, I regret selling Daisy to you. Can I buy her back?"

"Well, if you must," Farmer John replied, "for 2000 euros she's yours again."

Farmer Pete paid promptly and happily walked away with Daisy.

A week later, Farmer John was back at Pete's: "It's a funny thing Pete, but now I have regrets about selling Daisy. I would like to buy her back."

"Fine with me," Farmer Pete responded. "I'm selling her for 2250 euros."

They carried on like this until Daisy was sold at a price of 3500 euros. Then, on a bad day, the cow died. The two farmers got together to ponder Daisy's unhappy fate.

"It's a shame she is dead. Such a fine animal," Farmer John said.

"Indeed it is," Farmer Pete replied. "Luckily, we have both made a nice profit on her."

Part I

Introducing strategic performance management

1

Introduction

Something tells us that the way in which the two farmers in the tale are evaluating their performance is not quite right. It seems that they were either measuring the wrong thing or measuring it in the wrong manner, or perhaps even both. We could argue that these farmers are old-fashioned and behind the times and that modern-day organisations do not make the same interpretative mistakes as these two men. However, we could also argue otherwise.

1.1 AN AGE OF EXTREME COMPETITION

First of all, here are some facts from the business world you may not be aware of:

- More shareholder value has been destroyed in the last five years as a result of mismanagement, wrong decisions, and bad execution of strategy than through all the recent compliance scandals combined. A recent Booz Allen Hamilton survey among 1200 large companies showed that at the 360 worst performers, 87 per cent of the value destroyed was caused by strategic missteps and operational ineffectiveness. Only 14 per cent could be attributed to compliance failures or poor oversight of the corporate boards (Kocourek et al., 2005).
- The average time a CEO or managing director occupies his/her position is continually decreasing, from an average of more than ten years 20 years ago to two and a half years nowadays. The main reason for his/her dismissal is underperforming, not ethical issues or illegal behaviour (Lucier et al., 2005).
- More than 50 per cent of managers take decisions based on gut feeling, not on hard facts, and 36 per cent have "black boxes" in the organisation, areas of which they have little knowledge (SAS Institute Nederland, 2002).
- Despite the widespread conviction that employee satisfaction and

employee loyalty have a positive effect on customer satisfaction and loyalty, and thereby increase the company's turnover and profitability, four out of ten organisations do not actively stimulate employee loyalty (Manpower, 2002).

- The rate at which companies lose their leadership positions in their industry, the so-called topple rate, has doubled in the last 20 years. The rate at which new companies enter the Standard & Poor's 500 and old respectable firms disappear from this list has almost doubled in the last 50 years. Only 40 per cent of Fortune 500 companies in 1980 are still on that list today. The average life span of an organisation, irrespective of its size, is now 12.5 years (Rooij, 1996; Foster and Kaplan, 2001; Huyett and Viguerie, 2005).
- Seventy per cent of the population consider their government to be not very effective and therefore are losing trust in it. Almost the same percentage of civil service officials are of the same opinion. Public trust in for-profit companies has declined from 60 per cent in 1980 to 40 per cent in 2000, while only 28 per cent of the population trusts business leaders to tell the truth, which is still 10 per cent higher than the trust in politicians (Morton, 2003; McKinsey, 2005).
- Return rates and warranty costs are dramatically rising while at the same time customer satisfaction levels are steadily decreasing, a strong indication of the deteriorating quality of products (Kleiner, 2005).
- Of recent mergers and acquisitions, only 17 per cent are reported to have added value to the combined company, 30 per cent produced no discernible difference, and 53 per cent actually destroyed value (KPMG, 1999).
- The majority of companies that get into a crisis find themselves in this situation because of internal factors, of which dysfunctional management (48 per cent of the cases) and inadequate management information systems (42 per cent) are the most common causes (Eyck van Heslinga, 2002).
- Most companies operate well below their true capabilities. It was calculated that on average companies can reach productivity levels of up to 85 per cent. Productivity can never be 100 per cent as companies always spend time on non-value adding activities (like training and meetings). In practice, enterprises have an average productivity of 61 per cent of their optimum capacity. The causes of this reduced productivity are insufficient management planning and control (40 per cent), inadequate supervision (32 per cent), ineffective communication (9 per cent), poor working morale (8 per cent), inappropriately qualified workforce (7 per cent), and information technology-related problems (4 per cent). This comes down to a staggering 87 working days lost per person per year (Proudfoot Consulting, 2003, 2004).

What do these facts have in common? They all indicate that organisations, both profit and nonprofit, are starting to collapse under the increasing pressure of demands placed on them by competitors, stakeholders, legislators, the investment community, and stakeholders in general. It is said that this is the age of extreme competition in which the combined forces of global competition, technology, interconnectivity, and economic liberalization make life for companies tougher than ever before (Huyett and Viguerie, 2005). Ever since the 1980s, business writers have been claiming that the world was getting more dynamic, turbulent, unpredictable, and competitive. Jack Welch, former CEO of General Electric, once said that the 1980s would be a "white-knuckle" decade of intensifying competition and that the 1990s would be tougher still. From a business point of view, in retrospect the 1990s were easy compared with today where businesses have to compete in a highly complex and constantly changing world. Nowadays, many trends and developments are fundamentally reshaping the global business economy. The most important ones are:

- *Globalisation*. In the so-called borderless economy, competition can literally come from every corner of the world. The globalisation of companies and brands makes it difficult to determine the home country and home market of many corporations. Companies have to be able to do business in many different countries with many different cultures. Cultural differences increasingly cause problems in doing business and marketing on a worldwide scale. Global mergers create corporations that are rich and powerful and have a turnover greater than the gross national product of many individual countries. This often causes tension between a company and the country it operates in, as the latter sees the company as an invader. Concurrently, regional economic power blocs, like the growing European Union, NAFTA, and ASEAN, create strong economic bases around the world. Manufacturing capacity continues to shift from Western economies to nations with cheaper labour (Rosen, 2000; Lawrence, 2002; Sadler, 2002; Bakker et al., 2004; Light, 2005; Starbuck, 2005).
- *Impact of new technology*. Increased connectivity, caused by the increasing possibilities and the rapidly decreasing costs of telecommunications and the explosive growth of Internet use, have created what is known as "the death of distance": distance is no longer an issue for doing business. Strict office hours are abandoned because people can be reached 24 hours a day. A side-effect of this development is that it makes it difficult for businesses to discern traditional consumer groups in specific countries: people can order and ship products from any place to anywhere in the world. At the same time, the interconnectivity causes identity problems because people find it increasingly difficult to identify themselves with a certain group. The rate at which new technology is invented and put to use seems to be still accelerating, giving rise to new possibilities and at the same time new unforeseen threats. The only way for many companies to cope with this is to merge or forge strong bonds with former competitors and suppliers. New materials and new manufacturing techniques, like nanotechnology, have the

potential to disrupt complete industries (Rosen, 2000; Sadler, 2002; Malone, 2003; Bakker et al., 2004; Light, 2005).

■ *Rebound of Asian markets and ascension of China.* The hard-working nature of people in the Asian world, their strong social and family relations, and their raised educational levels are a strong foundation for Asian economics. It is expected that the existing industrial overcapacity will grow even more in the years to come, and that the struggle for raw materials like steel will intensify as a result of that. China is on the way to becoming the world's largest economy of this century (Rosen, 2000; Lawrence, 2002; Pacek and Thorniley, 2004).

■ *The gap between the haves and have-nots.* The gap between those who have and those who have not is widening in many countries, as is the gap between rich and poor nations. The rich get richer, the poor get poorer. This increasingly causes tension between large groups of people and between nations, causing ethnic conflicts, wars and the rise of terrorism, eventually resulting in potential worldwide disruptive effects (Farashahi and Molz, 2004; Laudicina, 2005; Starbuck, 2005).

■ *Environment.* Global warming and environmental pollution will accelerate, creating economic and political conflicts within and between countries, causing fights for scarce resources like water (Rosen, 2000; Laudicina, 2005).

■ *Demography.* The population of developed countries is rapidly ageing: people live longer and their life expectancy is rising because of the advances in medical science and technology. At the same time, population growth is decreasing, making it impossible to maintain the economic growth rates of the last decades of the twentieth century. This will result in an increased struggle for the most valued employees, growing importance of hiring people from less-developed countries to supplement the national workforce, and decreased spending because of the high number of relatively poor pensioners (Martin, 2002; Laudicina, 2005; Light, 2005).

■ *Intangibles.* Falling capital costs have caused enormous efficiency gains in operational management. In fact, capital is no longer a scarce resource today. It is intangible resources such as the knowledge, skills and mentality of the workforce that are important. In a world in which innovation becomes more and more important, organisations increasingly rely on the ingenuity and resourcefulness of their people. The "knowledge economy" is truly here (Doz et al., 2001; Bassi and McMurrer, 2005; Creelman and Makhijani, 2005; Niven, 2005).

■ *Leadership.* The trends mentioned above require a new type of leader: a globally literate leader who can inspire people from many different backgrounds and cultural diversities, and who can adapt quickly to change and is able to take the organisation along. On top of that, the behaviour and attitude of this leader should be beyond reproach, and the leader should be able to continuously balance the interests of all company stakeholders (not just his/her own) and gain or regain their trust. Unfortunately, only a few people qualify as this type of leader (Rosen, 2000; Davidson, 2002; Trompenaars and Woolliams, 2003; Davies, 2005; Useem, 2005).

■ *Transparency and information*. The recent accountancy scandals and the subsequent new laws and regulations have dramatically increased the need for transparency in company results and operations. Analysts, banks, and shareholders as well as society have taken great interest in what an organisation is doing and fails to be doing. At the same time, the possibilities for generating data and management information have increased a thousandfold, causing the by now infamous "information overload." Governments can no longer control the flows of information and neither can top management inside the company. Customers can easily get comparative quality and price information on every kind of product and service (Martin, 2002; Waal, 2003; Light, 2005).

As it is the task of every manager to realise the goals of the organisation by achieving outstanding performance in the organisational unit he or she is responsible for, managers are working under great pressure to deal effectively with the aforementioned trends and developments. They are forced to:

> adapt faster and faster to growing international demands for flexibility and speed and to compete simultaneously on the basis of development cycle time, price, quality, flexibility, fast and reliable delivery, and after-sales support for their products.
>
> (Kasarda and Rondinelli, 1998)

As a result of the changes in industry and also the influence of significant changes in society, government agencies too are subject to change. They have to rapidly reshape themselves into nimble and flexible organisations which centre on serving the interests of citizens, a movement which is known as "new public management" (Zeppou and Sotirakou, 2002; Pollitt, 2003).

1.2 CURRENT TRENDS IN ORGANISATIONS

Contemporary trends in global competition, rapid technological developments and increased use of management information systems and the Internet, developments in planning and control and management thinking, and changing demographics are putting pressures on profit and nonprofit organisations. As a consequence, companies are having more and more difficulty in achieving sustained performance. They are forced to look for new management methods and to develop cutting-edge processes to deal with existing trends and developments. An extended literature study has identified the trends that are likely to consume a lot of management time in the next three to five years (Waal, 2003). It lists the following trends:

- *Development of an e-finance function.* An increase of e-business applications in the finance function is observed, to make the finance processes more efficient and effective.
- *Development of an enterprise intelligence function.* More and more organisations are developing an enterprise intelligence function, to streamline and coordinate all the internal and external information flows of the organisation.
- *Development of strategic skills.* Organisations increasingly develop the strategic skills of managers, so that they can function as true business partners.
- *Focus on behavioural aspects.* More and more attention is paid to the behavioural aspects of management and improvement initiatives. This is illustrated by the increased focus on change management aspects of major projects.
- *Focus on corporate governance.* Organisations are increasingly interested in questions of good, fair, and respectable management of the company, so the reputation of the firm is safeguarded.
- *Focus on cost reduction.* In addition to turnover growth, organisations are continuously looking for cost reduction opportunities.
- *Focus on creating value.* Organisations more and more focus on adding value to their organisations. They do this, for example, by introducing value-based management and Economic Value Added™.
- *Focus on intangibles.* There is growing attention for the reporting and subsequent management of intangibles such as knowledge, brands, and patents in order to track the more intangible side of the business.
- *Focus on integrity.* Organisations spend more time on ethical and integrity dilemmas than they did several years ago, again to safeguard the firm's reputation.
- *Focus on risk management.* Organisations show an increased interest in identifying and managing the material risks that they are running or will be running in the future while doing business.
- *Focus on turnover growth.* Despite difficult economic circumstances, organisations are initiating activities not only to reduce costs but also to improve their turnover growth. They are for example paying more attention to innovativeness.
- *Implementation of new laws and regulations.* Creating transparency for the outside world about the performance and risks of the company has become a major concern for organisations as a result of, for example, International Accounting Standards/Financial Reporting (IAS/FRS), Basel II, and Sarbanes-Oxley.
- *Improved implementation of projects.* Organisations increasingly focus on implementing and realising action plans from beginning to end to obtain maximum return, instead of developing multiple plans simultaneously which are not finished.
- *Making information flows more reliable.* Under pressure from recent accounting scandals, organisations have to make internal and external information flows more reliable.

- *More use of ICT.* Information and communication technology is increasingly used for the support of the business processes.
- *More benchmarking.* By comparing their own performance with that of competitors (external benchmarking) or other internal organisational units (internal benchmarking), organisations aim to improve their business processes and their performance.
- *More efficient budgeting.* Organisations are making the budgeting process more efficient by adapting or even removing it (also referred to as "beyond budgeting").
- *More forecasting of the future.* Organisations focus more on looking ahead than they used to do, to be prepared for future developments. They do this by introducing rolling forecasts which predict results six quarters in advance.
- *Outsourcing of processes.* Processes are increasingly outsourced to third parties in order to achieve cost benefits and quality improvement.
- *Use of more nonfinancial information.* Organisations show a growing interest in the reporting and management of nonfinancial indicators to better track their activities and performance. An example is the rise in balanced scorecard implementations.

These trends formed the basis of a questionnaire which was distributed on four occasions to Dutch and Belgian managers between 2002 and 2006. The respondents were asked to indicate which trends they regarded as the most important to them and their organisations, by rating them on a scale of 0 (not important) to 3 (very important). On the basis of the scores, the relative importance of each trend was calculated by adding up all points per development and dividing the total by the maximum number of points available (= number of filled-in questionnaires times 3 points). If for example a trend was regarded as very important by all respondents, it would get a relative importance of 100 per cent. The resulting relative importance scores for the 2005/06 questionnaire can be seen in Figure 1.1.

Figure 1.1 shows that almost all trends are considered important (50 to 70 per cent) to very important (more than 70 per cent) by the respondents. This indicates that modern organisations have to address many trends concurrently, which makes them very busy places. In order to deal more effectively with these trends, businesses are looking for effective management techniques. There is growing consensus that effective approaches to management offer organisations competitive advantage (Lawler et al., 1998). As a result, and in the wake of the landmark book *In Search of Excellence* (Peters and Waterman, 1982) and the recent bestsellers *Built to Last* (Collins and Porras, 1994) and *Good to Great* (Collins, 2001), managers have become increasingly interested in identifying the characteristics of high performance to help them in their quest for excellence (O'Reilly and Pfeffer, 2000).

An increasingly popular management technique in this respect is "strategic performance management." It has been calculated that new publications about strategic performance management have been appearing at a rate of

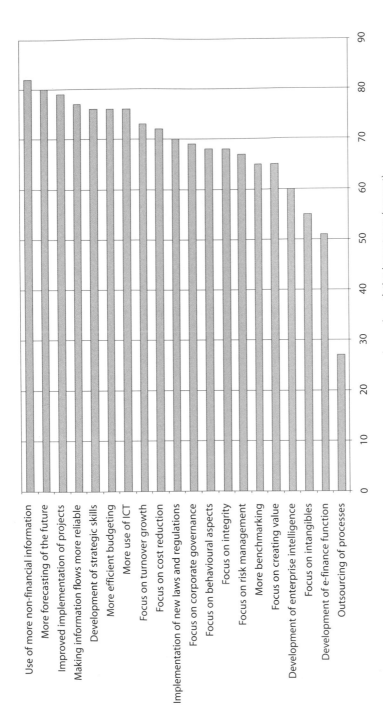

The chart shows the following items and their increasing relative importance (percent):

- Use of more non-financial information
- More forecasting of the future
- Improved implementation of projects
- Making information flows more reliable
- Development of strategic skills
- More efficient budgeting
- More use of ICT
- Focus on turnover growth
- Focus on cost reduction
- Implementation of new laws and regulations
- Focus on corporate governance
- Focus on behavioural aspects
- Focus on integrity
- Focus on risk management
- More benchmarking
- Focus on creating value
- Development of enterprise intelligence
- Focus on intangibles
- Development of e-finance function
- Outsourcing of processes

Figure 1.1 Current trends

one every five hours of every working day since 1994, and that there are now more than 12 million sites dedicated to this topic (Marr and Schiuma, 2002). This book describes how strategic performance management supports organisations in their pursuit of better performance. A well-designed performance management process stimulates managers to develop high-quality strategic plans, set ambitious targets, and track performance closely – all activities which help to achieve strategic objectives and consequently sustained value creation (Lobo et al., 2000). This book discusses new ideas and developments in the field of performance management which will help managers to improve the performance management process in their organisations.

1.3 HOW TO USE THIS BOOK

The aims of this book are to provide readers with an insight into the importance of strategic performance management for successful entrepreneurship, and to provide methods and techniques to implement strategic performance management and to make it work. Furthermore, the book aims to develop understanding and skills in handling the behavioural issues involved in strategic performance management. The text of *Strategic Performance Management* is based on material from my previous books, supplemented by much new material, which has been tried and tested during many university lectures and projects at organisations. After reading the book, readers will have an understanding of the theoretical and practical side of strategic performance management, including the following competencies:

- recognising and communicating the importance of strategic performance management for the success of the organisation
- analysing the quality and the intensity of use of the existing performance management system
- identifying the main challenges that an organisation faces during the improvement of its performance management system
- designing a high-quality performance management process and system
- promoting the behavioural aspects of strategic performance management; showing managers better ways of working with the performance management system
- discussing the latest developments in the field of strategic performance management.

The setup of this book is as follows. Chapter 2 starts with a short review of management control and information systems (the precursors of strategic performance systems) and of strategic performance management: the definition, the process, and its history. After that, the strategic performance management development cycle is introduced. This cycle, which consists of the various stages of the performance management process, is in this book used as a framework for Chapters 3–13. The various elements of the cycle are examined consecutively: designing a strategic management model, designing a strategic reporting model, and designing a perform-ance-driven behavioural model. Some of the subjects discussed are respon-sibility structure, critical success factors, key performance indicators, the balanced scorecard, information and communication technology, excep-tion and action reporting, performance-driven behaviour, competency management, performance management implementation, performance management in nonprofit organisations, and performance management in emerging countries.

Is this your organisation?

- Performance information is transparent, customised, and timely.
- Analysis of results are clear (*not only "what" but also "why"*).
- Management discussions (*vertically and horizontally*) are efficient.
- Management and employees understand and "think constructively" about the business processes.
- Swift (*corrective and preventative*) actions are taken if needed.
- "Everyone knows what to do."

If the answer to one or more of these statements is negative, there is a good chance that your performance management system needs to be improved.

Each chapter consists of two sections, theory and cases. In the theory section, the foundations of strategic performance management are discussed. In the case section, the theory is illustrated by one or more prac-tical cases. They describe how concepts discussed earlier in the chapter were applied at real-life organisations. The real-life cases are followed by a ficti-tious case study, in serial form, of a company named Ultra Violet Design (UVD). The reader is allowed into the world of UVD as it is trying to improve its strategic performance management system. Each time, the UVD case closes with a number of questions for the reader to ponder on. Each chapter starts with a short overview of the chapter's objectives, and ends with a summary of the main points of the chapter, to provide the reader with a quick overview.

I thank all the case companies for the opportunity they gave me to learn from them and to pass these lessons on to the readers of this book. And, as with each of my books, I am greatly indebted to my wife Linda who has gone "beyond the call of duty" to make the original manuscript into a readable document and enjoyable book.

Key points

☑ The age of *extreme competition*, in which forces of global competition, technology, interconnectivity, and economic liberalization combine, makes life for organisations tougher than ever before.

☑ It is the task of every manager (profit, nonprofit, and government) to realise organisational goals by achieving outstanding performance.

☑ Effective approaches to management offer organisations competitive advantage. An increasingly popular management technique is strategic performance management.

☑ A well-designed performance management process stimulates managers to develop high-quality strategic plans, set ambitious targets, and track performance closely – all activities which help to achieve strategic objectives and sustained value creation.

References

Bakker, H.J.C., Babeliowsky, M.N.F. and Stevenaar, F.J.W. (2004) *The Next Leap. Achieving growth through global networks, partnerships and cooperation*. London: Cyan Books.

Bassi, L. and McMurrer, D. (2005) What to do when people are your most important asset. *Handbook of Business Strategy*, 219–24.

Collins, J. (2001) *Good to Great: Why some companies make the leap ... and others don't*. London: Random House.

Collins, J.C. and Porras, J.I. (1994) *Built to Last: Successful habits of visionary companies*. New York: Harper Business.

Creelman, J. and Makhijani, N. (2005) *Mastering Business in Asia: Succeeding with the balanced scorecard*. Singapore: Wiley Asia.

Davidson, H. (2002) *The Committed Enterprise. How to make vision and values work*. Oxford: Butterworth Heinemann.

Davies, H. (2005) The twenty-first century manager book: working on (and on and on ...). In: C.L. Cooper (ed.), *Leadership and Management in the 21st Century: Business challenges of the future*. Oxford: Oxford University Press.

Doz, Y., Santos, J. and Williamson, P. (2001) *From Global to Metanational: How companies win in the knowledge economy*. Boston: Harvard Business School Press.

Eyck van Heslinga, H.C. van (2002) *Hands-on Crisis Management*. Deventer: Kluwer.

Farashahi, M. and Molz, R. (2004) A framework for multilevel organisational analysis in developing countries. *International Journal of Commerce and Management*, 14 (1), 59–78.

Foster, R. and Kaplan, S. (2001) *Creative Destruction: Why companies that are built to last underperform the market – and how to successfully transform them*. New York: Doubleday.

Huyett, W.I. and Viguerie, S.P. (2005) Extreme competition. *McKinsey Quarterly*, 1.

Kasarda, X. and Rondinelli, X. (1998) Innovative infrastructure for agile manufacturers. *Sloan Management Review*, Winter, 39 (2), 73.

Kleiner, A. (2005) Beware the product death cycle. *Strategy + Business*, 38, Spring.

Kocourek, P., Newfrock, J. and Van Lee, R. (2005) SOX rocks, but won't block shocks. *Strategy + Business*, 38, Spring.

KPMG (1999) *Mergers and Acquisitions Global Research Report*. London: KPMG.

Laudicina, P.A. (2005) *World out of Balance: Navigating global risks to seize competitive advantage*. New York: McGraw-Hill, Starbuck.

Lawler III, E.E., Mohrman, S.A. and Ledford Jr. G.E. (1998) *Strategies for High-Performance Organisations: The CEO report*. San Francisco: Jossey-Bass.

Lawrence, P. (2002) *The Change Game: How today's global trends are shaping tomorrow's companies*. London: Kogan Page.

Light, P.C. (2005) *The Four Pillars of High Performance: How robust organisations achieve extraordinary results*. New York: McGraw-Hill.

Lobo, C., Cochran, D. and Duda, J. (2000), Using axiomatic design to support the development of a balanced scorecard. In: A. Neely (ed.), *Performance Measurement: Past, present, and future*, 347–54. Cranfield: Centre for Business Performance, Cranfield University.

Lucier, C., Schuyt, R. and Tse, E. (2005) CEO succession 2004: the world's most prominent temp workers. *Strategy + Business*, 39, Summer.

Malone, T.W. (2003), Is empowerment just a fad? Control, decision making and IT. In: T.W. Malone, R. Laubacher and M.S. Scott Morton (eds), *Inventing the Organisations of the 21st Century*. Cambridge, Mass.: MIT Press.

Manpower (2002) *International Employee Loyalty Survey*. Manpower Inc., May 27

Marr, B. and Schiuma, G. (2002) Research challenges for corporate performance measurement: evidence from a citation analysis. In: A. Neely, A. Walters and R. Austin (eds), *Performance Measurement and Management: Research and action*. Cranfield: Cranfield School of Management.

Martin, C. (2002) *Managing for the Short-Term. The new rules for running a business in a day-to-day world*. New York: Currency Doubleday.

McKinsey (2005) *21minuten.nl*. The Netherlands: Research McKinsey.

Morton, C. (2003) *By the Skin of our Teeth: Creating sustainable organisations through people*. London: Middlesex University Press.

Niven, P.N. (2005) *Balanced Scorecard Diagnostics: Maintaining maximum performance*. New York: Wiley.

O'Reilly III, C.A. and Pfeffer, J. (2000) *Hidden Value: How great companies achieve extraordinary results with ordinary people*. Boston, Mass.: Harvard Business School Press.

Pacek, N. and Thorniley, D. (2004) *Emerging Markets: Lessons for business success and the outlook for different markets*. London: The Economist.

Peters, T. and Waterman, R. (1982) *In Search of Excellence*. Warner Books.

Pollitt, C. (2003) *The Essential Public Manager*. Manchester: Open University Press.

Proudfoot Consulting (2003) Missing millions: how companies mismanage their most valuable resource. *International Labour Productivity Study*, October.

Proudfood Consulting (2004) *International Labour Productivity Study*, www.proudfootconsulting.com

Rooij, E. de (1996) *A Brief Desk Research Study into the Average Life Expectancy of Companies in a Number of Countries*. Amsterdam: Stratix Consulting Group.

Rosen, R. (2000), *Global Literacies: Lessons on business leadership and national cultures*. New York: Simon & Schuster.

Sadler, P. (2002) *Building Tomorrow's Company: A guide to sustainable business success*. London: Kogan Page.

SAS Institute Nederland (2002) *Nederlandse topmanagers missen informatie uit eigen bedrijf bij strategische beslissingen*. SAS Nederland.

Starbuck, W.H. (2005), Four great conflicts of the twenty-first century. In: C.L. Cooper (ed.), *Leadership and Management in the 21st Century: Business challenges of the future*. Oxford: Oxford University Press.

Trompenaars, F. and Woolliams, P. (2003) *Business Across Cultures*. Chichester: Capstone.

Useem, J. (2005) From heroes to goats ... and back again? In: A. Leckey and J.C. Bogle (eds), *The Best Business Stories of the Year: 2004 edition*. New York: Vintage.

Waal, A.A. de (2003) *Ontwikkelingen en Trends in de Financiële Functie*. Deventer: Kluwer.

Zeppou, M. and Sotirakou, T. (2002) The stair model: a comprehensive approach for managing and measuring government performance in the post-modern era. In: A. Neely, A. Walters and R. Austin (eds), *Performance Measurement and Management: Research and action*. Cranfield: Cranfield School of Management.

2

Strategic performance management

This chapter examines first the predecessors of strategic performance management, namely management control and information systems, and then the history, development and advantages and disadvantages of strategic performance management systems.

Chapter objectives

- ☑ To provide the reader with an insight into the problems of current management information systems.
- ☑ To provide the reader with an insight into the need for and importance of performance management in creating a successful organisation.
- ☑ To enable the reader to study the subprocesses of the strategic performance management process and the strategic performance management development cycle.
- ☑ To teach the reader how to determine whether an organisation is ready for strategic performance management.

2.1 MANAGEMENT CONTROL AND INFORMATION SYSTEMS

To be successful in the long run, an organisation strives for organisational fitness. Organisational fitness is defined as an organisation's ability to adapt and survive in the ever-changing business environment, and is achieved through natural evolution, purposeful change, and continuous learning (Beer, 2003; Voelpel et al., 2004). To obtain organisational fitness, an organisation needs a clear and explicit management concept which is formulated by its most senior management (Bossert, 1993). This management concept is the basis for long-term development of the organisational strategy and the strategic objectives. The strategy has to be translated into business unit plans, budgets, and operational action plans at the lower organisational levels. The management concept needs to be supported by an unambiguous and well-organised planning and control cycle. In this cycle, clear feedback is given on the execution of the plans by means of a management control and information system. Having an effective planning and control cycle and management control and information system is essential for business success.

A management control and information system helps managers influence other members of the organisation in such a way that the organisation's mission and strategy are implemented, while simultaneously ensuring that resources are used effectively and efficiently (Anthony, 1965; Anthony et al., 1989; Zairi and Jarrar, 2000). A modern management control and information system distinguishes two components: the management control structure, which reflects which parts the system is composed of; and the management control process, which reflects what activities are involved in the system (Figure 2.1).

The management control structure is defined as the combination of the organisational structure (i.e. delegation of authority and responsibilities), the standards of performance measurement and evaluation, the infrastructure for the planning and control cycle, and the infrastructure for management information of an organisation. The management control process is defined as the activities undertaken by an organisation to set targets, allocate resources, evaluate performance, execute corrective actions, and realise targets. The manner in which the management control and information system is used by an organisation is referred to as the organisation's management style.

The management control and information system and the management style have to be formulated and organised in such a way as to support and advance the realisation of targets of all organisational units and of the organisation as a whole. It is essential that the management control and information system provides adequate management information. There are four ways in which an organisation uses management information:

- to keep scorecards, at regular intervals, usually as part of a standardised reporting process
- to improve the understanding of problem solving
- to align the business and direct learning in the organisation
- to legitimise decisions

(Simon et al., 1954; Vandenbosch, 1999; Lohman, 1999).

Performance management information, which is collected through performance measurement, is specifically intended for supporting decision-making processes to control the organisation (that is, not decision-making processes in general). The effectiveness of performance management information is determined by its contribution to organisational performance.

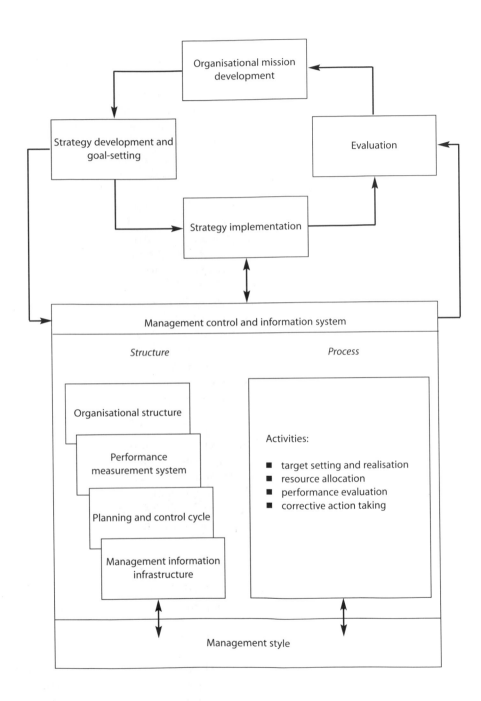

Figure 2.1 Relation between mission/strategy and the management control and information system

Source: based on Petri and Van der Vossen (1994).

In the literature performance measurement is defined as:

> the process of quantifying past action, in which measurement is the process of quantification and past action determines current performance. Organisations achieve their goals by satisfying their customers with greater efficiency and effectiveness than their competitors. Effectiveness refers to the extent to which customer requirements are met and efficiency is a measure of how economically the organisation's resources are utilized when providing a given level of customer satisfaction. A performance measure can now be defined as a metric used to quantify the efficiency and/or effectiveness of a past action.
>
> (Neely, 1998)

However, the term "measurement" is not quite correct because the process of performance measurement does not automatically lead to performance improvements. It should always initiate action through the use of appropriate measures. For this reason, performance *management* and performance *management* system are preferred (Rigas and Fan, 2000).

2.2 THE STRATEGIC PERFORMANCE MANAGEMENT PROCESS

Strategic performance management is defined as:

> the process where steering of the organisation takes place through the systematic definition of mission, strategy and objectives of the organisation, making these measurable through critical success factors and key performance indicators, in order to be able to take corrective actions to keep the organisation on track.
>
> (Waal, 2001)

Strategic performance management has many aims and purposes:

- helping to achieve sustainable improvements in organisational performance
- acting as a lever for change in developing a more performance-oriented culture
- increasing the motivation and commitment of employees
- enabling individuals to develop their abilities, increase their job satisfaction and achieve their full potential to their own benefit and that of the organisation as a whole
- enhancing the development of team cohesion and performance
- developing constructive and open relationships between individuals and their managers in a process of continuing dialogue which is linked to the work actually being done throughout the year
- providing opportunities for individuals to express their aspirations and expectations about their work

- creating continuous improvement
- supporting planning of organisational activities
- reinforcement of management rhetoric
- introducing pay for group performance
- influencing employees' attitudes
- performing benchmarks
- individual and organisational learning
- focus and justification of investments.
  (Armstrong and Baron, 1998; Martins, 2000; Simons, 2000).

The strategic performance management process consists of various subprocesses: strategy development, budgeting/target setting, execution/forecasting, performance measurement, performance review and incentive compensation. These integrated subprocesses create the perform-ance-driven behaviour of employees that is needed to become and stay world-class (Figure 2.2) (Waal, 2001).

- *Strategy development*. The strategy development process results in clear strategic objectives and action plans for measurable performance improvement. These are based on a thorough understanding of the

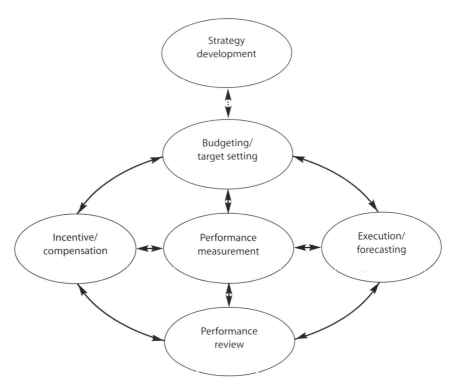

Figure 2.2 The subprocesses of the strategic performance management process

key value drivers that are aimed at achieving a competitive advantage. Business issues that drive organisations to improve the strategy development process are the lack of focus of the strategic plans and the low quality of the strategic targets. The strategy development process often focuses too much on meticulously calculating future financial results instead of planning for value creation. Strategic plans tend to look inward, resulting in unrealistic long-term views that do not take environmental developments into account and that focus insufficiently on competitive advantage and true differentiation. Strategic targets are often not clearly defined and can therefore not be appropriately measured. In addition, they are often over-optimistic and not accompanied by action plans on how to achieve the ambitiously set goals.

■ *Budgeting/target setting.* The budget/target setting process results in clear operational action plans for improving the key value drivers, for committing resources, and for setting financial targets for the coming year. Business issues that drive organisations to improve the budgeting/target setting process are the low reliability of the budget data and the too high level of detail of the budget. Because of the volatility of the business environment and the organisation itself and the early start of the budgeting process in the year, the targets in the budget tend to be out of date the moment it is set. This provokes manipulation by managers because fiddling the numbers often seems to be the only way to deal with the unrealistic targets. In addition, the budget tends to be too detailed with too many parameters on all management levels, and therefore takes too much time to prepare.

■ *Execution/forecasting.* During the execution/forecasting process organisational members execute the activities that have to lead to the desired results. Regular forecasts are made to predict whether the organisation is still on track or whether corrective and/or predictive actions are needed to solve current or predicted problems. Business issues that drive organisations to improve the execution/forecasting process are that activities and actions taken are not systematically tracked and evaluated. Also, forecasting is only infrequently done and as a consequence organisational members cannot behave in a proactive manner to deal with predicted problems and issues.

■ *Performance measurement.* The performance measurement process collects, processes (including consolidation), and distributes data and information to allow an effective execution of the other subprocesses. The information is represented in the form of critical success factors (CSFs) and key performance indicators (KPIs). A business issue that drives organisations to improve the performance measurement process is the low quality of management information and management reports. Often management information does not fully satisfy management's needs and does not stimulate proactive behaviour because the reports lack nonfinancial information, are not sufficiently exception-based, do not include corrective and preventive actions, and are incomplete because data collection is very time-consuming.

- *Performance review*. The performance review process periodically reviews actual performance, targets, and forecasts in order to ensure that timely preventive and corrective action is taken to keep the company on track. Business issues that drive organisations to improve the performance review process are the low quality of forecasts and bad timing of performance reviews. The added value of forecasts is relatively low because their accuracy is often insufficient, they are usually too financially oriented, they do not provide enough explanatory information about future issues, and it takes too much time to prepare them. Performance review meetings generally take place on a regular basis rather than as an exception when there really is a problem. As a result the performance reviews take up too much time when there are no problems in the organisation, and when there are real performance issues and problems the reviews are either not held or held too late.
- *Incentive compensation*. This process links strategic and operational actions for key value drivers, in a balanced way with compensation and benefits policies. The main business issue that drives organisations to improve the incentive compensation subprocess is that this process is not sufficiently aligned with the other subprocesses, therefore it does not reward the right performance-driven behaviour of organisational members.

It has to be noted that the strategic performance management process, in the context of a manager's work environment, resembles the planning and control cycle. The planning stage of the cycle starts after the long-term strategic objectives of the organisation have been formulated and the corresponding management information needs have been defined. The purpose of this stage is to translate strategic plans into tangible, short-term action plans for each business unit. Management has at its disposal the results of the previous period(s) and the analysis of these results. These are used to make an action plan for the next period. It is crucial for people to use the analysis of the preceding period to learn from incorrect assessments or mistakes.

Managers make use of a performance management system in the planning stage when they:

- take the performance management system analysis of the preceding period as the basis for setting financial and nonfinancial targets for the next period(s)
- set priorities for the targets because these can be conflicting
- determine which specific actions have to be taken to achieve these targets
- allocate resources on the basis of planned actions and targets
- discuss the action planning with superiors and colleagues

(Kloot, 1997; Mooraj et al., 1999; Vandenbosch, 1999).

Making action plans is followed by implementing these plans. The manager has to make sure that this is done efficiently. The primary tasks of the manager in the control stage, therefore, are to communicate clearly the strategy, targets and planned actions to all employees and to control their implementation. Additionally, the manager indicates which indicators need to be measured and the way in which this should be done.

Managers make use of a performance management system in the control stage when they:

- inform employees through the performance management system about the strategy, targets, planned actions and the results to be measured and reported
- motivate employees by regularly providing intermediate feedback via the performance management system on the organisation's results (Anthony and Govindarajan, 1995; Lynch and Cross, 1995).

The purpose of the measurement stage is to collect information on the results of activities so that management can determine if adjustment is required. The three basic steps of how people acquire and process information are determination of information needs, information seeking, and information use – each of which can be considered in terms of cognitive, emotional, and situational factors (Choo, 2000). Information needs arise when people experience cognitive gaps that hinder their progress and induce uncertainty. To bridge these gaps, they seek good, accessible information sources. During and after execution of activities, management makes sure that the organisation's results are collected and recorded in the performance management system. The performance management system is used to provide feedback (via screens or reports) to managers on the implemented action plans. The feedback is closely studied by management to identify areas for improvement or correction.

Managers make use of a performance management system in the measurement stage when they:

- collect information in the performance management system for feedback purposes
- study the results of the financial and nonfinancial targets and compare these with budget
- provide feedback via the performance management system to employees on the results and discuss these with them so that employees achieve the defined targets
- determine if there is a need for further analysis of the performance management system and which adjustments to the action plans are needed (Simons, 1995; Kaplan and Norton, 1996a; Kloot, 1997).

In the feedback stage, managers identify (based on the organisation's results) those areas that need further attention and detailed interpretation. Managers look for causal relationships between the various results, and try to find causes for lagging results in the internal and external environments. Feedback on the results to the employees and formulation and execution of corrective and preventive action then takes place. The performance management system is used to discuss frequently (mostly monthly) the execution and adjustment of action plans. In addition, the validity of the formulated strategy is discussed in periodic (less frequent, for example quarterly) meetings.

Managers make use of a performance management system in the feedback stage when they:

- interpret the KPI results and look for causal relationships between the different variables in the performance management system
- look into the internal and external environments for explanations for lagging results and then formulate corrective actions on the basis of this analysis
- discuss the information in the performance management system and possible adjustments to the action plans with colleagues
- discuss the validity of the formulated strategy and check the underlying assumptions in quarterly meetings
- share the information in the performance management system and the outcomes of periodic meetings with superiors and colleagues, thereby advising superiors about possible adjustments to strategic programmes
- record important data from the discussions as well as of the outcomes of review and analysis meetings in the performance management system for future use and learning
  (Leonard et al., 1996; Atkinson et al., 1997; Pfeffer and Sutton, 2000).

2.3 HISTORY OF STRATEGIC PERFORMANCE MANAGEMENT SYSTEMS

The development of management control and information systems (which include strategic performance management systems) in the first half of the nineteenth century can be divided into three stages (Johnson and Kaplan, 1987). These stages are closely linked to industrial developments:

- *Stage 1: Development of low-complex systems.* Many of the early business organisations limited their attention to coordinating and controlling labour-intensive tasks in a few closely linked manufacturing processes which tended to produce fairly homogeneous product lines. Management control and information systems mainly concentrated on the collection of financial and some nonfinancial data about efficiency of input and output conversion activities in processes, including non-accounting data about cost of process outputs. Nineteenth-century firms measured their costs and revenues meticulously (Meyer, 1999). However, they were careful to disclose very little information and often told their shareholders nothing about their performance.

■ *Stage 2: Development of medium to high-complexity systems.* By the late nineteenth century, large-scale organisations started to integrate mass production with mass marketing and offered a wide variety of intermediate and finished products. Frederick Taylor's scientific management was introduced around 1911, arguing that division and specialisation of labour would lead to greater productivity. Standard production methods were used and standard costing techniques applied (Zairi, 1996). In the period from 1920 to 1925 DuPont and General Motors experimented by introducing decentralised divisional structures with profit centres. As support for these reorganisations they also introduced the DuPont chart, and with it the concept of return on investment (ROI). This meant that from that moment on management was held responsible for the achievement of budgeted ROI, and it therefore focused not only on measures of margin and net income but also on return on investment.

■ *Stage 3: Development of systems of growing complexity.* Between the 1920s and the 1980s, large business organisations had to cope with growing organisational complexity. They organised internal activities according to product lines or geographic regions, creating multidivisional structures. Also, they increasingly decoupled functions and processes. This meant that more and more companies started to use the DuPont chart and the concept of ROI. The principles of capital investment appraisal, budgeting, performance measurement, and variance accounting were introduced in the 1920s. By the 1930s, fully integrated cost and management accounting systems were developed, regulated, subjected to independent auditing, and linked to external financial operating systems (Zairi, 1996). After the 1950s, management control and information systems focused on the growing use of accounting targets to control operating processes.

It can be stated that by the 1950s most standard cost accounting methods, such as budgeting, standard costing transfer pricing, and the DuPont model had been developed and incorporated in management accounting textbooks. New developments, such as the concepts of residual income and net present value, were only sporadically included in textbooks (Olve et al., 1999). However, after the Second World War it became increasingly apparent that management needed information other than that supplied by the traditional management control and information systems. This information was needed because the systems and procedures of cost accounting and managerial control used at that time were devised for manufacturing organisations with mass production (Kaplan, 1983, 1984). In these organisations cost-price calculation and responsibility accounting systems mainly focused on recording labour costs and minimising manufacturing costs.

In the 1980s the competitive environment changed dramatically because of new technologies, increased competition as a consequence of deregulations, and the emergence of foreign producers. Quality improvements, reduced inventory, more efficient production processes, and increased automation were needed to survive in this new environment. The changes reduced the direct and indirect labour content of products and services and increased overhead costs. The traditional management accounting and information systems can no longer offer proper support for modern organisations that have to deal with customer-specific production, short lifecycles, computer aided design/computer aided manufacturing technology, and (more) overheads. The shortcomings of traditional systems are depicted in Figure 2.3 (collected from Govindarajan and Gupta, 1985; Fitzgerald et al., 1991; Business Intelligence Research, 1992; Eccles and Pyburn, 1992; Govindarajan and Shank, 1992; Nanni et al., 1992; Nolan, Norton & Co, 1992; Euske et al., 1993; Gregory, 1993; Brancato, 1995; Neely, 1998; Marr and Neely, 2001; Niven, 2002).

In Figure 2.3 the shortcomings of traditional systems have been divided into two categories, hard and soft. "Hard" shortcomings are inadequacies in the management information reporting process, such as problems with collection, content, quality, and timeliness of information. "Soft" shortcomings are less tangible because they are not directly related to targets. They include problems concerning the organisation's communication, culture, and the support of managers by the system. These shortcomings are discussed in more detail below.

■ *One-sided information.* The management information in traditional systems is too financially oriented. This is caused by the fact that management control and information systems were often designed to satisfy legal requirements, which mainly require financial data. At the same time financial ratios, like ROI and working capital, are not used as much. Neither is nonfinancial information, which is usually restricted to personnel (number of full-time equivalents, absenteeism), projects (status of large investments), and external information

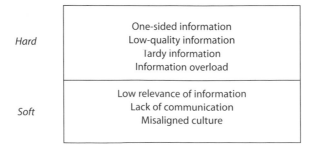

Figure 2.3 Shortcomings of traditional management control and information systems

(market share). Information about client satisfaction, vendor perform-ance, innovation, product quality, and intellectual capital is not, or not sufficiently, available. In addition, management information is mainly internally focused, on the activities of the organisation itself. Information on external factors, such as competitors and environmen-tal conditions, is missing. Also, information is often aimed at measur-ing the inputs, not the outputs. This forces management to focus on acquiring budgets instead of obtaining the desired results.

■ *Low-quality information.* The management information in traditional systems is too highly aggregated. The end results are measured, not the processes causing these results. The quality of analyses is low: too often only the differences between budget and actuals are reported without an adequate explanation, and there is no mention of actions to improve the results. In addition, the management information focuses too much on the past. Financial and nonfinancial targets are based on past results, not on up-to-date client information or benchmark data and certainly not on forecasts. Accurate measurement of past performance is commonplace; forecasting future performance is rare. This results in short-term behav-iour: managers go for quick wins instead of long-term development. Actions with a long-term effect are rarely executed because they regularly have a negative effect on the short-term financial result.

■ *Tardy information.* The management information in traditional systems is supplied to management at too late a stage. The value of the infor-mation has diminished by the time it reaches management. Consequently, necessary corrective actions are taken too late, making their effectiveness uncertain. Reports are still distributed in a paper format, which takes a long time. The management control and infor-mation system is often not linked to the supplying operational (infor-mation) systems, as a result of which reports have to be generated manually. Many managers do not use the reporting facilities of the operational and management control and information systems adequately. Management reports are often missing vital data needed by managers, resulting in many requests from them for additional information, which take a lot of time to fulfil.

■ *Information overload.* The management information in traditional systems does not contain ratios, trends, indicators, graphs, colours, and standardised layouts. The management control and information systems generate too much unrelated data. Conventional wisdom suggests that more data and more analysis lead to better decisions. However, research into information and decision making indicates that more is not necessarily better. Often, figures are stated and restated in reports without a short and concise explanation. As a consequence, formulated actions cannot be effective because they do not address the actual problems. Usually the expected impact of these actions is not described either, so the organisation is in the dark as to the effectiveness of its actions.

- *Low relevance of information.* The traditional management control and information systems are often based on outdated organisational concepts. They were originally built for manufacturing companies, but nowadays many organisations are in the first place service providers. In the course of time, organisations have put a lot of time and money into adapting the systems to the changing circumstances. However, instead of improving, the systems have become very difficult to maintain as they became more and more complex. The traditional systems measure the results of functions and organisational units, not the (interim) results of critical business processes that transcend the functions and units. In addition, traditional systems were originally designed to measure the use of budgets by managers, not the execution of strategy. As a result, there is not enough information available on the achievement of the strategic objectives at all organisational levels.
- *Lack of communication.* In traditional management control and information systems, communication about management information is not structural: discussions on organisational results take place irregularly and in an ad hoc manner. Management reports are rarely used for communicating the results to the organisation. Performance review meetings are often postponed which causes delays in taking action. If people agree on future actions, they do not use a structured scheme to monitor the execution, nor do they engage in structural communication or analysis of the results.
- *Misaligned culture.* The traditional management control and information systems do not foster a culture of trust and continuous improvement, as a result of which people do not act adequately on measured results. The focus is on performance measurement (collecting data), not performance management (acting on information). Because management control and information systems measure the wrong things they incite people to do the wrong things and display the wrong behaviour. The systems do not take into account ideas that managers have about information, causing a gap between delivered information and desired information.

Many of the problems discussed above are caused by the fact that organisations have been using virtually the same management control and information systems as they did in the 1930s (Johnson and Kaplan, 1987). However, in the last few decades a constant stream of new developments in production and processing techniques (such as flexible manufacturing systems, just-in-time production, materials requirements planning, enterprise requirements planning, supply chain management, and total quality assurance) has been matched by a series of new management information and accounting techniques, including: target costing, value engineering, strategic cost accounting, activity-based costing/management, kaizen costing, and nonfinancial performance indicators. Although many of these new accounting techniques are variations of older methods and ideas, they nonetheless provide a valuable contribution to managing an increasingly complex environment.

The idea of nonfinancial measures in itself is not new (Simon et al., 1954). In the 1950s, General Electric implemented a balanced set of performance measures (Kennerley and Neely, 2001). Daniel diagnosed that many organisations:

> were plagued by a common problem: inadequate management information, not in the sense of there not being enough, but in terms of relevancy for setting objectives, for shaping alternative strategies, for making decisions, and for measuring results against planned goals.
>
> (Daniel, 1961)

He argued that an organisation needed a combination of environmental, competitive and internal information based on financial and nonfinancial data. Daniel's idea did not exactly catch on. In the literature of the day not much reference can be found to nonfinancial indicators.

Then, in 1979, Rockart introduced a new idea to improve management control and information systems. He proposed a concept called critical success factors (CSFs):

> Critical success factors thus arc, for any business, the limited number of areas in which results, if they are satisfactory, will ensure successful competitive performance for the organisation. They are the few key areas where "things must go right" for the business to flourish. If results in these areas are not adequate, the organisation's efforts for the period will be less than desired. As a result, the critical success factors are areas of activity that should receive constant and careful management attention. The current status of performance in each area should be continually measured and that information should be made available.
>
> (Rockart, 1979)

These CSFs should, according to Rockart, be measured with prime measures, in later publications referred to as key performance indicators (KPIs).

Rockart's concept of CSFs and KPIs initially seemed to catch on. His concept was considered a breakthrough in management control as it considerably helped executives to narrow down the number of areas to focus on. The concept was therefore quickly picked up by other researchers. However, after the initial surge of interest, it once again became rather quiet on the implementation front because according to Olve et al. (1999) "managers were searching for even more simplified ways to represent cause-effect relationships at companies." This relative silence lasted until 1987, when Johnson and Kaplan published the important book *Relevance Lost*. In this book they argued the time had really come to improve traditional management control and information systems because they were severely out of date. They stated that organisations should make serious work of incorporating nonfinancial information, CSFs and KPIs.

Critical success factors and key performance indicators

A critical success factor (CSF) provides a qualitative description of an element of the strategy in which the organisation has to excel in order to be successful. The CSF is quantified, made measurable, by a key performance indicator (KPI). The use of critical success factors and key performance indicators enables measurement, and thus control, of strategic objectives. If performance indicators that measure the execution of the strategy and the creation of value are not included in the performance management process, it will remain unclear whether strategic objectives and value creation are being achieved.

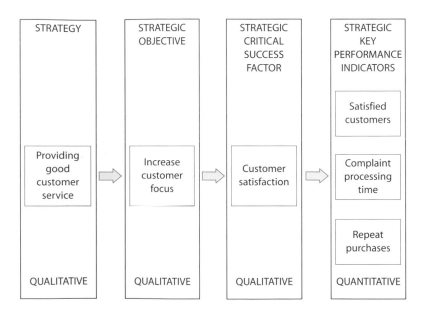

Figure 2.4 An example of a CSF and its corresponding KPIs

Providing good customer service is of critical importance to an organisation's success. One way to provide this service is by increasing the customer focus throughout the company, thereby increasing customer satisfaction. Whether customer service is satisfactory is reflected in the number of customers who repeatedly buy products or services ("repeat purchases"). Customer satisfaction can also be measured by proactively asking customers what they think of the services provided ("satisfied customers"). An important activity that helps to keep customers satisfied is to respond quickly to complaints ("complaint processing time").

In 1991, Eccles took it one step further when he published an important article in the *Harvard Business Review*. In this article, he predicted a "performance measurement revolution" which would take place in the next five years. During that revolution, traditional financial information systems would be replaced by nonfinancial information systems. According to Eccles, the revolution was necessary to improve managers' satisfaction with the information they receive and to satisfy the increased information requirements of modern organisations caused by new techniques like total quality management, focus on customer satisfaction, and benchmarking.

Kaplan and Norton expanded Rockart's theory by introducing the concept of the balanced scorecard (BSC) in a series of articles in *Harvard Business Review* and various books (Kaplan and Norton, 1992, 1993, 1996a, 1996b, 2000). This concept was based on a tool that was developed by the American company Analog Devices in the 1980s to support its strategic development process (Schneiderman, 1999). The BSC is used to represent the financial and nonfinancial performance indicators in a user-friendly format. Many management experts and the business community at large firmly believe that the BSC will form an integral part of modern management. They state that the BSC is "an idea whose time has come" as a result of organisations' growing frustration with traditional measurement systems coupled with an increasing need to cope with an ever more complex world. The concept is also well packaged and carefully marketed. Finally, it is said that the BSC is easy to comprehend: people who read about it for the first time can immediately grasp the concept (Marr and Schiuma, 2002).

The developments of management control and information systems can be summarised as follows:

- *Organisations pay more and more attention to the design of the systems.* Until recently, many organisations would, during the set-up of a new management control and information system, automatically have designed ROI criteria and deviation analyses without really looking at the effectiveness of these indicators. Nowadays, the choice of KPIs is the result of a structured process which centres around the strategy and CSFs of an organisation.
- *Organisations are increasing the number of CSFs and KPIs in the management control and information system to monitor the execution of the strategy.* In addition to traditional financial indicators, more and more CSFs and KPIs are included in management reports to monitor strategic goals like quality, delivery time, client satisfaction, competitor ranking, and employee retention.
- *Organisations are replacing absolute indicators with relative indicators and isolated indicators with a coherent set of indicators.* In the past, absolute targets were set for the KPIs that had to be achieved and which remained the same, no matter what. Nowadays, the striving for continuous improvement encourages organisations to regularly adjust targets upwards. In addition, the relations between KPIs are also made visible

and the KPIs are entered in a balanced measurement system, like the balanced scorecard.

From the beginning of the twenty-first century, these further developed management control and information systems became known as *strategic performance management systems*. A strategic performance management system is defined as a system in which the formal procedures that collect, analyse and report performance information, which is used by organisational members to steer and control business activities, are organised in such a way that everybody in the organisation strives towards achieving the strategic objectives of that organisation.

A strategic performance management system is organised on the basis of the chosen responsibility structure. It focuses on distributing financial and nonfinancial information to organisational members to support their decision-making and action-taking processes. Collecting, analysing, and distributing performance information are part of the routine procedures which are executed continuously in the organisation. A good strategic performance management system provides all relevant performance information on critical areas of the company, it is accepted and well used by organisational members, and leads to actions that improve operational and strategic performance. In addition, the system can be used for many more functions, like planning, performance evaluation, performance rewarding, benchmarking and learning (Figure 2.5).

Why did the strategic performance management system eventually experience a breakthrough? First, a possible explanation is that recent developments in information technology have created the right facilities for it. Introducing CSFs, KPIs, and the BSC requires collecting, storing, and reporting vast quantities of new data. In the 1990s, an increasing number of software vendors came to market with special applications, called executive information systems (EIS), that could to some extent meet the data and reporting requirements of CSFs and KPIs. These new applications, combined with dramatically improved price–performance ratios

Figure 2.5 Main uses of a strategic performance management system
Source: Martins (2000).

in hardware and breakthroughs in software and database technology, made it possible for organisations to generate, disseminate, analyse, and store more information from more sources for more people more quickly and cheaply than ever before (Holtham, 1994; Scapens, 1998).

With modern database technology, it is now possible to analyse information in a number of different ways and to have different information systems for different purposes. In general, it can be stated that information is becoming more and more widely available in organisations. Databases can easily be accessed through corporate networks, which enables managers to retrieve performance information from behind their desks. This has led to a decentralisation of information.

A second explanation for the breakthrough of strategic performance management systems is that, until recently, the significance of performance management was underestimated. This was largely because in the recent past managers had mainly concentrated on implementing total quality management (TQM), which focuses more on operations and less on management processes (Zairi and Jarrar, 2000).

A third explanation for the breakthrough can be found in the changing nature of the economy. In the traditional economy, which was dominated by tangible assets, financial measurements were adequate for recording investments and expenses associated with inventory, property, plant, and equipment. However, the new economy, in which intangible assets are the main sources of competitive advantage, requires information tools that describe knowledge-based assets and knowledge-based value-creating strategies. In 1982, a Brookings Institute study showed that tangible book values at the end of the 1960s represented 62 per cent of industrial organisations' market values, and that ten years later this ratio had dropped to 38 per cent. Later studies showed that by the end of the twentieth century the book value of tangible assets accounted only for 10 to 15 per cent of a company's market value.

It became obvious that a different type of management information was needed to keep up with the changing sources of value creation. These were changing from managing tangible assets to managing intangible assets, such as customer relationships, innovative products and services, high-quality and responsive operating processes, information technology and databases, and employee capabilities, skills and motivation. Performance information, based on CSFs, KPIs, and the BSC, met this demand (Kaplan and Norton, 2000).

2.4 BENEFITS OF STRATEGIC PERFORMANCE MANAGEMENT

The benefits from implementing strategic performance management are considerable, because it addresses many of the problems of traditional management control and information systems described in the previous section. Figure 2.6 positions the benefits along the categories "hard" and "soft" and "short-term" and "long-term." Short-term benefits are benefits

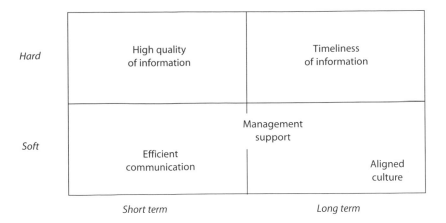

Figure 2.6 Benefits of performance management systems
(The figure is based on Jowett and Rothwell, 1998; Business Intelligence Research, 1992; Kaplan and Norton, 1996; Ashton, 1997.)

that can be obtained fairly quickly, because they require relatively simple alterations to the management control and information system. Long-term benefits, on the other hand, are benefits that become apparent only after some time because they require structural alterations to the system or changes that take a longer time to become effective, for instance in the case of changing the attitudes of managers or changing their use of the system.

- *High-quality of information.* CSFs and KPIs support effective planning and budgeting processes because they clarify the relationships between functions/activities and performance. Management reports are to a large extent complete and give a clear view of crucial business activities. CSFs and KPIs translate organisational strategy into qualitative and quantitative measures at all management levels. Through this, the execution of the strategy can continuously be measured and adjusted. This alignment will result in increased organisational performance (Bart and Baetz, 1998). Because only the most crucial items are tracked, information overload is counteracted. This benefit can be realised fairly quickly because organisational members can, if they are using a structured and focused approach, efficiently define the right indicators.
- *Timeliness of information.* When things go wrong, CSFs and KPIs function as an "early warning system," giving signals about potential issues before they actually happen or turn into real problems, and before they show up in the financial data. Organisational members can therefore anticipate new developments because they receive performance information at an earlier stage. This significantly lowers the chance of problems really becoming life-threatening to the organisation. It takes

a longer period of time to realise this benefit because the required information technology systems and registration procedures are often not yet present in the organisation.

- *Management support.* CSFs and KPIs support the concepts of continuous improvement and the "learning organisation" by focusing people's attention on continuous improvement and development, and by continuously raising performance expectations. CSFs and KPIs support total quality management by ensuring that organisational members are driven by customer expectations (internal and external). Because they have a better insight into and a better grip on organisational performance, cost reduction, organisational improvements, product quality and service improvements are made possible. It takes a longer period of time to realise this benefit because continuously setting and achieving new, higher targets takes time.
- *Efficient communication.* A set of clear CSFs and KPIs forms a common basis for communication and discussion in the organisation. This makes information easily transferable between departments and organisational units, making information less prone to being used as a means of executing power. Better transferable information makes it possible for organisational units to discuss common performance problems and exchange ideas, thereby building knowledge. This benefit can be realised fairly quickly because organisational members can decide straightaway to start sharing information.
- *Aligned culture.* The availability of high-quality information at all management levels makes "management by delegation" possible – that is, empowerment and front-line authority – which speeds up the decision-making process. Improved reporting enhances organisational members' self-management and self-control. They are more motivated because their goals and what is expected of them in regard to their behaviour and performance are clear, and they get regular feedback on how they are doing in these respects. As performance information is more standardised, it provides a better basis for discussion at all levels of the organisation. It takes a longer period of time to realise this benefit because a "mental reorientation" of managers is needed.

During the strategic performance management process efficient and effective steering and control of the organisation is achieved by:

- formulating the mission, strategy and objectives of the organisation
- translating objectives to the various management levels of the company
- measuring objectives with CSFs, KPIs and the BSC
- taking quick corrective action based on regular reporting of indicator results.

For efficient and effective management control, organisational members (managers and employees) also need to display performance-driven behaviour, which can be defined as goal-oriented behaviour (Lipe and Salterio, 2000; Martins, 2000). More and more research, both anecdotal and scientific, shows that the combination of performance-driven behaviour and regular use of effective strategic performance management system does lead to improved results (Ahn, 2001; Sandt et al., 2001; Stratton et al., 2005).

In one of the first research studies over a longer period of time (1996–99), senior executives from 58 organisations with a performance management system that focused on measuring a set of financial and nonfinancial data were asked to state how their organisations were ranked compared with their peers in the industry. The same was asked of senior executives from 64 organisations without such a performance management system. The opinions of the executives (1000 in total) were juxtaposed with the three-year ROI of their organisations. Figure 2.7 shows that the organisations with a structured performance management system achieved significantly better results than organisations without such a structured system (Schiemann and Lingle, 1999).

In this same study, it was observed that organisations with a "balanced" performance management system showed a number of different characteristics in comparison with fellow organisations with a non-balanced performance management system (Table 2.1).

In a study performed almost a decade later (2005) among 150 US, European, and Asian companies, the same positive picture emerged

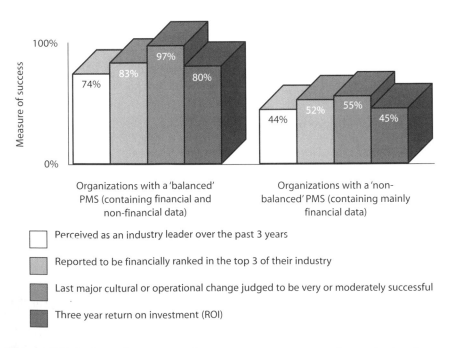

Figure 2.7 Relation between performance management and organisational performance

Table 2.1 Organisations with different performance management systems (PMS) have different characteristics

Characteristic	Organisations with a balanced PMS (percent)	Organisations with a non-balanced PMS (percent)
Clear agreement on strategy among senior management	93	37
Good cooperation and teamwork among management	85	38
Unit performance measures are linked to strategic company measures	74	16
Information within the organisation is shared openly and candidly	71	30
Effective communication of strategy to organisation	60	8
Willingness by employees to take risks	52	22
Individual performance measures are linked to unit measures	52	11
High levels of self-monitoring of performance by employees	42	16

(Figure 2.8). Organisations that are best in class with their performance management system achieved significantly better financial results than the average enterprise and the firms that were lagging in the development of their systems (Aberdeen Group, 2005).

In an online survey conducted by the Balanced Scorecard Collaborative among its members (2003), 250 of the 500 respondents reported that they used a BSC. Of these, 125 said it was still too early to tell what the impact of the scorecard on their organisation had been. Of the other 125, 19 reported they had achieved significantly better results, 80 said they saw some progress, and 26 said they had limited or no better results. The organisations with breakthrough results (among others) created a better sense of urgency for performance management, and the scorecard used strategy maps significantly more, and communicated more extensively than in those organisations with lesser results (Table 2.2).

In a scientific study (Waal, 2002), the hypothesis that "a manager's use of a performance management system influences organisational performance favourably" was tested among a group of companies. This group consisted of organisations with well-functioning performance management systems, organisations where performance management implementation projects had failed, organisations with good results, and organisations with bad results. The study demonstrated positive relations between the regular use of performance management and increased quality of work, increased innovativeness of organisational members, and increased performance. An overview of performance management implementations, most notably of the

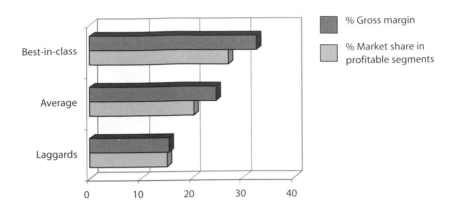

Figure 2.8 Relation between performance management and organisational performance

Table 2.2 What distinguished the winners?
Source: Waal (2003).

Action	Number of organisations applying the action (in percentage per category)		
	Breakthrough results	Some progress	No results
Executive team has created a sense of urgency	84	38	20
Strategy is translated into a strategy map and a balanced scorecard	84	41	0
Corporate/business unit measures are linked and aligned	72	39	0
Employees are aware of the strategy	56	32	0
Individual and team goals are aligned with the strategy	42	26	0
The balanced scorecard is an integral part of the strategic planning process	100	40	0
The budget is driven by the strategy	42	29	0

balanced scorecard, in Asia showed that all 11 documented companies experienced substantial improvements in their financial and nonfinancial performance, some even recovering from the brink of bankruptcy (Creelman and Makhijani, 2005).

The general observation in the literature seems to be that organisations that have implemented a performance management system and are using it perform better both financially and nonfinancially than organisations that are less performance management-driven. This is explained by the fact that performance management directs focus and motivates the organisation to act in a strategically desirable way. It creates clarity about:

- the goals to be achieved
- the responsibilities and tasks of all organisational members
- the results achieved
- the consequences of non-performance (both organisationally and individually)
- the support people can expect from their superiors (like coaching).

Performance management also counteracts escaping and shunning behaviour because it is stated clearly who has to act to solve certain problems. Consequently, excuses for not acting are no longer useful because they cannot shift the blame any more; problems become opportunities to analyse and improve the situation. Such a change in attitude will lead to better individual, departmental, and organisational results and foster professionalism throughout the enterprise. Of all the improvement techniques developed in the past two decades, only performance management seems to be able to provide better organisational performance – provided it is implemented and used properly (Waal, 2005). This gives a compelling argument for organisations to implement strategic performance management.

2.5 THE STRATEGIC PERFORMANCE MANAGEMENT DEVELOPMENT CYCLE

The way to introduce strategic performance management in the organisation is through the strategic performance management development cycle (Figure 2.9).

The strategic performance management development cycle is composed of the following stages:

1. *Design a strategic management model.* In stage 1 the organisation establishes the strategic structure that is the foundation for the development of the performance management process. This stage consists of setting up a consistent responsibility structure; developing scenarios; developing the organisational mission, strategy and strategic objectives; and developing strategic action plans.
2. *Design a strategic reporting model.* In stage 2 the organisation establishes the reporting structure to monitor and adjust the execution of the strategy and the progression of crucial business activities. This stage consists of developing CSFs and KPIs; developing exception and action reports; developing a balanced scorecard; setting-up a management information technology architecture; and setting-up a key processes model.

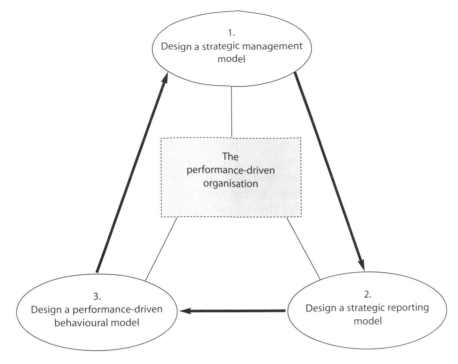

Figure 2.9 The strategic performance management development cycle

3. *Design a performance-driven behavioural model.* In stage 3 the organisation decides on the culture needed to become a performance-driven organisation. This stage consists of establishing the characteristics of performance-driven behaviour; aligning personal objectives with strategic objectives; and linking performance management with competency management.

The three stages of the strategic performance management development cycle are each discussed in three separate parts of this book. The stages are broken down into consecutive steps that an organisation has to take to set up the performance management system. Each step is illustrated with one or more cases, which are based on real-life organisations, followed by a description of the way in which the fictitious company UVD dealt with improving its strategic performance management system.

2.6 FEASIBILITY ANALYSIS

Not every organisation is ready for the far-reaching implementation of strategic performance management. Particularly if there is organisational turbulence (such as in the case of a reorganisation), disappointing financial results, or chronic overtime, organisational members have to focus on solving current problems. In such a situation, little support can be expected for an additional major improvement project. Thus, before implementing strategic performance management, an organisation has to determine whether its current situation is stable enough and whether organisational members are ready for it.

Feasibility analysis is an assessment tool which can be used to determine whether an organisation is ready for strategic performance management (Waal, 2001). This analysis consists of a questionnaire with 13 questions which relate to criteria that an organisation must meet before implementation is started. The questions have to be answered with "yes," "no," or "±" in case of doubt. The more often "no" or "±" is answered, the more advisable it is that the organisation carries out a number of preliminary activities before implementing strategic performance management. The feasibility analysis questionnaire can be completed by managers at all levels of the organisation.

1. *Do organisational members acknowledge that the current performance management system does not provide them with sufficient support?*
   If the answer to this question is "no," organisational members have no complaints about the performance information they receive. In itself this does not mean that the quality of the performance management system is satisfactory. But because there is no perceived need for new types of information, there will be little incentive for organisational members to put effort into developing it. It would make little sense to initiate a performance management improvement project.
2. *Do organisational members agree on the necessity and the importance of performance management?*
   The implementation of strategic performance management entails radical change to the organisation. If the answer to this question is "no," the organisation first has to concentrate on explaining and communicating the benefits and the necessity of performance management to the organisational members.
3. *Is the organisation itself stable?*
   The implementation of strategic performance management requires a lot of time and effort from the organisation. If the answer to this question is "no," the organisation has to focus its attention on other, more urgent matters such as reorganisations, mergers and takeovers, excessive personnel turnover, or financial problems. There will be too little time and attention left for an additional performance management improvement project.
4 *Is the organisation's working environment stable?*
   If the answer to this question is "no," there is a tense situation within the organisation characterised by conflicts, a lot of overtime, unfinished business, or a large amount of stress. The employees are too distracted by other issues or lack the energy to see the performance management improvement project through to the end.

Table 2.3 The feasibility analysis questionnaire

1.	Do organisation members acknowledge that the current performance management system does not provide them with sufficient support?
2.	Do organisation members agree on the necessity and the importance of performance management?
3.	Is the organisation itself stable?
4.	Is the organisation's working environment stable?
5.	Do organisation members agree on the starting time of the performance management improvement project?
6.	Are there enough resources available for the performance management improvement project?
7.	Are there any other change processes in progress within the organisation that are related to the performance management improvement project?
8.	Is the management team sufficiently involved in the performance management improvement project?
9.	Are there organisation members who have earlier positive experiences with performance management?
10.	Do organisation members have clear insight into the market and the position of the organisation in it?
11.	Has the organisation a mission and a strategy?
12.	Do organisation members have insight into the business processes, the organisational structure, and the relationship between these?
13.	Does the organisation have an open communication structure?

Start the strategic performance management improvement project?

5. *Do organisational members agree on the starting time of the performance management improvement project?*
   If the answer to this question is "no," organisational members think, for various reasons, that the moment chosen to start the performance management improvement project is not convenient. They will not or cannot free up enough time for the project. In the event the project is started, organisational members will cooperate insufficiently and the implementation will almost certainly take a long time.

6. *Are there enough resources available for the performance management improvement project?*
   If the answer to this question is "no," there are not enough resources available in the organisation to execute the performance management improvement project in an efficient and effective manner. Some examples of resources are time constraints of organisational

members, financial resources to pay for expert advice, and time and money for modifying existing information systems.

7. *Are there any other change processes in progress within the organisation that have a relation with the performance management improvement project?*
It is very possible that multiple change processes are simultaneously in progress in the organisation. If the answer to this question is "no," the change processes are not related to the performance management improvement project. This means that the projects will compete with each other, and they will both lay a claim to the organisation's scarce resources. The more unrelated processes coincide, the greater the chance that not enough resources will be available for the performance management improvement project. An example of a related change process is the restructuring of a department in which tasks and responsibilities are being changed and reallocated. This process requires that the performance management process and management information system also have to be changed to support the new structure.

8. *Is the management team sufficiently involved in the performance management improvement project?*
An organisation's management has two important responsibilities during the improvement project. First of all, it must continuously incite people to develop, realise, and use the new strategic performance management system. Second, it has an important exemplary function. If employees see that management is frequently using CSFs and KPIs and discussing them with other organisational members, it becomes clear that the new indicators are to be taken seriously. If the answer to this question is "no," there is not enough willingness among management to be involved in the performance management improvement project. As a consequence, managers are unlikely to live up to their responsibilities and organisational members will be discouraged from participating in the project.

9. *Are there organisational members that have earlier positive experiences with performance management?*
If the answer to this question is "yes," the organisation can assign a leading role to the people with performance management experience during the improvement project. These pioneers will function as "ambassadors" of strategic performance management because they can draw on their experience and communicate the benefits of performance management to the other organisational members.

10. *Do organisational members have clear insight into the market and the position of the organisation in it?*
When the organisation's strategy is formulated, the characteristics of the market and industry in which the company operates must be taken into account. If the answer to this question is "no," the organisational members do not have sufficient insight into the market position of the organisation. As a consequence, the organisation's mission

and strategy will be incomplete or inaccurate, and the accompanying CSFs and KPIs will not monitor critical business processes.

11. *Has the organisation a mission and a strategy?*

    If the answer to this question is "no," the strategic objectives that the organisation wants and/or has to achieve are unclear or unknown. Because of this, it is uncertain what should be measured and consequently the right CSFs and KPIs cannot be determined.

12. *Do organisational members have insight into the business processes, the organisational structure, and the relationship between these?*

    In order to be able to improve the CSFs and KPIs, and thereby achieve the organisation's objectives, organisational members need to know how they can influence the critical business processes. They also need insight in the organisational structure to know who has what responsibility in influencing these processes. If the answer to this question is "no," the quality of formulated actions to improve the CSFs and KPIs is insufficient and therefore actions will not be executed.

13. *Does the organisation have an open communication structure?*

    CSFs and KPIs make the performance and results of an organisation and its organisational members more transparent. If the answer to this question is "no," there is no open and honest communication about the achieved results and organisational members may, out of fear of "reprisals," be reluctant to use strategic performance management.

Table 2.3 lists all the feasibility analysis questions. There is no absolute number of negative answers that indicates an organisation should not initiate a performance management improvement project. In some cases, it is possible to carry out a number of corrective activities during the project itself. In other cases, a single "no" can mean that it is wise for an organisation to postpone the start of the performance management improvement project. The decision whether or not to start a project strongly depends on an organisation's specific circumstances.

2.7 CASE: FEASIBILITY ANALYSIS AT CNS

Communication Network Systems Inc. (CNS) specialises in communication systems for the business market. The company has four departments: Communication Systems supplies transmission and data communication networks and systems for videotext; Network Systems supplies local and wide area networks (LAN/WAN); the systems sold are installed and maintained by Operations & Maintenance; and Finance & Support provides internal support services, such as finance, systems support and personnel (Figure 2.10). With a staff of 140 employees the company has a turnover of $65 million.

The company was originally subdivided into traditional, functional units.

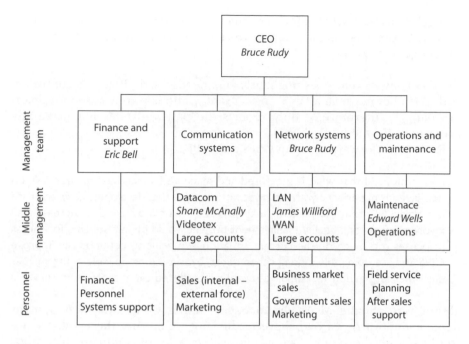

Figure 2.10 Organisation chart of CNS

CNS has suffered decreasing profit margins during the last couple of years. An analysis pointed out that this could have been caused by the inflexibility of both the organisational structure and the management systems. To combat the narrow-mindedness and the protecting of one's own turf that a functional structure often brings with it, CNS is currently creating a more flexible, process-oriented organisation. Part of the reorganisation consists of joining together the various sales disciplines within the Communication Systems and the Network Systems departments, so that they will be able to respond more quickly and decisively to customer wishes. The management systems are also being dealt with by implementing a new strategic perform-ance management system.

CEO Bruce Rudy explains the reasons that CNS wants to start a strategic performance management improvement project:

> On the basis of our new mission and strategy, we have started a reorganisation to adapt our organisational structure and systems to the direction in which CNS wishes to expand. We want to increase our turnover and margin by concentrat-ing on specific market segments and by becoming one of the three main suppli-ers in these market segments. We are looking for new outlets and acquisitions within these market segments. We are attempting to cooperate more with our clients in order to tie them more to CNS. Within each department, we have created a single point of reference for the customers. We support all this by constantly paying attention to efficiency and reducing costs. These changes

require a higher level of self-reliance and self-motivation from our personnel. We want to give them the appropriate tools for this, such as a new performance management system.

"The current system does not satisfy our needs," Eric Bell, the controller, adds. "It does not match CNS's new strategy and is purely based on financial data. Furthermore, it only reports the past and does not make any projections for the future."

Rudy looks forward to using CSFs and KPIs:

> I am convinced that what is measured and made visible can be improved. We do not have any experience with them yet, but I imagine that developing CSFs and KPIs is a playful way to measure items that now still are unknown and to increase staff involvement. A total quality management project would be less suitable for this as it focuses too much on the current situation. We want to continuously improve CNS and are doing this, among other things, by measuring new elements such as customer satisfaction. Yes, we have recently introduced client satisfaction surveys.

"Mind you," Shane McAnally, manager in the Communication Systems department, warns, "I do believe in this, but we are not there yet. We are still busy with the reorganisation and we get a lot of complaints from our employees. They say they do not know what is going to happen, what this is going to mean for them personally, and some people are even wondering out loud why we need a new system in the first place and why now. The common grievance is that "management never tells us anything.""

"Ah," Rudy dismisses Shane's comment, "Where there is a will, there is a way. They will come round to see our point. Of course we have to let go of some employees but that has nothing to do with this project. I know strategic performance management is the best thing CNS has come across in a long, long time, and it will certainly restore our profitability!"

Shane shakes his head and sighs. "I still wonder whether we should start the project now."

Table 2.4 shows the filled-in feasibility analysis questionnaire for CNS.

The reorganisation of CNS is a major project which demands a lot of time and effort from both managers and employees. Part of this reorganisation should be the implementation of a new strategic performance management system because this will provide the information CNS's organisational members need to manage in the new situation. However, the reorganisation effort together with several items which are currently not in order – employees questioning both the need and the starting time for a new system, and the rather closed communication structure – should be cause for CNS' management team, and especially the CEO, to take stock and maybe decide to first fully implement the new organisational structure. In the meantime they can work on growing a positive attitude towards the new performance management system. After the situation has settled, and people have become more receptive to the new system, CNS can start the introduction of performance management.

Table 2.4 The feasibility analysis questionnaire for CNS

Feasibility analysis questionnaire	Y/N/±	Remarks
1. Do organisation members acknowledge that the current performance management system does not provide them with sufficient support?	Y	The new organisational structure needs a new performance management system. At the same time, organisation members are not happy with the current system.
2. Do organisation members agree on the necessity and the importance of performance management?	±	Some employees question the need for a new system.
3. Is the organisation itself stable?	N	A reorganisation is in progress.
4. Is the organisation's working environment stable?	N	Everyone already works very hard. Some employees will be laid off because of the reorganisation, which is causing unrest.
5. Do organisation members agree on the starting time of the performance management improvement project?	±	Some employees question the timing of the new system.
6. Are there enough resources available for the performance management improvement project?	±	Currently, CNS is struggling with profit margins.
7. Are there any other change processes in progress within the organisation that are related to the performance management improvement project?	Y	The current reorganisation has to be accompanied by a new performance management system
8. Is the management team sufficiently involved in the performance management improvement project?	Y	The CEO especially is very enthusiastic.
9. Are there organisation members who have earlier positive experiences with performance management?	N	Strategic performance management is new to the company.
10. Do organisation members have clear insight into the market and the position of the organisation in it?	Y	Customer satisfaction surveys were recently introduced.
11. Has the organisation a mission and a strategy?	Y	A new mission and strategy were recently introduced.
12. Do organisation members have insight into the business processes, the organisational structure, and the relationship between these?	±	CNS comes from a situation of functional departments which only partly cooperate with each other and which do not always have knowledge of each other's activities.
13. Does the organisation have an open communication structure?	±	Some employees dared to air their dissatisfaction out loud.
Start the improvement project?	N	CNS is too much engaged in the reorganisation.

2.8 CASE STUDY: UVD'S FEASIBILITY ANALYSIS

The experiences of a fictitious company Ultraviolet Design Ltd (UVD) in developing a strategic performance management system are described in Chapters 2 through 12. In this chapter, UVD is introduced.

Description of UVD

In 1993, UVD was established by the Williams brothers. The company started with some promising designs of high-quality home products, including vases, lamps, and clocks. The CEO of the company is John Williams, who is also responsible for the design of the products. His brother Gary has responsibility for the manufacturing of the products and a third brother, Martin, is in charge of marketing and sales. The brothers strongly emphasise innovation, ecological soundness, quality, and market/customer orientation. This emphasis has produced results: over the past 12 years, the turnover has increased on average by 8 per cent per year. The number of employees has grown from an initial six to 256. UVD has now penetrated the top tier of the retail market segment: the top furniture stores, department stores, and specialist stores.

Initially, the Williams brothers were only focusing on the Dutch market. However Martin, who loves to travel in Europe during weekends and holidays, noticed that there was a market for UVD products in many European countries. Martin had a particularly good feeling about the UK. He developed a catalogue containing UVD's products and mailed this catalogue to retailers all over Europe. His marketing instinct was correct; European sales increased, especially in the UK. Four years ago, when the European sales surpassed the marketing and sales capacity of the Dutch office, a new office was opened in the UK. At that time, almost 35 per cent of UVD's sales were in the UK. Marketing, sales, and warehousing activities for the UK are done from the UK office (UVD UK).

Because Martin likes travelling, and since he was already responsible for marketing and sales, he was appointed as CEO of the UK office. The headquarters of UVD Europe, based in the Netherlands, is responsible for marketing and sales (excluding the USA and the UK), customer service, manufacturing of the products, research and development of the products, finance, and personnel. Figure 2.11 depicts UltraViolet Design's organisational structure.

UVD produces and sells four types of products: vases, lamps, clocks, and CD racks. Each product group contains a range of products (Table 2.5).

John Williams is most proud of his master creation, the Clock product group. All clocks, except the Appel, are made of lightweight, recyclable, synthetic material and have an ingenious clock mechanism that automatically adjusts to the local time zone. This means that in the UK, for example, the clock automatically adjusts to Greenwich Mean Time (GMT) and in the

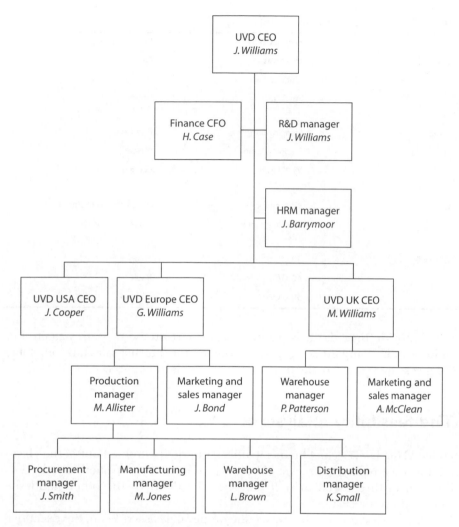

Figure 2.11 Organisation chart of UVD

Netherlands to Central European Time (CET). John's latest creation is an ecologically sound CD rack. It has a revolutionary click mechanism to facilitate the task of sliding the CDs in and out of the rack. Because of this click mechanism, the CDs can be stored very close together, reducing the size of the rack. The product (in all three sizes) was put into production at the end of 2002 and was brought to market in May 2003.

Recently the brothers decided to penetrate the North American market with their designer products. Setting up a complete distribution network all over the North American continent was far beyond the financial capacity of UVD. They decided to initially market and sell their products over the internet. John hired a new manager, Jack Cooper, whose task it was to set up the UVD website and outsource the warehousing and logistics handling of the products to a national

Table 2.5 Product portfolio of UVD

Product group	Product type	Product name
Vase	Large vase	Dali
	Medium vase	Brood
	Small vase	Escher
Lamp	Hanging lamp	Picasso
	Standing lamp	Monet
	Wall lamp	Gauguin
Clock	Wall clock	Mondrian, Rembrandt
	Standing clock	Appel, Van Gogh
CD rack	30 CDs	Mozart
	40 CDs	Bach
	50 CDs	Chopin

distributor. In time, UVD is planning to insource these processes again, but right now the company is focusing on making the internet sales take off. Table 2.6 gives an overview of the distribution channels by country.

The feasibility analysis at UVD

Helen Case, UVD's chief financial officer, hurriedly stepped out of the elevator onto the boardroom level. The stack of papers she frenetically tried to hold on to threatened to spill out onto the floor. In the other hand she clenched two briefcases.

"Can I please go in right away?" she desperately asked Ellen, the executive secretary.

"Yes, of course," she answered cheerfully. "He is expecting you."

Relieved, Helen balanced her way into the boss' room.

"Next time use a trolley!" Ellen called after her. "You are starting to look like a clown with all this juggling of yours."

"A trolley, that's a good idea," Helen thought. "I should have thought of that myself. I'll make a note of it, as soon as my hands are free."

The reception from John Williams, the boss, was not as she expected. "No, not again," John moaned as he saw his chief financial officer come staggering in. "Every month the same mountain of paper. It drives me crazy."

"But," Helen said bewildered, "these are the monthly figures you are always asking for."

"Of course I was waiting for them, but I can never find them in that pile of yours."

Table 2.6 Distribution channels of UVD

Area	Country	Regions	Distribution channels
Europe (UVD Netherlands)	Netherlands	North South West East Central	Furniture stores Department stores Specialist stores
	Belgium	Central	Furniture stores Department stores
	Luxemburg	Central	Furniture stores
	Germany	West	Furniture stores Department stores
	France	North	Furniture stores
	Spain	North	Furniture stores Department stores
	Italy	Central	Furniture stores
UK (UVD UK)	UK	North South West East Central	Furniture stores Department stores Specialist stores
Americas (UVD USA)	Americas	North America South America(with focus on the north)	Internet(warehousing and distribution are outsourced)

"Everything is in there," Helen replied triumphantly. "To measure is to know, you know."

"Have you never heard of information overload?" John asked.

Helen shook her head. "One can never measure too much."

"Is that so?" the boss snarled. "So you think you can find anything in that pile of papers? Tell me then, what is the reason we're experiencing those delivery problems in Germany?"

"Of course I can tell you that." Feverishly Helen started to flick through the reports. "Gee," she muttered, "where is it? I've seen it this morning somewhere."

"What's that, Helen?" John asked while observing the desperate CFO.

"Nothing, nothing, just give me a minute, I'm almost there. I'm sure it's here somewhere. After all, we measure literally everything in this company." Relieved, Helen looked up from the papers. "Here it is, the delivery problems are caused by .... because our suppliers have ... oh no, that was last month. Something else is going on. But what?"

John was starting to lose his patience. He slapped the table with the palm of his hand. "Shall I tell you what's going on? You have made our performance management system so elaborate, by cramming in everything you could lay your hands on, that the system is now virtually unworkable. It is as flexible as an oak door and the whole management team is complaining about it!"

"But, but ..." the poor CFO sputtered.

"Never mind, I'll find out myself," John roared. He pushed a button on the intercom. "Ellen, call the warehouse manager right now. That's how I get my information anyhow," he grumbled. He glared at Helen. "And I want you to prepare a proposal for an improvement project for our performance management system. We are growing so fast that it is unacceptable to continue with this old-fashioned system. We need a new strategy and good information on it, and we need it fast."

Helen started to make her way to the door. "Wait," John continued. "Include the project costs and I'll make sure we have the resources for it. And I want you to be personally responsible for the implementation."

"But John," Helen objected, "I have got my hands full with the new cost management system for our American operations and by the way, I'm grossly understaffed as I told you last month. This is not the best time to start a project, especially because the others are also busy with America so they don't have any hands to spare."

"Well, it shouldn't be such a problem," John questioned. "I remember you told me during your job interview that you have experience with these types of projects. In fact, it was one of the reasons for hiring you."

"OK, OK, I'll get cracking." Helen shuffled out of John's office, still holding on to her precious papers.

Case question: Should UVD start a performance management improvement project? Fill in the feasibility analysis questionnaire to support your argument.

Key points

- ☑ To be successful in the long run, an organisation strives for organisational fitness, which is defined as an organisation's ability to adapt and survive in the ever-changing business environment.
- ☑ A management control and information system helps managers influence other members of the organisation in such a way that the organisation's mission and strategy are implemented, while simultaneously ensuring that resources are used effectively and efficiently.
- ☑ Strategic performance management is the process where steering of the organisation takes place through the systematic definition of mission, strategy, and objectives of the

organisation, making these measurable through critical success factors and key performance indicators in order to be able to take corrective actions to keep the organisation on track.

☑ The strategic performance management process consists of the subprocesses strategy development, budgeting/target setting, execution/forecasting, performance measurement, performance review, and incentive compensation.

☑ Organisations that have implemented a performance management system, and are using it, perform both financially and nonfinancially better than organisations that are less performance management-driven.

☑ The way to introduce strategic performance management in the organisation is through the strategic performance management development cycle, consisting of these steps: design a strategic management model, design a strategic reporting model, and design a performance-driven behavioural model.

☑ Before implementing strategic performance management an organisation has to determine whether its current situation is stable enough and whether organisational members are ready for it, by using feasibility analysis.

References

Aberdeen Group (2005) *Closed Loop Corporate Performance Management Benchmark Report*.

Ahn, H. (2001) Applying the balanced scorecard concept: an experience report. *Long Range Planning*, 34.

Anthony, R.N. (1965), *Planning and Control Systems: A framework for analysis*. Boston: Harvard Business School Press.

Anthony, R.N. and Govindarajan, V. (1995) *Management Control Systems*, 8th edn. Chicago: Irwin.

Anthony, R.N., Dearden, J. and Bedford, N.M. (1989) *Management Control Systems*, 6th edn. Chicago, Irwin.

Armstrong, M. and Baron, A. (1998) *Performance Management: The new realities*. London: Institute of Personnel and Development.

Ashton, C. (1997) *Strategic Performance Measurement: Transforming corporate performance by measuring and managing the drivers of business success*. London: Business Intelligence.

Atkinson, A.A., Balakrishnan, R., Booth, P., Cote, J.M., Groot, T., Malmi, T., Roberts, H., Uliana, E. and Wu, A. (1997) New directions in management accounting research. *Journal of Management Accounting Research*, 9, 79–108.

Bart, C.K. and Baetz, M.C. (1998) The relationship between mission statements and firm performance: an exploratory study, *Journal of Management Studies*, 35 (6), November, 823–85.

Beer, M. (2003) Building organisational fitness. In: S. Chowdhry (ed.), *Organisations 21C*. New Jersey: Financial Times Prentice Hall.

Bossert, J. (1993) *De organisatie van besturingsprocessen, een exploratief onderzoek naar de vormgeving van besturingssystemen* (The organisation of management control processes, explorative research into the design of management control systems). PhD dissertation, Amsterdam: Vrije Universiteit.

Brancato, C.K. (1995) *New Corporate Performance Measures*. London: The Conference Board, 1118–95–RR

Business Intelligence Research (1992) *Business Intelligence survey: Business performance measurements*. London: Business Intelligence.

Choo, C.W. (2000) Closing the cognitive gaps: how people process information. In: D.A. Marchand, T.H. Davenport and T. Dickson (eds), *Mastering Information Management: Complete MBA companion in information management*. Harlow: Prentice Hall Financial Times, 245–53.

Creelman, J. and Makhijani, N. (2005) *Mastering Business in Asia: Succeeding with the balanced scorecard*. Singapore: Wiley Asia.

Daniel, D.R. (1961) Management information crisis. *Harvard Business Review*, September/October, 111–21.

Eccles, R.G. and Pyburn, P.J. (1992) Creating a comprehensive system to measure performance. *Management Accounting (US)*, October, 41–4.

Euske, K.J., Lebas, M.J. and McNair, C.J. (1993) Performance measurement in an international setting. *Management Accounting Research*, 4, 275–99.

Fitzgerald, L., Johnston, R., Brignall, T.J., Silvesto, R. and Voss, C. (1991) *Performance Measurement in Service Businesses*. London: CIMA.

Govindarajan, V. and Gupta, A.K. (1985) Linking control systems to business unit strategy: Impact on performance. *Accounting, Organisations and Society*, 10 (1), 51–66.

Govindarajan, V. and Shank, J. (1992) Strategic cost management: tailoring controls to strategies. *Cost Management*, Fall, 14–24.

Gregory, M.J. (1993) Integrated performance measurement: a review of current practice and emerging trends. *International Journal of Production Economics*, 30 (1), 281–96.

Holtham, C. (1994) *Integrating Technologies to Support Action*. Working paper, London: City University Business School, London.

Johnson, H.T. and Kaplan, R.S. (1987) *Relevance Lost: The rise and fall of management accounting*. Boston: Harvard Business Press.

Jowett, P. and Rothwell, M. (1988) *Performance Indicators in the Public Sector*. Basingstoke: Macmillan.

Kaplan, R.S. (1983) Measuring manufacturing performance: a new challenge for managerial accounting research. *Accounting Review*.

Kaplan, R.S. (1984) The evolution of managerial accounting. *Accounting Review*.

Kaplan, R.S. and Norton, D.P. (1992) The balanced scorecard: measures that drive performance. *Harvard Business Review*, January/February, 71–9.

Kaplan, R.S. and Norton, D.P. (1993), Putting the balanced scorecard to work. *Harvard Business Review*, September/October.

Kaplan, R.S. and Norton, D.P. (1996a) *The Balanced Scorecard: Translating strategy into action*. Boston: Harvard Business School Press.

Kaplan, R.S. and Norton, D.P. (1996b) Using the balanced scorecard as a strategic management system. *Harvard Business Review*, January–February, 75–85.

Kaplan, R.S. and Norton, D.P. (2000) *The Strategy-focused Organisation. How balanced scorecard companies thrive in the new business environment*. Boston: Harvard Business School Press.

Kennerley, M. and Neely, A. (2000) Performance measurement frameworks: a review. In: A. Neely (ed.), *Performance measurement: Past, present, and future*. Cranfield: Centre for Business Performance, Cranfield University, 291–8.

Kloot, L. (1997) Organisational learning and management control systems: responding to environmental change. *Management Accounting Research*, 8, 47–73.

Leonard, N.H., Scholl, R.W. and Beauvais, L.L. (1996) *The Impact of Group Cognitive Style on Strategic Decision Making and Organisational Direction*. Paper presented at the annual meeting of the Academy of Management, August.

Lipe, M.G. and Salterio, S.E. (2000) The balanced scorecard: judgmental effects of common and unique performance measures. *Accounting Review*, 75 (3), 283–98.

Lohman, F. (1999) *The Effectiveness of Management Information: A design approach to contribute to organisational control*. PhD dissertation, Delft: Technische Universiteit.

Lynch, R.L. and Cross, K.F. (1995) *Measure Up! How to measure corporate performance*, 2nd edn. Cambridge, Mass.: Blackwell Business.

Marr, B. and Neely, A. (2001) *Balanced Scorecard Software Report*. Gartner Inc and Cranfield School of Management

Marr, B. and Schiuma, G. (2002) Research challenges for corporate performance measurement: evidence from a citation analysis. In: A. Neely, A. Walters and R. Austin (eds), *Performance Measurement and Management: Research and action*. Cranfield: Cranfield School of Management.

Martins, R.A. (2000) Use of performance measurement systems: some thoughts towards a comprehensive approach. In: A. Neely (ed.), *Performance Measurement: Past, present and future*. Cranfield: Centre for Business Performance, 363–70.

Meyer, M.W. (1999), Permanent failure and the failure of organisational perform-ance. In: H.K. Anheier (ed.), *When Things go Wrong: Organisational failures and breakdowns*. Thousand Oaks: Sage, 197–212.

Mooraj, S., Oyon, D. and Hostettler, D. (1999) The balanced scorecard: a necessary good or an unnecessary evil? *European Management Journal*, 17 (5), 481–91.

Nanni, A.J., Dixon, J.R. and Vollmann, T.E. (1992) Integrated performance meas-urement: management accounting to support the new realities. *Journal of Management Accounting Research*, Fall, 1–9.

Neely, A. (1998) *Measuring Business Performance: Why, what and how*. London: Economist Books.

Niven, P. (2002) *Balanced Scorecard: Step-by-step, maximizing performance and maintaining results*. New York: Wiley.

Nolan, Norton & Co. (1992) *Measuring Performance in the Organisation of the Future*. Executive summary of a research study, Nolan, Norton & Co.

Olve, N.G., Roy, J. and Wetter, M. (1999) *Performance Drivers: A practical guide to using the balanced scorecard*. New York: Wiley.

Petri, R., and van der Vossen, G.J.A.M. (1994) Management control structure. *Handbook of Management Accounting*. D1100, 1–33, Deventer: Kluwer.

Pfeffer, J. and Sutton, R.I. (2000) *The Knowing–Doing Gap: How smart companies turn knowledge into action.* Boston: Harvard Business School Press.

Rockart, J.F. (1979) Chief executives define their own data needs. *Harvard Business Review*, March/April, 81–93.

Rigas, J. and Fan, I.S. (2000) Devising improvement action plans out of performance measurement by an operational model of performance indicators. In: A. Neely (ed.), *Performance Measurement: Past, present, and future.* Cranfield: Centre for Business Performance, Cranfield University, 483–90.

Sandt, J., Schaeffer, U. and Weber, J. (2001) *Balanced Performance Measurement Systems and Manager Satisfaction.* Germany: Otto Beisheim Graduate School of Management.

Scapens, R.W. (1998) Management accounting and strategic control, implications for management accounting research. *Bedrijfskunde, 1, 1–17.*

Schiemann, W.A. and Lingle, J.H. (1999). *Bullseye! Hitting your strategic targets through high-impact measurement.* New York: Free Press.

Schneiderman, A.M. (1999) Why balanced scorecards fail. *Journal of Strategic Performance Management*, January, 6–11.

Simon, H., Guetzkow, H., Kozmetsky, K. and Tyndall, G. (1954) *Centralization vs. Decentralization in Organizing the Controllers Department.* Controllership Foundation paper.

Simons, R. (1995) *Levers of Control: How managers use innovative control systems to drive strategic renewal.* Boston: Harvard Business School Press.

Simons, R. (2000) *Performance Measurement and Control Systems for Implementing Strategy: Text and cases.* Upper Saddle River, NJ: Prentice Hall.

Stratton, W., Lawson, R. and Hatch, T. (2005) Achieving strategy with scorecarding. *Journal of Corporate Accounting and Finance*, March/April.

Vandenbosch, B. (1999) An empirical analysis of the association between the use of executive support systems and perceived organisational competitiveness. *Accounting, Organisations and Society*, 24, 77–92.

Voelpel, S.C., Leibold, M. and Mahmoud, K.M. (2004) The organisational fitness navigator: enabling and measuring organisational fitness for rapid change. *Journal of Change Management*, 4 (12), 123–40.

Waal, A.A. de (2001) *Power of Performance Management: How leading companies create sustained value.* New York: Wiley.

Waal, A.A. de (2002) *The Role of Behavioural Factors in the Successful Implementation and use of Performance Management Systems.* Amsterdam: Vrije Universiteit.

Waal, A.A. de (2003) The future of the balanced scorecard: an interview with Robert S. Kaplan. *Measuring Business Excellence*, 7 (1).

Waal, A.A. de (2005), Forget value based management and the balanced scorecard! An interview with Ken Merchant. *Measuring Business Excellence*, 9 (6).

Zairi, M. (1996), *Benchmarking for Best Practice: Continuous learning through sustainable innovation.* Oxford: Butterworth Heinemann.

Zairi, M. and Jarrar, Y. (2000) Becoming world class through a culture of measurement. In: A. Neely (ed.), *Performance Measurement: Past, present, and future.* Cranfield: Centre for Business Performance, Cranfield University, 688–94.

Part 2

The strategic performance management development cycle

Stage 1

Designing a strategic management model

Stage 1 of the strategic performance development cycle deals with the design of a strategic management model. In this stage the organisation establishes the strategic structure that is the foundation for the development of the performance management process. This stage consists of three steps (see Figure P2.1). Each step is discussed in a separate chapter.

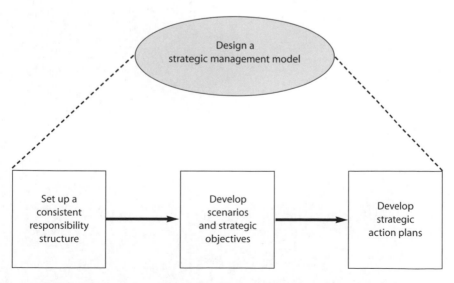

Figure P2.1 Steps to be taken to set up a strategic management model

3

Responsibility structure

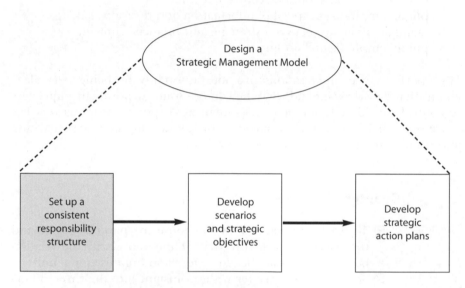

Figure 3.1 Setting up a consistent responsibility structure

The starting point of each strategic performance management system is setting up a consistent responsibility structure. It is essential that there is consensus throughout the organisation on "who is responsible for what." The roles and responsibilities of each management level must be clear, and the chosen management style must be applied consistently throughout the performance management process. Managers and employees need to know what they are held accountable for. Based on their accountability, they then can set up action plans for their own area of expertise. A clear responsibility structure makes it possible to align performance with the responsibilities of organisational members. In addition, the information requirements of management become predictable, instead of the constant stream of ad hoc information requests and differing information requirements that many organisations are dealing with. The responsibility structure also offers managers and other organisational members guidelines on what actions and reactions are expected from them. This is essential because consistent behaviour creates people's trust in management.

Research on high-performance organisations shows that these companies consciously strive to (Waal, 2003):

- establish a consistent responsibility structure with clear roles and accountabilities
- clearly define the roles and responsibilities of corporate headquarters and of business units
- reach consensus between corporate headquarters and the business units about what should be controlled where
- put an emphasis on speed of information and decision making
- maintain a balance between strategic and financial control
- put an emphasis on "no surprises."

High-performance organisations promote autonomy by being very clear about what they do want and what they do not want corporate headquarters to control. In this way senior management at corporate headquarters has more time for long-term tasks, such as strategy development and coaching and training managers who people can rely on.

Chapter objectives

- ☑ To teach the reader how to choose the parenting style and the parenting structure that define and clarify the relation between corporate headquarters and organisational units.
- ☑ To provide the reader with an insight into the three different parenting styles: strategic planning, strategic control, and financial control.
- ☑ To enable the reader to study the three different parenting structures: simple reporting, divided parenting, and duplicated parenting.

3.1 PARENTING STYLE

An organisation needs to make choices about the roles and responsibilities of corporate headquarters, the divisions, and the business units. For this purpose, the organisation can use the concept of parenting styles described by Goold et al. (1994). There are three styles – financial control, strategic control and strategic planning – which differ in the extent of influence that corporate headquarters has on the strategic development processes of lower levels in the organisation, and the method of control used by corporate headquarters.

The parenting styles were originally developed for large (multi)national companies but in practice they proved to be also useful for smaller companies. For those companies the term "corporate headquarters" should be thought of as "the management team."

The influence on the development of the strategy and the strategic objectives of lower organisational levels depends on the frequency and intensity with which corporate headquarters involves itself in the strategic development process of these lower levels. This influence determines whether important decisions are made top-down or bottom-up. The way lower organisational levels are controlled depends on the manner, frequency, content, and level of detail of reporting from these lower levels to corporate headquarters. Management procedures stipulate when corporate headquarters can intervene in the operations of lower organisational levels and what control tools (sanctions, incentives, promotion/demotion of managers) are available to corporate headquarters to do this.

The three parenting styles are depicted in Figure 3.2. A summary of the characteristics of each style is given in Table 3.1.

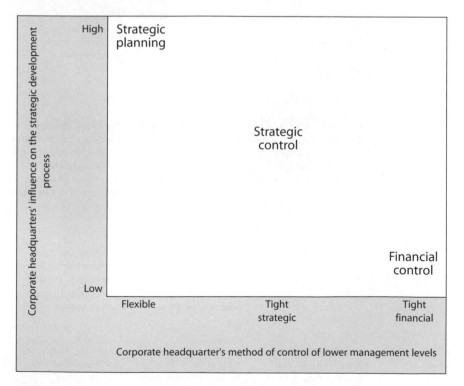

Figure 3.2 Influence of corporate headquarters on the strategic development process of lower organisational levels, and the method of control of these levels

Table 3.1 Characteristics of the three parenting styles

Aspect	Strategic planning	Strategic control	Financial control
Type of industry	Rapidly changing, fast-growing or fiercely competitive industries.	Mature industries and stable competitive situations.	Wide variety of industries.
Parent role	Headquarters is closely involved with business unit in formulation of plans and decisions. Clear sense of direction.	Planning is decentralised to business units. Parent role consists of checking, assessing, and sponsoring.	Headquarters insists that all decisions are "owned" by the business units themselves.
Division/business role	Divisions and business units seek consensus with headquarters and other units for business initiatives (in line with strategic targets).	Divisions and business units have own responsibility for strategies, plans, and proposals.	Divisions and business units are independent entities, sometimes working together to achieve mutual benefits.
Organisational structure	Large or powerful func-tional staff at centre. Shared service departments (marketing, R&D, etc.)	Decentralised with focus on individual performance of division and business unit. Headquarters operates as strategic controller.	Minimal staff at headquarters level, focused on support and financial control.
Planning process	Resource allocation driven by requirements of long-term strategies. Planning influence of headquarters is high.	Negotiation of financial and strategic performance targets. Planning influence of headquarters is medium.	No formal strategic planning, process focuses on division/ business unit annual budget and financial targets. Planning influence of headquarters is low.
Control process	Headquarters puts low priority on monitoring monthly financial results; control is flexible.	Headquarters regularly monitors actuals against planned, on financial and nonfinancial targets; control is strategic.	Headquarters concentrates on financial targets and results (contracting); control is strictly financial.
Value creation focus	Creation of new business units for long-term business development.	Long-term strategies and goals of the divisions/business units (facilitating and coordinating).	Operating improvements and financial control.

Strategic planning

In the strategic planning style, corporate headquarters plays an active part in the strategy development process of the divisions and business units. The planning process is intensive and time-consuming. Because corporate head-quarters is working so closely with the divisions and business units, it is at all times informed about their status. Therefore, the focus of control is mainly on achieving longer-term strategic objectives. Corporate headquarters will only officially react to large deviations of operational results, which makes the control process flexible, taking second stage to the planning process. The staff departments needed to support corporate headquarters in this style are relatively large. In short, corporate headquarters is heavily involved in planning, developing, deploying, and monitoring the execution of the strategy at the divisional and business unit levels.

Strategic control

In the strategic control style, corporate headquarters issues strategic guidelines but the divisions and business units independently make their own strategic plans. These plans are evaluated and prioritised by corporate headquarters. The focus in the plans is on defining both short and longer-term financial and nonfinancial objectives, which are regularly checked by corporate headquarters. The size of the staff departments at headquarters is average. In short, corporate headquarters monitors the execution of the strategy, while the planning, development and deployment of the strategy is done by the divisions and business units themselves.

Financial control

In the financial control style, the responsibility and authority to plan, develop, deploy, and execute strategic plans is totally delegated to the divisions and business units. Corporate headquarters in principle does not evaluate these plans, but is only interested in whether or not the divisions and business units achieve the financial targets as forecasted in their strategic plans. Corporate headquarters effectively manages a portfolio of businesses. The size of the financial department at corporate headquarters is relatively large; the other staff departments at headquarters are small. In short, corporate headquarters only manages on (key) financials from the divisions and business units.

During the definition of a new management control model, it is of the utmost importance that an organisation chooses one parenting style and applies this style consistently throughout the performance management process. Consistent application results in:

- clarity about the roles and responsibilities of the different management levels in the organisations
- consistency in management and control of the various organisational levels
- clear expectations about responsibilities
- clarity about which strategic objectives should be achieved by who
- consensus about intervention by higher management levels in the management process of lower management levels.

Despite the above statement that an organisation should choose only one parenting style, in practice it appears that large and complex organisations can have several parenting styles. Of course organisations should aim at having a single, consistent parenting style, as this sends out a clear signal to the organisational members. However, if an organisation operates in heterogeneous business environments in a wide variety of industries, it is not inconceivable that different divisions should have different parenting styles. It should not be a problem as long as the chosen parenting style for a specific division is applied consistently throughout that division and its underlying business units.

For some divisions, corporate headquarters will choose financial control as the parenting style. This style is often used in divisions that meet financial targets consistently over a period of time. These divisions are mainly managed on the basis of financial figures, and their business units have a fair amount of freedom in their strategic planning processes. Divisional management only gets involved in business unit management if a particular business unit shows serious deviations from the targets agreed upon. In other divisions, corporate headquarters will opt for strategic planning as its parenting style. This is the case in divisions that operate in a highly dynamic, volatile and competitive environment, in divisions that are young and/or have a young, relatively inexperienced management, and in divisions that consistently do not achieve their targets. In those cases, experienced senior management has to step in to coach divisional management.

3.2 PARENTING STRUCTURE

The parenting style of an organisation, and consequently the responsibilities of the different management levels, strongly influences the parenting structure of that organisation. A parenting structure indicates how the control processes between corporate headquarters and the division and its underlying business units are organised (Figure 3.3). Selecting a parenting structure also forces the organisation to make choices about the desired relations between senior management and divisional and business unit management, regarding its control and information processes.

There are various parenting structures for organisations to choose from, as Figure 3.3 illustrates. They differ in the number of parent levels, the level

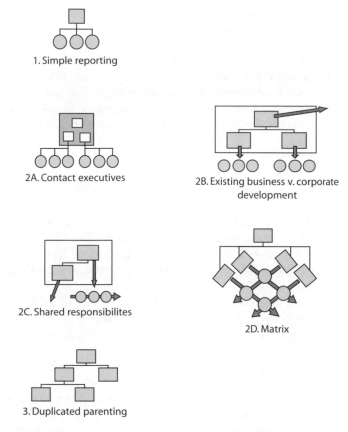

1. Simple reporting

2A. Contact executives

2B. Existing business v. corporate development

2C. Shared responsibilites

2D. Matrix

3. Duplicated parenting

Figure 3.3 Parenting structures
Source: adapted from Goold et al. (1994).

of parenting authority, and the parenting focus. The parent level is the management level that has authority to manage and control one or more management levels that are placed underneath. The horizontal squares in Figure 3.3 represent the parent levels, which are usually the highest management levels, such as corporate headquarters management and division management. The round symbols represent the management levels that have a lower authority and consequently have a parent relation with fewer management levels, usually business unit managements which have a relation with their departments. The arrows show the direction of the parenting focus.

1. *Simple reporting*. Corporate headquarters stands directly above the business units, as a result of which the two management levels can communicate directly and frequently. This parenting structure is often found in small, relatively simple organisations.
2. *Divided parenting*. Specialist groups are set up at corporate headquarters, which increases the management capacity of corporate headquarters.

This parenting structure is often found in organisations which are (getting) bigger. There are four substructures:

    A. *Contact executives*. At corporate headquarters, there are representatives appointed who are responsible for one functional or organisational area in the organisation, or for part of the portfolio. Business units will still go to corporate headquarters to get approval for their plans and budget, however in the remainder of the year they will have frequent (in)formal contact with their contact or sponsoring executive.

    B. *Existing business vs. corporate development*. There are two parenting levels in the organisation, each one concentrates on different tasks. Corporate headquarters focuses on corporate development and external relations, and the division management level focuses on managing the business units.

    C. *Shared responsibilities*. There are two parenting levels in the organisation, each one concentrates on different tasks. However, corporate headquarters not only focuses on corporate development and external relations, but is also heavily involved in controlling the business units. The division management level focuses on managing the business units and the linkages between these units.

    D. *Matrix*. Corporate headquarters is placed directly above the divisions. There are two types of division management levels which focus on different functions: regional/geographic and product/brand/services. They are placed on either side of the matrix. The business units report to both types of divisions. Corporate headquarters settles disputes between the two sides of the matrix, and further focuses on corporate development and external relations.

3. *Duplicated parenting*. This parenting structure involves repetition of the same basic tasks, at different management levels. Each level controls the level below and has influence beyond that level. An example is the case of both the division and corporate headquarters directly controlling business units. This parenting structure is often found in very large organisations.

Once an organisation has established a clear parenting style and parenting structure, and has aligned the rest of the organisation to this style and structure, it can begin to analyse the consequences for the performance management system. The parenting style and structure have consequences for the strategy development, budgeting, forecasting, reporting, and review processes, as well as for the content and layout of reports and for the systems supporting the performance management process.

Table 3.2 Characteristics of the parenting structures

Aspect	1. Simple reporting	2. Divided parenting				3. Duplicated parenting
		A. Contact executives	B. Existing business vs. corporate development	C. Shared responsibilities	D. Matrix	
Organisation structure	Single parent level above business units	Portfolio specialisation of individuals on a single parent level	Two parent levels: one for development and one for parenting portfolio	Two parents both with active role in influencing businesses	Parents for two functions: regional and product/brand/service	Multiple parenting levels
Company size	Small companies with few business units	Mostly medium-sized to large companies	Mostly medium-sized to large companies	Mostly large companies	Large companies	Very large companies
Relation of business unit with corporate	Direct formal and informal contact with corporate	Formal contact with corporate, frequent informal contact with contact executives	Direct formal and informal contact with second parent layer	Formal contact with corporate for strategic and budget control, regular contact with division	Direct relationship with different parents for different functions	Repetition of basic tasks, at different levels of management
Advantages	Simplicity	Single parent level	Parent close to important business issues	Distinct roles for divisional and central levels	Specialisation of parenting	None
Disadvantages	Difficult to expand	Lack of clarity about position of contact executives	Duplication risk	Overlap of influence on business units	Lack of clarity/excessive overlap	Cash/time costs of duplication not justified by additional value creation

3.3 CASE: PARENTING STYLE OF ELECTRICAL CONSTRUCTION GROUP

Electrical Construction Group (ECG) was founded in Cleveland, Ohio, just after the Second World War. The company manufactures a wide range of electrical, electronic, and electromechanical products for commercial, industrial, and consumer markets. ECG is a global company which is present in many countries and has been growing steadily over the years. The enterprise consists of six divisions which each have multiple business units (Figure 3.4).

The executive team at ECG's headquarters formulates strict strategic guidelines and targets for KPIs for all its divisions. All divisions receive the same set of indicators. The targets set for these indicators are not negotiable. Examples of these indicators and targets include operating profit and inventory turnover, which should improve by more than x per cent over the next y years. The targets are very challenging and cannot be achieved by simply improving current business compared with last year. Therefore, divisions and business units are forced to think of new ideas and actions, aimed at both cost improvement and revenue growth. Since ECG is an established business and operates in a relatively stable competitive environment, the company is able to use the same set of financial performance indicators for each division and business unit. More than that, this set of performance indicators can even be kept the same for quite a number of years. This constancy keeps the organisation focused on the same value drivers and improves

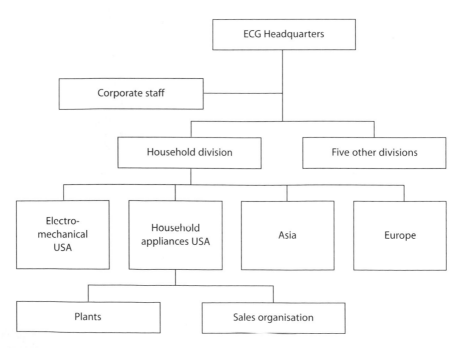

Figure 3.4 Simplified organisational chart of ECG

comparability of performance over the years. It also gives the senior management team the opportunity to benchmark business units against each other.

The strategic guidelines make the expected strategic performance of all organisational levels explicit beforehand, and can therefore be used by divisions and business units as input for their strategic planning processes. The divisions and business units can spend their time on formulating strategic actions that help to achieve the strategic targets instead of renegotiating targets with senior management at corporate headquarters. As a result, the quality of the strategic action plans and initiatives increases. ECG's culture is such that people accept that senior management at corporate headquarters sets strict targets for the divisions and business units. Both the heavy involvement of senior management in the planning process and its in-depth knowledge of each business make sure that the divisions and business units accept the strict targets. This acceptance eliminates the need to involve divisions and business units in the strategic company-wide target-setting process.

During the strategic planning process the senior management team pays a lot of attention to reviewing and testing the divisional plans on logic and feasibility. Senior management has a genuine desire to understand the plans and underlying actions. Once the plans have been approved, it limits its evaluation of the units to four formal reviews per year. In addition to these regular reviews, special reviews are held for capital investments or changes in strategic direction. The divisions have their own responsibility for executing the strategic plans. On a monthly basis, each division reports financial and operational information to the senior management team at corporate headquarters. ECG's parenting style can be characterised as strategic control which is applied consistently throughout the organisation (Table 3.3).

3.4 CASE: RESPONSIBILITY STRUCTURE OF SOUTH-MIDDLE ECOLOGICAL LABORATORY LTD

This case is an example of an organisation which, because of internal and external forces, had to change its parenting style and parenting structure to be able to deal with these forces. This particular organisation operates in a rapidly changing industrial environment with many opportunities but also with many threats. The management team has spent a lot of time restructuring the organisation to make it more agile and ready to take advantage of the changes.

The organisation's background

South-Middle Ecological Laboratory Ltd (SMEL) is currently one of the biggest waste management organisations in the mid-south of the country.

Table 3.3 ECG's parenting style

Aspect	Strategic planning		Strategic control	Financial control
Type of industry	Rapidly changing, fast growing or fiercely competitive industries.	✓	Mature industries and stable competitive situations.	Wide variety of industries.
Parent role	Headquarters is closely involved with business unit in formulation of plans and decisions. Clear sense of direction.	✓	Planning is decentralised to business units. Parent role consists of checking, assessing, and sponsoring.	Headquarters insists that all decisions are 'owned' by the business units themselves.
Business role	Divisions and business units seek consensus with headquarters and other units for business initiatives (in line with strategic targets).	✓	Divisions and business units have own responsibility for strategies, plans, and proposals.	Divisions and business units are independent entities, sometimes working together to achieve mutual benefits.
Organisational structure	Large or powerful functional staffs at centre. Shared service departments (marketing, R&D, etc.).	✓	Decentralised with focus on individual division and business unit performance. Headquarters operates as strategic controller.	Minimal staff at headquarter level, focused on support and financial control.
Planning process	Resource allocation driven by requirements of long-term strategies. Planning influence of headquarters is high.	✓	Negotiation of financial and strategic performance targets. Planning influence of headquarters is medium.	No formal strategic planning, process focuses on division and business unit annual budget and financial targets. Planning influence of headquarters is low.
Control process	Headquarters puts low priority on monitoring monthly financial results. Control by headquarters is flexible.	✓	Headquarters regularly monitors actuals against planned, on financial and nonfinancial targets. Control by headquarters is strategic.	Headquarters concentrates on financial targets and results (contracting). Control by headquarters is strictly financial.
Value creation focus	Creation of new business units for long-term business development.	✓	Long-term strategies and goals of the divisions and business units (facilitating and coordinating).	Operating improvements and financial control.

The organisation services the complete chain of waste treatment: from collecting waste at the point of origin to the end-processing and disposal of waste, including pre-treatment and recycling. The organisation is currently changing its image from a mere incinerator company to a full-service waste management company.

The main strategy of SMEL is to work in partnership with governmental agencies and industrial companies. Through these partnerships, the firm stays closer to its customers and can offer better service. Moreover, SMEL also wants to grow by means of acquisitions and alliances, and through cooperation with other waste treatment companies.

In general, the waste management industry deals with two main categories of waste streams (Figure 3.5). The primary waste streams deal with untreated waste which is produced by industrial companies, governmental agencies, municipalities, and households. Efforts to reduce the amount of waste (prevention) mainly take place in this stream. The untreated waste is collected, sorted into different types and then processed by waste treatment companies. The secondary waste streams consist of landfilling or storing in depots waste materials that cannot be recycled or incinerated, such as toxic waste and metals.

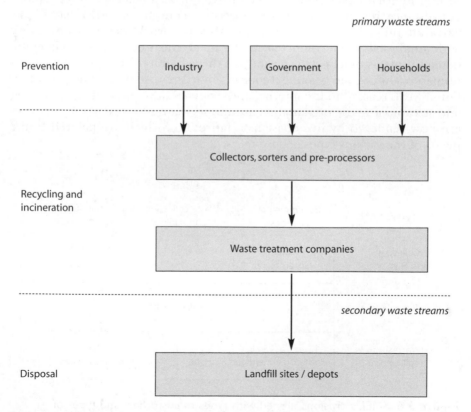

Figure 3.5 Schematic overview of waste sources and streams

In the past few years, waste treatment has developed into a fierce marketplace. Competition is getting stronger, margins are getting slimmer, legislation is becoming stricter, and customers are placing higher demands on services. There are several concurrent developments that are causing this fiercely competitive market. First of all, the government is withdrawing from the physical treatment of waste and is concentrating more on environmental legislation and ensuring compliance with the law and regulations. Waste treatment is now strictly carried out by specialised companies that may originate from the local domestic market or from neighbouring states and countries. Many waste treatment companies are reacting to these developments by merging with other companies or by setting up strategic partnerships. In this way, they can offer services for the treatment of all types of waste. This means that they can become a 'one-stop shop' for waste treatment, increasing customer convenience.

Making the change

While the external environment was changing rapidly, SMEL experienced several internal developments which threatened its ability to react rapidly. For instance, because of a number of recent acquisitions, SMEL had to pay extra attention to internal processes. Also, the workforce had to acquire additional skills and competencies to meet the growing and changing demands of customers. This meant that there had to be a stronger focus on human resources and training, requiring more management time and attention. SMEL reacted to the internal and external developments by changing and streamlining the organisation around its main services. SMEL's services are now rendered by five divisions (Figure 3.6), which are tailored to the needs of the various types of customers.

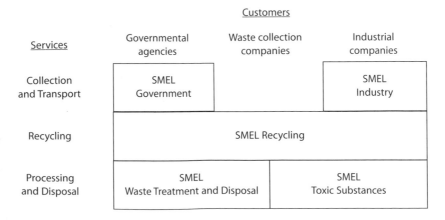

Figure 3.6 SMEL's divisions, aligned with types of customers and types of processes

There are two commercial divisions that aim at selling services to specific markets, SMEL Government and SMEL Industry, and three waste treatment divisions that specialise in specific treatment techniques, SMEL Toxic Substances, SMEL Waste Treatment & Disposal, and SMEL Recycling. The waste treatment divisions work for the commercial divisions, but they can also receive waste directly from pre-processing companies. The new organisational structure made it possible for SMEL to develop an integrated service. Through this service, a one-stop-shop service is offered to customers, by taking care of all their waste. This kind of service requires close cooperation between SMEL's divisions. It also demands strict coordination between the divisions. A critical success factor therefore is the availability of timely and relevant information throughout the process.

In order to make the new service possible, SMEL needs a clear picture of the responsibilities and tasks of the various management levels in the organisation. Looking at the current situation, it becomes quickly evident that the various acquisitions and subsequent restructurings have caused vagueness about responsibilities in the organisation. In the old, more stable situation, SMEL was a centrally managed organisation in which corporate headquarters had the most important voice. In the new situation, it was not yet clear who had responsibility for which process.

SMEL's management team decided to conduct two workshops to make things clearer. In the first workshop, senior management at corporate headquarters discussed the current parenting style and structure of SMEL. They also discussed the desired parenting style and structure that would support SMEL's strategic ambitions. The results of this workshop were presented to division management during a second workshop. Consensus was then reached between corporate headquarters and the divisions on the changes needed to the parenting style and parenting structure. All participants in this second workshop were confident that the organisation was about to be well prepared for the future.

A shift in parenting style and parenting structure

In the old days, SMEL was a centrally managed company. This was because at that time SMEL was a small organisation which operated in a relatively stable environment. Management could still be very close to operations and was consequently well informed. However, external pressures (as described in the previous section), which occurred at the same time as the organisation was growing, meant that this central management style was no longer tenable. A change in management style was needed. During the workshops, the different parenting styles were discussed and a choice was made for each aspect, i.e. which style best described SMEL's current situation (✓ in Table 3.4). The arrows in Table 3.4 indicate the shifts on aspect level from the existing to the desired situation.

It became clear that all the changes that ensued from the new situation

Table 3.4 SMEL's changing parenting style

Aspect	Strategic planning	Strategic control	Financial control
Type of industry	✓ Rapidly changing, fast-growing or fiercely competitive industries	Mature industries and stable competitive situations	Wide variety of industries
Parent role	✓ Headquarters is closely involved with business unit in formulation of plans and decisions. Clear sense of direction.	✓ Planning is decentralised to business units. Parent role consists of checking, assessing, and sponsoring.	Headquarters insists that all decisions are 'owned' by the business units themselves
Business role	Divisions and business units seek consensus with headquarters and other units for business initiatives (in line with strategic targets)	✓ Divisions and business units have own responsibility for strategies, plans, and proposals	✓ Divisions and business units are independent entities, sometimes working together to achieve mutual benefits
Organisational structure	✓ Large or powerful functional staffs at centre. Shared service departments (marketing, R&D, etc.).	✓ Decentralised with focus on individual division and business → unit performance. Headquarters operates as strategic controller.	Minimal staff at headquarter's level, focused on support and financial control.
Planning process	Resource allocation driven by requirements of long-term strategies. Planning influence of headquarters is high.	✓ Negotiation of financial and strategic performance targets. Planning influence of headquarters is medium.	No formal strategic planning, process focuses on division and business unit annual budget and financial targets. Planning influence of headquarters is low.
Control process	Headquarters puts low priority on monitoring monthly financial results. Control by headquarters is flexible.	✓ Headquarters regularly monitors actuals against planned, on financial and nonfinancial targets. Control by headquarters is strategic.	✓ Headquarters concentrates on financial targets and results (contracting). ← Control by headquarters is strictly financial.
Value creation focus	Creation of new business units for long-term business development.	✓ Long-term strategies and goals of the divisions and business units (facilitating and coordinating).	Operating improvements and financial control.

had muddled the company's responsibility structure. Sometimes several parenting styles were used at the same time! After discussing this issue, a clear preference was expressed by SMEL's management for the "strategic control" style. The company could then be managed in a "hands-off" manner with more entrepreneurship in the divisions. Consensus was reached that senior management at corporate headquarters and divisional management should start acting according to the guidelines of this control style (➔ in Table 3.4).

There is currently still a relatively large staff department at corporate headquarters as a remnant of the centralised past. In the near future, the staff will move to the divisions because the main operational processes take place at that level. The corporate staff will then be cut down in size.

During the workshops, it became apparent that in SMEL's existing situation a hybrid mix of parenting structures was used. This mix consisted of the "contact executives," "shared responsibilities," and "matrix" parenting structures as detailed in Table 3.5.

SMEL's management team decided to switch to the "contact executive" parenting structure (Figure 3.7).

Two corporate senior managers each have the responsibility for two divisions. It is their job to make sure that enough information about their divisions is shared with the other senior managers at corporate headquarters, and that directives from the senior management team are communicated to their divisions. Because of the relative newness of the organisational structure, these senior managers are quite involved in the day-to-day operations

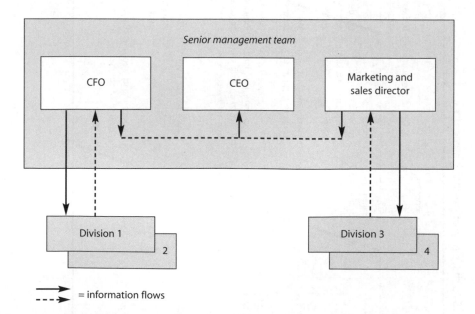

Figure 3.7 SMEL's parenting structure: two senior managers are contact executives for two divisions

Table 3.5 SMEL's mix of parenting structures

Aspect	1. Simple reporting	2. Divided parenting				3. Duplicated parenting
		A. Contact executives	B. Existing business vs. corporate	C. Shared responsibilities	D. Matrix	
Organisation structure	Single parent level above business units	Portfolio specialisation of individuals on a single parent level	Two parent levels: one for development and one for parenting portfolio	Two parents both with active role in influencing businesses	Parents for two functions: regional and product/brand/service	Multiple parenting levels
Company size	Small companies with few business units	Mostly medium-sized to large companies	Mostly medium-sized to large companies	Mostly large companies	Large companies	Very large companies
Relation of business unit with corporate	Direct formal and informal contact with corporate	Formal contact with corporate, frequent informal contact with contact executives	Direct formal and informal contact with second parent layer	Formal contact with corporate for strategic and budget control, regular contact with division	Direct relationship with different parents for different functions	Repetition of basic tasks, at different levels of management
Advantages	Simplicity	Single parent level	Parent close to important business issues	Distinct roles for divisional and central levels	Specialisation of parenting	None
Disadvantages	Difficult to expand	Lack of clarity about position of contact executives	Duplication risk	Overlap of influence on business units	Lack of clarity/ excessive overlap	Cash/time costs of duplication not justified by additional value creation

of their divisions and the underlying business units. However, the senior management team is of the opinion that divisions have to take a stronger and more visible role in managing and controlling their underlying business units in the near future. This will move SMEL more toward the "shared responsibility" parenting structure. The new one-stop-shop service makes yet another structure viable, the "matrix" parenting structure. Because SMEL is divided into customer-oriented and product-oriented divisions, there is a certain need for a matrix organisation to ensure that the customer–product relations are managed well.

3.5 CASE STUDY: UVD'S RESPONSIBILITY STRUCTURE

So far, the brothers Williams have managed the UVD organisation hands-on. They and their direct reports are a tightly knit team and personnel turnover is low. However, lately a marked decline in enthusiasm has been noted in comparison with the eagerness and excitement that everyone experienced when the business was still in the building-up stage. The UK and US operations both benefit from the fact that they are newly set-up divisions, as it gives them the opportunity to organise their divisions, which energises the employees. However, employees in the Netherlands, in particular, find expanding the company increasingly difficult and stressful as they feel burdened by an increasing number of new bureaucratic procedures they have to adhere to. In addition, it is unclear to them in which direction UVD wants to go with its new activities and new products, and how they can play a role in this.

UVD management realises that many things have changed in the past few years. In the old days, the Williams brothers formulated the strategy themselves while at the same time being heavily involved in day-to-day operations. However, the company has grown to such an extent that this is no longer possible. Because of the expansions in the UK and the United States, there is a tendency towards decentralisation, with management being less directly involved in operations. In the new set-up, local managers have become much more responsible for their own performance.

The UK office has indicated it wants to apply a different marketing strategy than the one used in the Netherlands, to improve results. This has resulted in many discussions about who is allowed to make which decisions, who sets the targets and who is responsible for achieving them. The controller of UVD, Helen Case, realises that the recent changes have also created the need for a new strategic performance management system. She has decided to start her search for a new system by looking at the current and desired parenting style and structure of UVD.

Case question 1: What are the existing parenting style and parenting structure of UVD?

Case question 2: What should the desired parenting style and parenting structure of UVD be?

Case question 3: What are some of the consequences of the chosen parenting style and parenting structure for UVD's existing strategic performance management system?

Key points

- ☑ High-performance organisations establish a consistent responsibility structure with clear roles and accountabilities for corporate headquarters and business units, and reach consensus between corporate headquarters and the business units about what should be controlled where.
- ☑ Choosing a parenting style and parenting structure defines and clarifies the relation between the organisational structure (roles and responsibilities) and the performance management process.
- ☑ The parenting style stipulates the extent in which corporate headquarters influences the strategic planning and operational control processes on lower levels in the organisation.
- ☑ The parenting structure stipulates the way in which the control process between corporate headquarters and the division and its underlying business units is structured.
- ☑ Every management level has to stick to the chosen and communicated parenting style and structure: consistently "walk the talk."

References

Goold, M., Campbell, A. and Alexander, M. (1994) *Corporate Level Strategy: Creating value in the multibusiness organisation*. New York: Wiley.

Waal, A.A. de (2003), *On the road to Nirvana: Building the real adaptive enterprise*. Hyperion white paper, www.andredewaal.nl.

4

Scenarios and strategic objectives

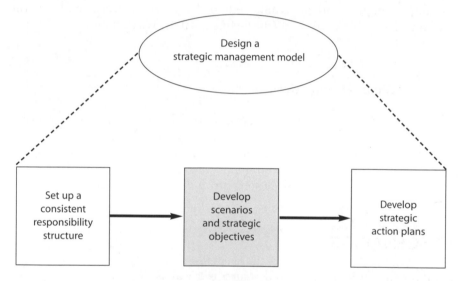

Figure 4.1 Developing scenarios and strategic objectives

In these dynamic times, in which many trends are both threats and opportunities to companies, it has become increasingly important for organisations to "think ahead." Thinking ahead makes organisations proactive: they can react more quickly and effectively to threats and opportunities, and develop strategies to benefit from them. Research has shown that taking longer-term trends into account in daily decisions leads to superior results (Hart and Banbury, 1994). There are other advantages as well: a long-term planning focus limits the need to react in an off-the-cuff manner to crisis situations, it creates a learning system because organisational members learn from comparing forecasts with actual results, and it instils a proactive mentality throughout the company. Above all, "an inability to predict means an inability to plan" (Mintzberg et al., 1998).

Research on high-performance organisations shows that organisations of this type monitor the environment constantly and respond adequately to shifts and opportunities in the marketplace. They do this by surveying the markets and identifying trends and exploring scenarios. They balance long-term focus and short-term focus in order to safeguard the long-term continuity of the business, while at the same time obtaining short-term results which make it possible to plan against possible futures.

High-performance organisations deliberately create clarity and a common understanding of the company's direction and strategy, which results in a commonly held strategic mind-set among organisational members. In addition, they create a company-wide understanding of individual, group, departmental and divisional contributions, and clarity of purpose and action. Finally, they ensure they build robust, resilient, and adaptive plans by applying scenario thinking and "what-ifs," and drafting resilient strategies and plans tailored to the levels of uncertainty in the environment (Goldsmith and Clutterbuck, 1998; Waal, 2005).

Chapter objectives

☑ To teach the reader how to develop scenarios – possible futures of an organisation – in a practical way.

☑ To teach the reader how to translate the strategy of the organisation in tangible, concrete strategic objectives which can be communicated throughout the organisation.

4.1 SCENARIOS

Thinking ahead in a formal and structured way is known as scenario planning or scenario building. Scenario planning is defined as:

> the process of positing several informed, plausible and imagined alternative future environments in which decisions about the future may be played out, for the purpose of changing current thinking, improving decision making, enhancing human and organisation learning and improving performances.
> (www.personal.psu.edu/faculty/t/j/tjc18/scenario-planning.html)

There are two types of scenarios, internal and external. External scenarios are derived from shared and agreed-upon mental models of the external world. They outline a range of possible future developments and outcomes in the external world. The organisation is essentially unable to influence the proceedings of these external developments and outcomes, but if they materialise they will have an impact on the organisation. Internal scenarios also outline a range of future developments and outcomes, but this time of the organisation itself. They are derived from the organisation's anticipation of future situations, which is arrived at by linking its own (intended) actions to anticipated external developments (based on Heijden, 1996). Both types of scenarios lead to anticipated results and the consequences thereof which may affect the company to some degree. Therefore, the results of scenarios have to be taken into account in the mission and strategy of the organisation (Figure 4.2).

Many development methods have been devised and many books have been written on the topic of strategic planning, of which scenario planning forms a part (for a comprehensive overview see Mintzberg et al., 1998). These methods can be quite elaborate, which can diminish their value for everyday practical use. A pragmatic way to develop scenarios is as follows:

- *Set a goal and timeframe for the scenario planning.* Make sure the participants in the scenario planning process understand the goal of the exercise: to assess the impact of external and internal developments on the organisation's mission and strategy. Set the timeframe of the scenario, considering how fast changes take place in the industry concerned and the extent to which it is possible to predict common trends in, for instance, demographics. A practical timeframe is three years.

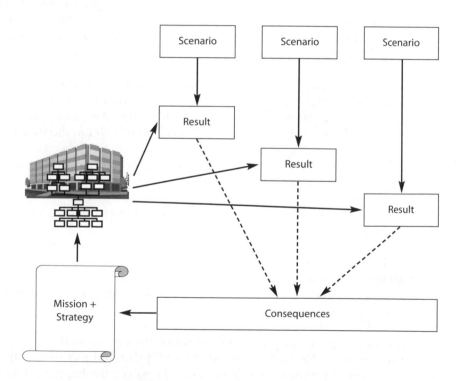

Figure 4.2 The relationship between scenarios and the mission and strategy of an organisation

- *Identify the participants in the scenario planning process.* Decide on who can and should have input, based on knowledge of the industry, and who has an vested interest in the possible outcomes of the process. As a rule, the entire management team will be involved, but department heads and other persons interested may also participate.
- *Prepare the scenario planning process.* Ask a (senior) staff member to map and describe the basic trends and driving forces in the industry. Ask the participants in the scenario planning process to list the three key developments (which can be external and/or internal) that they see happening around them. Collect and distribute the information to all participants.
- *Conduct the scenario planning session.* Let all participants brainstorm on the current and expected trends. Make sure all trends are seriously thought of and discussed before they are assessed. List the scenarios that everybody agrees upon and let the participants estimate the chance that the scenario will materialise in the next three years. Let them also stipulate whether each scenario represents an opportunity or a threat to the company, and whether it will have a low, medium, or high impact on the organisational strategy. Try to combine scenarios to make a shorter list.
- *Write out the scenarios.* Prepare a short document that concisely describes all the scenarios and the reasons for the likelihood of each scenario occurring. Distribute the document to all participants and other interested parties and ask for feedback. Adapt the scenarios based on the received input.
- *Conduct the strategic objectives session.* Collect the current strategic objectives and map them in a matrix against the scenarios. Estimate the effect of the scenarios on the current objectives. Are these strong enough to address the trends which are likely to unravel in the future? Use the matrix to decide what to do with the objectives: keep them, reformulate them, remove them, or add new ones. The case of the Laboratories at Blackwood (later in this chapter, see page 87) gives an example of such a matrix. Assess the impact of the new objectives on the current mission. Does it have to change to better depict what the organisation will be going through in the future?
- *Write out the new mission and strategic objectives.* Prepare a short document in which the mission and all the strategic objectives are described. Distribute the document to all participants and other interested parties, and invite feedback. Finalise the mission and strategic objectives based on the received input.

Technically speaking, the approach just described does not lead to "real" scenarios in the sense that they are elaborate and quantified pictures of the future state of the organisation and its industry. However, the big advantage of this approach is that it is fast, with maximum input of the people who have to steer the organisation in the near future. The support for the newly formulated mission and strategic objectives will be high, which is an excellent starting point for the remainder of the performance management implementation process.

4.2 STRATEGIC OBJECTIVES

One of the most important tools of every organisation is the strategic development process. A recent survey conducted among 960 organisations found that strategic development is applied by 79 per cent of them, and that these companies are very satisfied with this technique: a 4.14 score on a scale of 1 – 5 (Rigby, 2005).

The starting point in the strategic development process of every organisation is that it states its reason for being, its mission. The mission is formulated by answering the question, "What do we, as an organisation, want to accomplish: what is our mission?" After that, the organisation can formulate its strategy by answering the questions, "How are we as an organisation going to achieve our mission?" and "How can we accomplish what we want?" A well-formulated strategy indicates how the organisation wants to anticipate changes in its environment and the consequences these changes will have on the quality, price, and delivery times of its products and services.

The strategy (which often can be quite an elaborate statement) is made concrete in what are known as strategic objectives. These are short and powerful statements that can be communicated easily throughout the company, covering one aspect from the strategy and clearly stating what the organisation is going to do. Suppose an organisation has the following mission: "to be the premier customer-driven organisation with a social conscience." The strategy for this company reads: "to double in size by focusing on the customers, while retaining a socially conscious image." Possible strategic objectives are then to focus the organisation more on customer satisfaction, to develop new environmental-friendly products, and to sponsor local environmental projects.

During the development of strategic objectives there are a number of quality criteria that each objective has to satisfy in order to make it manageable:

- it has to describe an activity that leads to the desired final result
- it has to be defined in concrete, not abstract terms
- it must express action (e.g. "Improve …")
- it must relate to the area of responsibility of the manager for whom the objective is developed
- there should be a limited number of objectives per manager, preferably no more than seven

In addition, a strategic objective should be SMART:

- *Specific:* the objective is concrete, unambiguous (susceptible only to one explanation to prevent misunderstandings), and relevant.
- *Measurable:* the achievement of the objective can be measured by using critical success factors and key performance indicators (see Chapter 6).
- *Acceptable:* the objective is acceptable and motivating for the employees.
- *Realistic:* the objective is ambitious yet achievable (with regard to time, money, and capacity needed).
- *Time bound:* the objective has to be achieved in a specific timeframe.

The strategic objectives have to be translated to lower levels in the organisation to make sure everybody in the company works towards achieving the same organisational goals. For this, the Christmas tree model can be used (Figure 4.3).

The starting point is the strategy which is formulated by the management team and which is made concrete by developing it further into strategic objectives. The formulated strategy and strategic objectives form the basis for the next level down. Each division has to ask itself the question, "How can our division contribute, in a tangible and concrete way, to the realisation of the company's strategy and strategic objectives?" The answers to this question form the divisional objectives. These divisional objectives form the basis for the next level down, the business units. In turn, each business unit has to ask itself the question, "How can our business unit contribute, in a tangible and concrete way, to the realisation of the divisional objectives, and thereby the company's strategy?" The answers to this question form the business unit objectives. This process is repeated until the lowest level in the organisation, the individual employees. An organisation can go as far as formulating personal objectives for each employee, thereby creating a personal balanced scorecard.

Figure 4.3 Aligning the strategy throughout the organisation

By using the Christmas tree model, a company can be sure that all levels in the organisation are strategically aligned. Because each objective on each organisational level has been derived from the strategy, management can be confident that each individual knows what is important for the company and will aim to achieve this.

4.3 CASE: SCENARIOS AND STRATEGIC OBJECTIVES AT THE LABORATORIES AT BLACKWOOD

The Laboratories at Blackwood (LAB) is a prominent research laboratory for water, food, waste, and environmental testing. The company has subsidiaries all over Europe. Its clients are municipalities, engineering firms, food and chemical companies, and building and construction companies. LAB processes large numbers of samples in three shifts per day, which gives the laboratory the characteristics of a production environment in which logistics and information technology play an important role. The company employs 500 people, and is financially healthy. The organisational structure is flat with only four layers: management team, department heads, team leaders, and lab assistants. It has been a conscious decision to work in small teams as it increases the commitment and accountability of the employees.

The mission of the company is: "LAB is the no. 1 independent provider of high-quality food and environmental testing in Europe and is a reliable partner for its customers." On the basis of this mission and a strategic analysis performed five years ago and still in place today, the following strategic objectives have been developed:

1. Improve delivery reliability.
2. Develop a service portfolio which satisfies the customers' needs.
3. Safeguard a healthy financial management.
4. Improve the quality of the processes.
5. Improve the flexibility and adaptability of operational processes.
6. Develop a customer-oriented innovation process.
7. Foster knowledge-sharing in the organisation.
8. Improve the information systems.

During the last decade LAB has grown rapidly because of the increasing interest in Europe in environmental affairs and the Kyoto Protocol. Part of the growth has been autonomous and part has been through acquisitions all over Europe. The growth has attracted competitors, which created a price war in recent years. In addition, the needs of customers have changed quite dramatically. While in the old days only the quality of the testing was important, nowadays speed, costs, and reliability in process delivery time are also important. LAB has been slow to react to the increased competitive pressures and demands, but has realised it needs to pay more attention to efficiency and costs. The management team is of the opinion that the time has come to look critically at the organisation and its mission and strategy. Further professionalism in performance management is seen as the condition to make sure that the three spearheads of the firm are assured: delivery on time, high client satisfaction, and good profitability. As a starting point, the management team feels a new mission and strategy are needed that are better suited to the new competitive environment.

As a first step, scenarios are developed by asking all management team members to describe three trends in the environment that are likely to affect LAB in the next three years. These trends are discussed, considering whether they are a threat or an opportunity, and the impact and likelihood of each scenario becoming reality is estimated, with the following result:

S1.   Growth in the profit industry, decreasing in orders from governmental agencies. Both an opportunity and a threat. High impact. Likelihood: 95 per cent.

S2.   New legislation which requires less environmental testing. A threat. High impact. Likelihood: 30 per cent

S3.   New legislation which requires different environmental testing. An opportunity. Medium impact. Likelihood: 80 per cent.

S4.   Increased scaling-up in the industry, requiring LAB to acquire more competitors. An opportunity. Low impact. Likelihood: 40 per cent.

S5.   Increased competition and therefore even more price erosion. A threat. High impact. Likelihood: 75 per cent.

S6.   Increased shortage of qualified laboratory personnel. A threat. High impact. Likelihood: 85 per cent.

The second step is to evaluate whether the existing strategic objectives can deal with the consequences of each scenario. The evaluation shows whether the objectives will still be valid in the next three years or whether they have become obsolete, and whether they have to be reformulated to stay relevant. The evaluation is performed by constructing a matrix in which the management team puts its judgment of the effect of the scenarios, according to the following scoring table:

++   =   The objective is very important in addressing and dealing with the consequences of the scenario and certainly has to be upheld.

+   =   The objective in its current form can address and deal with the consequences of the scenario.

−   =   The scenario has no consequences for the objective; the objective does not address the scenario consequences.

Δ   =   The objective in its current form partly addresses and deals with the consequences of the scenario, but it needs to be reformulated in order to become more effective.

Table 4.1 Effects of scenarios on LAB's existing strategic objectives

Scenario	S1(95%)	S2(30%)	S3(80%)	S4(40%)	S5(75%)	S6(85%)
Opportunity /Threat	O/T	T	O	O	T	T
Impact	H	H	M	L	H	H
1. Improve delivery reliability	++	–	–	+	++	–
2. Develop service portfolio	++	Δ+	Δ+	–	++	–
3. Safeguard healthy financial management	++	++	+	Δ+	++	–
4. Improve quality of processes	+	Δ+	Δ+	–	Δ+	–
5. Improve operational processes	Δ+	+	++	+	++	–
6. Develop innovation process	–	–	++	–	+	–
7. Foster knowledge sharing	+	–	++	++	+	+
8. Improve information systems	–	–	–	+	–	–

From the table, the management team composes the new strategic objectives by looking at each objective and deciding whether it can be removed (many "–"), kept (many "+" or "++"), or kept in a reformulated form (many "Δ").

This results in the following draft objectives:

- Improve delivery reliability (same).
- Improve match between service portfolio and profit and nonprofit customers (reformulated).
- Safeguard a healthy financial management (same).
- Improve match between process quality and customer needs (reformulated).
- Improve the flexibility and adaptability of operational processes (same).
- Increase knowledge sharing in the organisation (reformulated).

The current objectives 6 and 8 are removed.

Then for each scenario, and especially the ones with a high impact and high likelihood, it is checked whether the new objectives address the scenarios enough. This reveals that scenario 6 is not addressed, so another strategic objective is added:

■ Increase attractiveness of LAB to highly skilled personnel (new).

Finally, the current mission is looked at to evaluate whether it has to be reformulated because of the new strategic objectives. It is decided to reformulate it as follows:

LAB is the no. 1 independent provider of high-quality food and environmental testing in Europe. It is a reliable partner in satisfying the needs of its customers and an attractive employer for its employees.

4.4 CASE: STRATEGIC ALIGNMENT AT PACKAGED FOODS LTD

Packaged Foods Ltd is a medium-sized company which selects, sorts, washes, cuts, and packages vegetables and fruits. Its clients are the major supermarkets, whose customers pay a premium for what is considered to be a convenience food. The firm started as a small family business and has grown through the years to more than 600 employees who work in three eight-hour shifts. The products are distributed all over the country and to two neighbouring countries. Packaged Foods has a flat organisational structure with a management team of three people (chief executive officer, director of operations, and director of support staff), who manage the various departments (such as Purchasing, Production, Logistics, Sales, HRM, Finance).

Packaged Foods enjoyed healthy profits until recently. However, the attractive margins on convenience foods have drawn in more competitors, causing Packaged Foods to suffer a decline in turnover growth and a pressure on margins because the company has been forced to lower some of its prices and to increase its service. At the same time, clients expect more quality from the company. This is the reason for Packaged Foods to turn to performance management as a technique to increase the professionalism of the firm.

As a first step in the professionalism process, the strategy of the company is redeveloped. Until now Packaged Foods lived according to the basic rule of "just sell more." This however is no longer adequate as a guiding principle for a company that finds itself in increasingly turbulent waters. Therefore a workshop is organised with the management team in which a SMART strategy is developed that can easily be communicated throughout the company. This strategy reads: "Profitable growth with preservation of quality." The rationale for this strategy is that Packaged Foods, as a family business, wants to stay independent. To guarantee this the company has to keep growing to be larger than its competitors, but this growth has to be profitable in order to fund it. Also, the profit has to be used for continuous investments in new machinery, new working processes and procedures that increase turnover and quality.

The second part of the strategy is prompted by the unique selling point of Packaged Foods: the quality of its products. This quality has always been excellent and therefore does not need to be improved. However, the growth of the company specifically threatens this aspect of the business. The quality has to be maintained, keeping in mind that quality does not just mean the quality of products but also the quality of processes, personnel, and clients. The latter may, to some extent, cause a culture shock because in the old days no client was turned away. Now the company has to make choices because it cannot afford to keep on servicing unprofitable clients. Packaged Foods has to part company with these types of client.

Although the new strategy of Packaged Foods looks deceptively simple, it is SMART. The strategy is:

- *Specific*: because it is susceptible to only one explanation: growing while keeping an eye on both profit and quality.
- *Measurable*: growth, profit, and quality all can be tracked with performance indicators.
- *Acceptable*: this strategy will guarantee the survival of the firm and thereby safeguard the jobs of employees.
- *Realistic*: depending on the targets which are set by the management team for the performance indicators.
- *Timely*: although at first glance there is no time period mentioned: this strategy will be valid "until further instruction".The company – as long as it wants to stay independent – has to strive for this strategy.

The strategy can be converted into two strategic objectives: "Strive for profitable growth" and "Preserve quality in all business processes."

The next step in the professionalism process is to translate the strategy into departmental objectives. As an example the strategic objective "Preserve quality in all business processes" is taken and applied to several departments of Packaged Foods (Table 4.2).

4.5 CASE STUDY: UVD'S STRATEGIC OBJECTIVES

One morning, when visiting a supplier's office, Martin Williams was introduced to Pete Fields, a management consultant. Fields had worked with the supplier's management team and employees during the previous year to increase performance by improving their organisational effectiveness. Martin noted the supplier's openness to UVD's requirements and was impressed by the improved responsiveness he had experienced during this time. Martin decided to invite Pete to a meeting to discuss how the consultant could help UVD improve its performance.

Pete arrived early on the morning of the meeting but he only just made it to reception on time as he couldn't find a parking space anywhere in the UVD car park. Breathless, Pete stood at the front desk as he waited for the receptionist to finish on the telephone. After a few minutes, the receptionist looked up from her conversation and indicated that Pete should sign the

Table 4.2 Some of the departmental objectives derived from Packaged Foods' strategy

Department	Departmental objectives	Argument
Purchasing	▪ Guarantee quality and continuity of raw material deliveries	Basis for the high-quality Packaged Foods products are the excellent raw materials (fruit, vegetables, package materials) that are used in the manufacturing process, so the quality of these raw materials must be monitored at all times. The company also has a reputation of delivery reliability, so the production process cannot be interrupted because of lack of ingredients.
Production	▪ Maintain manufacturing quality	As stated, the quality of the manufacturing process is currently high so this should be kept on at least the same level during growth.
Logistics	▪ Increase delivery reliability	More growth means more delivery routes and points. As a consequence logistic planning and transportation have already become more complex with several ensuing problems. The department therefore has to increase the reliability of its operations.
Sales	▪ Improve client satisfaction ▪ Improve complaint response time	In the old days, the management team – and especially the CEO – could dedicate their attention to a relatively small number of clients. These days this is not possible any more, which means the entire company has to focus and work towards client satisfaction. More clients inevitably also means more complaints which must be dealt with swiftly.
HRM	▪ Increase quality of personnel	More growth means more people are needed. Formerly, employees were first drawn from the family and then from the local population. These sources are no longer sufficient, which means that people from further away and often with less skills need to be employed. These new employees have to be trained in the operations so they can deliver quality products. Current employees also need to be trained in the more complex operations.
Finance	▪ Improve financial systems and reporting	When Packaged Foods was a lot smaller, finance was relatively simple. Nowadays, the increased size and complexity means the financial systems need to be upgraded to make sure the management team receives the information they need to manage the company efficiently and effectively.

guest book. When he was finished, the receptionist nodded him to a seat where Pete sat waiting to be taken to the meeting. By the time Martin and John arrived to escort him into the meeting room, Pete had had a good opportunity to observe more employees of UVD as they hurried into work.

Following introductions, John briefed Pete on the company background. He then asked what Pete thought his services could bring for the company. Pete looked directly at John and then Martin and said, "I am very impressed with what you have done with your business so far and how you arrived at this point. What I am not clear about is why you or your employees work so hard. Or why you would want to improve performance. What are you working for? What I hear about the future of UVD sounds like more of what you have had in the past, and that doesn't sound like it really inspires you."

John and Martin sheepishly looked at each other. Then Martin sighed and replied, "I'm embarrassed to say that it has really become just a job for me and I don't know any more why I'm doing it. Habit, I guess. Isn't that how it usually is? People join companies full of ideas but after a while they just get used to it."

"It doesn't have to be that way. I've seen many people and organisations get out of the kind of rut you are honest enough to describe, just by changing their practices, by substituting new habits for old," replied Pete. "The most important thing is that you want to make it happen. Do you?"

"Absolutely!" responded John. "It's what I've been trying to do but I asked you here because I think I need a coach. It's so frustrating. I'm trying to drive and everyone keeps putting the brakes on."

"Yes, *everyone* puts the brakes on," interrupted Martin. They looked at Pete to continue.

Pete nodded and said, "OK, the first step to improve performance is articulating *why* you are doing what you do. It may sound simplistic but a shared vision or mission helps to direct energy in a focused way. But you might not be ready to create an aligned vision yet."

John shrugged his shoulders. "If I say what my vision is, I don't think I believe that we would ever stick to it, even less fulfil it. I know it sounds weak but I don't think my staff is ready to do it. We have been through a lot together and it just isn't as easy to motivate people any more."

"Some CEOs take a day of convincing before they get to the clarity which you have just shown. The resistance comes from the fact that you and your team have a lot of history, John," said Pete. "We all make decisions and assumptions that shape the way that business looks to us based on our experiences, so we rarely look at something we know really well as if we are looking at it for the first time. Most management teams work in a swamp of old problems, issues, and perceptions. Before you can create something new, you have to 'clear the swamp' of all the things you and your team already know about the business. I suggest that everyone at UVD goes through a process of clearing the swamp before defining an aligned vision that you can work on together. Draining the swamp and creating a vision is the first step towards creating a new paradigm for working together in your team."

John and Martin looked and nodded at each other with an expression which said, "Oh yeah? Prove it!" Martin spoke for them both with a challenge. "If you can do that, we'll be impressed."

"I can't, you can," answered Pete. "I can coach and support you, just as you can coach and support your team. When the rubber hits the road it will be you and them that make it work. I can help you to take the brakes off of UVD but it's up to you to grab the steering wheel and start driving. It's always down to the management team to make it happen, and it is often confrontational for them to do what is needed."

Martin nodded, "I guess that's us!"

Challenged, John smiled and looked at Pete and then at Martin, saying, "It sounds like a game worth playing. What do we need to do? What would you say I need to face up to?" By this time, John, Martin, and Pete were excited.

Pete replied, "Your job is to lead. To believe there is a way even when you can't see it. To let it go when you feel like throttling one of your team, and to know that anything that works is down to you, and anything that doesn't work is down to you, too."

John and Pete had several subsequent meetings, in between which John was asked to clear his own swamp of issues and concerns, and to create a vision of what was possible for his team and his business. Over time, he found himself getting more excited. The brakes seemed to be coming off – for him at least. Pete coached him to be ready to facilitate the first session with his whole management team.

John arranged the management team meeting. He was nervous. It was the first time he had actually brought the team together for such an important conversation. John introduced Pete as the meeting facilitator, describing his impressive track record to build credibility with his team. He knew how difficult they could be to impress.

John cleared his throat and began, "I'll hand you over to Pete. He will explain the kind of work he has done with other companies and the kind of work we'll be doing because today we are going to participate in a unique event at UVD. Over to you, Pete."

Pete provided context for the meeting. "In my work with organisations, I have found that high-performing organisations are high performing because they manage to articulate a vision *and* to implement that vision." He drew two axes on a flipchart. "A vision answers the question *what* are we going to do. Implementation is about *how* we are going to do it. Most organisations find it easy to create a vision but much harder to implement it. When we fail to implement a vision, we give up on it. We avoid talking about vision and work becomes monotonous. No one wants to work for either an organisation without a vision or an organisation that fails in implementing the vision. "You have a lot going for you at UVD. John has set my goal for working with you. My goal in working with you is to help you to make this an organisation that you are all proud of. To do this, you will create a shared vision and a shared plan. A shared vision has to excite you – so it's you who will create it. The problem is that if you are anything like the other teams I've worked with, you've had your challenges in the past and you've learned some tough lessons. Every day you cross a swamp full of alligators to do your jobs. That swamp is full of debris from everything that went wrong in the past. We need to clear away the debris of the past so we can create a vision for the future. Actually, even when we've cleared the debris, we're going to find some alligators in there – the real business issues you are dealing with. So to begin at the beginning, let's drain the swamp. What are all the issues and problems which stop UVD from being a great place to work and an effective organisation? John, do you want to say anything before we continue?"

John spoke. "After today's meeting, I guarantee that each of us will begin to tap into a new creative energy around our work. How are we going to accomplish this? We are going to put to rest any niggles, resentments, and complaints, we are going to say things that we have been putting off saying and anything else that has been blocking your enjoyment or effectiveness at work – even if it's me! You are probably wondering why we are doing this. Martin and I see that it is possible to have a company that is driven by a vision. A company where the whole team helps to create the vision and contribute to its fulfilment. We know that UVD's success depends on you, and we want to give you the opportunity to recreate UVD with us."

Martin continued. "We know you are all committed to the success of UVD. But what are we *all* working toward? Oh, I know that each of us could give a vague answer but what we are looking to create is an organisation where we *all* feel we have a part to play. But before we can create a vision, there may be attitudes, disappointments, niggles, complaints, or resentments that need to be cleared away first. Once we have completed this exercise our company will be a safe place to say anything we want, allowing us to move forward. Who would like to go first?"

The management team, who had initially squirmed in their seats uncomfortably, were now sitting forward attentively. This sounded different! Mark Jones, manager of Manufacturing, cleared his throat and began, "Well, Manufacturing was put under a lot of stress by the late design revisions and, I know this for sure, the team is very demoralised right now."

"But we couldn't send out faulty ..." replied John.

"Whoa," interrupted Pete. "A ground rule of a 'swamp clearing' meeting is that no one needs to defend anything. No one has done anything wrong. In fact, everyone is responding perfectly given the environment in which they have been working. If there are any really sticky points, then we can list them and make sure that something is done to rectify them. For now, just listen and list."

Mark and John both sighed in relief.

A few weeks later, after several swamp-clearing sessions with all managers facilitated by consultant Pete Fields, UVD had formulated its new mission. It captured the spirit of innovation, accomplishment, and making a difference that united the entire company (see Figure 4.4).

Figure 4.4 UVD's new mission

After formulating the mission, the strategic objectives of UVD were identified:

- *Establish an ecologically sound image.* A key to growth was identified as establishing an ecologically sound image. This is important to UVD for two reasons. First, new legislation in the Netherlands pertaining to waste management stipulates that all manufacturers, retailers/distributors, and consumers must contribute to the disposal of products. The Dutch government will probably take the lead in developing the European environmental legislation that needs to be effective in all European countries within the next six years. In this respect, by producing ecologically sound products UVD could gain a competitive advantage, since most companies are not yet taking advantage of the marketing potential provided by the new legislation. This also reduces the costs of waste disposal. Second, when customers purchase UVD products in markets where the new legislation has not yet taken effect, they need to associate UVD's slightly more expensive products with their eco-friendliness. When customers buy UVD products, they are buying into a lasting planet.
- *Create international coverage.* In order to be in a strong position for future growth and to achieve at least a minimum value of sales in each country, UVD wants to deliver to the majority of stores in selected regions in each country. National coverage will strengthen their position as the number one supplier and will increase customer familiarity with UVD's products. In the US, UVD is "going virtual": products will be sold over the Internet, with distribution from a central warehouse.
- *Enhance customer satisfaction.* In order to keep existing customers and obtain new ones, customer satisfaction is an important goal. Satisfied

customers are loyal customers who buy repeatedly and, in addition, provide UVD with free word-of-mouth advertising.

- *Increase profitability.* As for all commercial organisations, being profitable is a necessity for the continuity of the organisation. Profitability is also needed to fund the considerable research and development (R&D) activities of UVD, especially now it is adding an eco-friendly product range to its business.
- *Be innovative.* To stay competitive UVD products need to provide something that none of the competitor's products do. In the highly competitive retail marketplace, innovation is important in terms of design, features, and functionality. Another key area of innovation is the company's marketing method in the United States, which leverages web marketing, ordering, and outsourced warehousing and delivery.
- *Produce high-quality products.* In order to gain and retain customers in the top tier of the retail market, offering high-quality products is vital.

Case question: Are the strategic objectives of UVD SMART? If not, how would you reformulate them? Would you keep all the existing objectives, or add, or remove, or replace them? Could UVD use these strategic objectives as objectives for lower organisational levels?

(This case study first appeared in de Waal and Fourman, 2000.)

Key points

- ☑ Research has shown that taking longer-term trends into account in daily decisions leads to superior results.
- ☑ High-performance organisations build robust, resilient, and adaptive plans by applying scenario thinking and "what-ifs" and drafting resilient strategies and plans tailored to the levels of uncertainty in the environment.
- ☑ Thinking ahead in a formal and structured way is known as scenario planning or scenario building. External scenarios are derived from shared and agreed-upon mental models of the external world, and they outline a range of possible future developments and outcomes in the external world. Internal scenarios outline a range of future developments and outcomes of the organisation itself.
- ☑ A well-formulated strategy indicates how the organisation wants to anticipate changes in its environment, and the consequences these changes will have on the quality, price, and delivery times of its products and services. The strategy is made concrete in strategic objectives.
- ☑ A strategic objective should be SMART: specific, measurable, acceptable, realistic, and time bound.

References

Goldsmith, W. and Clutterbuck, D. (1998) *The Winning Streak Mark II: How the world's most successful companies stay on top through today's turbulent times*. Orion Business.

Hart, S. and Banbury, C. (1994) How strategy-making processes can make a difference. *Strategic Management Journal*, 15, 251–69.

Heijden, K. van der (1996) *Scenarios: The art of strategic conversation*. New York: Wiley.

Mintzberg, H., Ahlstrand, B. and Lampel, J. (1998) *Strategy Safari: A guided tour through the wilds of strategic management*. New York: Free Press.

Rigby, D. (2005) *Management Tools 2005*. Bain & Company

Waal, A.A. de (2005) *The Foundations of Nirvana: The characteristics of a high-performance organisation*. Hyperion white paper, www.andredewaal.nl.

Waal, A. de and M. Fourman (2000) *Managing in the New Economy: Performance management habits to renew organisations for the new millennium*. Arthur Andersen & ShowBusiness.

5

Strategic action plans

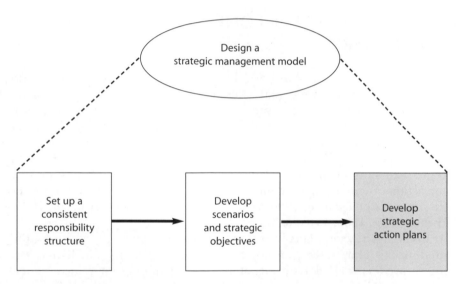

Figure 5.1 Developing strategic action plans

A strategic action plan is a document that describes the activities that need to be executed in order to achieve the strategic objectives and reach measurable performance improvement. The long-term orientation of the strategy (often three to five years) is translated into realistic and workable short-term actions (often annually). The development of the strategy and strategic objectives is based on a thorough knowledge of the value drivers of the company. Therefore, the strategic action plans aim at improving these value drivers. In this way, an organisation works on achieving short-term results which improve the long-term survival and thriving of the enterprise.

Chapter objectives

- ☑ To discuss the importance of a dual focus on the short term and the long term.
- ☑ To provide the reader with insight into the hockey stick effect.
- ☑ To teach the reader how to split the strategic development process into two different processes, resulting in a separate growth action plan for the long term and operational action plan for the short term.

5.1 BALANCE OUT THE LONG-TERM WITH THE SHORT-TERM

In practise many organisations have difficulty in turning their strategy into actions that achieve strategic goals. Research indicates that although many companies often have a good strategic plan, more than half of them are not able to articulate and communicate this strategy effectively to the organisation. Delivering on their strategy also appears to be consistently difficult for many. The main problem for these companies is that they lack the ability to execute their strategy properly. At the same time, most companies state that clear, action-oriented deployment of their strategy significantly influences their success (Renaissance, 1996; Charan and Colvin, 1999; Drucker, 1999; Redwood et al., 1999; Ernst & Young, 2000).

Translating strategic plans into short-term action plans proves to be the main difficulty. The strategy development process focuses too much on calculating future financial effects in detail instead of planning for value creation and looking at the effects of nonfinancial indicators on the business. Strategic plans do not sufficiently focus on concrete actions to achieve the strategic targets, and the link to the short term (i.e. the budget) is often obscured. At the same time, long-term expectations should be more realistic, meaning that organisations should take into account the "hockey stick" effect. This infamous effect occurs when organisations make financial projections for future years that are ill-founded, over-positive and therefore unrealistic.

The reason that organisations often fail to execute their strategy is because their strategies focus on achieving two types of objectives – growth and operational improvement – through *one and the same* strategic development process. However, the strategic actions needed to achieve these types of objectives are different in nature and require different time spans and resources. This creates an area of tension in the organisation. A lot of managers have difficulty distancing themselves from day-to-day operations, and as a result the innovative part of the strategic plan (which deals with growth) gets too little attention. To allow an organisation to better focus on

The hockey stick effect

The hockey stick effect is the unfounded prediction that after a period of moderate positive results, company performance will suddenly increase dramatically. The hockey stick effect results in unrealistic forecasting of results.

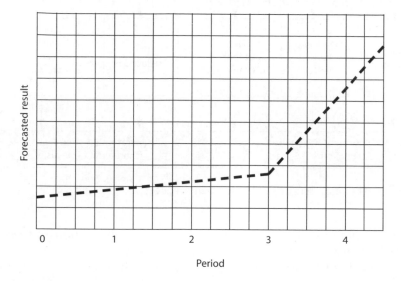

Figure 5.2 The hockey stick effect

Whether the strategic plan is having the desired result can be evaluated by translating long-term strategic plans into realistic short-term strategic action plans, and by predicting the effects of these action plans on the results, using a combination of financial indicators (for the short term) and nonfinancial indicators (for the long term).

both types of objective, the strategic development process should be split into two different processes: one that focuses on growth (continuity) and one that focuses on improvement of operations (profitability). The two strategic development processes each result in their own action plan: the growth action plan and the operational action plan (Figure 5.3).

The strategic *growth* development process focuses on actions that create breakthrough growth opportunities, often applying "discontinuous innovation" (i.e. innovation leading to complete new things, not elaborating on previous inventions). The growth action plan focuses on finding new

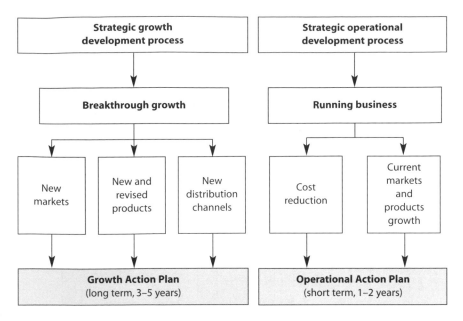

Figure 5.3 The "split" strategic development process

markets, distribution channels, and products. It results in new sources of revenue for a organisation in the next three to five years.

The strategic operational development process focuses on actions that improve operations of an organisation ("running the business"). The operational action plan aims specifically at cost reductions and on sales growth with current products and current market channels. It leads to incremental improvement in the following one to two years. Splitting the strategic development process into a growth and an operational process entails two distinct processes, a different timing of the plans, the involvement of different people (mainly manufacturing in the operational process and mainly marketing and sales people in the growth process), and results in two distinct strategic action plans.

The link between the strategic plan and the budget can also be adapted and improved. As shown in Figure 5.4, the budget for year 1 (Y1) is created from a combination of the latest actuals and forecasts, a trend analysis, and input from the strategic plans: the growth action plan and the operational action plan. For each action in the growth action plan, the expected positive effects on the key value drivers are calculated for the next five years. These effects are each given a certain value (Δ). In addition, the resources needed to execute the proposed growth actions are calculated. The same is done for the actions in the operational action plan (now for the next two years), resulting also in values (Δ) and needed resources. The Δ values for year 1 are combined with the trend analysis of the latest actuals and forecasts, to arrive at the budget for the coming year. This means that the development of the

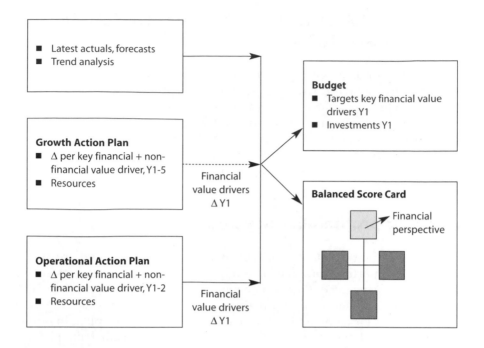

Figure 5.4 The link between strategic action plans and budget

two strategic action plans have to follow each other quickly, because Δ values from both plans are needed for the budget calculation. The needed resources are also combined, to arrive at the investment plan for the coming year. The Δ values are also an input for the balanced scorecard's financial perspective for the coming year.

A split in strategic attention for improvement of operations and strategic growth opportunities has the benefit that the split forces management to focus more on each of the aspects of strategic planning, which enhances the content of these plans. Management has to think "out of the box" to look for new growth opportunities, and subsequently has to clearly articulate strategic actions solely aimed at achieving these opportunities. Management gets a clear idea of the boundaries of the strategic goals, as the operational action plan represents the minimum performance required of the business. Because the budget is based mainly on the Δ values from the operational action plan, the budget targets are more realistic. They do not include the uncertainties that are embedded in targets derived from over-ambitious growth plans. In the budget, some Δ values from the growth action plan can be incorporated, but only for those growth actions that already have an effect in year 1 (the dotted arrow in Figure 5.4). Because of the nature of growth actions, most effects are expected in the longer term. Conversely, the growth action plan represents the "realm of possibilities," the turnover and revenue that can be obtained when the organisation's creativity gets going.

5.2 CASE: STRATEGIC ACTION PLANS OF ELECTRICAL CONSTRUCTION GROUP

Electrical Construction Group (ECG: see Chapter 3 for a description of the company) has split the strategic development process into two separate processes. This allows the company to better focus on each type of objective and to improve the overall quality of its strategic plans. The strategic profitability development process focuses on actions that improve the running of the business. The strategic growth development process focuses on actions that create breakthrough growth opportunities.

Strategic profitability development process

The business units, in close cooperation with the division, prepare action plans and supporting financial data aimed at realising the targets set by ECG's senior management team. The manufacturing department spends 80 per cent of its planning time on the strategic profitability development process, while Marketing and Sales spends 20 per cent of its planning time. The input from all the business units is combined into a profitability plan for the division (Figure 5.5). The plan's layout is standardised by using a mandatory set of forms. This enables easy consolidation of the business unit plans, and also makes it possible for the senior management team to compare the divisional plans. The profitability plan has a time span of 11 years: looking back five years, looking at the current year, and looking forward five years. In this way, ECG can keep track of past and future performance. Differences in the results forecasted last year have to be explained. A huge advantage of this constantly looking back and forward is the reduction of the hockey stick effect, as managers always have to explain deviations to ECG's executive team.

Next the divisional profitability plan is submitted to corporate headquarters where it is analysed by corporate analysts. Based on this analysis, questions are communicated to the divisions so that they can prepare themselves for the upcoming review by ECG's senior management team.

The profitability meeting takes place three to four weeks after submission of the plan. It takes place at the divisional location and takes two days. The chief operating officer, other members of the senior management team, and

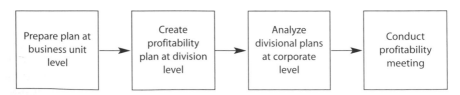

Figure 5.5 The steps in the profitability development process

analysts represent corporate headquarters. Divisional management and functional managers from the business units (mainly manufacturing) are present to explain the divisional plans. During the meeting, the division gives an overview of the strategy, major initiatives, and key issues it is currently facing. Marketing information underlying the plans, such as sales quantities and pricing assumptions, is discussed and the plans of the engineering, purchasing, manufacturing, and human resources departments are reviewed. Finally, the financial summary is examined.

ECG's senior management team tests and challenges the plans, based on its knowledge of the division and industry as well as on the results of the corporate analysis. The purpose of this testing is to ensure that the actions defined by the division are sufficiently rigorous to achieve the targets set by the senior management team. Division and business managers present and defend the parts of the profitability plan for which they are responsible. This results in strong ownership of the plans. ECG's culture is aimed at creating this ownership: "You have to stand up to talk about how to fix things. You may not be the cause of the problem, but you are still expected to fix it." When the plan is approved, a manager has gained the trust and ownership of the project. However, as one manager put it: "If you waver, they will grill you." This leads to redoing or improving the plan. A deep and thorough understanding of the business by the senior management team is critical to the acceptance of its advice by the divisions and business units.

The strategic growth development process

Divisional marketing managers start the strategic growth development process by collecting information from the strategic business review. This review consists of a series of strategic brainstorming sessions conducted between ECG's chief executive officer (CEO) and each division. Key issues facing the division and its business units are addressed and "out of the box" ideas are generated. Topics include new markets, synergies between divisions, and potential acquisitions. At the end of these sessions, key actions are identified to be further pursued. Another source of information is the corporate planning conference that is conducted once a year. This conference looks at the overall strategy of ECG, examining the past five years and the next five years. All divisions are present at this conference, which is led by the CEO. The overall strategic direction resulting from this meeting is input for the divisional development process.

With the collected information, market intelligence storylines are built. These explore new ways to create double-digit revenue growth. The storylines result in specific strategic action plans aimed at achieving each identified revenue opportunity. The action plans are collected in the growth plan, which must show that sales volumes can increase aggressively. It takes approximately four to six weeks with ten team members to create the plan.

The plan has standardised, obligatory financial exhibits that form a basis for benchmarking and analysis. The time span of the growth plan is four to six years, looking back one year and forward about three to five years.

Corporate headquarters then conducts a growth conference with each division to discuss the growth plan in detail. This meeting is attended by the senior management team including the CEO, divisional management, and a representation of business unit management (mainly marketing and sales). The conference consists of presentations and dynamic discussions. The meeting begins with a brief overview of the business, its environment, and its strategy. Then, five to seven growth plans are presented. During the conference, the atmosphere can get rather tense because the CEO questions the plans and the underlying assumptions quite aggressively. The division and the business units have to withstand this without wavering. As one manager explained: "ECG is not about asking questions but about issuing challenges." The meeting results in a list of well-founded growth plans and related actions, such as further investigations of ideas or programmes.

Integrating the profitability plan, growth plan, and the budget

The profitability plan and the growth plan set the boundaries of the business. The profitability plan focuses on the performance required to run the business profitably. The growth plan gives "the realm of possibility." These different outlooks cause a natural tension, as the profitability plan has to be conservative (to keep costs in check), while at the same time the growth plan has to set stretch targets. Balancing the two is a challenge. Growth initiatives that have been tested in the marketplace and have been judged to be ready for implementation become part of operations. The expected results of these growth actions are incorporated in the next profitability action plan and become real targets at that time.

The first year of the profitability plan is the basis for the budget. The growth plan is not part of the budget and is managed separately. Thus, the budget only represents the actual business, making budget targets firm. These targets represent the minimum performance level and do not include new, unproven plans for which results are unsure. All divisions explicitly build in margins to deal with deviations from the budget. All parties understand that the budget cannot be forecast with exact accuracy, encouraging ECG to accept deviations to a certain extent. The margin is expressed as a percentage and is negotiated with the executive team. Since the budgeting process occurs in the last quarter of the year and the profitability meeting is held some time during the first three-quarters of the year, the division faces a time delay between the two events. During this time, changes in external and internal factors may occur. If these changes result in deviations between the profitability plan and the budget, the senior management team requires a detailed explanation from the division. ECG calls itself an analytical company that "manages by numbers, not by anecdote." The company values its ability to compare the budgets with the predictions.

Key points

- ☑ Many organisations have a good strategic plan but are at the same time not able to articulate and communicate this strategy effectively to the organisation, let alone consistently deliver it.
- ☑ A strategic action plan is a document which describes the activities that need to be executed in order to achieve the strategic objectives and reach measurable performance improvement. It translates the long-term orientation of the strategy (often three to five years) into realistic and workable short-term actions (often yearly).
- ☑ Organisations have to be aware of the hockey stick effect: the unfounded prediction that after a period of moderate positive results, company performance will suddenly increase dramatically. The hockey stick effect results in unrealistic forecasting of results.
- ☑ Organisations should split the strategic development process into a process that focuses on growth (continuity) and a process that focuses on improvement of operations (profitability). This will result in a separate growth action plan and operational action plan.

References

Charan, R. and Colvin, G. (1999) Why CEOs fail, *Fortune*, June 21.

Drucker, P.F. (1999) *Management Challenges for the 21st Century*. Harper Business.

Ernst & Young (2000) *Measures that Matter*. Research report.

Redwood, S., Goldwasser, C. and Street, S. (1999) *Action Management: Practical strategies for making your corporate transformation a success*. Wiley.

Renaissance Solution Ltd (1996) *Translating Strategy into Action*. Research report.

Stage 2

Designing a strategic reporting model

Stage 2 of the strategic performance development cycle deals with the design of a strategic reporting model. In this stage the organisation develops the reporting structure that is used for monitoring and adjusting the execution of the strategy and the progress of crucial business activities. This stage consists of four steps (see Figure P2.2). Each step is discussed in a separate chapter.

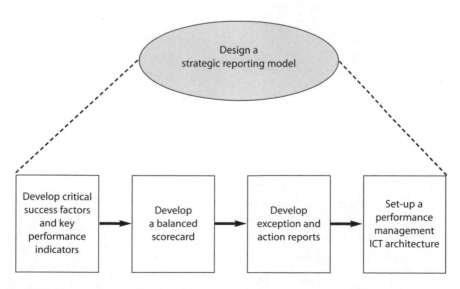

Figure P2.2 Steps to be taken to set up a strategic reporting model

6

Critical success factors and key performance indicators

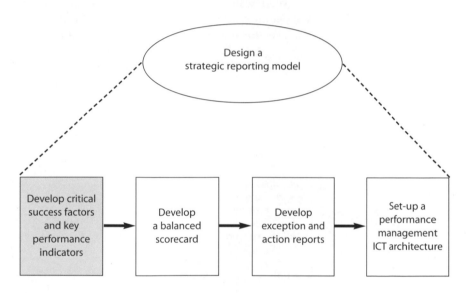

Figure 6.1 Developing critical success factors and key performance indicators

Intangible assets like patents, trademarks, and human capital are increasingly seen as major value sources of an organisation, in addition to the more traditional, tangible assets like physical capital and financial capital. Even today, many of these intangible assets are not yet included in the formal reporting systems of organisations, because most of these systems were built to report financial information (Boulton et al., 2000; Doz et al., 2001; Foster and Kaplan, 2001; Marr, 2006). This creates a problem for modern-day organisations: they want to move to more value-based, nonfinancial indicators and better performance management, yet they cannot because their existing management information systems are not designed to deal with these. The implementation of CSFs and KPIs provides a solution to this problem as it combines nonfinancial leading indicators with financial lagging indicators in one system. This way it offers management a balanced overview of the organisation's performance and a means to check whether the organisation's strategy is being executed successfully.

The development process of CSFs and KPIs is depicted in Figure 6.2. In this process, which departs from SMART objectives, two types of CSFs are developed for each objective: result CSFs and effort CSFs. After that the KPIs are developed for each CSF. In the following sections, the development process of CSFs and KPIs is described in more detail.

Chapter objectives

☑ To teach the reader how to develop critical success factors and key performance indicators throughout the organisation, to measure the execution of the strategy and of key processes.

☑ To teach the reader to distinguish between results and critical efforts indicators.

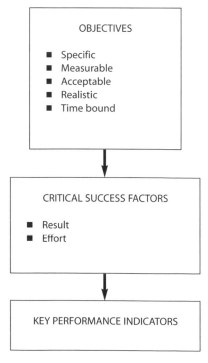

Figure 6.2 Development process of CSFs and KPIs

6.1 CRITICAL SUCCESS FACTORS AND KEY PERFORMANCE INDICATORS

A critical success factor (CSF) is defined as "a qualitative description of an element of the strategy in which the organisation has to excel in order to be successful." The CSF is made quantifiable with a key performance indicator (KPI). The use of CSFs and KPIs enables the measurement, and thus the management, of strategic objectives. If performance indicators that measure the execution of the strategy and the creation of value to the organisation are not included in the performance management process, it will be unclear whether or not strategic objectives and value creation are being achieved.

The development of CSFs and KPIs is at the centre of the effort to build a performance management system. In this section, the development process of these indicators is described, using the performance measurement pyramid (Figure 6.3).

The performance measurement pyramid has five building blocks:

1. *Mission and strategy.* First of all, an organisation has to formulate its mission by answering the question, "What do we, as organisation, want to accomplish: what is our mission?" To formulate a strategy, an organisation has to answer the questions, "How are we, as organisation, going to achieve our mission?" and "How can we accomplish what we want?"

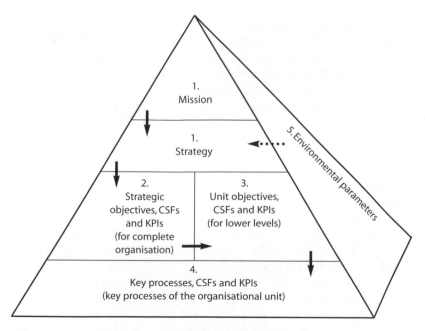

Figure 6.3 The performance measurement pyramid

2. *Strategic objectives, critical success factors and key performance indicators.* In order to make the organisational strategy tangible, strategic objectives need to be formulated. A strategy is often expressed in abstract terms. By formulating one or more strategic objectives, it becomes clear to the organisation which activities it has to perform to implement its strategy. If the organisational strategy is already expressed in specific, measurable terms, the strategy and the strategic objectives will be virtually the same. Whether strategic objectives are being achieved or not, they can be monitored with strategic CSFs and KPIs. These "strategic indicators" are included in the management reports that are used by the board of directors or senior management team. Often the balanced scorecard (see Chapter 7) of an organisation is composed of these strategic indicators. For an organisation with very diverse operating activities, designing an all-encompassing balanced scorecard on corporate level may not be that meaningful, because nonfinancial KPIs for one subsidiary are not necessarily useful for another. In such a case, it is more appropriate to include a limited number of financial KPIs in the balanced scorecard and to formulate, in addition to that, nonfinancial KPIs on the subsidiary level.

3. *Unit objectives, critical success factors and key performance indicators.* Organisational units like divisions, business units, and departments can support an organisation's mission and strategy by translating the strategic objectives into objectives for their own unit. The extent to which these unit objectives are achieved is monitored with unit CSFs and KPIs (Figure 6.4). These "unit indicators" are included in a balanced scorecard and used by unit managers to measure progress. Because each organisational unit contributes in its own way to achieving the strategic objectives, units should determine their objectives independently of each other. It is management's responsibility to make sure that the unit objectives are aligned with the strategic objectives. If this is not, or is no longer, the case, the unit objectives need to be reformulated. This is an effective way for the organisation to secure alignment.

    Suppose the R&D department of an organisation translates the strategic objective "Improve customer focus" into the departmental objective of conducting more innovative research. After all, the more products are developed that meet customer demands, the more satisfied customers will be. It is critical to the R&D department, therefore, to monitor whether the department succeeds in developing enough new products that are attractive to customers. Whether customers appreciate these new products can be measured by the sales of new products. Whether the number of new products developed is sufficient can be measured on the basis of the share that these new products have in the product portfolio.

4. *Key processes, critical success factors and key performance indicators.* In order to achieve the objectives, every organisation has key processes. There are two types of key processes. The first type of key process is one that directly influences the achievement and results of an objective, and can

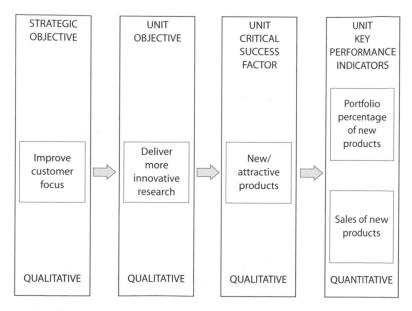

Figure 6.4 Example of unit CSFs and KPIs (for an R&D department)

therefore be directly linked to that objective. The second type is one "that makes the business tick" and that must always be executed well in order for the business to survive, regardless of the chosen strategic objectives. The execution of key processes is monitored by means of key process CSFs and KPIs (Figure 6.5). These operational indicators are used by managers who are directly involved in the execution of the key processes. The operational indicators are included in the balanced scorecard for the organisational unit, which is often a department. Section 6.3 (page 120) goes into more detail on the identification and improvement of key processes and their underlying activities.

An organisation has to make optimal use of its assets to prevent product costs becoming too high. Suppose an organisation's strategy is "to bring high-quality consumer products to the market at a low price." The organisation then has to watch the production costs closely so they do not become too high, resulting in a profit margin that is too small for the organisation to be able to continue investing properly. As a consequence, one of the organisation's key processes is to produce as efficiently as possible, which means utilizing its resources optimally. The capacity utilization of these resources has to be tracked, by measuring the machine utilisation and the FTE (full time equivalent) utilisation.

5. *Environmental parameters.* If an organisation wants to know how it is influenced by its environment, it needs to identify indicators that provide information on the environment it operates in, and on developments that affect the organisation. These are usually factors over which the organisation has little or no control, and that at the same

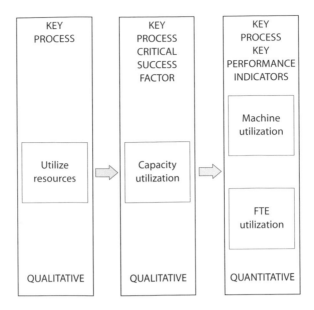

Figure 6.5 Example of key process CSFs and KPIs

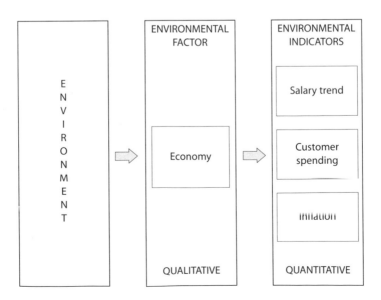

Figure 6.6 Example of environmental factors and environmental indicators

time may have considerable effect on the results of the organisation (Figure 6.6). This is why, especially during the target-setting process for KPIs, managers have to take into account the influence of environmental factors. These business environment indicators should therefore be included as an extra perspective in the balanced scorecard of the organisation.

Economic developments usually have a direct influence on an organisation's business results, and are therefore critical to the organisation's success. Many indicators, such as salary and wage developments, inflation (and interest rates), and the accompanying consumer spending indices, provide important input for estimating the expected turnover. If the economy grows more slowly than expected, this phenomenon may be accounted for by adjusting the target sales budget downwards. If the sales manager does not succeed in realizing the adjusted target, the most obvious explanation ("We had a downward economic trend") cannot be used and the manager has to look for the real causes of not achieving the target.

6.2 RESULT AND EFFORT INDICATORS

The critical success factors that are important for monitoring the results of an objective or a key process (which are known as result CSFs) can be determined by answering the following questions: "What is the result when we achieve the objective successfully?" and "What is the result when we execute the key process successfully?" The CSFs that are important for monitoring the efforts that are critical for achieving an objective or a key process (which are known as effort CSFs) can be determined by answering the following questions: "What do I absolutely need to do to achieve the objective successfully?" and "What do I absolutely need to do to execute the key process successfully?" There are many efforts that may lead to achieving the final result, but only the ones that are the most critical need to be monitored. A "critical effort" is an action that is most likely to lead to achieving the desired result.

After identifying the CSFs, the organisation needs to answer the following questions to identify the KPIs for each critical success factor: "How do we measure the critical success factor?" and "How can we see the result of the critical success factor?" A KPI is usually defined as a ratio or a percentage (numerator and denominator). After all, a KPI result expressed as an absolute figure, for instance "10," in itself does not mean much. A KPI result is only meaningful if it is expressed in percentages, for example: "10 complaints per 1000 customers (1 per cent)" or "10 complaints per 100 customers (10 per cent)." Figure 6.7 gives an example of a strategic objective with the corresponding result and effort CSFs and KPIs.

In Figure 6.7, the strategic objective of the company is "Better development of personnel." The final result of this objective is to have qualified

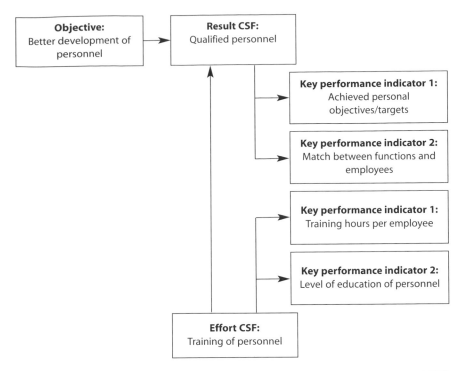

Figure 6.7 Example of the use of result CSFs and KPIs and effort CSFs and KPIs

personnel, which means personnel of a higher quality than before (a result CSF). Whether the organisation's personnel are indeed qualified can be measured in terms of the percentage of personnel that is actually capable of achieving the agreed personal objectives for the current year (KPI 1). A high percentage of personnel who are in the wrong job position can, for example, indicate the absence of well-qualified personnel (KPI 2). Whether personnel quality has improved compared with the previous year can be measured by comparing the present results of the above-mentioned key performance indicators with those of the previous year. One of the main efforts to improve personnel quality is providing training for employees (an effort CSF). Whether employees get enough training can be measured by the number of training hours per employee (KPI 1) and the final education or skill level achieved by an employee (KPI 2).

It is important to distinguish between result CSFs and effort CSFs. If an organisation monitors only its efforts, it may be that it performs the wrong activities very well ("a" in Figure 6.8). However, performance is not just about "doing things right" but about "doing the right things right." Therefore managers should always keep in mind the desired end result to make sure that the organisation is heading in the right direction. In addition, managers have to monitor whether the organisation is doing the right things to achieve the desired end result (also called "critical efforts"). They can do this by measuring whether their efforts and those of other employees are having the desired

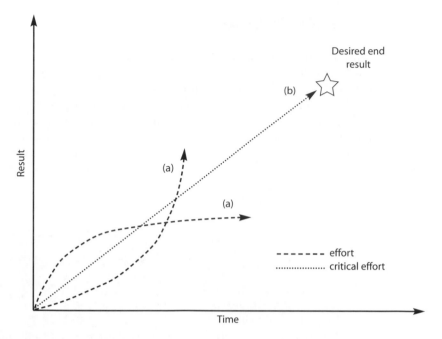

Figure 6.8 Balance between efforts and result

effect ("b" in Figure 6.8). These "interim results" offer managers the opportunity to adjust activities along the way.

During the development of CSFs, KPIs, and targets for the KPIs, there are a number of quality criteria that indicators have to meet to be useful to management. These criteria are listed below.

Critical success factors

- Each objective should be measured with at least one result CSF and no more than two effort CSFs.
- For each CSF, no more than three KPIs should be developed. This is to limit the amount of information, development time, and costs, and to make sure that only relevant information is included in management reports.
- CSFs should cover not only financial information but also nonfinancial information, to ensure a well-balanced view of the objective.
- A CSF is a qualitative notion that describes in words how a certain objective can be measured. It is therefore never quantitative (a number or percentage). For example, it is not "the number of satisfied customers," but "customer satisfaction."
- A CSF is clear, concise, and unambiguous (it can only be interpreted in one way).

Key performance indicators

- The definition of a KPI should be concise, easy to understand, and complete (i.e. every term used in the definition is described in such a way that the definition can only be interpreted in one way).
- A KPI can be measured by the organisation. An organisation should have the procedures, resources and (some) information systems to make measuring possible.
- The definition of a KPI preferably includes a comparison or a relationship between things. Percentages and ratios provide more valuable information than absolute figures.
- The definition of a KPI includes a reporting frequency (e.g. monthly, quarterly, yearly).

Targets

- The target for a KPI should be realistic: the manager responsible should think it is feasible.
- The target for a KPI has a certain margin. Corrective action should only be taken if the result is not within this margin (either above or under).
- The target for a KPI is determined together with the manager responsible for the result of the indicator concerned. This fosters support within the organisation.

6.3 KEY PROCESSES

In stage 2 of the strategic performance management development cycle the organisation thus far has identified how the strategic and unit objectives can be monitored using CSFs and KPIs. However, just measuring these objectives is not enough; the organisation also has to know how to improve them. For this, the links between the objectives and the key processes that influence them have to be made explicit. Once this is done, organisational members know which processes to improve when results on specific CSFs and KPIs fail to materialise or deteriorate. In order to identify the key processes, an organisation has to set up a key processes model containing all the key processes an organisation has to excel at during their execution.

A process is defined as an activity or collection of activities that add value to a certain input and subsequently produce a specific end product, such as a product or service for an internal or external customer. A process can be uncomplicated and cover just one activity, or it can be complicated and comprise several activities or even subprocesses. At the highest level, there are three types of processes: operational, support and management processes (Verweire and Van den Berghe, 2002). There are various types of operational processes such as:

- manufacturing processes that produce products and services
- development processes that create new products, services, markets, and manufacturing processes
- resource processes that provide the resources needed for other processes
- management processes that steer and manage the organisation and its processes.

An organisation executes literally hundreds of processes a day. It is virtually impossible to closely monitor all these processes and their underlying activities. For strategic performance management it is important to identify the key processes of the organisation, i.e. the processes which directly influence the results of strategic, unit, and operational objectives. If the organisation manages to optimise these key processes, it will be able to better achieve its objectives and thereby improve its performance. Optimising the key processes can be done by applying techniques like business process management and business activity monitoring (Burlton, 2001; Smith and Fingar, 2002; Harmon, 2003; White, 2005).

An organisation can link the key processes to the organisational objectives by taking the following steps:

1. *Identify the key processes.* Select from the hundreds of processes in the enterprise only those processes that cover multiple functions and departments and that involve many people.
2. *Describe the key processes.* Give a short description of the process: its input, its activities, its output, and its owner(s).
3. *Relate the key processes to the organisational objectives.* Construct a matrix for each type of objective (strategic, unit, operational). The rows of the matrix should list all the objectives of a certain type; the columns should represent all the key processes of the organisation. Then indicate whether the objectives are or are not covered by the key processes by placing a tick ($\checkmark$), meaning *yes*, or a cross ($\times$), meaning *no*, in the appropriate box. The resulting matrix will provide an overview of the existing links between the organisation's key processes and its organisational objectives (Table 6.1).
4. *Analyse the matrix.* Each objective should be covered by at least one key process, and each key process should influence at least one objective. Table 6.1 shows that strategic objective 3 is not covered by any of the key processes. This could pose a problem, so it has to be determined whether this is because the organisation cannot influence the objective (which means that it is not SMART and should therefore be removed), or because the organisation does not have a process in place to influence and achieve the objective, or because the process has not been

Table 6.1 Matrix of strategic objectives and key processes
Source: Geelen and Van de Coevering (2005).

	Key process A	Key process B	Key process C	Key process D
Strategic objective 1	✓	✗	✗	✗
Strategic objective 2	✗	✓	✓	✗
Strategic objective 3	✗	✗	✗	✗
Strategic objective 4	✓	✓	✗	✗

identified as a key process during step 1. Whatever the cause, corrective action is required here. In Table 6.1 key process D does not influence any objective. By definition it therefore cannot be a key process, and the organisation should consider whether it really needs this process at all.

5. *Update the matrix.* After executing the corrective actions, the matrix has to be updated. This should be repeated until each objective is covered by at least one key process in the matrix. Only then can the organisation be sure that it has processes in place that contribute to achieving its objectives.

6. *Define process CSFs and KPIs.* Process CSFs and KPIs provide information on the execution and result of a specific process. A process CSF describes the result the organisation expects from the particular process. A process KPI is used to measure the input, activities, or output of the process (Figure 6.9). The links between strategic management, which uses result and effort CSFs and KPIs to measure the execution of the strategy, and process management, which measures and improves the key processes of the organisation, are the effort KPIs because these are directly influenced by the key processes.

For each key process, the organisation should define one or more process CSFs and the accompanying KPIs. This can be done by making a table of definitions for each type of objective that is influenced by the key process (Table 6.2).

In Table 6.2 the first column in the table lists (in this example) a strategic objective and the effort KPIs that measure the effort made by the organisation to achieve this objective. No result KPIs should be included here, because result KPIs do not directly concern the actual process of achieving the strategic objective, but rather assess the effectiveness of the process to achieve the objective (whether or not the objective has been achieved). The second column lists the key processes that influence the objective, given in the first column, and the process CSFs, which indicate the results expected from the key processes. Underneath each process CSF, the accompanying process KPIs (input, activity, output) are given.

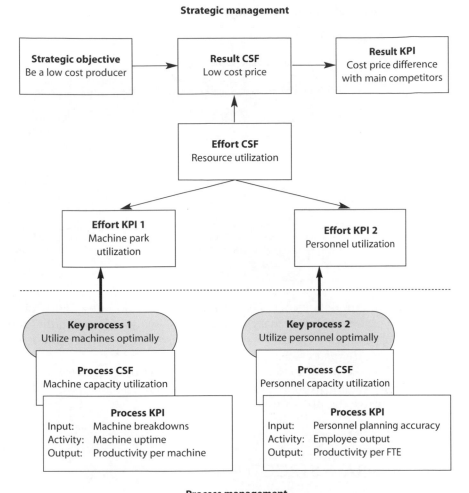

Figure 6.9 Link between strategic objective and processes

7. *Break the key processes down into subprocesses.* The key processes can, if necessary, be subdivided into more detailed processes to make them more tangible for organisational members. Each subprocess should be measured with its own process CSFs and KPIs, which can be developed by detailing the CSFs and KPIs of the key processes it belongs to. Once the objectives have been translated into (sub)processes, the result will be a key processes model comprising the organisational processes that can be positively influenced by employees throughout the organisation.

8. *Determine process improvements.* Define targets for the process KPIs. Then measure the current results of the process KPIs and compare them with these targets. If there are differences, identify the necessary

Table 6.2 Table of definitions: one strategic objective and its process CSFs and KPIs

Strategic objective	Key processes		
Be a low-cost producer	Utilise machines and personnel optimally		
	Process CSF: Machine capacity utilisation		
Effort KPI	Input KPI	Activity KPI	Output KPI
Machine park utilisation	Machine breakdowns	Machine availability	Productivity per machine
	Process CSF: Personnel capacity utilization		
Effort KPI	Input KPI	Activity KPI	Output KPI
Personnel utilisation	Personnel planning accuracy	Employee output	Productivity per FTE

improvement, define corrective actions, and execute these. For example, an organisation can make a process cost analysis that identifies the costs of each process and explores possibilities to reduce these by improving the processes.

9. *Make a process information report.* Make a report that regularly depicts the results on the process KPIs so operational management can analyse and improve the processes.

6.4 CORPORATE STRUCTURE

In the first section of this chapter, "Critical success factors and key performance indicators", a description was given of how to develop CSFs and KPIs using the performance measurement pyramid. The pyramid methodology applies to organisations with a relatively uncomplicated organisational structure. In organisations with a group structure of headquarters and organisational units (i.e. divisions and business units), like a multinational, the methodology can also be applied with some adjustments to take account of the different accountability set-up in a holding structure (Figure 6.10).

Formulating CSFs and KPIs for a group is largely done in the same way as in companies with a less complicated organisational structure. First, the group formulates its mission and strategy by answering the question, "What do we want to accomplish as a group?" Then the group defines its strategic objectives: "How are we going to accomplish our mission?" To define the strategic indicators (CSFs and KPIs), however, the group has to follow a more complex route.

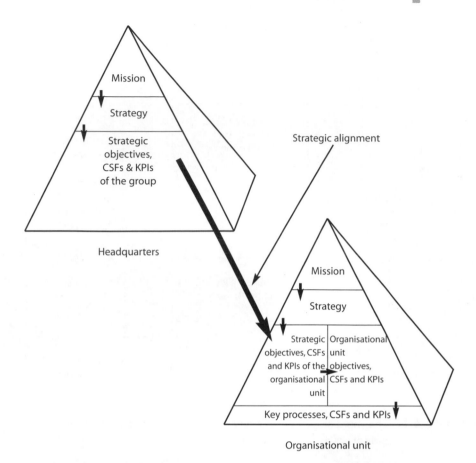

Figure 6.10 Relationship between headquarters and organisational units

- The performance on the strategic objectives is monitored by means of strategic CSFs and KPIs for the group as a whole. These strategic indicators are developed by and used by group headquarters. Because the divisions and business units often form an autonomous organisation, with their own mission, strategy, and strategic objectives, they have their own performance measurement pyramid. Therefore, these organisational units also have their own specific strategic CSFs and KPIs which are used by the management teams of these units. In the case of a group structure, multiple performance measurement pyramids are used concurrently: one for group headquarters, and one for each division and business unit.
- The strategies of the divisions and business units should be aligned with the strategy of the group. In the same manner, alignment is needed between the indicators developed at group level and the indicators developed at divisional and business unit levels.

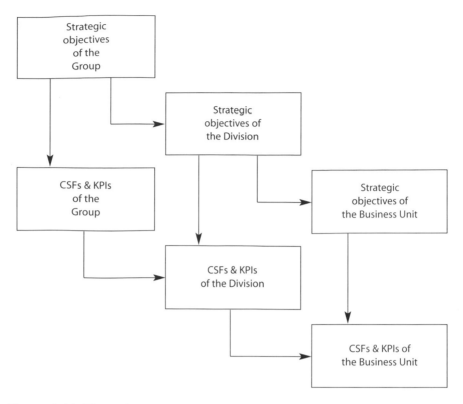

Figure 6.11 The multi-staged development plan of strategy and strategic indicators in a group structure

In summary, the strategic objectives of group headquarters determine the direction of the divisional objectives. Between a division and its business units a similar relationship exists. Objectives of business units should therefore be derived from divisional objectives, which are derived from group objectives. In a similar way, the different sets of CSFs and KPIs are aligned: the group CSFs and KPIs determine the direction of the CSFs and KPIs of the division, which in turn determine the direction of the CSFs and KPIs of the business units (Figure 6.11).

6.5 CASE: CSFs AND KPIs AT CNS

After finalising the reorganisation at Communication Network Systems Inc. (CNS, see Chapter 2 for a description of the organisation), chief executive officer Bruce Rudy and chief financial officer Eric Bell decided to develop CSFs and KPIs for the company. They distributed some articles on performance management and workshop documentation among the management team members. Then, during a brainstorming session at a remote location, the management team formulated CNS's mission for the coming years. One of the things they based the mission on was the direction in which the market CNS operated in was expected to develop. Subsequently they formulated CNS's company strategy, and derived a list of strategic objectives from that. Finally the management team developed CSFs for every strategic objective (Table 6.3).

After the strategy development session, Rudy and Bell consulted my colleague and me about how to proceed. We advised them to involve middle management in any further developments as soon as possible in order to create the support basis they needed for their new reporting system. The executives followed our advice, and during a session with middle management they explained CNS's mission and strategy, and the concept of CSFs and KPIs. In addition, they saw to it that a study group was set up for each department, and asked the study groups to develop KPIs, with targets, for all the CSFs that the management team had developed earlier. The study groups set to work independently. More than once, they consulted someone from the management team during the improvement project. After that, the study groups presented their findings to the management team. The proposed number of KPIs was considerable. The management team decided to reduce them to a controllable number (Table 6.4).

Expectations at CNS

CNS's management team determined the CSFs and KPIs that were going to be used and the targets for them. It also decided to get the new reporting

Table 6.3 CNS's critical success factors

Mission	To become the most valued supplier for our professional customers and to be one of the three leading suppliers in the market segments that we selected	
Strategy	Growth will be realised by continuously exceeding customers' expectations through use of high-quality resources	
Strategic objectives	**Critical Success Factors**	
Exceed customers' expectations	■ High customer satisfaction (result) ■ High service level (effort) ■ Good customer intelligence (effort)	
Maintain high quality standards of personnel, products, and organisation	■ CNS's quality image (result) ■ Training of personnel (effort) ■ High-quality products (effort) ■ Improved internal communication (effort)	
Realise substantial and sustained growth	■ Turnover growth (result) ■ Increased name and brand recognition (effort)	

Table 6.4 Some of CNS's key performance indicators

Critical success factor	Key performance indicator
High service level	▦ Breakdown percentage ▦ "Out of service" time
Training of personnel	▦ Number of courses in training plan ▦ Number of employees trained
Turnover growth	▦ Market share ▦ Percentage of successful proposals ▦ Cash flow

system, which included the new indicators, started as soon as possible. In instances that CNS's current information system was unable to supply certain data, or when it would take too long, some data fields would remain blank for the time being. CNS would then try to gather the missing data at a later stage. According to Bell, the reason for this was "to keep the process going." CEO Rudy explained to us what CNS's management team expected from the CSFs and KPIs:

> We expected our staff to become more aware of what is important to CNS as a company and of the things they are engaged in. We thought we could make CNS's strategy more tangible to our staff by using key performance indicators. By concentrating on these indicators, we thought the strategy would automatically become reality. We also hoped that people would propose improvements on their own initiative, so that we could implement the strategy quicker and better.

When we asked which of these expectations were eventually realised, Rudy answered:

> The indicators sure enough indicate the important aspects and problem areas of our company. This makes it possible to detect and initiate corrective actions earlier than before. However, I do believe that the pace at which the organisation picks up the KPIs is too slow. Because the advantages of these indicators are so self-evident to me, I thought the concept would sell itself. But it turned out that people are quick to think that this idea is a new kind of plaything for managers. I must constantly see to it that people are actively using the performance indicators. I show them that I really value those KPIs by adding explanatory notes in the new reports. In those notes, I inform them about changes and developments, and indicate what we must keep an eye on in the coming month.

Rudy and Bell summed up the four advantages of implementing CSFs and KPIs to their company up till now:

> Firstly, the CSFs and KPIs make people quicker at detecting situations that tend to go wrong and that force them into action. When, for example, the "breakdown

percentage" last month increased too much, people immediately examined which machines were the cause of this. These machines were taken out in the same month, which immediately caused a decrease of the breakdown percentage. Formerly, we would not have noticed the strong increase in repair costs until the end of the month. By the time we took action it was, of course, already too late.

Secondly, the employees now think more about increasing CNS's success. Turnover is no longer the only thing that counts. They have gained more insight into factors that are important to the success and profitability of CNS. The indicators make two things more tangible: what is important in the markets in which CNS operates, and where costs are increased for the company.

Thirdly, we are now able to ask more direct questions about the progress of certain issues. Instead of asking general questions like "How are things going?" we can now ask specific questions like "How many malfunctions have we had this week?" People are now able to answer these specific questions immediately. We have tightened our grip on the company. Finally, in the old days there was mostly one-way top-down communication between management and staff. But the use of CSFs and KPIs has given rise to discussions between management team and departments, and also among departments themselves. This stimulates two-way communication and encourages a strategic dialogue.

Experiences of CNS

Rudy and Bell told us about their experiences during the implementation of strategic performance management at CNS. At first, the company thought it could finish the entire development process in a limited number of sessions. The management team had never thought that development and implementation of a strategic performance management system was going to take six months. They had to communicate with middle management and staff a great deal more than they initially expected. Some of CNS's administrative systems, including those that were computerised, turned out to be less adequate than expected. There also proved to be quite a few stand-alone and manual databases in use. This caused difficulties in collecting the data, which often were not available in time. As a result, management reports were often released too late.

It would have been better if the organisation, prior to introducing the new reporting system, had examined which data the existing systems were able to supply. In addition to that, someone should have been in charge of checking whether the information in the systems supplying data was up to date or not. Staff were rather reluctant to disclose the results for the KPIs. They found it very frustrating when a particular indicator remained below or far below target. They found it even more frustratingly that the KPIs openly demonstrated "their" failure to management. Consequently, indicators were initially looked upon as "liquidators."

According to Bell:

Working with performance management requires people to be mentally strong. Indicators are more confrontational than financial figures. The financial figures depict past results and not much can be done about that any more. KPIs, on the other hand, involve people more directly. Because they are available all the time or within one month, people can react almost immediately. One should bear in mind, however, that "negative motivation" is not a good way to encourage the use of KPIs. By negative motivation I mean that managers discuss only the poor results for indicators with staff. Positive motivation exists when managers and staff together try to find a solution to disappointing results, which encourages people to use KPIs in their daily routines.

Bell told us that CNS had an unpleasant experience during the implementation:

As you may have gathered from the organisation chart, Bruce Rudy is CEO as well as interim head of Network Systems. This is because we had to lay off Ben Perkins, the former head of department, partly as a result of this project. CNS's traditional management reports showed for Network Systems a cumulative turnover which was slightly behind budget. We expected to obtain most of the turnover in the last months of the year, as this was always the case. So not surprisingly, Perkins said that the order portfolio looked quite promising and that he did not expect any trouble in realising the budget.

The moment we decided to use KPIs and targets to gain a better insight into our present condition and future expectations, we asked Perkins to include these indicators in his departmental reports. But the Network Systems department was not able to do this as it did not have the right systems to supply the required data. Perkins was given the task of solving this problem as quickly as possible. He tried to accomplish this by putting his staff under extreme pressure, which caused a great deal of unrest. In the end, Perkins was not able to support his claims of the expected turnover by means of KPI results. Both management team and staff lost all confidence in him and we were forced to dismiss him.

In the end, the incident with Perkins would have led to his dismissal anyway. It was because of the CSFs and KPIs that we could signal future problems for CNS at an earlier stage. This is why Perkins had to face the consequences earlier than expected. After the managers of Network Systems and I had developed the indicators, it became clear that Perkins's turnover expectations were much too optimistic. If we had known this earlier, we could have reacted sooner. We aim to create an atmosphere of openness at CNS, and performance management is helping us to accomplish this. The indicators actually also serve as a means of control. As the lesser functioning areas will show up anyway through KPIs, we can better be open and honest about the results.

When we interviewed some of CNS's middle managers, we discovered a discrepancy between their attitude towards CSFs and KPIs and their actual use of these. On the one hand, middle managers thought positively about using indicators. They considered the fact that the indicators can measure the extent to which CNS's strategy was being realised was a major advantage. It motivated them enormously: to see that the company's success in the market was a direct result of their work. On the other hand, middle managers objected to the manner in which the indicators were developed. As maintenance manager Edward Wells commented:

> Emotionally we were not involved in the development project. The management team had already visualised the CSFs. They were simply presented to us and we were told to develop KPIs for them. Due to this, the CSFs were not supported by middle managers. This is less the case for the KPIs, as we were at least allowed to determine those partly ourselves. I did this together with my staff. The management team then evaluated our input and decided among themselves which indicators and targets were important to my department. Some of my indicators were not included and others had been redefined in such abstract terms that I cannot do anything with them.

Datacom manager Shane McAnally added:

> The markets and activities of the departments within CNS are quite distinct from each other. This is why the generic indicators set developed by the management team had little relevance to the departments. For example, we generally negotiate for a very long time in preliminary discussions with our larger clients. We are dealing with potentially large orders and large sums of money. By the time we are ready to make an offer, we are 100 per cent sure that we will get the order. To run my department with the KPI "percentage of successful offers" is of little use: we always score 100 per cent anyway. It's a completely different story for the Network Systems department. To this department, the KPI is quite relevant because here it involves short-term, smaller orders.

During the discussions at CNS it became clear to us that the implementation of CSFs and KPIs required consistent and continuous control by the management team. For example, LAN manager James Williford remarked:

> The need for control starts with the strategy. If we are evaluated by the way we execute the strategy, it must be clearly formulated and communicated by the management team. It is essential that we see the connection between the strategy and the indicators we have been given. We now fail to see this, because we were not involved in the development of the CSFs. What we also lack is a proper consultative structure in which the KPIs are discussed. In addition, managers need to speak to their people about the actual results of the KPIs for which they are responsible. As long as management does not show enough interest in the KPIs, no one will be willing to base their actions on them.

A few additional issues surfaced from our talks with CNS middle managers, who were of the opinion that the inclusion of CSFs and KPIs in their reports had advantages for CNS as a whole. The advantages that they mentioned most often were: what is happening inside the organisation has become more visible; there is the chance to react more quickly and take action quickly; and there is better control of business processes. It was also expected that the parameters would have a positive effect on the balance sheet and profit-and-loss account. The people surveyed tended to be less positive about the advantages for their own performance. The reason given for this was that too little consultation and cooperation had taken place during the development process. How middle management could use the parameters remained unclear.

The efforts that went into the gathering of required data made middle management feel that the cost–benefit analysis would turn out to be negative at that moment. Most departments were made responsible for from one to five KPIs. The middle managers generally thought that this was an appropriate and feasible number. There was uncertainty about who was responsible within a department for a particular indicator. This uncertainty worsened because the management team did not officially provide feedback on the progress of the KPIs.

The future at CNS

Within CNS there was a general feeling that the implementation of performance management was useful to some extent. Unfortunately, the project came to a halt. Several months after the new performance management system was put into practice, management reports started coming out late or not at all. There were a number of reasons for this.

- The management team had indicated that daily operations were the first priority. As a result, staff at CNS never got to the point of actually working with the KPIs. They therefore did not really experience how these indicators could help them in becoming more efficient and effective.
- The management team had beforehand decided that they would not oblige staff to act on the basis of the results of specific KPIs. People had to decide for themselves what to do. The management team would only carry out a trend analysis. They feared that if they insisted on action, the new system would never get off the ground. Staff may have thought that their evaluation would be based on the action plans. But the effect of all this was that the reports with the KPIs insufficiently incited staff to take action. This was unfortunate because those actions would actually have been quite suitable for inclusion in people's daily routine. In fact, it would also have had a positive effect on the level of acceptance of the new performance management system.
- The methods developed for supplying the required data were either insufficient or nonexistent. Because of that, staff put too much time into manually compiling the figures. In addition, the layout of the new

reports was unclear and unattractive. The new reports were also not, or insufficiently, discussed during work meetings by middle management and staff. As a result, the KPIs were of little interest to staff.

During a meeting to discuss the findings of our interviews, Rudy and Bell assured us that CNS would continue with performance management. They acknowledged the causes of their problems, and were glad that our interviews had indicated that basically everyone at CNS subscribed to the usefulness of utilizing CSFs and KPIs. Both expressed the wish to devote themselves to revitalizing performance management and generating enthusiasm among staff. Rudy wanted to increase self-activation among staff with the use of the KPIs, by expanding their authority to act so that they could influence the result of the KPIs themselves. Both executives acknowledged that in future the management team would play an important, exemplary role in utilising performance management during its daily operations.

We advised CNS's management team to conduct an "update round." During this round, managers would assess the relevance of the developed CSFs and KPIs to the company's mission and strategy. If necessary, the indicators could can be adjusted or replaced by new ones. Subsequently, managers in each individual department thoroughly examined how the data for the KPIs could be generated. Facilities for this were created by modifying existing ICT systems or implementing new systems. The right kind of reporting system would help them create appealing report layouts.

Lessons learned

A lot of lessons can be learned from CNS' implementation of a new strategic performance management system.

- The CNS case clearly showed that early involvement of employees in the implementation of performance management is crucial for creating support for the new performance management system in the organisation. Not only do employees better understand which business variables are important for the proper functioning and performance of the company, they also see how they themselves can contribute to accomplishing the company's strategy. In addition, employees are usually in a better position than the management team to indicate what is important within their own departments. The only concern of the management team should be to ensure that these matters are in line with the company's mission and strategy. Imposing CSFs from the top down will only produce the opposite effect: employees will not be able to relate to these CSFs and consequently they will use the KPIs insufficiently or not at all.
- All CSFs at CNS turned out to be linked to the company's strategy. In addition to this, all the KPIs were identical for all departments.

Because no unit and operational indicators had been defined, the various characteristics of the distinct departments were insufficiently reflected in the performance management system. Despite the fact that the responsibilities of the management team and middle managers were completely different, the indicators that were defined for them showed no distinction. This partly explains the lack of support for this new approach at CNS. As middle managers got involved too late in the implementation, there was no mechanism to signal and control this.

- CEOs often wish to implement change in a short period, which makes them rather impatient. As Rudy indicated, an organisational change will not catch on by itself, despite the obvious advantages. To guide an organisation through the transitional period from the old to the new situation requires the constant attention of CEO and management team. The general duration of a transitional period is estimated to be approximately three years: three to six months to develop the indicator set of CSFs and KPIs, three to six months to set up the ICT systems in such a way that they can produce the information required, one year in which people within the organisation learn to work with the new performance management system and receive coaching from their management team, and another year before performance management is really "in the genes" of the organisation.

- The data required for calculating KPIs must be produced easily and on time. Measurement of performance must not be experienced by organisational members as an extra burden on top of their normal workload, as this would immediately lower their motivation. KPIs need not be 100 per cent accurate; it is mainly their signalling function that is important, that is, their capacity to alert the organisation of changes in performance. If data are not readily available, "substitute indicators" may be used instead. These are KPIs which actually do not completely provide the information that is required but only an indication of the direction in which certain business processes are developing. The substitute indicators can be replaced by "real" KPIs as soon as new ICT systems and/or registrative procedures have been implemented.

- There were discussions at CNS about directly linking KPIs to salaries. It was decided not to do this because the punitive aspect of bonus payment could start to dominate the use of performance management and cause resistance. Handing out apparently insignificant nonfinancial rewards in public, like champagne or cakes for good performance, is probably a better way of showing acceptance. Whether people have used the KPIs effectively in their daily routines or not will automatically manifest itself in the person's overall performance.

- The case description of CNS clearly shows that implementing performance management will not automatically lead to success. Whether management and staff have a positive attitude towards CSFs and KPIs will generally not be a problem, because the advantages of the method are usually obvious to everyone. However, this alone is not enough. A structured approach which involves everyone in the organisation during the implementation at an early stage is also crucial. Only then can the required internal support, which forms the basis for the daily use of performance management, be generated.

6.6 CASE STUDY: SPOT FREE'S CSFs AND KPIs

During one of the performance management workshops that my colleague and I conducted, we came into contact with Mr Forrest, CEO of Spot Free Inc. He told us that he found our vision on performance management very interesting and that he wanted to implement CSFs and KPIs at Spot Free. After a short conversation, we wished him every success and said that he could call us any time, should this be necessary.

We watched Forrest as he enthusiastically strode out of the room and asked ourselves whether we would ever hear from him again. As always, we were very interested in his experiences with implementing performance management based on CSFs and KPIs and the results he would gain.

Three months later Forrest called and invited us to his office. He wanted to discuss what he had done to improve the company's performance management system and the results he had gained so far. He felt he was not making enough progress. Of course we were quite willing to help him, and two weeks later we visited Spot Free's headquarters for the first time. The following case study describes what happened.

The organisation

Spot Free is a specialised cleaning service company and is part of one of the largest conglomerates in sanitary services in the world. Spot Free focuses on the cleaning and maintenance of equipment and buildings. The company has four distinct departments: commerce, production, personnel and organisation, and finance (Figure 6.12). The turnover is $84 million and the company employs 695 people, working both full-time and part-time. The company's position in the market is especially strong in one specific market segment in which 95 per cent of its turnover is realised.

Spot Free operates in a constantly changing environment. Clients' demands regarding the services rendered by Spot Free are changing: they increasingly want more value for less money. At the same time, the regulations and laws that have to be observed, like environmental legislation, are multiplying and getting more and more stringent. Competition is intensifying, as a result of which Spot Free can no longer take automatic renewal of contracts by customers for granted. Forrest summarised it as follows during our meeting: "Change is the only constant factor in Spot Free's operations."

Spot Free is characterised by reliability, expertise, vast experience, and

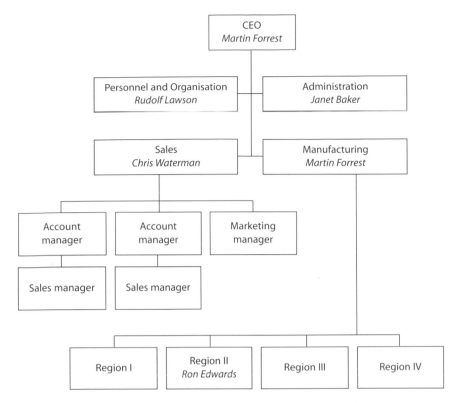

Figure 6.12 Spot Free Inc.'s organisational chart

superior quality. This is generally acknowledged in the market. However, the lion's share of the firm's turnover was "easy money" as it came from a single market segment in a fairly easy way for several years. Because of this, the organisation had over the years developed time-consuming procedures and a fairly inflexible attitude towards customers. Forrest felt that "this organisation is dozing off because until now the market didn't expect us to change." Management acknowledged that the organisation's characteristics did not sufficiently safeguard Spot Free's strong market position in the future. This is why, as part of their latest strategic development process, they initiated a change process to maintain and, if possible strengthen, Spot Free's position in the market. The most important strategic objectives were:

- *Secure continuity*: spread turnover over multiple market segments and clients.
- *Develop existing and new markets*: become more active in acquisitions and product development, by establishing a new commercial department.
- *Increase flexibility*: make the organisation and its employees more flexible so that they can adequately and promptly anticipate and respond to clients' wishes.

▪ *Monitor the right level of quality*: make sure the service rendered by Spot Free corresponds with, but does not exceed, the agreements made with clients.
▪ *Improve efficiency*: lower operating costs to improve the company's position in the market.

Forrest was pondering the following question: "How can I communicate to the management team and staff that the proposed changes are necessary?" He told us that:

> Our employees often adopt a wait-and-see attitude towards clients when they ask questions or express wishes. But we have to focus on quality and customer satisfaction and develop a proactive attitude towards our clients and the market. People should be given and assume more responsibilities, so that they will think more about whether their activities add value to the clients and Spot Free's future.

One of the techniques that Forrest wished to use to bring about a change in attitude was strategic performance management. Forrest told us:

> CSFs and KPIs are often much more tangible and closer to operational activities than financial figures. This is why they should be more of interest to middle managers. By using KPIs, middle managers will be better equipped to manage and control their units. I do not intend to use performance management to check up on my managers. On the contrary, I want to use it to incite managers to take the first step towards improving themselves and their units.

Phase I

In a previous job Forrest had gained experience in implementing strategic performance management, yet he was not overly positive. The people at that company did not feel responsible for the KPIs and the management team did not do much with the actual results. Forrest wanted to prevent the same thing from happening at Spot Free, and therefore prepared himself well, for instance by consulting some of the literature about the subject. He came across what is known as a "performance standard." A performance standard compares a person's performance with a previously agreed standard. Forrest decided to develop performance standards in consultation with the members of the management team and the regional managers. Forrest explained:

> I asked each manager a couple of questions which dealt with the actual responsibilities and tasks of that manager. Questions like: "Which tasks do you carry out?" "Why do you carry out these tasks?" and "Under which circumstances do you carry out your tasks well?" Together we identified each manager's five most important responsibilities. Subsequently, we determined the results that the

managers had to achieve. We quantified these results by means of performance standards [Table 6.5].

The responsibilities, results and performance standards were determined and agreed by both the CEO and the manager responsible. After the performance standards had been used for a number of months, Forrest took stock of the situation. Although he was content with the results so far, there were still some issues that needed to be addressed. Forrest commented:

> It became clear from the monthly talks about the performance standards that not everyone was using them properly. About half of the managers were actively using the performance standards while the other half were primarily looking for excuses not to use them. These managers stated they had problems with the way in which performance standards were measured and found it difficult to indicate the exact progress that had been made. It turned out that some performance standards were not specific enough. In addition, people questioned how and to what extent performance standards would contribute to the company's overall result. To them there was no visible link with Spot Free's strategy.

It was in this period that Forrest visited our workshop and learned about performance management based on CSFs and KPIs. Forrest pointed out:

> This technique seemed to be exactly what I needed to get the performance standards further entrenched in my organisation. The method was practical to such an extent that I thought I would be able to apply it at Spot Free right away.

Phase 2

Forrest continued his story:

> When I was evaluating the use of the performance standards, I was also drafting the medium-term plan. I was looking for a way to give this plan more body and credibility. To use CSFs and KPIs derived from the company's strategy seemed to me a suitable method to help implement the changes proposed in the plan.

As a starting point for drafting the medium-term plan, Forrest decided to organise a series of workshops for the management team to develop CSFs and KPIs. Table 6.6 gives the results of the first workshop: the strategic CSFs of Spot Free, some organisational unit CSFs, and key process CSFs for the Marketing and Sales, Finance, and P&O departments.

Case question 1: In Table 6.6, what are the result CSFs and what are the effort CSFs? Are there any result CSF and/or effort CSFs missing?

Case question 2: What are the KPIs for each CSF mentioned in Table 6.6?

Table 6.5 Some examples of performance standards

Responsibilities	Results	Performance standards
P & O manager		
Check progress of improvement projects	Continuously improve the quality of operations	80 percent of the formulated objectives are realised by the improvement teams
Southeast region manager		
Monitor absenteeism	Perform work as efficiently as possible, without people leaving and with a high level of social acceptance	At the end of year, the average sick leave does not exceed 10% over the last 13 periods

Table 6.6 Spot Free's CSFs

Objectives	Critical success factor	Description
Organisation	Strategic	
Realise a good sales margin	Margin expected by shareholder	Spot-Free will remain attractive to its shareholders by realising the agreed margin on sales.
Spread current turnover risk	Turnover ratio of different product-market combinations	A strong basis for continuity will be created by reducing the relative share of the most prominent client
Improve image	Professional and customer-friendly image	The image of product-oriented supplier should be changed to that of customer-oriented supplier
Marketing & sales department	Organisational unit	
Prevent competitors from penetrating Spot Free's customer base	By customer accepted price/quality ratio	By lowering the price level customer X will be less apt to switch to another supplier
	Key process	
Develop effective sales team	Promotional effectiveness	Boost sales through a balanced promotional campaign or communication strategy
	Sales profitability	Gross profit can remain at an acceptable level because of a keen price policy and optimum production
Finance department	Organisational unit	
Improve quality of administrative process	Management reporting system	Corrective actions can be taken in time because of an effective system with financial and nonfinancial figures
P & O department	Key process	
Clarify tasks, responsibilities, authorisations, performance standards and procedures	HRM procedures	The quality of operation can be improved and costs can be lowered by simple and adequate HRM procedures, for hiring, firing, training, evaluating, and rewarding

6.7 CASE STUDY: UVD'S CSFs AND KPIs

Pete Fields, management consultant, addressed the management team of UltraViolet Design (UVD), who had been listening intently to his explanation of CSFs and KPIs. He asked: "What is the starting point when you want to develop CSFs?"

CEO John Williams took the lead. "The strategic objectives, of course."

"That's right. We have determined those in the past few weeks. Now, how are you going to achieve the company's strategy?" Pete continued.

"We have to derive the CSFs for the strategic objectives. Things which are of utmost importance to UVD so that we have to constantly keep an eye on them," CFO Helen answered.

"Excellent. Let's start with an easy one – UVD's image, for example. What strategic actions could we formulate for it?"

"What exactly do you mean by strategic action?" Gary Williams asked.

Before Pete had a chance to, Helen answered. "To be able to execute the strategy we have to describe what we want to accomplish with the strategic objectives, the 'outcome' so to speak. And to monitor the progress of these actions, we need KPIs."

"Could you give an example?" Martin Williams asked.

"Take, for instance, again UVD's image," Helen continued. "We want to distinguish ourselves from our competitors by emphasizing the eco-friendly image of our products, to sell more products. The outcome we need is a positive image, as this makes customers buy UVD's position instead of the competition's."

"Why?" asked Pete.

"Well," replied Helen, "we currently use high-priced, and I mean really expensive, recyclable raw materials in our products because we are extremely aware of the effect of manufacturing plastics on the environment. We need to convey this environmental awareness to our customers, otherwise we can't really explain why our prices are higher than those of the competitors."

She took a deep breath before continuing. "Another reason to pursue an environment-friendly image is that end-consumers may turn away from our products because they are unaware of the fact that these are made from recycled, biodegradable plastics. Without their knowing, our clients may decide to no longer buy our products, and we may well end up with a warehouse full of goods that cannot be sold."

"How would you translate this into a CSF?" Pete asked.

Helen replied, "I think our first CSF would be an environment-friendly image."

Pete quickly wrote this down on the flipchart. "I agree with you. If UVD doesn't keep track of its image, it will never be able to execute its strategy."

"But," Gary objected, "how can you measure this CSF?"

Pete replied, "That's a good question, Gary. You can measure the environment-friendly image, the first CSF, by means of a KPI."

John straightened up. "It seems logical to me that if you want to find out how the market views you, you go out and investigate that in some way."

"What do you think about asking our clients for their opinion?" said Martin, putting in his bit.

John gave his younger brother a questioning look. "What do you mean by that?"

"Well, we can conduct a client survey in which we ask our clients about our image. For example, how they see us, whether they think that we make environment-friendly products, or to check if they have an opinion at all. And if they don't, then we seriously have to work on our image!" Martin replied.

John commented, "Sounds good. So the KPI for our image is 'client responses'. We want to know the number of positive client responses as compared to the total of all client responses. We can measure that by conducting a special survey."

"Or we make this a continuous survey, so that we can see the number of positive responses per period," said Martin enthusiastically.

Helen commented, "Wait a minute, Martin. Do you have any idea what it costs to carry out these surveys continually? Money doesn't grow on trees here – trust me, I know!"

Jeanette Barrymoor, HRM manager, came to Martin's aid. "But Helen, we just decided that image is crucial for UltraViolet Design's success. Having decided that, we have to accept the consequences as well as the rewards. We cannot put our faith in random signals from the market or from our clients. We have to conduct a structured survey."

Helen nodded, and Jeanette went on, "Yes, this could be rather expensive, particularly if you've never done it before and you have to start from scratch. But think, just for a second, about the alternative: being in the dark about information that is of great importance to our company. We'll never be able to direct anything, let alone redirect anything!"

Jeanette put Helen's mind at ease. "Of course we would look for less costly alternatives to the continuous measurement method. Just as long as we get the results somehow."

"In that case," Gary commented flippantly, "we could carry out spot-checks to ask if our clients have any complaints about the quality of our products."

"Excellent idea," John commented. "This data can then be entered in our sales system, which is also used to register complaints."

Case question 1: For each strategic objective, what would be the result CSFs and effort CSFs? Identify at least one result CSF and one effort CSF.

Case question 2: What are the KPIs for each identified CSF?

Case question 3: Could the CSFs and KPIs that you just defined be used at lower management levels of UVD? If not, what has to be done to obtain lower-level indicators?

Key points

☑ Intangible assets are increasingly seen as major value sources of an organisation in addition to the more traditional, tangible assets, yet many of these intangible assets are not included in the formal reporting systems of organisations because these have been built to report mainly financial information.

☑ Implementation of critical success factors and key performance indicators combines nonfinancial, leading indicators with financial, lagging indicators in one reporting system which offers management a balanced overview of the organisation's performance and of the execution of the strategy and key processes.

☑ A critical success factor is a qualitative description of an element of the strategy in which the organisation has to excel in order to be successful. It is made quantifiable with a key performance indicator.

References

Boulton, R.E.S., Libert, B.D. and Samek, S.M. (2000) *Cracking the Value Code: How successful businesses are creating wealth in the new economy.* New York: HarperBusiness.

Burlton, T. (2001) *Business Process Management: Profiting from process.* Sams.

Charan, R. and Colvin, G. (1999) Why CEOs fail. *Fortune,* June 21.

Doz, Y., Santos, J. and Williamson, P. (2001) *From Global to Metanational: How companies win in the knowledge economy.* Boston, Mass.: Harvard Business School Press.

Foster, R. and Kaplan, S. (2001) *Creative Destruction: Why companies that are built to last underperform the market – and how to successfully transform them.* New York: Doubleday.

Geelen, P. and Coevering, R. van de (2005) *Integral Performance Management.* Deventer: Kluwer.

Harmon, P. (2003) *Business Process Change: A manager's guide to improving, redesigning and automating processes.* San Francisco: Morgan Kaufmann.

Marr, B. (2006) *Strategic Performance Management: Leveraging and measuring your intangible value drivers.* Oxford: Butterwoth-Heinemann.

Smith, H. and Fingar, P. (2002) *Business Process Management: The third wave.* Tampa: Meghan Kiffer Press.

Verweire, K. and Van den Berghe, L. (2002) Integrated performance management: adding a new dimension. In: A. Neely, A. Walters and R. Austin (eds), *Performance Measurement and Management: Research and action.* Cranfield, UK: Cranfield School of Management, 587–94.

White, C. (2005) Is BAM alive and well? *DM Review,* September.

7

The balanced scorecard

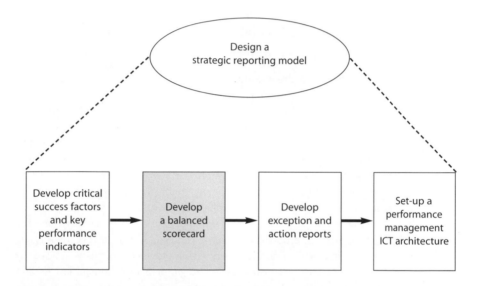

Figure 7.1 Developing a balanced scorecard

These days, performance management is attracting more and more attention, among both academics and practitioners. It has been calculated that new publications about performance management have been appearing at a rate of one every five hours of every working day since 1994, and that there are now more than 12 million sites dedicated to this topic (Marr and Schiuma, 2002). However, it seems that only a few authors and a few concepts dominate the field of performance management. At each biannual conference of the Performance Management Association (PMA), a citation analysis is made on the basis of the papers that are presented. For the 2002 PMA conference in Boston, 115 papers were accepted in which 2248 authors were cited (Marr and Schiuma, 2002). Of these authors, 95 per cent were cited less than three times. Over 80 per cent were only cited once.

In contrast, Robert Kaplan and David Norton were cited 154 and 120 times respectively. It comes as no surprise that, looking at the citation analyses of the 1998, 2000, and 2002 PMA conferences, the most cited literature sources were all publications by Kaplan and Norton: *The Balanced Scorecard: Translating strategy into action* (Harvard Business School Press, 1996), 'The Balanced Scorecard: Measures that drive performance' (*Harvard Business Review*, January/February 1992), and *The Strategy-Focused Organisation: How balanced scorecard companies thrive in the new business environment* (Harvard Business School Press, 2000), making the balanced scorecard (BSC) one of the most successful concepts in the performance management field. A recent survey conducted with 960 organisations on five continents found that the BSC is being used in 59 per cent of the companies, and that the use of the scorecard increased 18 per cent in the period 1996–2004 (Rigby, 2005). In addition, the BSC has been hailed as one of the 75 most influential business ideas of the twentieth century (Niven, 2005).

According to Professor Kaplan, the success of the BSC can be explained as follows:

> There is a huge gap between the vision and strategy developed at the top and the things people down in the organisation, at the frontline, are doing. Peter Drucker already noticed this almost 50 years ago when he coined the phrase 'Management By Objectives', but at that time there was no language with which the gap could be closed. This gap became even more apparent in the 1970s. First, Michael Porter and consultancy firms such as the Boston Consulting Group, formalized the theory and practice of strategy for senior-level executives. At the same time, employees' everyday actions were affected by total quality management programmes, the drive for empowerment and the introduction of personal objectives. However, no bridge was made between these two initiatives: strategy and employee empowerment for continuous improvement. The BSC provides the required language, it is the missing link. The scorecard links vision and strategy to employees' everyday actions by translating the abstract strategy into clear strategic priorities and initiatives and relating these to clear tangible strategic outcomes the organisation and its employees have to strive for: satisfied shareholders, delighted customers, efficient and effective processes and a motivated workforce. In this way, the BSC makes strategy everyone's job. And because all organisations face the aforementioned gap, especially when they transfer from the traditional command & control style, which used to work well in the old days, to the empowerment style of modern times, they need something like the BSC to help them bridge the gap. Another point is that more and more company value comes from intangibles – see for instance the work of Baruch Lev of the Stern School of Business. The traditional financial system cannot convey the importance of these intangibles such as people, processes, innovation to senior executives and to front line employees. The BSC can.
>
> (Waal, 2003)

It can be stated that for many organisations the BSC has such a reputation that is helps define modern management for them. It now is an institutionalised object that is difficult to object against, and as such, every manager should know about it (Hansen and Mouritsen, 2005).

Chapter objectives

- ☑ To teach the reader how to develop the four perspectives of the traditional balanced scorecard.
- ☑ To teach the reader how to develop a strategy map and connect it with the balanced scorecard.
- ☑ To provide the reader with an insight into the criticisms of the balanced scorecard.
- ☑ To enable the reader to study the connection between the parenting styles and the balanced scorecard.

7.1 THE BALANCED SCORECARD

Traditionally, a BSC has four perspectives or areas: innovation of products/services or people (including learning and development of people), effectiveness of internal processes, experiences of customers, and financial performance (see Figure 7.2).

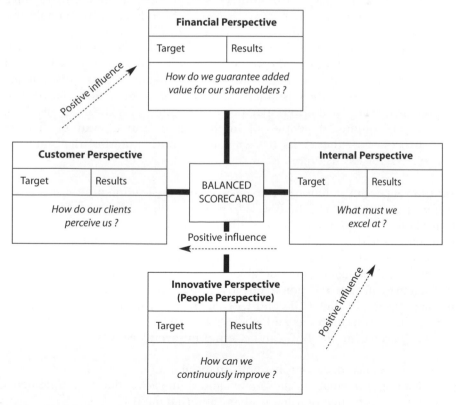

Figure 7.2 The set-up of the BSC

- The *innovative (or learning)* perspective measures how often an organisation introduces new products, services, or (production) techniques. In this way, the organisation makes sure that it does not become complacent but continuously renews itself. Sometimes organisations include people aspects in this perspective. These are used to measure the well-being, commitment and competence of people in the organisation. The people aspects measure cultural qualities like internal partnership, teamwork, and knowledge sharing, as well as aggregate individual qualities like leadership, competency, and the use of technology.
- The *internal (or process)* perspective measures the effectiveness of the processes by which the organisation creates value. It comes after the innovative perspective because innovation and people influence the ability of the organisation to create value by implementing and managing effective processes. The contribution of innovative people to the ability of the organisation to create value consists of implementing and managing effective processes. The internal perspective measures how effective processes are. It precedes the customer perspective because efficient processes make it possible for an organisation to stay competitive, or become more competitive.
- The *customer* perspective measures performance in terms of how the customer experiences the value created by the organisation. It comes after the internal perspective, because efficient processes enable the organisation to provide better service to its customers.
- The *financial* perspective measures the bottom line, such as growth, return on investment and the other traditional measures of business performance. It comes after the customer perspective because higher appreciation by the customers translates into higher financial results. It is the last of the four perspectives because it is the final result of good, committed people, of implementing and operating effective processes, of the ability to renew and innovate, and of the ability to create for its customers.

In different organisations, the perspectives and the leading indicators can be different, but the idea of the BSC is to provide a "balanced" set of indicators that allows an organisation to measure the cause and effect chain by which customer and shareholder value is created. If value is created by people working on and in processes to satisfy customers and to produce financial results, then managers must be able to measure and monitor all of these perspectives of value creation to effectively manage the business. By combining lagging and leading CSFs and KPIs, managers gain an understanding of where the organisation was and where it is going.

The "balance" in the BSC can be found in several aspects:

- nonfinancial data complements financial data
- leading information (customer and innovative data) complements lagging information (financial and internal data)

- internal information (financial, internal and innovative data) complements external information (customer data).

Figure 7.3 gives an example of the four perspectives of a balanced scorecard. It has been enhanced (compared with the traditional format) with some extra columns. For each of the four perspectives, it shows in the first column the actual performance of this period compared with the actuals of last period (+, – or 0, with traffic light colouring: red = below budget, orange = on budget, green = above budget), in the centre column the CSFs (grey) and accompanying KPIs (white) which are colour-coded to show actual performance this period versus budget this period, and in the right-hand column the expected performance for the next period (↗,→ or ↘, again with traffic light colouring). For instance, the KPI "multiskilled employees," belonging to the CSF "quality employees" in the internal perspective, could be coded + and green in the first column, meaning the actual result is better than the actuals of the last period, and coded orange in the centre column, indicating actual performance is equal to budget this period. However, there could be a red arrow pointing downward in the right column, meaning that the organisation expects to do worse in the next period. This is a clear signal for the organisation that it should act now, to prevent negative developments.

Financial perspective

	Top line growth	
0	Margin growth	↗
0	Sales volume growth	↗
	Succesful new products	
+	New product sales	↘

Customer perspective

	Customer satisfaction	
+	Customer satisfaction	↗
–	Days sales outstanding	↘
	Promotion	
0	Promotional campaigns	↗

Internal perspective

	Effective processes	
+	Process goal achievement	↗
	"Quality" employees	
+	Multiskilled employees	↘
	Productivity	
0	Qualified employees	↗

Innovative perspective

	Quality brand portfolio	
–	Big brands	↗
0	Brand reduction	↗
	Quality investments	
+	Big brand investment	↗

Figure 7.3 Example of the BSC

The main benefit of managing with a combination of financial and nonfinancial information is that the use of leading, nonfinancial indicators facilitates proactive control and the ability to take preventive action. A balanced set of key financial and nonfinancial CSFs and KPIs enables management to focus on the really important issues that drive business performance, and to monitor the achievement of strategic goals more closely. Using nonfinancial information improves the analysis capabilities of managers because they can identify the root causes of financial performance. The nonfinancials can include external information, making it possible for management to compare the internal results with external trends and drivers.

It is interesting to see how Kaplan and Norton extended ideas proposed earlier by other authors. For instance, their "lagging" and "leading" indicators were mentioned earlier by Rockart as "monitoring" and "building" CSFs. A well-known predecessor of the BSC is the *Tableau de Bord*. It emerged in France at the end of the nineteenth century, having been developed by process engineers who were looking for ways to improve the production process by better understanding its cause–effect relationships (Lebas, 1994; Epstein and Manzoni, 1997; Bourguignon et al., 2004).

The same principle was then applied at top management level to give senior management a set of indicators that would allow them to monitor the progress of the business, compare it with the goals that had been set, and take the corrective actions needed. Each organisational unit had its own *Tableau de Bord*, which was not limited to financial indicators but extended to operational measures. Just as with the BSC, the development of the *Tableau de Bord* involved translating an organisational unit's vision and mission into a set of objectives, from which the unit identified its CSFs, which were then translated into a series of quantitative KPIs. To provide managers with information they could use for decision making, the *Tableau de Bord* primarily contained performance indicators that the organisational unit especially could control.

7.2 STRATEGY MAP

(This section is for a large part based on Kerklaan and Dresens, 2005.)

In addition to the BSC, Kaplan and Norton introduced the strategy map (Kaplan and Norton, 2000, 2004). This is a logical architecture that defines a strategy by specifying the relationships between shareholders, customers, business processes, and competencies. A strategy map guarantees that the balanced scorecard is linked to the organisation's strategy, using the causal links that exist between the various elements of the strategy, which can be placed in the various perspectives of the BSC (Figure 7.4).

The reason Kaplan and Norton developed the strategy map was that during implementations of the BSC they found that many companies had great difficulty translating their strategy into a scorecard. Kaplan and Norton stated that for the successful execution of the strategy, three components are

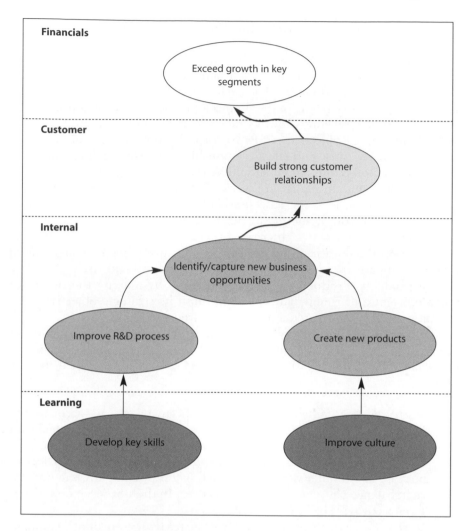

Figure 7.4 Causal links between the BSC perspectives

needed: describing the strategy, measuring the strategy, and managing the strategy. Measuring is taken care of with the BSC, managing by applying the concept of the *strategy focused organisation*, and describing the strategy can now be achieved with the strategy map.

With the strategy map the organisation's strategy is visualised by making the internal factors that determine the successful execution of the strategy explicit, and identifying the cause and effect relations between these CSFs. In this way, the map supports management in making their ambitions, plans, and strategic objectives concrete. But because the strategy map is so visual, it is also an excellent communication tool to disseminate the strategy and critical business processes throughout the enterprise. In this way, the strategy map is the "missing link" between strategy and measurable indicators. Figure 7.5 gives an example of a strategy map.

The strategy map in Figure 7.5 includes the well-known BSC perspectives, which are mentioned on the left-hand side. Each perspective has its own horizontal field (domain). For each perspective, a limited number of strategic objectives is given. In the financial perspective, for example, there are the objectives "revenue growth strategy" and "productivity strategy." For each of the strategic objectives, CSFs are formulated which are connected by arrows to indicate cause and effect relationships. The strategy map has to be built from top to bottom, and it should be read the same way.

The strategy map in Figure 7.5 shows that the central strategic objective of the organisation is to increase shareholder value. The company wants to realise this through increasing its revenues while at the same time becoming more productive. Increased revenue has to be achieved by selling more products to existing customers and attracting new customers, and by being a low-cost supplier with perfect quality and the right selection of products. Productivity will be improved by making the processes more efficient and timely. For achieving both its strategic objectives, the company needs a motivated and well-prepared workforce.

The purpose of the strategy map is to give the reviewer a clear picture of the organisation's strategic objectives and the critical success factors of importance for achieving these objectives. The map is developed in four steps.

1. *Describe the financial perspective.* This perspective concerns, according to Kaplan and Norton, the main objectives of the company that deal with creating shareholder value. This perspective is relatively simple to operationalise as a company usually has to sell more and spend less to increase shareholder value. The main task for the company is to find the right balance between these two objectives. In the BSC each objective is given its own set of CSFs and KPIs.

2. *Describe the customer perspective.* This perspective, according to Kaplan and Norton, concerns the central strategic objectives of the organisation because it describes how the company will become successful in its chosen customer segments. It contains the value proposition to customers, which differentiates the firm from its competitors and provides the way in which the organisation wants to create added value for its customers.

3. *Describe the internal perspective.* This perspective covers the translation of the strategic objectives, recorded in the customer perspective, to the internal processes of the company. The processes have to be organised in such a way that the selected customer segments can be serviced as chosen in the customer perspective. For this, the crucial business processes or activities, which mostly influence the successful achievement of the various strategic objectives, have to be selected so they can receive the most attention. The enterprise has to choose "the vital few

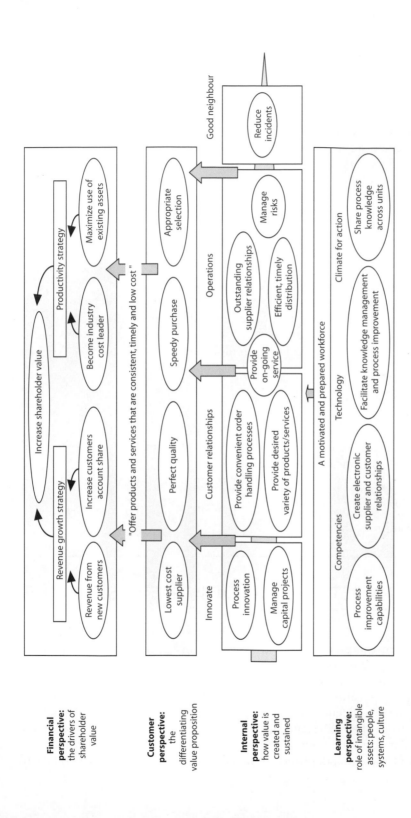

Figure 7.5 Example of a strategy map

Source: Kaplan (2002).

versus the trivial many." Kaplan and Norton distinguish four types of internal processes which all have to be provided with objectives: operational processes (the key processes of the organisation), innovative processes (processes to invent new products, services and processes), customer relationship processes (processes to strengthen relationships with major customers), and social processes (processes that make the organisation a "good neighbour" to society).

4. *Describe the learning perspective.* The objectives in this perspective have to create the ideal combination of people (competencies), technology (information systems and architecture), and organisational culture ("climate for action") that fosters the successful achievement of the various objectives in the three other perspectives.

Strategy map checklist

A well-constructed strategy map translates the organisational strategy into operational terms. Whether the constructed strategy map satisfies this condition can be verified with the following checklist.

Does the strategy map:

- show the business strategy clearly?
- contain a comprehensive view of the strategy?
- contain plausible cause and effect relations?
- contain concrete and tangible strategic objectives?
- give clear critical success factors?
- make the development of corresponding key performance indicators fairly easy?
- form a communication tool for disseminating the strategy throughout the company?

7.3 THE LINK BETWEEN PARENTING STYLES AND THE BALANCED SCORECARD

As described in Chapter 3, there are three main parenting styles: financial control, strategic control, and strategic planning. The choice of parenting style dictates the influence that corporate headquarters has on the strategic planning and operational control processes of the divisions and business units. This in turn dictates the content and level of detail of the information flow going from these divisions and business units to corporate headquarters. To make a link between a specific parenting style and the shape of a matching BSC, we can adapt the model of Weber and Schaffer (1999) which

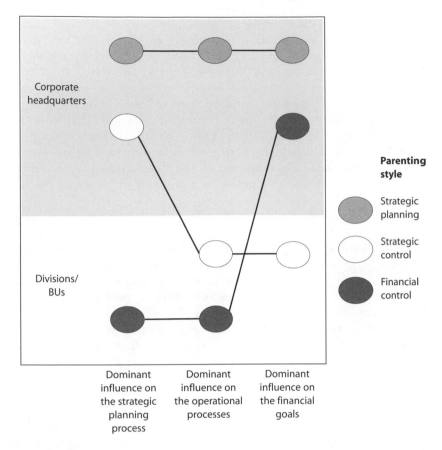

Figure 7.6 Influence of corporate headquarters on the content and use of the balanced scorecard, depending on the parenting style

matches types of corporate structures with types of BSC, by putting in the types of parenting styles and adapting the types of control (Figure 7.6).

In the *strategic planning style*, corporate headquarters plays an active and dominant part in the strategy development process of the divisions and business units. It is also heavily involved in deploying and monitoring (the execution of) the strategy. Because corporate headquarters has to stand close to the divisions and business units, it needs the same type of information from all lower organisational units. The scorecard indicators of the divisions, business units, and corporate headquarters are so similar that these can be consolidated into one balanced scorecard. This consolidated scorecard is checked in detail by corporate headquarters, which makes it possible to intervene on lower levels. In the strategic planning style, corporate headquarters has a dominant influence on both the development and use of the BSC.

In the *strategic control style*, corporate headquarters issues strategic guidelines but the divisions and business units make their own strategic plans independently. These plans are evaluated and prioritised by corporate headquarters. The divisions and business units define both short and longer-term financial and nonfinancial objectives, which are put in "local" balanced scorecards. These indicators are then collected (but not consolidated!) into one scorecard, and complemented by indicators that show the added value of corporate headquarters. This scorecard is checked at a high level in corporate headquarters. In the strategic control style, corporate headquarters has a dominant influence on the development of the scorecard. The divisions and business units have dominant influence on the use of the BSC.

In the *financial control style*, the responsibility and authority to develop strategic plans is totally delegated to the divisions and business units. Corporate headquarters in principle does not evaluate these plans, but is only interested whether or not the divisions and business units are achieving the financial targets as forecasted in the strategic plans. Corporate headquarters manages a portfolio of businesses and does not need complete BSCs of the divisions and business units nor of itself. Corporate headquarters can use the financial indicators in the "local" scorecards as input to evaluate the portfolio. In the financial control style, the divisions and business units have dominant influence on both the strategic and the operational use of the BSC. Corporate headquarters uses parts of the BSC for financial control purposes.

These links between parenting styles and types of BSC use should be regarded as guidelines. Every organisation has to work out for itself whether the links described here are in keeping with the guidelines and agreements made between organisational levels.

7.4 CRITICISM AND THE "TEN COMMANDMENTS"

Despite the popularity of the BSC, it is not without criticism. Most criticism focuses on the imbalance in the number of stakeholders that is accounted for. For instance, suppliers are absent from the scorecard. It is implicitly assumed by the scorecard developers that if the business itself excels, all is well. But in these days of increased outsourcing, business interdependencies are continually growing.

A second criticism is that the social context and the environment do not have an "official" place in the standard scorecard layout. Some organisations have had bad experiences with BSC implementations: they have abandoned their scorecards after a few years without consistent results or as a result of difficulties during the implementation phase. These organisations have reported problems in defining the measures, especially in areas where performance is more qualitative than quantitative, and in decomposing the measures to lower levels in the organisation.

The third point of criticism is that the BSC disregards the human element: it does not go into the effect that a BSC can have on managerial attitudes and the question of whether a BSC is suitable for every type of manager. Intellectual capital and intellectual property are also under-represented in the scorecard approach.

It is interesting that some case studies show that dividing performance indicators over the perspectives of the BSC makes the performance information less understood by lower-level managers, which creates the opposite effect from what senior management intended (Brignall, 2002; Nørreklit, 2000; Malina and Selto, 2004; Marr and Adams, 2004; Mauritsen et al., 2004; Waweru et al., 2004; Smith, 2005).

In addition, the one-way linear cause and effect relations that Kaplan and Norton are suggesting are a much-debated issue. Several authors argue that there are no causal relationships between the four perspectives because they are interdependent. This means a change in one perspective by definition causes a like change in the other perspectives. A causal relationship can only exist if both variables are logically independent. These authors state that Kaplan and Norton are confusing logical relationships with causal ones.

There can be as many as five different relationships within a causal relationship: multiple phenomena may be co-related (or not), coexist (or not), co-vary positively or negatively (or not), be similar or opposite phenomena, and be independent or dependent phenomena in a causal relationship. Many of these interrelationships are possible among the performance variables and their measures in the four perspectives of a BSC. This may help to explain the weak and conflicting results from tests of causal relations among claimed performance drivers and their outcomes which have been reported in empirical research to date (Ittner and Larcker, 1998a, b; Nørreklit, 2000). Some of these studies even show a detrimental relationship between the results of nonfinancial KPIs and overall performance of the organisation (for example, as measured in its stock price). A possible explanation could be that there is a time lag between good results on nonfinancial indicators and their expression in the overall company result (Pandey, 2005).

Despite the criticism, the BSC remains the management accounting innovation that has had the biggest impact on scientific theory and organisational practice in the past two decades. It therefore deserves more research on ways to effectively implement it in companies. A good first start in this regard has been given by Lewy and Du Mee (1998), who proposed "ten commandments" for a successful implementation of the BSC (McCunn, 1998). These commandments are a checklist of dos and don'ts that are based on successful BSC implementations in seven European companies. It is not absolutely necessary to meet all ten commandments: in practice satisfying six or seven of them seems to be enough for a successful implementation. However, if an organisation meets less than six dos and don'ts, the chances of implementing the BSC successfully are slim.

Dos

1. Ensure a clearly defined strategy: strategic objectives, and strategic goals are in place before developing a BSC. Do not invent or formulate the strategy during the project, because that will cause much confusion.
2. Use the BSC as a platform for implementing the strategy, strategic objectives, and strategic goals throughout the company. It is an ideal tool to communicate and disseminate the strategy in a graphic manner throughout the organisation.
3. Ensure the implementation of the BSC is sponsored at senior management level (the *project champion*) and commitment for the scorecard exists with all relevant line managers. The implementation of performance management and the BSC is so important that it has to be the top priority.
4. First implement a pilot to gain experience with the scorecard, before introducing the BSC company-wide. This provides valuable lessons and avoids "big bang" problems and risks.
5. First conduct a feasibility analysis (see "Feasibility analysis" in Chapter 2) in each individual organisational unit, before proceeding to implement the scorecard in that unit. This minimises the risk of starting the project in unfavourable circumstances, and provides information on how the project needs to be customised.

Don'ts

6. Do not use the scorecard as an extra tool for strengthening hierarchical control. This will cause employees to resist and sabotage the new tool.
7. Do not use a standardised implementation approach. The BSC has to be tailored to the specific needs of each individual organisational unit. After all, each organisation and even organisational unit is unique.
8. Do not underestimate the need for training and communication. The idea behind the BSC is relatively simple but difficult to implement in practice. The resulting changes in processes and especially behaviour will be huge.
9. Do not overcomplicate the scorecard by striving for perfection: use the 20–80 per cent rule. Avoid "paralysis by analysis."
10. Do not underestimate the costs associated with tracing, recording, administrating, and reporting the data needed to fill in and report the BSC. Gathering data for the BSC can be very time-consuming and costly, especially when this data is collected for the first time.

7.5 CASE: STRATEGY MAPPING AT BABS

(This case is based on a case study in Kerklaan and Dresens, 2005.)

The chief executive officer (CEO) of the building conglomerate BaBs (Build all Bricks) had formulated, together with the controller, a draft strategic plan. The purpose of the CEO was to let the management team react to the draft and then to develop a BSC. However, this well-intended action did not arouse the expected reaction from the management team. The managers dismissed the review by sending e-mails to the controller with texts like "Agreed!" or "Success with the further development."

During a special management team meeting which was dedicated solely to discussing the draft plan, no progress whatsoever was made. The management team members found the plan rather abstract but nicely formulated, so they could not really be "against" it. Although the link between the plan and their own activities was not transparent to them, they thought that in time there would come more clarity and they were quite willing to wait for that.

The CEO found this an unacceptable course of action, and decided to change tactics. She called in a consultant who proposed to convert the draft strategic plan into a strategy map. A workshop was organised with the management team, and a strategy map was constructed from top to bottom (Figure 7.7).

The strategy map shows that the main strategic objective of BaBs is to be a healthy independent corporation with a prominent role in the market for development, building, and maintenance. In the construction industry risk management is very important and influences, to a large extent, the type of projects that BaBs undertakes. At the same time, the financial return has to be improved, which can be achieved by working for profitable customers. From these strategic objectives, objectives and success factors have been developed for each perspective. The perspectives mentioned in the strategy map deviate somewhat from the standard four BSC perspectives: an additional perspective "market position" has been added and the "learning" perspective has been renamed "competencies."

Central to the customer perspective is the objective "supply what the customer wants," entailing that BaBs will supply a high-quality product that fits the customers' needs within the agreed-upon budget and time frame. In order to achieve this objective, BaBs wants to work with carefully selected co-manufacturers, suppliers, and subcontractors. It is essential for the quality experience of the customer that there is regular communication between them and BaBs, because this gives the company the opportunity to get to better know the customers' needs and wishes and to build a strong relationship. Preconditions for a high-quality product are optimal processes, high efficiency, and synergy of the organisational units of the conglomerate BaBs. The basis for this lays in the competencies and attitude of the employees and their professional expertise.

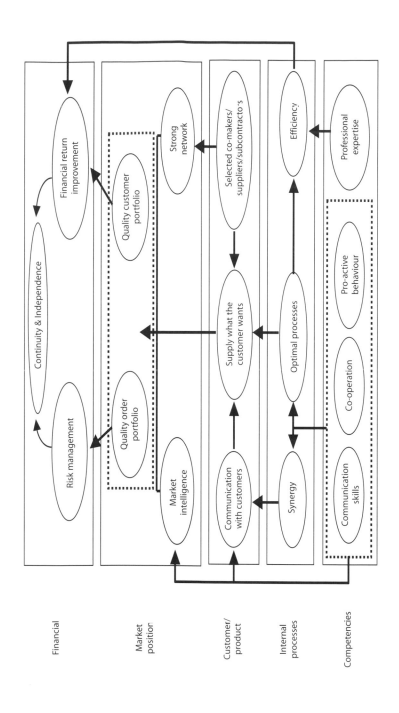

Figure 7.7 BaBs' strategy map

Financial

Market
position

Customer/
product

Internal
processes

Competencies

Financial return
improvement

Continuity & Independence

Risk management

Quality customer
portfolio

Quality order
portfolio

Strong
network

Market
intelligence

Supply what the
customer wants

Communication
with customers

Selected co-makers/
suppliers/subcontracto's

Efficiency

Optimal processes

Synergy

Professional
expertise

Pro-active
behaviour

Co-operation

Communication
skills

Key points

☑ The BSC is one of the most successful concepts in the performance management field.

☑ The traditional BSC consists of four perspectives: innovation of products/services or people (including learning and development of people), effectiveness of internal processes, experiences of customers, and financial performance.

☑ The "balance" in the BSC can be found in several aspects: nonfinancial data complements financial data, leading information complements lagging information, and internal information complements external information.

☑ The strategy map is a logical architecture that defines a strategy by specifying the relationships between shareholders, customers, business processes, and competencies.

☑ The strategy map guarantees that the BSC is linked to the organisation's strategy, using the causal links that exist between the various elements of the strategy and which can be placed in the various perspectives of the BSC.

References

Bourguignon, A., Malleret, V. and Nørreklit, H. (2004) The American balanced scorecard versus the French *tableau de bord*: the ideological dimension. *Management Accounting Research*, 15 (2), 107–35.

Brignall, S. (2002) The unbalanced scorecard: a social and environment critique. In: A. Neely, A. Walters and R. Austin (eds), *Performance Measurement and Management: Research and action*. Cranfield, UK: Cranfield School of Management, 85–91.

Epstein, M.J. and Manzoni, J.F. (1997) Translating strategy into action: the balanced scorecard and tableau de bord. *Management Accounting*, August, 28–36.

Hansen, A. and Mouritsen, J. (2005) Strategies and organisational problems: constructing corporate value and coherence in balanced scorecard processes. In: C.S. Chapman (ed.), *Controlling Strategy, Management, Accounting and Performance Measurement*. Oxford: Oxford University Press.

Ittner, C.D. and Larcker, D.F. (1998a) Innovations in performance measurement: trends and research implications. *Journal of Management Accounting Research*, 10, 205–38.

Ittner, C.D. and , Larcker, D.F. (1998b) Are nonfinancial measures leading indicators of financial performance? An analysis of customer satisfaction. *Journal of Accounting Research*, 36, supplement, 1–35.

Kaplan, R.S. (2002) Building strategy focused organisations with the balanced scorecard. Presentation during the third International Performance Measurement and Management Conference, Boston, July. Published in: A.A. de Waal, (2003) The future of the Balanced Scorecard: an interview with Robert S. Kaplan. *Measuring Business Excellence*, 7 (1).

Kaplan, R. S. and Norton, D.P. (1992) The balanced scorecard: measures that drive performance. *Harvard Business Review*, January/February, 71–9.

Kaplan, R.S. and Norton, D.P. (2000) T*he Strategy-Focused Organisation: How balanced scorecard companies thrive in the new business environment*. Boston, Mass.: Harvard Business School Press.

Kaplan, R.S. and Norton, D.P. (2004) *Strategy Maps: Converting intangible assets into tangible outcomes*. Boston, Mass.: Harvard Business School Press.

Kerklaan, L. and Dresens, D. (2005), *Strategy Mapping: de ontbrekende schakel*. Management Executive.

Lebas, M. (1994) Managerial accounting in France: overview of past tradition and current practice. *European Accounting Review*, 3 (3), 471–87.

Lewy, C. and Du Mee, L. (1998) The ten commandments of balanced scorecard implementations. *Management Control and Accounting*, April, 2.

Malina, M.A. and Selto, F.H. (2004) *Causality in a Performance Measurement Model*. Monterey Calif.: Naval Postgraduate School.

Marr, B. and Adams, C. (2004) The balanced scorecard and intangible assets: similar ideas, unaligned concepts. *Measuring Business Excellence*.

Marr, B. and G. Schiuma (2002) Research challenges for corporate performance measurement: evidence from a citation analysis. In: A. Neely, A. Walters and R. Austin (eds), *Performance Measurement and Management: Research and action*. Cranfield, UK: Cranfield School of Management, 355–62.

Mauritsen J., Bukh, P.N. and Marr, B. (2004) Reporting on intellectual capital, why, what and how? *Measuring Business Excellence*.

McCunn, P. (1998) The balanced scorecard ... the eleventh commandment. *Management Accounting*, December, 34–36.

Niven, P.N. (2005) *Balanced Scorecard Diagnostics: Maintaining maximum performance*. New York: Wiley.

Nørreklit, H. (2000) The balance on the balanced scorecard: a critical analysis of some of its assumptions. *Management Accounting Research*, 11 (1), 65–89.

Pandey, I.M. (2005) Balanced scorecard: myth and reality. *Vikalpa*, 30 (1), 51–66.

Rigby, D. (2005), *Management Tools 2005*. Bain & Company.

Smith, M. (2005) The balanced scorecard. *Financial Management*, February, 27–28.

Waal, A.A. de (2003), The future of the Balanced Scorecard: an interview with Prof. dr. Robert S. Kaplan. *Measuring Business Excellence*, 7 (1).

Waweru, N.M., Hoque, Z. and Uliana, E. (2004) Management accounting change in South Africa: case studies from retail services. *Accounting, Auditing and Accountability Journal*, 17 (5), 675–704.

Weber, J. and Schaffer, U. (1999) Fuhrung im konzern mit der balanced scorecard. *Kostenrechnungspraxis*, 43e jrg., H.3.

8

Exceptions, actions, and rolling forecasts

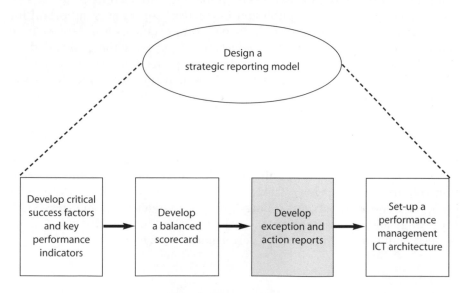

Figure 8.1 Developing exception and action reports

Developments in the performance management field enable managers to gain much better insight into their business. At the same time, the developments described in Chapter 1 demand different types of information than before. The traditional way of dealing with information needs was by adding new information to the old stack. This resulted in reports getting more and more voluminous and an increasing amount of data being stored in the company's information systems. A major challenge for modern-day managers therefore has become the management of information overload. At the same time, for data to become really useful to management, it has to go through what is known as the "value creation cycle." Raw data, originating from the primary and secondary processes of the organisation, is processed, consolidated, modelled, and reported. Through this treatment, data becomes information. This information is presented and discussed (for instance during management team meetings), and interpreted. This dialogue creates knowledge for the participants. Managers then take action based on the gained knowledge to keep the organisation on course. This finally creates the desired added value for the company.

It is a challenge to not try to know every detail. The art of management is not to know everything that is happening in a organisation, but to know what the key issues of the business are, keep track of them, and take action on them. Reports should function as an enabler for action. Focusing on what is truly important entails focusing on key value drivers that are crucial to the business, identifying exceptional events or figures, analysing financial and nonfinancial results, drawing up corrective action plans, and the impact of those action plans. This creates two major benefits for the company: more transparency and more focused decision making and action.

Transparency is a key requirement for focusing on what is important for a organisation. If there is a focus on truly important issues, decisions are centred on solving crucial business issues, thus improving the quality of decisions. Decisions are no longer based on piles of paper, but on those key value drivers that matter to the organisation. When, at the same time the proactivity of managers and employees is fostered, a major step is taken towards focusing and improving what is important.

In the ideal situation, managers and employees know exactly what to do and what not to do, thus helping the organisation to focus on truly important issues. The reporting procedure is an important enabler in this process.

There are several reporting methods that help to structure the information required by managers. These methods, of which the most prominent ones – exception reporting, rolling forecasts, budget contingencies, STAP reporting, and action reporting – are discussed in this chapter, can be applied simultaneously as part of performance management.

Chapter objectives

☑ To enable the reader to study the development of management reports that are more action and future oriented.

☑ To teach the reader how to focus on exceptions through using traffic light reporting.

☑ To provide the reader with insight in the two types of rolling forecasts: the quarterly flash forecast and the strategic rolling forecast.

☑ To teach the reader how to apply budget contingencies.

8.1 EXCEPTION REPORTING

Exception reporting gives the actual results on all KPIs but highlights performances that are outside a certain margin (under or above) from the forecasted targets. For the KPI results that are within the margin, no additional information is required. However, for every KPI result that is outside the margin, the organisation obliges the manager responsible for the indicator in question to provide additional information, containing an analysis of the causes of deviation and a list of corrective actions.

"Traffic light" reporting is a way to quickly highlight exceptions (Figure 8.2). The first page of a traffic light report gives a summary that depicts deviations from the plan by highlighting these. Specific colours are used to express the percentage of deviation from target. For example: the colour red stands for more than 10 per cent under target, yellow for 5–10 per cent under target, green for on target, and blue for above target.

Exception reporting enables management to steer the business more efficiently and effectively by quickly focusing on deviations. Problems in the business are immediately noticed, fostering swift analysis and action without spending too much time on matters that do not need immediate attention. Some companies may find that exception reporting does not fit in their culture. Their culture may be such that management always wants to have a complete and detailed view of performance, which means that all data must be available. A consequence will be that the overload of information is not reduced and much valuable management time will be wasted on discussing less urgent issues.

8.2 ROLLING FORECASTS

The forecasting process is for many organisations a time-consuming, too detailed, and too complicated number-crunching exercise. The forecasts lack relevance because organisations try to make a prognosis in great detail over a long forecast period, which is difficult and results in many inaccuracies because of the nature of looking into the future. This makes managers, used to detailed accurate figures, uncomfortable. Because of the diminished relevance, the forecasting process lacks ownership in the organisation, and therefore nobody wants to be accountable for the forecasts.

To remedy these problems, an organisation should first of all start to forecast only on a limited set of key financial indicators (KFIs). An organisation should only analyse the differences between forecast and budget for these KFIs in order to formulate preventive actions for improving the results on these indicators. The second step is to split the forecast into two types: a short-term and a long-term forecast. At the middle of the quarter an outlook for the end of quarter is made. This short time span enhances the accuracy of the forecast. At the end of each quarter, a forecast is made for from four

Division X	EVA		Sales		Margin		IFO		Volume		CAPEX		Cash flow	
	Actual	Budget	Actual	Budget	Actual	Budget	Actual	Budget	Actual	Budget	Actual	Budget	Actual	Budget
Product a	200	180	4,200	4,000	3,200	3,130	1,120	1,100	2,500	2,480	230	235	760	758
Product b	45	43	1,540	1,540	900	880	512	500	270	286	60	80	98	95
Product c	57	51	450	448	410	400	60	58	430	300	35	60	115	103
Product d	156	148	1,700	1,680	768	750	234	230	601	589	40	40	280	270
Product e	10	10	280	220	95	94	30	60	100	90	2	2,1	23	23
Other products	15	14	130	125	160	150	20	20	40	35	30	31	-12	-8
Total	483	446	8,300	8,013	5,533	5,404	1,976	1,968	3,941	3,780	397	449	1,264	1241

Light grey represents green, medium grey represents yellow, and dark grey represents red.

Figure 8.2 Example of an exception report.

to six quarters ahead. This forecast can be used for external purposes, to give year-end predictions.

The organisation should watch out for a discrepancy that can occur between the time horizon management is focused on and the time span that is covered in the forecast. Management is primarily focused on the time horizon that is covered by the management compensation programme, which most often is one year. The forecast horizon may well be longer, such as six quarters ("rolling forecasts"). This results in management not paying enough attention and not putting enough effort into preparing the (rolling) forecast, thereby decreasing the added value of this process. Therefore, aligning the forecasting horizon with the time horizon that is subject to management compensation improves the quality and reliability of the forecasts. Instead of adjusting the time horizon of the forecast to the time span covered in the management compensation, the opposite can be applied. In that case the management compensation period can be extended to include longer-term (strategic) achievements.

8.3 BUDGET CONTINGENCIES

Organisations may decide to use contingencies in the budgeting process. Because budgets are a "snapshot in time," management can never fully guarantee that budgets will be achieved exactly as planned. Contingencies can be defined that constitute performance ranges representing acceptable deviations from the budget (Figure 8.3). Only if business performance is outside the agreed contingency area will corporate headquarters or divisions intervene and take on a more active (coaching) role. This active role includes requiring more frequent performance reviews and requesting more detailed reporting.

In order to implement this type of "management by exception," budgets are agreed at the business level for a limited set of financial KPIs. Examples of such indicators are economic value added™, net operating profit, return on capital employed, and contribution margin. For each of the KPIs, contingencies are set between business unit and corporate headquarters, as well as between business unit and division (1 in Figure 8.3). The contingencies are based on sensitivity analyses performed during the strategy development process. Management reports include traffic lights that make it clear whether actual or forecasted performances on the KPIs need divisional intervention (for example by using yellow to indicate the results are in the division intervention area; 2 in Figure 8.3), or corporate headquarters intervention (for example by using red to indicate the results are in the corporate intervention area; 3 in Figure 8.3). Performance reviews take place on an exception basis, as corporate headquarters or divisional management only intervene if the results are outside the contingency areas. Figure 8.4 shows some situations that can occur during the control process. The solid line signifies the actuals, the dotted line the forecast.

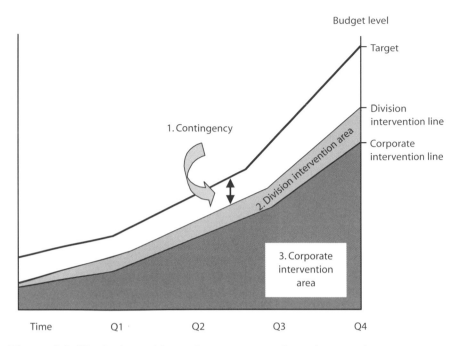

Figure 8.3 The budget with contingency area and two intervention areas

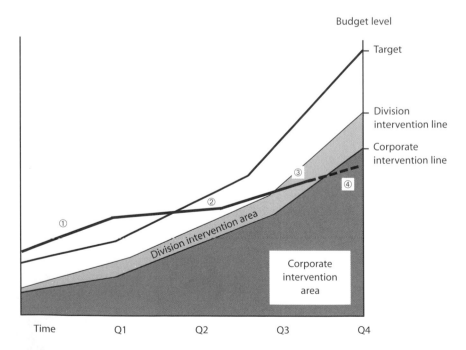

Figure 8.4 Examples of control situations

In quarter 1, the business unit performs better than budget (1 in Figure 8.4). Only financials and strategic leading nonfinancial KPIs are reported monthly to the division and corporate headquarters. Monthly review meetings are held with divisional management. Large business units conduct once a year a (strategic) review meeting with corporate headquarters.

In quarter 2, the business unit performs as planned, not as good as target but still in the contingency area (2 in Figure 8.4). Only financials and strategic leading nonfinancial KPIs are reported monthly to the division and corporate headquarters. Monthly review meetings are held with divisional management.

In quarter 3, the business unit performs below the division intervention line, and thereby arrives in the division intervention area (3 in Figure 8.4). Detailed financials and strategic leading nonfinancial KPIs are reported at least monthly, and maybe more frequently, to the division. Still, only financial and strategic leading nonfinancial KPIs are reported monthly to corporate headquarters. Longer review meetings are held monthly with divisional management. The division now acts as custodian of the business unit.

The forecast predicts that the business unit performance will end up in the corporate intervention area in quarter 4 (4 in Figure 8.4). Detailed financial and strategic leading nonfinancial KPIs are reported at least monthly, and maybe more frequently, to the division and corporate headquarters. Monthly review meetings are held with corporate headquarters. Corporate headquarters now acts as custodian of both business unit and division.

Working with budget contingencies means that setting up the budget takes up less time than in traditional budgeting, because only key financials are used, and because there are clear targets and contingency areas for lower levels to work with. Defining the contingency areas requires business unit management to know its industry and market very well. Discussions about the feasibility of the budget are held only during the budget-setting process and no longer during the year. There is no need to talk about or renegotiate the budget every time changes occur, because the boundaries between which the business unit can operate are clear. Because contingency areas have been defined, the absolute accuracy of the forecast is no longer relevant. Control is no longer aimed at forecasting accuracy, but at drafting preventive actions aimed at obtaining the budget. These preventive actions are based on a rigorous analysis of cause-and-effect relationships, thereby increasing the knowledge of managers about their business.

The definition and use of contingency areas provides a clear structure for corporate headquarters and divisional management regarding the timing of interventions. Ownership and entrepreneurship are stimulated because there is less danger of higher levels stepping in too soon. Budget contingencies enable "management by exception," thus allowing management sufficient time to focus on the real problem areas. When budget contingencies are used, they can be translated into exception reports, thereby enhancing management's focus and saving time, as less information is required for performance review. There are direct and clear consequences when actuals or forecasts go off track, which increases accountability. The level of detail of the budget affects the concept of contingencies. Setting contingencies for every budget line item is rather time-consuming and can become unmanageable. Consequently, it is advisable for an organisation to use a limited set of financial KPIs in the budgeting process.

8.4 STAP REPORTING

Incorporating CSFs and KPIs in management information reports enables an organisation to monitor the implementation of its strategy. However, even with these indicators the emphasis can still be on reporting the past, just as in the traditional financial reporting system. An organisation has to set up a future and action-oriented reporting system, using the STAP reporting cycle. STAP stands for STrategy, Action, and Projection. The STAP reporting cycle's primary objective is to formulate actions on the basis of expected results on a company's CSFs and KPIs, and to monitor the implementation of these actions to evaluate whether they yield the desired results. The cycle consists of the following steps (Figure 8.5):

1. The organisational mission, strategy, and strategic objectives are translated into tangible points of measurement in an organisation, the CSFs and KPIs.
2. The management team sets targets for the KPIs, for instance during the yearly budgeting process, which are based on the changes in the company's internal and external environments and the actual values that were realised in the past.
3. The organisation performs its business processes and activities.
4. Periodically, preferably monthly, the actual results achieved on the KPIs are compared with the targets by the managers responsible for these KPIs, using an exception report. These targets can be the original ones set during the budgeting process, or updated ones to reflect changes in the internal and/or external environment of the company. The comparison can be favourable (actuals are above target) or unfavourable (actuals are below target).
5. Subsequently, the managers produce a forecast for the expected future results on the KPIs for the next periods, and compare this with the targets for the next periods. If the comparison in Step 4 was unfavourable, it is very likely that there will be a gap between the forecast result and the targets. In that case, actions are formulated to make sure that the targets will be realised after all in the next periods. If the comparison was favourable, however, there still is a chance that a gap will develop, and that actions will have to be formulated. In both cases another comparison has to be made between the forecast results after executing the actions and the targets. If this comparison is still

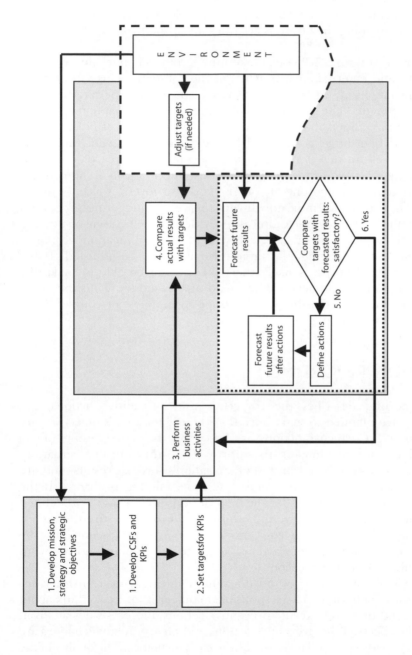

Figure 8.5 The STAP reporting cycle

unfavourable, additional actions will have to be formulated and reformulated until the comparison is favourable. Actions are laid down in an action plan. Their definition and implementation are the responsibility of the manager who is in charge of the KPI.

6. If the comparison in Step 4 was favourable, the managers continue with performing the business activities and processes.

The forecast result for a KPI must take into account changes that occur in the internal and external environments of the company. This can be done by adjusting targets upwards or downwards for the coming periods based on these developments. The advantage of dynamic targets is that managers will not be bound by targets that have become unrealistic as a result of change. In addition, when things go less well than expected, it prevents managers from hiding behind deteriorating factors beyond their area of influence. The following example serves to illustrate this. Suppose you are a manager of a department store and one of your KPIs is "turnover." You have determined the target for this indicator during the yearly budgeting process on the basis of the consumer index forecast provided by the Consensus Bureau. If the Bureau adjusts its figures in the course of the year, meaning economic circumstances are changing, the target also needs to be adjusted. If the consumer index drops, it is likely that you will not be able to make the budgeted target as consumers will be spending less money. Thus the target needs to be lowered accordingly. The opposite applies, of course, if the consumer index goes up.

8.5 ACTION REPORTING

Action reporting describes the corrective and preventive actions that managers have planned to make sure that the organisation's objectives are being achieved. Corrective actions are based on the actual results of the organisation, and are meant to improve an unfavourable situation. Preventive actions are based on the organisation's forecast results, and are intended to solve minor issues before these become big problems. If the forecast results and the targets for the next periods are outside a predefined margin, preventive actions have to be formulated to make sure the targets still can and will be achieved later on. The action plan also includes the projected results of the various actions, as effects of these may not show up in the results until in later periods.

The implementation of preventive action reporting, based on forecasts, instils proactive behaviour. The responsible manager is forced to think about the future, and plan and execute preventive actions if forecasts deviate from targets. The effects of the preventive actions and environmental changes are described, providing a good forecast of future performance. The quality of the performance reviews increases because the reviews are more future-oriented,

CSF	KPI	Fore-cast Q2	Target Q2	Analysis	Actions	Due date	Res. person	Projected result		
								Q2	Q3	Q4
Time to market	Average lead time	15	12	Lead time will increase because several experienced people are leaving shortly after one another	1. Build multi-disciplinary teams to increase synergy 2. Invest in new manufactur-ing software 3. Increase expertise through recruiting	Q2 Q3 Q4	X Y Z	14	14	12

Period: second quarter
Date: 3 – 4 – xx

Figure 8.6 Example of an action report

and preventive actions and their effects have already been incorporated in the projected results.

Figure 8.6 depicts a preventive action report for one CSF and KPI. It shows an unfavourable deviation between forecast (15) and target (12), the root cause analysis, the description of preventive actions, and the projected results for the KPI in the next periods.

8.6 CASE: STAP AT SPOT FREE INC

Spot Free is a specialised cleaning service company focusing on cleaning and maintenance of equipment and buildings (see Chapter 6 for a detailed description of the company). The firm recently introduced CSFs and KPIs, and next on the agenda was the improvement of the management reports that were in use at Spot Free. Chief executive officer Forrest and the regional managers were not content with these reports. Regional manager Ron Edwards explained:

> They are awkward and it takes an awful lot of time to extract, out of all the data, the right kind of information. It takes too much effort to determine what we do well and what we do not so well and to establish problem areas.

By using the STAP reporting cycle Forrest wanted to offer his regional managers a tool that would help them use management reports more effectively. Forrest commented:

We are going to highlight a number of problem areas and incorporate these in the STAP reporting cycle. We are going to monitor the developments within these problem areas and take action to improve the results. Of course, we will also monitor the results gained from our actions.

Forrest decided to first test the STAP reporting cycle in one of Spot Free's regions, so that the company could get familiar with its application. The decision to implement the reporting method in the other regions would be based on this test. After deliberation, it was decided that the test was going to take place in Region II. The reason was that this region was currently coping with a number of problems that required extra attention. Regional manager Ron Edwards expressed his satisfaction:

> The new reporting cycle is needed because Spot Free has to change. The customer is becoming ever more demanding and expects from us a high degree of efficiency. At the moment, we are not competitive enough in the market. The new reporting cycle will help us bring about change as it emphasises exactly those factors that are crucial to the company: costs, productivity, and quality. These three factors need to be in line with agreements made with customers: that is, they should be not less and not more than agreed. Offering a higher quality level than agreed is not recommendable because it may give customers the idea that they can also ask for a lower quality level at a lower price. This will undoubtedly have a negative effect on our turnover.

Forrest and Edwards jointly defined the report, focusing on one of the most urgent issues in Region II. One of the larger clients had been extremely demanding regarding the quality and the price of the services rendered, and Region II appeared unable to meet all these demands. Satisfying the client's needs was an urgent matter as the contract was about to expire and it was not certain that the client would renew the contract. Table 8.1 gives one CSF and one of the corresponding KPIs as an example.

Table 8.1 One CSF and KPI for Region II

Unit: Region II's objective	Critical success factor	Description	
Offer professional products	Product quality as perceived by customers	A guaranteed product quality will strengthen Spot Free's position	
Critical success factor	Key performance indicator	Definition	Target
Product quality as perceived by customers	Percentage of rejects	Number of rejects as a percentage of the total number of random spot checks performed (per period)	3 %

The CSF "product quality as perceived by customers" is measured with the KPI "percentage of rejects." The percentage of rejects is determined on the basis of quality spot checks. The contract with the customer stipulates a 3 per cent target, which means that not more than 3 per cent of the spot checks should find that the quality of the performed work is below standard. This is a very important piece of information for the client because it provides feedback on the extent to which Spot Free delivers the agreed quality. The information is of course also very relevant to Spot Free itself, because the company aims to deliver exactly the quality mentioned in the contract. If the quality level of the performed work turns out to be below standard (the KPI actual is above 3 per cent), the customer will be discontented. If, conversely, the actual result of the KPI is lower than the agreed 3 per cent, it means that the quality of the work delivered is too high and that too many working hours have been put into the cleaning activities. By lowering the number of working hours, Spot Free can either increase its margin (pay less working hours with same turnover), or lower the service price if the client wishes to renew the contract.

Because Spot Free's current reporting system is not able yet to produce the new exception and action reports, these reports for the time being will be produced manually every month. It is not recommended to purchase a new reporting information system during the trial period. The actual results of the various KPIs will be forecast on the basis of reports currently available. Edwards and Forrest will forecast independently of each other, as a way of preparing for their monthly review meeting. Edwards will forecast the expected results for his KPIs for the following period, and will think of possible actions and the effects that these actions will have on the KPI results for the next three periods. Forrest and Edwards will discuss the actuals in their meeting, and together determine which actions are needed to realise the targets. They will include the outcome of this meeting in the STAP report (Figure 8.7).

The actuals over period 8 show that the quality of the services rendered has been too high in this period. The KPI "percentage of rejects" is 2 per cent instead of the targeted 3 per cent. Edwards formulated two actions to ensure that the organisation would meet the 3 per cent target in period 10. The defined actions were to consult the team leaders in order to arrange to work fewer hours, and instruct employees to stop dotting the i's and crossing the t's too feverishly, as it were.

After a few months Forrest commented on the STAP reporting cycle:

> I am very happy with the results so far. The STAP reporting cycle is very useful, as I have noticed that Edwards and I have started to look at the reports and the results differently. One reason for this, of course, is the use of CSFs and KPIs. Another reason is that I think we have started to communicate more often with each other about the achieved and forecasted results in critical areas, such as quality and cost. Edwards now takes more initiatives than ever before, and that is exactly what I wanted to accomplish.

| STAP REPORT | | SPOT FREE INC. |
| Region II | Ron Edwards | |

Actuals			
Period : 8/2006 Date : 9/15/2006	Target value	Actual value	Deviation
Percentage of rejects	3%	2%	–1%

Action Plan							
Period : 9/2006 Date : 9/17/2006	Target value	Projected results excl. actions	Action description	Projected result			
				9	10	11
Percentage of rejects	3%	2%	■ Consult with foremen ■ Instruct employees	2.5%	3%	3%

Figure 8.7 Spot Free's STAP report for Region II

Edwards distinguished several advantages of the STAP reporting cycle in combination with CSFs and KPIs:

> I can now see in one glance how Region II is doing in the areas that require special attention. Also, the interrelationship between activities that are to be performed, activities that already have been performed, and the results has become more visible. The new action report is motivating to me, I deal with issues more often and more swiftly to make sure that the targets are realised and to carry out the actions successfully. It also causes a learning effect in the region. Through defining and executing the actions and monitoring the effects, people learn to see how to anticipate certain developments in order to prevent problems from happening again, or to solve them efficiently.

Based on the experiences so far with the STAP reporting cycle, Forrest has decided to implement the cycle company-wide. He introduced this idea in a meeting with all regional managers. Forrest was rather surprised when six weeks later one of the regional managers called him to ask when they were going to discuss the new report for his region. The meeting had enthused the manager to such an extent that he had immediately begun to develop an exception and action report. Forrest was extremely pleased to hear this:

> The STAP reporting cycle brings out the best in my managers. They themselves take steps to use it. Daring to take the initiative is an essential quality for the use of exception and action reports. Fortunately, the managers in my company possess this quality. We're definitely ready for the future!

8.7 CASE STUDY: UVD'S EXCEPTION AND ACTION REPORTS

It was Monday morning and Helen Case, UVD's chief financial officer, had just received the latest monthly report, which included the recently defined CSFs and KPIs (Figure 8.8). She was very content with this report as it gave her a better insight into those factors influencing UVD's success.

While examining the report more closely, Helen wondered about what seemed to be missing. The report mentioned targets, actual results, and deviations. It also showed her that, until now, some departments had managed to realise the targets whereas others required extra attention. The percentage of returned products, for instance, turned out to be 7 per cent above target. Helen asked herself which corrective actions the production manager had planned for the following periods to stop the percentage increase and to realise the target value.

Monthly report UVD				
MANUFACTURING			Period : Jan 06 Date : 2-1-06	
Critical success factor	Key performance indicator	Target value	Actual value	Deviation
Manufacturing process quality	Percentage of rejects	8%	8%	–
	Percentage of returned products	9%	16%	–7%
Manufacturing process flexibility	Reset times	55 min.	53 min.	+2 min.

Figure 8.8 Part of UVD's monthly report

Helen called Mike Allister, production manager, to get the answers to her questions. Mike appeared enthused about the new report he too had just received. Although initially he had been somewhat alarmed by the actual percentage of returned products, he now assured Helen that he was going to put all his efforts into changing it. When, however, Helen asked what he exactly had in mind, there was a short silence on the line. Mike got hold of himself fairly quickly and said he was still contemplating the subject. He had not yet formulated his thoughts into specific actions that could improve the percentage of returned products. He hesitated to say in what direction he expected the percentage of returned products to develop in the following periods. "That is written in the stars," he said jokingly.

The phone call with Mike had not been particularly reassuring to Helen, but before she could act she got an urgent call.

Some time later, Helen stepped hurriedly out of the elevator on the boardroom floor. The stack of papers she frenetically tried to hold on threatened to spill on the floor.

"Can I please go in right away?" she desperately asked Ellen, the executive secretary.

"Yes, of course," Ellen answered, not so cheerfully. "He is expecting you."

Relieved Helen balanced her way into the boss's room. "You're still not using a trolley!" Ellen called after her.

"Darn, I forgot – again," Helen thought.

"I'm experiencing *déja vu*," John moaned as he saw his chief financial officer come staggering in. "Every month the same pile of paper. It's driving me mad".

"But," Helen said, bewildered, "we now have CSFs and KPIs!"

"Yeah, sure, even more data. Just what I've been waiting for," the boss said sarcastically.

"Anyway, now I'm really sure everything is in there," Helen said triumphantly.

"Have you never heard of indicator overload?" John asked.

Helen shook her head. "One can never measure too much."

"Is that so?" the boss snarled. "So you can find anything in that stack of yours, can you? I really have the feeling we had this conversation before; in fact many times before. I will give you one last chance."

"What – what do you mean?" the poor CFO said nervously.

John glared at Helen. "We have spent a lot of time developing strategic objectives, critical performance thingies, and key indications ..."

"You mean critical success factors and key performance indicators," Helen interrupted.

"I don't really care what they are called," John exclaimed. "All I want is management reports I can really use. So get out and don't come back until you have a reporting set which will make me happy. And I'll start making my calls again to the regional managers."

"OK, OK, I'll get cracking." Helen hurried out of John's office, still clutching the ever-growing stack of reports.

Case question 1: What are the main problems in UVD's current management reporting set?

Case question 2: How can UVD's management reporting set be improved in such a way that both John Williams and Helen Case are happy?

Key points

- ☑ A major challenge for modern-day managers is the management of information overload. The art of management is not to know everything that is happening in a organisation, but to know what the key issues of the business are, keep track of them, and take action on them.
- ☑ For data to become really useful to management, it has to go through the value creation cycle: from raw data to information, to presentation, dialogue and interpretation, to knowledge, to action.
- ☑ Focusing on what is truly important entails focusing on key value drivers that are crucial to the business, analysing exceptional results, making and executing corrective and preventive action plans, and analysing the impact and results of those actions.
- ☑ A short-term forecast predicts the results at quarter-end. A long-term forecast predicts the results six quarters ahead.
- ☑ Contingencies for performance indicators constitute performance ranges representing acceptable deviations from the budget.
- ☑ The STAP (STrategy, Action and Projection) reporting cycle's objective is to formulate actions on the basis of expected results on a company's CSFs and KPIs, and to monitor the implementation of these actions to evaluate whether they yield the desired result.

References

Waal, A.A. de (2001) *Power of Performance Management: How leading companies create sustained value*. New York: Wiley.

9

Performance management ICT architecture

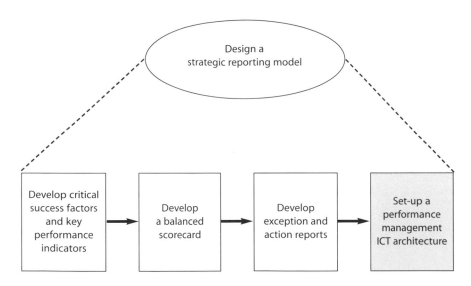

Figure 9.1 Setting up a performance management ICT architecture

Across industries, organisations share certain features that characterise today's performance management information and communication technology (ICT) architecture. For instance, every organisation has a range of information needs, including the widespread need for relatively simple information, the need for business analysis tools, the need for online analytical processing (OLAP) tools, and the need for specialist tools (e.g. for data mining). The majority of information requested is fairly straightforward and can be subdivided into two categories:

- performance management information (indicator results, financial data, nonfinancial data)

■ information supporting performance management (data/documents employees may need to ensure effective performance management).

An organisation normally has a backlog of management information and reporting requests, leaving analysts stressed and overworked. These analysts typically spend between 30 to 70 per cent of their time as information "gophers" preparing and distributing reports. The solution of making complex query tools available to everyone in the organisation is costly, and normally fails if the software requires more than minutes to provide the information requested. The most effective solution to the request for widespread delivery of reports is to automate reports and to deliver them through an easily accessible electronic catalogue. The value derived from reporting, OLAP, and data mining tools can be increased dramatically by effectively cataloguing and publishing the reports they produce.

It turns out that the delivery of simple performance management information accounts for 80 to 90 per cent of the business value that can be added through a performance management system. In most organisations, delivering this 90 per cent requires 10 per cent of the functionality and complexity, and a relatively small proportion of the cost (Figure 9.2) of the information systems. The goal of a good performance management ICT architecture is to first and foremost fulfil this need for performance management information adequately (Elbaum, 2005).

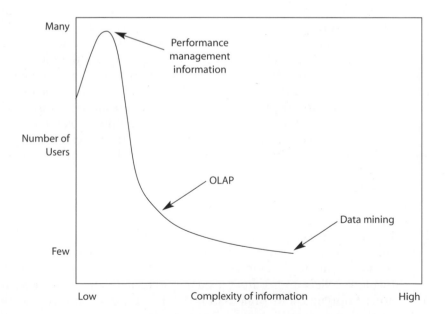

Figure 9.2 The 90–10 per cent rule of performance information business value
Source: Waal and Fourman (2000).

Chapter objectives

☑ To provide the reader with an insight of how to set up an ICT infrastructure that can support performance management efficiently and effectively.

☑ To enable the reader to understand the terms corporate performance management (CPM) and business performance management (BPM).

☑ To teach the reader how to choose between the various ways to implement the desired ICT architecture.

☑ To enable the reader to understand the concept of push-and-pull information.

9.1 HISTORY OF INFORMATION REPORTING SYSTEMS

Management information reporting systems have existed since the 1960s. The term "management information system" (MIS) also dates from that period. The primary purpose of this system was the generation of periodical reports that compared budgeted and actual results. These systems produced a lot of paper which was a great burden to the management team, because reading it cost them a lot of time. Only operational managers were able to benefit from the flood of information, because they received and used some reports that had relevance to their operational field. As they had a much more detailed knowledge of their functional area than the senior management team, they could go through these reports more efficiently.

Bad experiences with MIS resulted in the 1970s in the development of decision support systems (DSS). By using a DSS, a manager was able to make decisions using decision support models. This offered managers the possibility of calculating several alternative plans and using the outcome for their decision process. However, this system too was not ideal because using the system required a lot of time and specific knowledge. Thus the system absorbed a lot of managers' valuable time.

After DSS came executive information systems (EIS). This system's design was more user-friendly, and included presentation facilities with colours and graphics. Suppliers of these systems usually emphasised the extensive possibilities for including external data on markets and competitors. The system was meant as a tool for executives. But the EIS also failed to live up to expectations because it mainly presented (historical) financial data, or data that were difficult to collect and compare, such as external data on markets and competitors. Suppliers and organisations did not sufficiently realise that when implementing an EIS, it is necessary to pay attention not only to the presentation of the data (which these systems did extremely well), but also to the type of information (content) that should be included in reports.

Frequently there was a mismatch between the information available in the EIS and the information needed by managers, as a result of which managers often consulted the system sparingly.

At the end of the 1990s, a new breed of management information systems emerged, with various names: corporate performance management (CPM), business performance management (BPM) and enterprise performance management (EPM). These systems, which were very much alike, focused on supporting the decision-making process in the organisation by integrating the various processes of the company – planning, budgeting, forecasting, and reporting – into one software system. In the literature, several definitions for CPM and BPM can be found (taken respectively from Gartner, BPM Forum, and Heliview in 2005), such as:

An umbrella term that describes the methodologies, metrics, processes and systems used to monitor and manage the business performance of an enterprise.

A technology driven discipline which synchronises and aligns company strategies and business objectives through real time availability and continuous exchange of relevant and essential information.

Software applications that at a strategic level in an organisation provide management with an insight into financial performance concerning budgets, planning of strategic activities and the attainability of targets and plans. Information is usually made accessible via a business intelligence platform, which makes it possible to access, analyse and publish data held in various systems within the organisation like enterprise resource planning systems and customer relation management systems. The data is accessible via data warehouses and data mining applications and is presented on an intranet.

In this book the term CPM is used, since it is one of the more popular for the systems currently in use by organisations. A well-designed CPM system has the following characteristics (Coveney et al., 2003; Buytendijk et al., 2004; Eckerson, 2004):

- It offers complete integration of management processes like strategy formulation, budgeting, forecasting, goal setting, performance feedback, and business activity monitoring, over the complete enterprise and aimed at collaboration.
- It incorporates methodologies such as the balanced scorecard, six sigma, EFQM (European Foundation for Quality Management), activity-based management, value-based management, and intangible asset management.
- It encompasses measures such as the financial, nonfinancial, short-term, long-term, lagging, and leading indicators, and is focused on creating insight by means of exception and action management.
- It uses technologies such as business intelligence, data warehouses,

CPM suites and dashboards, cockpits, and scorecards in a user-friendly way so that users can easily work with the system.

An organisation can expect the following benefits from implementing a CPM system (Waal, and Geelen, 2002; Geelen, 2004):

- Increased transparency because all information on mission, vision, strategy, objectives, CSFs, KPIs, targets, actions, results, and forecasts is available throughout the organisation.
- Increased flexibility because objectives and organisational structures can be easily adapted in the system.
- Higher speed of execution of planning and reporting processes, with less maintenance.
- Higher reliability of data because all data elements are recorded only once in the system.
- Better integration of hard data (like actuals and targets) with soft data (like analyses and descriptions of actions).
- Increased relevance to users because each user gets access to tailored information.
- Better knowledge management because each user has access to a wealth of information, analyses, descriptions of actions and results, and lessons learned.
- Better scalability because the system can easily grow or decrease in size with the growth or decline of the business.
- Increased mobility because users can access the data through the internet at any time and from any place.

9.2 CHARACTERISTICS OF ICT ARCHITECTURE

ICT is a key factor in creating an efficient and effective performance management system. There are several characteristics that make up a high-quality ICT architecture. These characteristics are described below (Waal, 2003).

- *The ICT architecture is highly flexible.* The strategy and objectives of the organisation are regularly changing. The ICT systems have to provide the flexibility to deal with this. Organisational units should be able to change, add, or remove information items, information definitions, KPIs, actions, and lessons learned, as long as these conform to the agreed data and reporting standards, and as long as they are in line with the strategy and objectives of the company. Organisational changes (of, for instance, organisational structure or business processes) should be carried out effortlessly in the ICT systems. The ICT architecture displays information in all the formats required by users. It incorporates measures from survey tools and other systems, and allows the publishing of reports from other systems (e.g. desktop OLAP tools, ERP systems, data warehouse, operational systems, legacy systems).

- *The ICT architecture supports exception reporting, trend analysis, and simulations.* The ICT systems use tables, graphs, and data series set out in time (actuals, budgets, forecasts) to quickly detect problems and to show trends and developments. Rules for exception boundaries (like budget contingency areas) can be defined, both across the organisation and specifically for each organisational entity, and traffic lighting is used based on the boundaries. In the systems, KPIs can be calculated (ratios, percentages, etc) from source data. The ICT systems are also used to answer what-if questions and to calculate strategic, budget, and forecasting scenarios.

- *Information is easily accessible.* Unlocking data from underlying operational systems is simple, so additional detailed data can easily be found. The ICT architecture allows "drill-downs" (going to more detailed information) along the lines managers are interested in: organisational hierarchy, products, customers, markets, distribution channels, and so on. Data, financial and nonfinancial, is standardised so its reliability and consistency is guaranteed. Much of the nonfinancial data is present in the ICT systems, but they can also easily be entered manually in these systems. The functioning of the ICT systems is easy to comprehend.

- *The ICT architecture is safe, scalable, and supports mobility.* Information in the ICT systems is 100 per cent safeguarded. The ICT architecture is easy to implement and is scalable, to follow and support the growth of the company. At the same time, every organisational unit can tailor the ICT systems to its own needs and wishes. The performance information can be personalised by using, for example, individual BSC, CSFs, KPIs, exceptions, and actions. Members of the organisation can access performance information irrespective of where they are, because they have copies of the performance management system on their PCs, which are automatically synchronised after plugging into the system.

- *A performance management portal makes information easy to access.* The performance management portal provides a one-stop shop for performance information from multiple sources. In this way, performance information is distributed in a cost-efficient way throughout the organisation and it is accessible to all managers at the time and place they need it. The portal has the following characteristics: it delivers reports from all existing ICT systems; it catalogues reports and information in relation to strategy; it is easy to learn and use; it supports analysis of data; it supports workflow for requesting and improving the content of information; it supports manual entry of data, analysis, actions, and lessons learned. The portal makes management by surfing around on the management web possible: every manager is self-supporting in retrieving the required information from anywhere in the company.

- *Push and pull information leads to efficient information retrieval.* Each management level requests from lower management levels a certain amount of data and information that is needed on a regular basis. The higher the management level, the less information is required. The data is standardised for all these lower levels and is pushed upwards. The other management information is not standardised. This means that lower-level organisational units are free to define the information items that are specific to them in the way that they like. The data are collected and consolidated in an efficient and timely manner. A precondition is a standard chart of accounts, which should not have too many lines. Each management level is able to access, by itself and on an ad hoc basis, management information as well as nonstandard data from lower level organisational units. This information is pulled out of the local systems at these lower levels.

▪ *The organisation makes sure information is transparent.* Transparency of information is obtained by storing "pushed-up" information in a data warehouse, which is maintained by the management level that collects the information. Business intelligence tools (e.g. executive information systems) allow user-friendly drill-down and "slice and dice" capabilities on the data in the warehouse, which makes it possible to view and analyse information from different perspectives. Management information is made available on the intranet and also, thanks to advanced security capabilities, on the internet. A standard web browser provides access to management information at each organisational level, by providing access to standard homepages containing periodic management information such as the BSC, financial (traffic light) reporting, rolling forecasts, analysis, action reporting, and strategic plans. These homepages are standardised across the organisation to create a common, consistent, and therefore user-friendly view of periodic management information. Hyperlinks are added to the homepages to make links to other webpages on the Internet and intranet, thereby connecting related data and enhancing the overall value of the information. When information transparency is obtained, time is created for added-value activities. Because it takes users less time to "hunt" for and collect the data they need, managers have more time to actually process the information and to take action.

▪ *E-business applications make processes efficient.* Relatively simple primary processes are executed by ICT systems. These systems are web-architected, which means that they use web technology and the internet to process transactions. The results are fewer interfaces, more reliable data, shorter throughput time, and lower cost per transaction. Processes that are handled this way are, among others, purchase to pay, order to cash, virtual close, risk and process management, e-reporting, and e-performance. Through e-control there is a tight control on the safety of these e-based processes. EXtensible Mark-up Language (XML) is used to exchange information between applications (internal but also external, with partners and customers). EXtensible Business Report Language

(XBRL) is used for management reporting and for external reporting to shareholders, the stock exchange, and regulatory agencies.

■ *The corporate intelligence network provides managers with timely and important information.* The performance management portal makes it possible for managers to find the information they need themselves. In addition to this, there are dedicated employees who read and select available internal and external information on relevance and importance, and who put this information on the management web. Analysis of competitors and other business intelligence information is also made available this way. Ad hoc questions from managers are answered by these information providers and also placed on the web.

What a high-quality ICT architecture looks like is described in more detail in the following section.

9.3 ICT ARCHITECTURE FOR PERFORMANCE MANAGEMENT

(This section is based on the chapter "Prestatiemanagement en informatietechnologie" written by Kees Groenveld MBA QC RI, from Waal and Kerklaan, 2004.)

Many organisations suffer from such a fragmentation in their ICT systems that it is virtually impossible for them to have high-quality performance management information at their disposal in a timely fashion.

There are basically two methods businesses can use to improve their internal information supply. The first one, *uniformising*, starts with straightening out the internal data management. First a uniform information architecture model is created, in which all ICT systems are aligned. Then the information supply process itself is improved. The second method, *improvement*, starts with improving the information supply process using the current fragmented ICT systems, followed by development of a uniform information architecture model. Theoretically speaking, uniformising is the best method but it takes considerable time and effort before the first improved performance management is produced. In addition, information needs of managers change over time, which makes it impossible to work out all needed data beforehand. The improvement method is more practical because in a relatively short time span relevant information can be produced. This method is discussed in five steps.

Step 1: Determine the required data: push and pull

The first step commences with determining which performance data is needed and how often, in order to be able to manage the enterprise. Each management level in the organisation has to find a balance between the information that is collected and stored structurally on its own level and that has to be sent regularly to higher management levels (known as the information push), and the information that has to be available to lower management levels and that can be accessed on an ad hoc basis by higher management levels (known as the information pull). The concept of information transparency is applied, ensuring that a minimum of information goes to the top of the corporation while additional information is easily retrievable at lower levels of the corporation, and the top level can also access it if they want to (Figure 9.3).

The organisation defines a set of standardised performance information. This is information that each organisational unit needs to report, and that is used to not only manage the unit itself, but also report to corporate headquarters on the performance of the complete organisation in a uniform manner. Examples are specific financial and nonfinancial CSFs and KPIs and a BSC (1 in Figure 9.3). The remainder of the performance information is not standardised. This means each organisational unit can define information items that are specific to the unit. Examples are adding certain KPIs to the required, standardised BSC to make it more relevant to the unit, and adding specific accounts to the standardised chart of accounts to be able to capture extra unit-specific information (2 in Figure 9.3).

Each organisational unit requests from lower organisational units certain data and information that is needed to obtain a consolidated view of the performance of the lower units the organisational unit is responsible for. This data is common for all these lower units and is pushed upwards. The

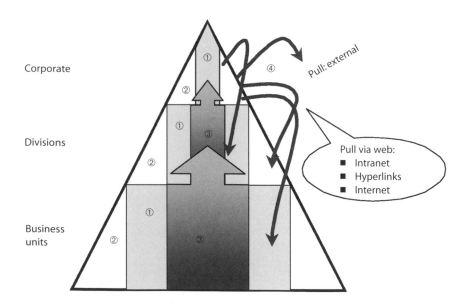

Figure 9.3 Information push and pull

higher the organisational unit, the less information is needed. The information is collected and consolidated in an efficient and timely manner. This is possible when strict agreements have been made concerning the data items to be pushed upward and the data definitions, which need to be standardised across the organisational units for these specific data items. A precondition for this is a standard chart of accounts, which should not be too detailed: that is, it should not contain too many categories (3 in Figure 9.3).

Each organisational unit is able to access, on its own and on an ad hoc basis, management information and nonstandard data from lower-level organisational units (for example, corporate from divisions and business units, divisions from business units). This information is pulled out of the local systems which reside at these lower levels (4 in Figure 9.3).

A standard web browser provides access to performance information at each organisational level. The web browser provides access to the standard homepages of every organisational unit, containing periodic management information such as BSC, traffic light reporting, forecasts, analysis, action reporting, and strategic plans. These homepages can be standardised across the organisation to create a common, consistent, and thereby user-friendly view of periodic management information. Hyperlinks can be added to the homepages. These provide links to other webpages on the intranet and internet, thereby connecting related data and enhancing the overall value of the information. This set-up is called "management by surfing around," which is based on the premise that management levels get only what is required by the organisation as standard. Other, extra, information can be retrieved by surfing the management web. Consequently, this implies a shift from databases towards "linkages." Instead of building a hierarchy of data warehouses, the web links all "stand-alone" information systems together. This includes internal linkages as well as relations with external stakeholders, such as customers and suppliers. Data is stored in one (local) place only.

Step 2: Determine the data sources

The second step starts with determining the sources for the required data. Can the data be generated within the organisational unit or does it have to come from external sources? Is the data freely accessible? In which systems is the data currently captured and registered? Which definitions are in use in the various organisational units? In particular, the last question is a real headache for many. Often, different organisational units use different definitions for the same data element, which makes it very hard to consolidate data. A factor complicating this issue is that many organisational units use ICT systems that are not linked to each other, so they act effectively as data islands. This brings with it the problem that several editing activities need to be performed on data originating from multiple ICT systems: checking the data on consistency of definition, matching the data to make sure the organisation is dealing with the same data elements, making the registration frequency uniform (a four-week reporting period is not the same as a monthly frequency), and aggregating the data to the organisational unit (for example from department to business unit) and/or time period (for instance from days to a week). Performing these activities manually is often not an option because the chances of making mistakes are too high, and it takes too much time and effort to do this every period. A good alternative is using a data warehouse coupled with a CPM system (Figure 9.4).

In the data warehouse, which is, simply put, a data collection reservoir, a data structure is organised which contains both data elements from separate underlying systems and information on the links between these elements. This way, information requests can be satisfied at any time by delving in the data warehouse. The data warehouse allows user-friendly drill-down and "slice and dice" capabilities on the data in the warehouse, thus allowing information to be viewed and analysed from different perspectives.

To make the data in the warehouse accessible, a CPM system is installed on top of it. This system is based on a three-layer model. The bottom layer is the database, often in the shape of one big data warehouse or several smaller warehouses, known as "data marts." The middle layer contains the unlocking program that extracts the data from the data warehouse. The top layer is the graphical user interface, supported by a web browser such as Windows Explorer. This architecture is known as the "performance management portal" (Collins, 2001). The advantages are that data are accessible from every workplace through the intranet and the internet, and the maintenance and

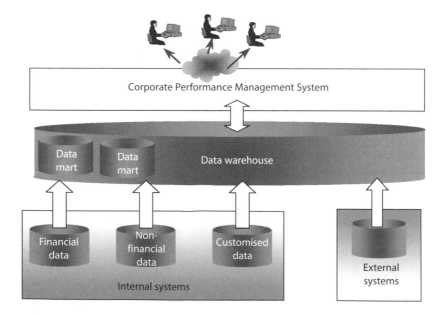

Figure 9.4 Using a data warehouse for the purpose of creating integrated performance management information

management costs are relatively low because the software needed for the portal is only installed once and then maintained in a central place.

When taking a performance management portal approach, it is best to use the same portal framework (though with different content) for different organisational units. Even where different organisation units use different operational systems, the performance management portal provides a standard template for information transparency. Taking the portal approach gives every organisation unit the ability to manage and organise its own information and knowledge and to control the access to this information. It is an effective way to create standardisation across a large organisation, without having to standardise every operational system, data warehouse, and reporting tool. This allows the organisation to work effectively without requiring a massive investment in replacing existing systems with new organisation-wide standards.

Step 3: Determine the frequency and manner of reporting

The integrated performance management information generated by the ICT architecture described makes it possible to define decision rules in such a way that the system can provide tailored information to individual users. The CPM system depicts actual results graphically, using traffic light colouring and contingency areas. In this way, an early warning system can be set up that generates "management by exception" information and gives off warning signals through the colour coding and also by sending mails to e-mail addresses, mobile phone numbers, and WAP telephones, pointing users to issues that require immediate attention. The CPM system also makes the links between objectives, CSFs, and KPIs clearly visible so a user can easily drill down to analyse certain results. To facilitate the analysis, many CPM systems offer OLAP support. OLAP makes it possible, in a user-friendly manner, to put data from the data warehouse in multidimensional cubes and add to it additional data and forecasts (based on scenarios). In this way multidimensional analyses can be made, which offer more insight.

Step 4: Design action management

To be able to adjust the course of the organisation, corrective actions have to be defined and tracked in the ICT architecture. Workflow functionality can be used to schematically represent the actions, as Figure 9.5 shows. In Figure 9.5 the "streams of information" that flow between the activities ("the blocks") are depicted. The CPM system can track for each objective what the progress towards the targets is and how actions are running. Through the integral recording of results, analyses, and actions, integral accountability is possible. (Scanned) decision and policy documents can be attached to each action in

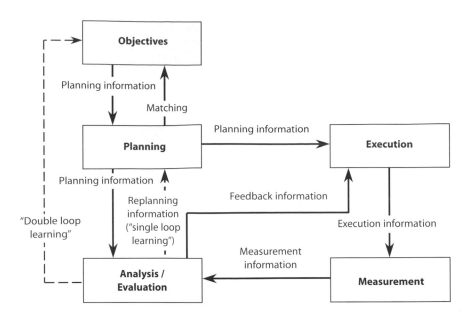

Figure 9.5 Action management within a CPM system

such a way that the basis of certain decisions is always retraceable. In addition, because the time component can also be recorded, information through time can be followed and analysed. In this way, an audit trail develops of the creation, development, and termination of information.

Step 5: Establish the integrated ICT architecture

Through the introduction of a data warehouse, the data from underlying ICT systems is standardised. However, the input of these data in the individual systems does not change. This means that the same data has to be entered regularly in several independent systems, increasing the risks of faults. Most companies have acknowledged this risk and have installed an integral system, the enterprise resource planning (ERP) system. Such a system is modular in structure, meaning that financial data from the financial module can easily be integrated with strategy information from the planning module, project data from the project management module, and personnel data from the human resource management module. Unfortunately this does not solve all information problems. Most companies still have so-called "legacy systems." These are ICT systems that have been tailored to the company's needs and circumstances and which cannot be standardised in such a way that they can become part of the ERP system. In addition, some information originates from places outside the company, so this also cannot be incorporated in a uniform ICT system.

To prevent multiple inputs of data in many ICT systems, an application integration platform can be installed (Figure 9.6). This platform makes it possible to exchange data between multiple systems in a controlled and authorised manner without having to make physical couplings between these systems. The thin lines between the ICT systems in Figure 9.5 are no longer needed because one link is made between each system and the application integration platform, which basically serves as a "transfer station." Through this set-up new ICT systems can be easily hooked on and old systems can quickly be replaced, while all the time safeguarding an integral information supply.

The architecture in Figure 9.6 is called the "hub and spoke" model. The individual ICT systems no longer communicate with each other directly (the thin lines in Figure 9.6) but through the application platform, on the basis of standardised messaging (the thick arrows in Figure 9.6). The platform tracks the status and progress (workflow functionality) of the information requests and the processing of these. In this, way the platform becomes a source of information on the monitoring and steering of actions. The performance management portal offers the user predefined standardised performance management information and the possibility of requesting ad hoc information. The user's request is routed through the portal to the application integration platform, which decides which systems have to

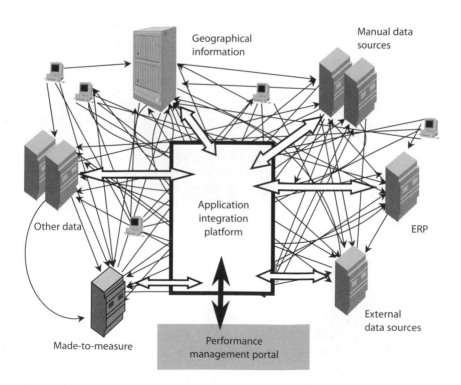

Figure 9.6 The application integration platform

provide the data for fulfilling the request. This answer is then efficiently routed back to the user by the platform.

When an ICT architecture has been installed that supports information transparency, managers have the opportunity to access management information on a "need for" basis. Managers' capabilities are improved by the easy access they have to underlying ICT systems and data warehouses. Information can be shared among managers and updated online in the systems, thereby keeping track of changes and making more timely, up-to-date information available. Organisation-wide, user-friendly and consistent views of information are presented, based on standardisation of (parts of) the architecture. The time spent on information gathering and searching for information is significantly reduced. Security is an important issue, and needs appropriate attention during the implementation and use of the ICT architecture.

9.4 CRITERIA FOR ICT PACKAGE SELECTION

In practice many companies are still using a combination of spreadsheets and PowerPoint slides to put together their self-made scorecards. This has mainly to do with the initial high investment that has to be made for CPM systems. A spreadsheet is in the short term much cheaper, and is often already present in the business (Creelman and Makhijani, 2005). However, in the long run, when the organisation grows and becomes more complex, it will take an enormous amount of resources to maintain and analyse the spreadsheet. Spreadsheets are notoriously difficult to scale up in a growing business and are very time-consuming to update and to tie together. In addition, communication between spreadsheets becomes increasingly difficult, producing a fragmented view of the company's performance (Marr and Neely, 2002). Then it is the moment to start thinking about purchasing a more robust solution. When organisations are selecting a CPM system to build the ICT architecture needed to support the performance management process in the organisation in an efficient and effective way, they often call in software suppliers. The IT market for CPM systems can be split roughly in three:

1. Vendors of ERP packages develop their own CPM systems to be put "on top of" the ERP system. Although these vendors claim their ERP systems are open to CPM systems from other vendors, in practice there are often problems with imperfect couplings or with system performance. When organisations choose these CPM systems, they are obliged to also purchase the data warehouse used in this system. These CPM systems regularly contain extra functionality, like financial consolidation and business planning, which the organisation may not need.
2. Suppliers known as "suite vendors" offer CPM systems that contain several modules for performance management, business planning,

consolidation, and reporting in one package. These suites are often developed in an OLAP environment which is open to other data sources and ICT packages, making it easy to couple them with ICT systems from other vendors. The organisation can choose to install the suite directly on top of the primary ICT systems or via a data warehouse. Modules in the suite can often be bought separately, allowing the company to "grow into" total functionality.

3. Best of breed vendors focus completely on CPM systems that offer a lot of dedicated functionality for performance management. Functionality that does not fit into the performance management picture, like business planning or financial consolidation, is not included or available. Their software is open, meaning it is easy to make links with applications from other vendors. Changes in this set-up are difficult and costly to make unless the organisation decides to install a special data warehouse between the various ICT packages.

Which type of vendor is best for an organisation depends on the current ICT architecture, the vision of the future in this respect, and the resources available. The following criteria can be useful for selecting ICT packages.

Strategy and CSF/KPI/BSC reporting

- *BSC*. Can the package support the required BSC display formats?
- *Documentation of strategy*. Does the package make it possible to document the strategy?
- *Documentation of cross-organisation KPIs*. Does the package allow for sharing of KPI definitions across the organisation and unique KPI definitions for individual organisational units?
- *Capture of soft measures*. Does the package make it possible to capture measures and indicators from survey tools, ISO 9000 systems, etc?
- *Reports from other systems*. Does the package allow the incorporation and publishing of reports from other systems (including desktop OLAP tools, ERP systems, data warehouse, operational systems, legacy systems, etc)?
- *Subset selection*. Does the package allow a focus on a subset of KPIs that drive value, without excluding other KPIs which also need to be tracked from the overall system?
- *KPI calculation from source data*. Does the package support calculation of KPIs (ratios, percentages, etc) from source data, either internally or by using an external OLAP database?
- *Organisational drill-down*. Does the package allow drill-down along the organisation hierarchy?
- *Internal partnership support*. Can everything be personalised: scorecards, CSFs, KPIs, BSC, presentation displays, forecasts, and actions?
- *Security*. Does the security of the package allow privacy as well as transparency?

Exception and action reporting

- *Flexible exception settings*. Does the package allow the definition of rules for exception reporting of each KPI, both across the organisation and specifically for a business unit?
- *Exception boundaries*. How easily can exception boundaries across organisation units be specified? Does the package use traffic light colouring based on exception boundaries? Can exception boundaries be different for each organisation unit and KPI?
- *Action reports hyperlinked to the BSC*. Does the package allow drill-down from the BSC to detailed information and activities for the KPIs?
- *Commentary and analysis*. Does the detailed information include analysis, or commentary to allow collaboration and shared learning?
- *Corrective action and preventive action management*. Does the package support definition and tracking of corrective and preventive actions, and can the action workflow integrate with the messaging and groupware standards of the organisation?

Technology

- *Ease of use for users*. Is the package easy for users to use?
- *Ease of deployment*. Is the package easy to deploy to networked, disconnected, and mobile users?
- *Manual report addition*. Can data and reports be added manually?
- *Web/intranet delivery*. Can the reports be published on the intranet?
- *Data and role dependent security*. Are data, role, and organisational unit-based security supported?
- *Workflow for user requests and additions*. Does the package support workflow for requesting and improving the information content?
- *Enterprise security model*. Can the package use the existing security and sign-on?
- *Ease of security maintenance*. If a separate security system is required, is it easy to maintain and will it scale to every user in the organisation? If not, how far will it scale and is that enough?
- *Organisational unit related rights*. Does the package allow organisational units to "own" their own implementation but still provide secure access to people in other parts of the organisation?
- *Use of existing hardware*. Will the package require deployment of more hardware?
- *Use of existing software*. To what extent does the package use existing software: OLAP databases, data warehouses?
- *Use of existing intranet/groupware*. To what extent does the package use the hardware, network bandwidth, and server processing power, provided for the intranet and groupware?
- *ERP system data*. Can the package use data from the ERP system(s) in

use in the organisation? What facility is provided for collecting data from remote and multiple ERP systems?

- *Operational systems data.* What links are available for operational systems data?
- *Data warehouse data.* What links are available for data warehouse data?
- *OLAP data feeds.* What links are available for OLAP database data?
- *Web data capture (or groupware).* What facilities are provided for web or groupware survey and data capture?
- *KPI calculation.* What facilities are provided for KPI calculation, and can these be replaced by best of breed (OLAP and modelling) tools?
- *Surf data.* Can the user "surf" across data from different KPIs and organisational units, subject to security?
- *Drill-down.* Can the user drill down to details?
- *Operating systems and platform support.* Are the preferred operating systems supported for both client and server?

Implementation

- How easy is the configuration (for instance of the BSC)?
- How easy is access to source data?
- How easy is KPI calculation?
- How easy is integration (for instance with reporting tools)?
- Can the package start small and scale to every user?
- Can the package support the changing of the strategy/CSFs/KPIs easily?
- Can the package support a change in an individual's role easily?
- Can the package support a change in the security classification of information easily?
- Can the package be implemented at multiple locations?
- Can the package be implemented as a quick win within one organisational unit, without limiting the future scope for wider use?
- What are the costs in the first year, and what is the total cost of ownership of the package, including software, hardware, configuration, installation, training, additional maintenance, and additional support?

9.5 CASE: PERFORMANCE MANAGEMENT IT ARCHITECTURE AT GLOBAL HYATT CORPORATION

(This case is courtesy of Hyperion Solutions Corporation. It is based on Hyperion, 2005.)

There are 211 hotels and resorts (over 90,000 rooms) in 44 countries around the world operating under the Hyatt, Hyatt Regency, Grand Hyatt, and Park Hyatt brands.

Currently, there are an additional 34 Hyatt hotels and resorts under development, including 12 new hotels in China. Hyatt Corporation (domestic US, Canada and Caribbean hotels) and Hyatt International Corporation (international properties) are subsidiaries of the Chicago-based Global Hyatt Corporation (GHC). The corporation is also the owner of Hyatt Vacation Club, Inc. (timeshare), Hyatt Equities LLC (hotel ownership), and US Franchise Systems, Inc. (which franchises Hawthorn Suites, Microtel and Best Inns). In 2005, GHC added 143 US properties to its growing portfolio with the acquisition of the AmeriSuites hotel chain.

Spreadsheet-based system obsolete

With the establishment of the Global Hyatt Corporation, there arose a need to more quickly and efficiently consolidate the hotels' financial data and streamline the planning processes throughout the business units worldwide. "Our manual aggregation of financial data had become far too time-consuming," says Gebhard Rainer, vice president for Hotel Finance and Technology at Hyatt International Corporation:

> We used to consolidate our operating results and the company's financial performance results through Excel spreadsheets. We consolidated operating results from a management perspective, to gauge our hotels' operating performance on a monthly basis, which typically took 15 days. And then we had to consolidate the results from our legal entities into the corporate structure, which took anywhere from 45 to 75 days. Plus, our old budgeting process took anywhere from three to five months. In addition to the amount of time needed, we had issues with the accuracy of the data. Using the Excel spreadsheets for consolidation was a highly error-prone process. So putting the two concerns together we needed a system that would automate these processes, and allow us to do global consolidation across all of the business units.

To sum up the challenge for GHC, the company had to replace the manual financial consolidation process, consolidate financial data from 200+ global business units, create budgets for all divisions and business units, and provide executives with clear view of financial results and forecasts.

Reduced planning cycle time

To reduce the time required in its planning process, GHC implemented a CPM software system that made scalable web-based collection of data, financial consolidation, and reporting and analysis possible. The system also contains a centralised web-based planning, budgeting, and forecasting module. It offers the company a collaborative integrated event-based planning solution that works throughout the enterprise, to track and monitor business plans and forecasts, and significantly enhance the financial planning process.

The implementation took less than one year. Rainer comments:

> Some of the selection process, in terms of choosing which applications to roll out first, was dictated by our business processes. We knew Global Hyatt Corporation was going to become significantly larger in January of 2005 because of the acquisition of AmeriSuites. That meant that for the first quarter we would need to have systems in place that would allow us to do our global consolidation accurately and in a timely fashion. We decided that we would be able to dramatically cut down on the planning cycle time by streamlining the amount of detail that we were previously required to submit with our budgets. By using a CPM solution, we saw the ability to push back the accountability to our hotels, which would make the budgeting process much faster, and more efficient.

GHC now pulls and consolidates its source financial data from over 230 locations, where it resides in an Oracle database and several local data marts. Data is collected from an array of transactions systems housed in the hotels and subsidiaries, then sent to a staging area. Next, the data is brought into Hyperion Financial Management via Hyperion Application Link, with UpStream WebLink used for external uploads and integration between the Hyperion products. At present the system is used by several hundred GHC employees in over 40 countries. Ultimately, that user base will expand to over 3000.

Rainer notes, "Every Hyatt-managed hotel in North America, Europe, and Asia is using the CPM system for financial consolidation," and continues:

> Since we're a global corporation, we must deal with a lot of variation in our general ledgers and accounts. We have to maintain an extended set of accounts for local requirements. And we actually follow both US and local accounting rules. In the past that had led to a pretty complex accounting process, but with the new system we've been able to reduce our chart of accounts from 4,000 to about 750 accounts, which has been an enormous benefit to us. Plus, it has helped us automate and document our accounting processes. This documentation in turn ensures our compliance with Sarbanes-Oxley.

Additional benefits

Additional benefits of GHC's CPM implementation include a greatly reduced time frame for financial consolidation and significantly improved accuracy in the forecasting process. Rainer says this reduction has been dramatic.

Rainer reports, "Where it used to take us three to five months to roll up our financial data and create a forecast, we're now down to six to eight weeks." He continues:

We've cut the closing cycle to two days, which means that by the end of the second business day of the following month, we can consolidate all of the hotels' operating results. Thanks to the new system, we've made a huge improvement in our corporate close and reporting, which now is within 30 days from quarter end, over the previous 50 to 75 days.

Rainer says that the single most important benefit of the CPM system is that GHC's executives can now track their data directly to its source. "In the past, the cumulative reports we received at corporate did not always correspond to the local reports produced by the hotels," he says. He continues:

But with the new CPM system everyone has "one version of the truth" because we know exactly where the data comes in. We have automated the process of loading data from the business unit level into the repositories at corporate, and the web-based delivery means everyone is looking at the same thing. We have cut back on our overall consolidation and planning time frame because our error checking has been greatly reduced, and in some cases, eliminated. As a result, we have faster closes, and much higher quality data.

GHC continues to review and evaluate its financial infrastructure, with a goal of making ongoing improvements. Currently it is upgrading the planning application to include an 18-month rolling forecast, and a move to what Rainer terms a "scorecard approach" to the budgeting process: analysts can take a snapshot of financial performance for a specific period, incorporate other types of data as desired, then use that view as a business plan.

Rainer predicts that:

In the years ahead we will extend our CPM solution into the whole business intelligence area, in order to make other, nonfinancial information available to GHC's management. That will lead us to a scorecarding approach, where we will be able to compare the results with targets and key performance indicators, and get almost real-time feedback on our financial results from the business units. In this way, CPM will help us respond in a much more proactive fashion than has ever before been possible.

9.6 CASE: CORPORATE PERFORMANCE MANAGEMENT AT PHARMACEUTICAL COMPANY

(This case is courtesy of Oracle Corporation, www.oracle.com. On request, the company is anonymous.)

Pharmaceutical Company, a top-tier global pharmaceutical company, develops and delivers innovative medicines. With over 25,000 employees and annual revenues that top $12 billion, its research and development areas include cancer, arthritis, inflammation and pain, infectious disease, cardiovascular and metabolic disorders, and women's health. Pharmaceutical Company makes well-known over-the-counter and prescription medications.

For pharmaceutical companies, the product development cycle takes seven years or longer, and researchers typically investigate about 40 compounds in the course of finding one that leads to a successful product. Financially, the stakes are high: Pharmaceutical Company spends more than $1 billion annually on research and development (R&D). Despite the high level of investment, the pharmaceutical industry as a whole lacks discipline and performance management in its research operations.

"Traditionally, pharmaceutical companies behaved like academic institutions, treating drugs as the by-products of research and development," the project manager for the balanced scorecard implementation at Pharmaceutical Company explains:

> In earlier days, restricted by limited budgets, researchers focused on the most promising projects, and the resulting drugs allowed pharmaceutical companies to expand with increased sales and to flourish financially. Since new drug development budgets were tied to sales figures, increased financial resources resulted in a loss of focus. Compounded with lack of accountability and some external factors, this led to a crisis in the drug development pipeline. Although Pharmaceutical Company's pipeline is in good shape, we needed a better view of information in order to more effectively use the money allocated for research. We chose Oracle's Balanced Scorecard solution to reveal comprehensive operational information and allow strategic decisions about the company's R&D efforts. The goals of the CPM system implementation were to allow the entire company to coordinate operations; provide detailed, comprehensive information to support management decisions; and bring discipline to R&D operations.

Details that make executives' dreams come true

The new CPM system has introduced a new performance management process and a new management mechanism to Pharmaceutical Company's R&D operations. For the first time, executives have a centralised, transparent view of the company. "One head of US clinical operations said this is something he has dreamed of for years," the project manager reveals.

> He appreciates the dynamic, timely way that business information is presented to him. It helps him understand how his organisation is positioned in relation to the corporate objectives and other parts of the company. The head of clinical operations for Asia said she could spend hours in front of the BSC because all of the data is so relevant to her business and she can get all the details she needs.

Several unique aspects of the pharmaceutical industry make company-wide coordination both challenging and crucial. Utilising the highly educated, highly paid workforce as effectively as possible is a key consideration. In addition, at any given time Pharmaceutical Company has thousands of patients enrolled in clinical studies and trials. "It's mind-boggling in terms of the resources we need to move around to accommodate priorities in different parts of the organisation, always making sure the cost objectives can be met," the project manager explains. "The new CPM system gives a comprehensive picture we haven't had in the past."

To meet its overriding objective of bringing new drugs to market, Pharmaceutical Company must carefully track the attrition rate of new compounds under study, work closely with physicians to bring a steady stream of appropriate patients into trials, and be sure it makes wise use of the funds allocated for research. The CPM system lets the company keep a close watch on all its milestones to make sure it is on track to meet its business goals. Pharmaceutical Company's R&D executives rely on the BSC to help them walk a fine line between encouraging innovation and acting as good stewards of research budgets. "Innovation is our lifeline, the key to our success. We need to have innovation supporting the top objective, supporting customer satisfaction, and supporting the process," the project manager stresses. "With the CPM system, we have a much better handle on the initiatives we put in place. We can measure an initiative at the outset to see what its relevance is, then review it at wrap-up to see whether its objectives were achieved."

Pharmaceutical Company links Oracle Balanced Scorecard to its applications databases through a data warehouse. "So far, about 30 per cent of our key performance indicators are automated," says the project manager. "We are continuing to automate with the intention of linking the maximum number of indicators to the data warehouse."

Besides automating data collection, linking to the data warehouse helps ensure high data quality. "Because Oracle Balanced Scorecard collects data in a dynamic, current way, we have much greater visibility into the data itself than ever before," the project manager explains further. "That's helping us improve the quality of the data we feed into the system." Pharmaceutical Company is rolling out the CPM system to all its divisions worldwide, which will give an even more comprehensive view of the company's R&D operations.

9.7 CASE STUDY: UVD'S INFORMATION SUPPLY

John Williams has an uneasy feeling. UVD has invested a lot of time and effort in developing a new performance management system, based on CSFs, KPIs, and the BSC. Everyone was very enthusiastic about the new system, so John expected all managers to energetically start using the new performance reports. Instead, he is hearing more and more critical opinions about the new system. He remembers yesterday's management team meeting.

Barrymoor kicked off the discussion about the new reports. "It took me quite a long time to decipher the new management reports. In fact, it took a long time before I started to get a feel of how to read and interpret all the numbers in the reports. There are so many of them."

Helen Case immediately launched a counter-attack. "The new reports look good, don't they? They contain all the information we need about the business units. I for one can see easily now how the units are performing against their targets and which units need special attention."

"But," Mark Allister asked, "do you know what needs to be done to get these units back on track?"

Helen did not understand the question. "I don't see the problem. We have leading indicators in the BSC which make it possible to look ahead. That gives enough input for steering these units, doesn't it? We don't have to tell them everything. Let them come up with ideas."

Gary didn't agree. "Helen, let's be fair. It not only takes a long time to collect, consolidate, analyse, and report the new data, it also takes ages to find out what corrective actions the units are planning, or worse, already have undertaken without our knowledge. It all takes too long."

Barrymoor sighed. "You know I was in favour of the new system, but this is no fun any more. The BSC is excellent, no doubt about that. But every time I want to see more detailed data to analyse something, I have to put in a request with the ICT people and then wait ages for the info. If something isn't done quickly, I'll stop using the system and go back to my old reports!"

"So what do you want me to do about it?" Helen exclaimed almost desperately.

"Well," said John, "I had somebody from the staff collect some examples of the way information is processed in our company, and I can tell you, that it's not always done very efficiently. Please take a look at this short report and tell me what you think. Or even better, let me have your ideas."

Case question 1: What are the main problems with UVD's performance management system?

Case question 2: How can the system be made more user-friendly? What role should ICT play in this?

To: John Williams
From: Martin Duvall, phone extension 564
Date: 25 August
Topic: Information processing at UVD
This memo describes everyday occurrences at UVD during the use of performance management information and performance reports by UVD's personnel. A possible new ICT architecture for the company has to be able to deal with these cases. I have observed four different situations, which are described in this memo. For each situation, the actions taken by the manager are listed and an analysis is given of the situation.

Situation 1

Mike Jones, UVD's manufacturing manager in Europe, notices that his KPI "personnel utilisation" over the past week is below target.

Actions 1

1. Mike retrieves the actual production hours and the number of available hours from the time registration system.
2. The actual production hours are lower than budgeted, whereas the total available hours are about the same as budgeted.
3. Mike asks for an itemisation from the production system of the actual production hours per machine. It turns out that the actual production hours of machine 1 are considerably lower than planned.
4. Mike contacts the foreman in charge of machine 1 to find out what caused this deviation and what they can do to improve over the next period.

Analysis 1

Mike uses aggregated data from several different systems, which he analyses to an increasingly lower detail level. To do this, Mike makes use of an integrated database which includes data of different levels of detail from several operational systems. He has to make sure that all data elements he needs have the same definition, so he knows he is looking at the same information. When he wants a different cross-section of the data, he has to start all over again.

Situation 2

Jack Bond is responsible for Marketing and Sales at UVD Europe. He does not want sales reported per product, because this results in a voluminous report which takes him too much time to analyse. The only thing he is interested in is which products do not sell well.

Actions 2

1. Jack asks Helen Case, financial manager, for her advice.
2. Helen offers to make a report which includes only those products that show sales results at least 10 per cent below budget.
3. Four working days later Jack receives the report which consists of only two sheets of paper. Within 10 minutes he can put his finger on the sore spots. He can now spend his time making plans to increase the sales of the products in question.

Analysis 2

Jack poses Helen an ad hoc question right after he has consulted the sales report. Because Helen can make use of a flexible reporting system, she is able relatively easily to generate an extra report that matches Jack's needs. However, as soon as Jack wants a different cross-section, Helen has to go to the reporting system and manually make a different report. Jack is not able to get the information he wants without help from Helen.

Situation 3

Helen Case has introduced the STAP reporting cycle. Each manager has to make projections for the KPI for the coming periods and include these in a rolling forecast report. They also have to report these forecasts to the management team.

Actions 3

1. On the tenth day of the new month, the managers get the results of their responsibility areas on paper. They cannot access this information through their own personal computer.
2. Each manager has one day to analyse the results and make projections.
3. In the rolling forecasts report, a manager has enter the projected results and actions manually.

Analysis 3

UVD does not have an integrated database system which includes actuals, target values, and KPI projected results. Users cannot enter descriptions of actions. Actuals are not automatically copied from the operational systems. Target values are not copied from the budgetary system. The managers have to manually enter their projected results and actions themselves, which takes a lot of time and effort and is accident prone.

Situation 4

Based on the management report of last month, Gary Williams, General Manager Europe, notices that the net result of the Lamps product group is 30 per cent below target and below the forecast given by Donald Reed, product manager of Lamps.

Actions 4

1. Gary analyses the product group results.
2. The product group's turnover and gross margin correspond with budget and projected results. The costs, however, do not correspond.
3. When Gary looks at an itemisation of the costs, it turns out that the advertising costs were twice as high as projected.
4. Gary puts his findings in a memo. He sends this memo to Donald via the internal mail. Donald however is often behind with his mail because he has to travel a great deal. Donald will probably get to see Martin's message after one or two weeks. A copy of the memo is sent to CEO John Williams.

5. Two weeks later Gary receives a memo from Donald in his mail. Donald explains that the sales of lamps were behind budget last month. Gary calls Donald to set up a meeting and to analyse the problem further. One week later they discover during their meeting that two months ago they decided to launch an extra advertising campaign to boost sales. But when Donald contacted advertising agency WOMA (Word Of Mouth Agency), the company that performs all advertising and promotional activities for UVD, it turned out that it could not start the campaign within the desired time frame. The contract between UVD and WOMA stipulates that orders should be made known at least one month ahead. As this was not the case, Donald had to find another agency that was able to execute this rush order. However, the costs turned out to be twice as high as WOMA's usual charges. The good news, though, was that the product group's turnover by now seems to back on target, although the latest figures are not in yet because of a computer malfunction.

Analysis 4

People at UVD desperately want to make use of the facility to send each other electronic messages via their personal computer. They could include data taken from the reporting system in these messages. By sending electronic messages, managers need not be physically present in the same place to discuss management reports, which is efficient as so many of them have to travel regularly. The time put into communication, taking action and decision making has to be reduced considerably.

Key points

☑ The majority of information requested in an organisation can be subdivided into two categories: performance management information (indicator results, financial data, nonfinancial data), and information supporting performance management (data/documents employees may need to ensure effective performance management).

☑ The goal of a good performance management ICT architecture is to first and foremost fulfil this need for performance management information adequately.

☑ The concept of information transparency entails that a minimum of information goes to the top of the corporation, while information is easily retrievable at lower levels of the corporation for top level to get it themselves if they want to ("push and pull information").

References

Buytendijk, F., Wood, B. and Geishecker, L. (2004) *Are you ready for corporate performance management?* Research Note, 30 January, DF-21-9550.

Collins, H. (2001) *Corporate Portals: Revolutionizing information access to increase productivity and drive the bottom line*. New York: Amacom.

Coveney, M., Ganster, D., Hartlen, B. and King, D. (2003) *The Strategy Gap: Leveraging technology to execute winning strategies*. New York: Wiley.

Creelman, J. and Makhijani, N. (2005) *Mastering Business in Asia: Succeeding with the balanced scorecard*. Singapore: Wiley Asia.

Eckerson, W. (2004) *Best Practices in Business Performance Management: Business and technical strategies*. Seattle: Data Warehouse Institute.

Elbaum, S. (2005) *CIO Disruptors Benchmark Report: The 2005 CIO agenda*. Aberdeen Group.

Geelen, P. (2004) *Corporate Performance Management: Sturen in een dynamische markt*. Deventer: Kluwer.

Heliview (2004) *Business Performance Management Survey*. Research report.

Hyperion (2005). *Global Hyatt Corporation: A Hyperion customer story*. www.hyperion.com

Marr, B. and Neely, A. (2002) *Balanced Scorecard Software Report*. Cranfield, UK: Cranfield School of Management.

Waal, A.A. de (2003) *On the Road to Nirvana: Building the real adaptive enterprise*. Hyperion white paper, www.andredewaal.nl.

Waal, A. de and Fourman, M. (2000) *Managing in the New Economy: Performance management habits to renew organisations for the new millennium*. Arthur Andersen and ShowBusiness.

Waal, A.A. de, and Geelen, P. (2002) Prestatiemanagement en informatietechnologie: een perfect paar? *FSR Forum*, 5.

Waal, A.A. de, and Kerklaan, L. (2004) *De resultaatgerichte overheid, op weg naar de prestatiegedreven overheidsorganisatie*. The Hague: SDU.

Tales of ... too bad!

A few years ago, a hamburger chain introduced a new type of chicken burger. After a while, it came to the notice of the regional manager that the litter bins of many of the branches were filled up with these new burgers at the end of the day. Not really surprising, as one of the company guidelines was to throw out products that had not sold within a certain period of time. Evidently the new burger was not selling very well.

The regional manager considered all these thrown-away products a waste and ordered the branch managers to reduce the wastage. From now on the regional manager was going to measure the waste and address the branch managers on this issue. A week later the regional manager visited the outlets again and checked the bins. To his great satisfaction there were no chicken burgers to be found. Relieved he walked into one of the stores where he saw, to his dismay, a large line of customers waiting in front of the ordering counter. He immediately looked for the branch manager and asked her what was going on. "Well," the branch manager replied, "because you wanted no wastage, we now make the chicken burger to order. Of course this takes a bit longer and because it is now a fairly popular product we get people waiting ..."

At a call centre, the average duration of a telephone conversation was measured for each employee. This indicator was important for management because the shorter the dispatch time of complaints and questions, the more calls an employee could handle per hour, and the fewer employees were needed, which meant a substantial difference in personnel costs. After some time, the average length for a call had dramatically decreased because if a conversation was taking too long, an employee would think up an excuse to end the call. The beauty of this for employees was that often the customer would immediately call the employee back, so another call was logged which improved the performance indicator of the employee ...

The management of a supermarket chain was looking for a key performance indicator to evaluate the effectiveness of its buyers. It was decided to measure the availability of products on the supermarket shelves: when it was too low the buyers obviously had not bought enough. However, unbeknown to management every time there was a problem with products not being present on the shelves the buyers were accustomed to resetting the performance indicator in the information system back to 100 per cent when the problem was not their fault (for example the supplier shipment was too late or the supplier could not deliver that week). Off course most of the problems were outside the control of the purchasers. The management of the supermarket chain is still trying to figure out why it is that the performance indicator clearly shows there is no problem, while in reality the supermarket shelves are empty ...

In the air force a specific type of fighter plane was stationed at two air bases. Because this plane had to be operational at all times, a key performance indicator was in use that measured the availability of a reserve cover for the cockpit as a replacement in case the original cover became damaged. Because this cockpit cover was extremely expensive and damages were sporadic and far between, air force management of the two bases decided to keep only one cover in store. The cover was put at base 1, which therefore satisfied the availability performance indicator. However, during inspection, management of base 2 was reprimanded because it did not have a cockpit cover on standby. Management immediately put in a request at base 1 to transfer the cover to base 2, so it would satisfy the performance indicator. During the next inspection, base 2 now was in the clear but this time base 1 got reprimanded. Management of this base immediately put in a transfer request for the cover at base 2, which shipped the cover over. Probably the cockpit cover at this moment still gets shipped back and forth ...

In a hospital, the average waiting time for an operation was far too long according to management. To decrease this time, management decided to evaluate and reward the doctors on the indicator "average waiting time per patient." After six months the average waiting time had decreased to the new, lower target, which was cause for celebration. However, the number of deceased patients had increased quite rapidly. Analysis showed that the average waiting time for all types of operations was about the same now: the non-emergency treatments were done earlier than before but the emergency treatments were done later than had been customary. That because of this more patients who needed an emergency procedure never made it to the operating table was seen as an "unfortunate side-effect" of the lower average waiting time. As the rate of deceased patients was not a performance indicator used in the hospital, no questions were asked and performance was considered up to standard ...

Stage 3

Designing a performance-driven behavioural model

Something tells us that the way in which performance management was applied in the organisations in the various tales was not quite right.

Performance management is a powerful technique to improve the results of an organisation, but as always there is another side to the coin: performance management can easily be used in the wrong manner with all kinds of detrimental effects. At the heart of many of the problems is the human factor – the way people handle performance management.

Stage 3 of the strategic performance development cycle deals with the design of a performance-driven behavioural model. In this stage the organisation decides on the culture needed to become a performance-driven organisation. Based on Edis's (1995) definition of achievement culture, "performance-driven" means a combination of performance orientation and professional excellence. It consists of the following steps: fostering the performance-driven behaviour of the organisation, fostering the performance-driven behaviour of individuals, and aligning personal objectives with strategic objectives. Each step is discussed in a separate chapter.

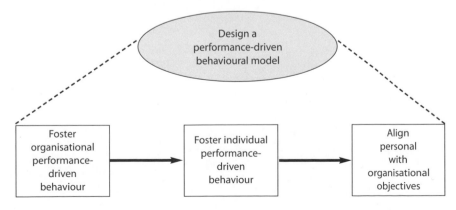

Figure P2.3 Steps to be taken to design a performance-driven behavioural model

10

Organisational performance-driven behaviour

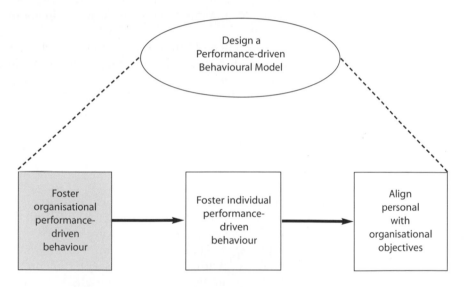

Figure 10.1 Fostering organisational performance-driven behaviour

Despite the many advantages of performance management, its implementation and especially its use are littered with problems (Bourne and Neely, 2000; Barrows Jr., 2004). It has been reported that 56 per cent of performance management projects fail, especially in the usage stage (Waal, 2002; Waal and Counet, 2006). This could be because the introduction of performance management is either not easy or underestimated. As Otley remarks:

> It seems clear that the BSC approach has something to offer, but also that the study of management control is more complicated and more contingent than previously recognized.
>
> (Otley, 1994)

Another reason might be, as Neely contemplates:

> The traditional view of measurement as a means of control is naive. As soon as performance measures are used as a means of control, the people being measured begin to manage the measures rather than performance.
>
> (Neely, 1998)

Before starting the performance management improvement process, it is therefore wise for an organisation to familiarise itself with the issues surrounding performance management and possible solutions.

Chapter objectives

☑ To provide the reader with an insight into the negative effects of performance management – and what to do about them.

☑ To discuss the importance of building trust in the workplace and establishing performance-driven values, in order to achieve successful change.

☑ To teach the reader the elements of a performance-driven organisational culture.

10.1 PERVERSE EFFECTS

It has been known for a long time that performance measurement and performance management can cause unintended and negative side-effects in organisations (Argyris, 1952; Simon et al., 1954; Ridgway, 1956). These effects are often referred to as "perverse." They can be harmful to an organisation because they cause more costs: in addition to the costs of implementing and maintaining the performance management system itself, cost is also incurred in reducing the effects of the dysfunctionalities and the accompanying lower performance. These costs are often difficult to notice and determine, let alone combat. Therefore it is better to know and understand what the perverse effects are, so an organisation can prevent them. The perverse effects can be divided into five categories (Jowett and Rothwell, 1988; Jaworski and Young, 1992; Hope and Hope, 1995; Smith, 1995; Merchant, 1998; Vosselman, 1999a,b; Holloway, 2000; Thiel and Leeuw, 2002; Koning et al., 2004):

1. *Behavioural displacement.* The performance management system encourages behaviours that are not consistent with the organisation's strategy and objectives. There are many examples of this. Managers pursue narrow local objectives, at the expense of the objectives of the

organisation as a whole (*suboptimisation*). On top of this, the priority areas of strategic importance to the organisation to target for performance measurement systems may be strongly contested. In addition, many outputs are the result of team efforts rather than individual efforts. As a result, if the implicit reward structure is directed at individuals, suboptimisation can arise. There is an inherent trade-off between the beneficial incentive effects of a formal control mechanism and the dysfunctional consequences of suboptimisation.

Managers pursue short-term targets at the expense of legitimate long-term objectives (*myopia*). This is caused by the fact that performance indicators are imperfect reflections of the efficacy of current management because they can indicate the results of managerial endeavour over many years, and they cannot always reflect the future consequences of current managerial actions. The problem is exacerbated by the short-term career perspectives of many workers.

Managers emphasise measures of success rather than the underlying objective (*measure fixation*). If a measure does not fully capture all dimensions of the associated objective, managers may be encouraged to pursue strategies that enhance the reported measure rather than further the associated objective.

Finally, management emphasises phenomena that are quantified in the performance management system, at the expense of nonquantifiable aspects of performance (*tunnel vision*). Most organisations usually hold a large number of diverse objectives, and it is often impractical or impossible to identify and track all of these objectives. It is impossible to devise a managerial reward structure that satisfactorily reflects achievement in more than three or four dimensions. In addition to that, specifically for the public sector, the ramifications of public sector services extend well beyond the immediate target of service delivery.

2. *Gamesmanship*. Managers take actions that are intended to improve their performance indicators without producing any positive economic effects for the organisation. Managers deliberately manipulate data so that reported behaviour differs from actual behaviour. For instance, they minimise the apparent scope for productivity improvements, as reported improvements in one year will result in increased expectations (and targets) for future years.

Gamesmanship can come in the form of "creative reporting" and fraud. If excessive reliance is placed on KPIs to control the organisation, there is clearly an incentive for managers to manipulate the data under their control to show their organisation's performance in the most advantageous light (*misrepresentation*). In addition, managers can adjust their activities in such a way that measurements on irrelevant KPIs lead to satisfactory results. This misrepresentation of results may lead to misallocation of resources and inequitable treatment of staff and clients.

Although in possession of all the facts, a manager might systematically misinterpret them, and thereby send the wrong signals to his or her superior (*misinterpretation*). This can be caused because the KPI reporting that is provided by the financial department is incomprehensible for managers. In addition, evaluation of performance measurement activities is often constrained by a lack of understanding of causal links between performance measurement and performance improvement.

Finally, management does not use the BSC consistently and reverts back to discussing financial measures when things go bad (*regression*). This happens in part because of their familiarity with financial measures, and because financial data apparently seems to be more objective and therefore leads to fewer discussions.

3. *Operating delays*. These are caused by administrative and bureaucratic procedures installed to exercise control, such as requiring an excessive number of signatures on a requisition form. These delays create frustration with, and resistance to, the performance management system.

A special form of delay, called *inertia*, occurs when there is not enough attention paid to following up the results on KPIs. Employees are not given (enough) feedback on their results and action is not taken on lagging results. There are no other control mechanisms in place that support the performance management system, such as human resources systems that reward good results on KPIs, accountability structures that make clear who is responsible for which KPIs, and a regular review of the quality of management in dealing with KPIs.

Organisational paralysis is brought about by an excessively rigid system of evaluation, thus inhibiting innovation. This danger arises because of the inevitable delay in designing and putting in place an evaluation scheme and the effort required to change it subsequently.

Organisations can also improve their performance by selecting the input that requires not a lot of work (throughput) to obtain the desired output. This means that the "easy cases" are dealt with before the more difficult cases. Because of this, the organisation seems to be more successful than it really is (*creaming or cherry picking or picking the low hanging fruits*). A consequence of this can be that the focus on optimisation of the processes becomes so strong that the drive for innovation is shut out of the business. After all, innovation can in the short term be detrimental to the output of the organisation because being innovative means taking risks (*ossification*).

4. *Negative attitudes*. The performance management system causes negative attitudinal effects like job tension, conflict, frustration, and resistance because managers do not want to feel controlled, or think that the performance management system is not effective, sensible, or ethical.

Managers object to being evaluated and judged by outsiders or other people in the organisation (*clouding the transparency*). People suffer from a perceived reduction in autonomy and start objecting to sharing their knowledge of the processes they have been put in charge of. That is why they object to KPIs which make their performance transparent.

In addition to this, managers constantly question the relevance of KPIs and also question the economic foundation of the KPI calculations (*beating the system*). They simply label the management information as "plainly wrong." Managers also state that the KPIs are not an accurate representation of their activities, that targets have been set in the wrong way, or that measuring nonfinancial indicators does not lead to increased profitability or growth. Many times managers have developed their own sources of information. In addition, selecting relevant and valid approaches that are also culturally and politically acceptable in the organisation can be highly problematic (*cultural mismatch*). There can be cultural barriers in countries where organisations approach performance measurement based on tradition and the accepted way of doing things. These traditions or embedded cultural norms are formidable barriers to change, and can cause many negative feelings.

5. *Structural deficits*. Development methods that work well in some organisations may fail to deliver in apparently similar organisations (*incompatibility*). In addition, the system can become too complex with too many separate measures, causing *indicator overload*. It is said that people can keep only about seven things in their heads at any one time (Pfeffer and Sutton, 2000). This means that having many indicators dilutes the attention people can pay to any single issue, or even a small set of issues.

Structural deficits can be created during the implementation phase, when the provision of resources (time, skill, and information) for systematic implementation is resisted from above and below, and consequently the resources are inadequate for the implementation project (*resource shortage*). Also, many organisations have a track record of starting and later abandoning initiatives such as the BSC. Many employees may have grown weary of such change efforts.

Finally, an organisation can suffocate by the large number of audits and evaluations that are conducted to show to external parties that the firm does satisfy the requirements of modern-day management techniques such as performance management.

Many of the problems described above can be seen as "facts of organisational life" that are related to change management, culture, and power (Holloway, 2000). These may be addressed by organisations acknowledging the issues and being sensitive to them when designing performance measurement systems, applying techniques that have established theoretical bases together with managerial flair. The problems reflect the natural evolutionary cycle that is at work in the development of theory and practice in the field of performance management systems:

> In the late 1980s and early 1990s, managers were concerned that they were measuring the wrong things. Hence, they began to explore and then adopt new and alternative measurement frameworks, such as the BSC. Throughout the

1990s, they struggled to implement these measurement frameworks. Now the most advanced organisations appear to be asking the next question in this natural evolutionary cycle: How do we use the data provided by our measurement systems?

(Neely, 2000)

It is therefore important to acknowledge that many of the perverse effects are not caused by shortcomings of the performance management technique itself, but are merely indications of the "clumsy way" such techniques and systems are implemented (Pidd, 2005).

10.2 PERFORMANCE MANAGEMENT: THE ALTERNATIVE USE

The best way to deal with the perverse effects of performance management is, of course, to prevent them from occurring in the first place. This requires performance management to be applied in the correct manner. Looking more closely at the perverse effects, it can be noticed that many of these effects are caused by performance information being used in an incorrect manner: it is solely used for evaluating people on their results and then rewarding or punishing them for their performance, and consequently often deteriorates into settling accounts. And because most people do not like to be punished, they start acting in a way that minimises the chance that information originating from the performance management system can be used to harm them: they start to manipulate the system. It therefore is crucial to be aware of how management levels use performance information in their dealings with lower management levels. If they use it in the wrong way, only for accountability and not for improvement, lower management levels will start to show perverse effects.

But behaviour is not only a case of evaluation and accountability: commitment of the employees is becoming more and more important for achieving good performance. "Soft" aspects of old, like attitude, enthusiasm, treatment, mentality, and disposition of employees, are in modern-day organisations decisive for the way service is given to customers, the innovativeness of the firm, the degree of absenteeism and employee turnover, and the willingness "to go the extra mile." But increasing commitment in combination with performance management is not that easy. It touches on change management aspects such as feelings of security and the range of influence people have. Giving authority to organisational members requires management to provide indirect steering and control.

Performance management cannot only focus on achieving targets, because organisational members then become a tool of performance management instead of performance management being a tool of organisational members. They will start to feel controlled and checked upon, which immediately harms their feeling of commitment to the organisation and its goals. Performance management has to be shaped in such a way that organisational members themselves can translate the organisational objectives and targets to objectives and targets of their own accountability areas, and can subsequently and independently achieve these themselves. The final results of their efforts should be evaluated, not the way they achieved these.

Performance management can be said to have four functions (based on: Albeda, 2002):

1. *Self-control function.* Organisational members continuously monitor themselves with KPIs to check whether they achieve their objectives and targets.
2. *Steering function.* Organisational members monitor which interventions have been successful and which not, to learn which actions are useful and can be taken again in the future.
3. *Learning function.* Organisational members evaluate whether direct links exist between the actions and the results of the KPIs, to learn how to improve these results continuously.
4. *Supervisory function.* Management observes whether organisational members achieve the required results.

The first three functions make it possible for organisational members to measure their own results and to improve these. These functions are mainly intended for self-management, not for accountability purposes. The main tools are the CSFs and KPIs that are used by organisational members to measure critical activities and results in their responsibility areas. A subset of these indicators can be used to provide higher management levels with some insight into the performance in these critical areas. This fulfils the fourth function of performance management. However, it should be kept in mind that the KPIs fulfil a signalling role and should not be used for punishment. Higher management levels can, on the basis of this signalling, start a dialogue with the organisational member in question about his/her results and corrective actions.

The functions of performance management should be institutionalised in the organisation (Figure 10.2). Every organisational unit has its own set of CSFs, KPIs, and management reports to track its strategy and crucial business processes (1 and 2 in Figure 10.2). The indicators act as input for the management reports of the organisational units (3 in Figure 10.2), and are used for self-management and self-control by management of the units (4 in Figure 10.2).

In addition to the regular obligatory financial reporting from organisational unit to corporate headquarters (5 in Figure 10.2), a subset of the most important CSFs and KPIs – those that give the best insight into the performance of the organisational unit and that are used by the unit's management itself – is regularly reported to corporate in a summary accountability report (6 in Figure 10.2). Corporate headquarters uses this information to fulfil its supervisory and controlling function (7 in Figure 10.2).

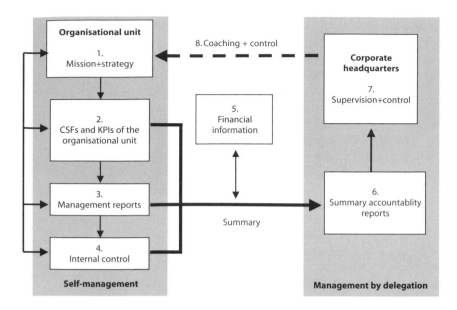

Figure 10.2 Framework for the management reporting flow from organisational units to corporate headquarters

Only when the organisational unit does not achieve its targets for a certain period of time should corporate headquarters step in (this also depends on the defined contingency areas: see "Budget contingencies" in Chapter 8) and start coaching and controlling the organisational unit (8 in Figure 10.2). This framework works for the combinations of corporate–divisions, divisions–business unit, business unit–departments, departments–teams, and even manager–employee.

Because the framework puts the emphasis on self-management and places accountability in the second place, using a subset of the KPIs, there is reduced or no pressure on organisational members to start manipulating the performance information. After all, they are not directly addressed on the KPIs and can without having qualms be innovative, experiment, and draft and execute action plans without directly being punished by superiors.

10.3 TRUST

An important precondition for a successful implementation of performance management is the involvement of organisational members in the development and implementation of the scorecard. To encourage employees to participate, management first has to gain their trust, because building trust in the workplace is crucial to successful change and organisational performance (Erdem and Ozen, 2003; McEvily et al., 2003; Morgan and Zeffane,

2003; Canen and Canen, 2004; Costigan et al., 2004; Lee, 2004; Perry and Mankin, 2004). Therefore it is imperative to establish an organisational culture of trust in people. In this culture, managers not only give employees the responsibilities and the tools to achieve agreed-upon results, they also give them freedom to achieve these results in the manner that the employees see fit. So there is no more interference in other people's responsibilities, no more repeatedly asking for more detail, no more review meetings that redirect focus, and no more changes in the parenting style, because all these send confusing signals to the organisation.

Management has to consciously and consistently work towards building employee trust before, during, and after the implementation process of performance management. Managers need to apply management techniques that allow them to coach the employees through the change. They need to understand the needs of employees, and address their concerns, while managing their performance during the change. This kind of support by managers helps to build trust in the change and increases employees' loyalty (Morgan and Hunt, 1994; Andaleeb and Charles, 1996; Calabrese, 2002; Korsgaard et al., 2002; Martins, 2002). In addition, managers who successfully promote trust increase employees' commitment to organisational goals (Long et al., 2005).

Definition of trust

In the literature, many different definitions of trust can be found, such as "a psychological state comprising the intention to accept vulnerability based upon positive expectations of the intentions or behaviour of another" (Rousseau et al., 1998), "one's expectations, assumptions or beliefs about the likelihood that another's future actions will be beneficial, favourable, or at least not detrimental to one's interest" (Robinson, 1996), and "the expectation that arises within a community of regular, honest, and cooperative behaviour, based on commonly shared norms, on the part of other members of that community" (Fukuyama, 1992). This suggests that people who do not trust one another will end up cooperating only under a system of formal rules and regulations, which have to be negotiated, agreed to, litigated, and sometimes enforced by coercive means (Martins, 2002). This is not a healthy climate to implement performance management in.

Managerial integrity is the quality that increases employees' trust in new changes (Turner, 2002). In turn, trust is the basis of strong relationships: without it there can be no good working relationship. Thus, an organisation whose employees lack trust will not be able to build the climate of loyalty that is so important for sharing opportunities and creating innovative ideas. In this respect, when introducing a major change, such as implementing a new performance management system, an organisation's greatest asset is the loyal support of employees which is based on trust.

Trust helps employees to come to terms with change, and helps them to understand that change is necessary and that they can contribute by helping to successfully implement the change. They learn to accept that their role in the company needs to change, and they should be ready to improve themselves in order to adjust to the new situation. It is the job of managers to ensure that employees adjust to such changes. Managers therefore need to master the competencies of trust:

- displaying congruence of word and deed
- expressing positive regard and belief in others
- manifesting accountability, predictability, and reliability
- articulating and embodying a moral code that cares about people
- relying on people and enabling them to enrich their lives
  (Charlton, 2000).

The benefits of building trust during the implementation of the BSC are:

- improved employee satisfaction
- ability to meet stakeholder expectations
- employee commitment to the use of the BSC
- increased employee trust in management
- improved quality of work
- improved productivity
- increased value
- increased access to new capital
- an increased number of long-term investors.

Trust is linked with predictability, consistency, openness, reliability, mutuality, honesty, competency, and caring about employees (Foster et al., 1996; Sharif et al., 2005; Smith, 2005). In order to stimulate predictability, it is important for managers to be consistent in their behaviour and reactions. It is also crucial to make real personal contact with employees, which requires an attitude of openness and integrity.

Trust in management requires consistent behaviour on all management levels. Consistency and transparency in organisations therefore call for bringing management and employees together to create mutually beneficial conditions. Predictability means management will always try to resolve issues communicated to them by employees. Managers have to be perceived by employees to be competent so they can rely on the discharging of duties and responsibilities by their managers in a professional and considerate manner. By focusing on transparency, an organisation's leadership creates conditions in which bias diminishes, parties set aside their natural defensive reactions, and learning occurs. Thus, focusing on the process of building trust centres on human relationships, the understanding that goes into building those relationships, and the caring that is shown toward employees. It is from relationship building that the process allows parties to work in solidarity and to learn to cooperate to achieve mutually beneficial outcomes.

Stanley (2005) provides 13 guidelines for developing trust in an organisation:

- Always tell the truth.
- Look for the good in people.
- Never take advantage of each other.
- Assign work to each employee fairly.
- Treat all employees with respect and dignity.
- Go to bat for your employees when they are right.
- Keep employee conversations and records confidential.
- When you tell someone you are going to do something, do it.
- Do everything you can to help all your employees to be successful.
- When your organisation is successful, share the credit with the employees.
- Be a good role model by projecting an integrity that is beyond reproach.
- Remain positive and reinforce employees during organisational change.
- Evaluate all employees objectively.

Mistrust is a primary cause for the withholding of support and information by employees. The majority of organisations that have ignored employee involvement have gone through painful experiences of dealing with unmotivated employees. High absenteeism, high turnover rates, conflicts that prove to be destructive and can lead to costly lawsuits, long grievance processes, and low productivity levels are just a few problems they had to deal with. It is therefore imperative that managers refrain from the following behaviours: constantly reminding employees (in word and deed) that they are the subordinates, not following through on promises and commitments, lying, and withholding praise and credit to employees for a job well done (Smith, 2005).

Building of trust

In the literature several theories and models can be found for building trust in an organisation (Dwivedi, 1983; Mayer et al., 1993; Mishra, 1996; Shaw, 1997; Galford and Drapeau, 2004; Herting and Hamon, 2004; Ramchurn et al., 2004). In this section a trust-building cycle is developed which is based on Goodman's trust-building model (2001). Goodman's model was chosen because it seemed to provide clear and detailed steps that in practice should be relatively easy for an organisation to implement. The cycle consists of six distinct steps, in a continuous cyclical process, that the organisation has to take in order to build or restore trust during the implementation of performance management (Figure 10.3).

In Step 1, the current situation has to be appreciated (Preston and Hayward, 1999; Reina and Reina, 1999; Korsgaard et al., 2002; Waal, 2002). Managers need to understand how employees perceive the BSC as their new performance management system. They need to know the opinions of employees, because otherwise they will end up working on

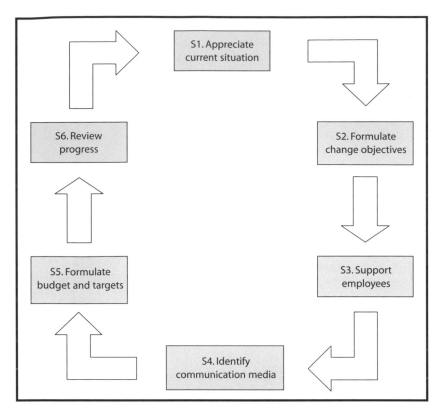

Figure 10.3 The trust-building cycle during implementation of performance management

assumptions which could be misleading. In appreciating the current situation, the main focus of the manager is to find out what employees know and do not know about the BSC, how they feel about this new system, and what their concerns are.

During Step 2, objectives for the change are formulated (Creelman, 1998; Eagleson and Waldersee, 2000). The manager formulates objectives for the performance management implementation, in consultation with employees. These objectives are meant to spell out which results the organisation wishes to achieve during and after the implementation. By setting objectives, the manager is attempting to create an atmosphere of trust by clarifying the objectives of the change. Once the objectives are known, everyone is aware of the intentions of the organisation.

Step 3 centres around creating support for employees, who greatly influence operations of the company and are in turn greatly affected by the operations of the company (Reina and Reina, 1999; Schneiderman, 1999; Nickols, 2003; Costigan et al., 2004). Hence it has to be taken into account how the new performance management system affects them and their interests. On the basis of the formulated change objectives, the significance of the change is explained to employees and discussed with them. Managers also make it clear how they will guide them through the change process. This guidance should be based on the manager's credibility, competence, and enthusiasm.

The required communication media are identified during Step 4 (Becerra and Gupta, 2003; Korsgaard et al., 2002; Morgan and Zeffane, 2003; Beslin and Reddin, 2004; Child and Rodrigues, 2004; Perry and Mankin, 2004). The manager makes sure that everyone continuously receives information on the progress of the performance management implementation and the results achieved so far. Such information can be communicated through meetings, notice boards, e-mails, workers' representatives, or a combination of these. Continuous communication ensures that employees do not spread rumours about performance management (its purpose, its results, its consequences) that cause tension within the organisation. If information is freely available, employees are better able to give feedback to management about any unclear issues and (potential) problems. Communication remains important after performance management has been introduced, to create a free flow of information for decision-making purposes to all concerned.

In Step 5, resources and change targets are formulated (Johnson and Kaplan, 1987). The resources available to achieve the change successfully are discussed with the employees, in order to determine their adequacy, effectiveness, and efficiency. Because there is almost always a lack of resources in the budget, employees need to understand the budget so they know what resources are at their disposal. On the basis of these resources and the formulated change objectives, targets for the change process are set so everybody knows what has to be achieved during the implementation of performance management.

The progress of the implementation is reviewed during Step 6 (Vroom and Yetton, 1993; Bourne et al., 2000; Kim and Mauborgne, 2003; Tzafir et al., 2004). This review entails evaluation of the progress made in achieving the objectives and targets of the change. This means regular assessments of the progress made towards achieving the desired change. This ensures that problems during the change process are identified early, so they can be solved quickly. It also gives managers the opportunity to regularly communicate with their employees about what is expected from them, and to discuss items which went wrong, whether this was the manager's or the employee's fault. It also entails checking whether both parties have kept their promises, whether managers have treated employees in a fair and consistent manner, and whether employees have been rewarded for (intermediate) results achieved during the change process.

Employees' trust is an important factor for the successful implementation of far-reaching changes such as the introduction of performance management. The trust-building cycle is a useful tool in creating or recreating this necessary trust.

10.4 PERFORMANCE-DRIVEN VALUES

An organisation can help focus its employees on performance management by formulating a set of performance-driven values. These are the values by which people in the organisation are going to live, in order to make performance management a success and thereby make themselves and the organisation successful. To put together the set, organisational members discuss during a workshop which values should apply within the firm. Some examples are:

- Mistakes are allowed.
- Risks can be taken.
- There is complete transparency of results.
- There is a delegating management style which encourages self-management and taking responsibility.
- There is a duty for employees to report deviations to management as soon as possible.
- There is a focus on performance and continuous improvement.
- There is focus on knowledge transfer within the company.

In essence, by introducing performance-driven values organisational members learn a new way of working and interacting with each other.

A practical way to develop performance-driven values is to organise separate workshops for each organisational unit, and to ask each workshop participant to write down, on three separate sticky-backed notes, the three values he or she thinks are the most important to make performance management a success and the organisation successful. This can be certain behaviour that needs to change or to stay the same, processes that have to be adapted, resources that need to be used more effectively, and so on. Anything is possible. After that, all sticky-backed notes are collected and put on the wall. The participants divide the sticky-backed notes into categories and make a summary of each category. The summaries, which are in fact the performance-driven values, are then written on a flipchart. Finally, all items on the flipchart are reviewed once more and details are added. The final result of the workshop is a complete set of performance-driven values for a certain organisational unit. By combining and summarising all workshop results, a performance-driven value set is obtained for the entire organisation.

10.5 CASE: TRUST AT ZIMASCO MINING AND SMELTING COMPANY

(This case originates from Waal and Nhemachena, 2005.)

Trust can be observed from individual behaviour and can therefore be measured experimentally (Möllering et al., 2004). In this case, the trust-building cycle is put to the test.

The mining industry plays a major role in the Zimbabwean economy by contributing 4 per cent to the country's GDP, and supporting 6 per cent of employment. It is the second major foreign currency earner after agriculture, at 13 per cent. However, the mining industry in Zimbabwe is currently experiencing a reduction in investments despite the abundance of mineral resources that can be exploited. Some established mining conglomerates have closed down while others are threatening to do the same.

The Zimbabwe Mining and Smelting Company (Zimasco) is a multinational mining and smelting company that is a major player in the Zimbabwe mining industry. The company consists of four divisions: Shurugwi and South Dyke Division (chrome mining), Middle and North Division (chrome mining), Mimosa Mining Company (platinum mining), and Zimasco Kwekwe Division (smelting). The vision of Zimasco is to have the lowest cost and to be the leading producer of high-quality carbon ferrochrome in the world. The strategy is to continuously look for cost-cutting measures in every activity carried out by all Zimasco's employees.

There are some major challenges in the near future for the company. First of all, ferroalloy has to be transported to new outlets such as the ports of Beira (Mozambique) and Durban (South Africa). Then a new smelting plant has to be established as soon as possible, to start processing high-grade coal originating from South Africa. This new coal is needed because Zimasco's main market, Japan, has stringent quality measures for the coal used in smelting chrome. Finally, in the past the company has not been able to meet employees' expectations about bonuses and dividends that have been promised by the company, causing some resentment among the workforce.

Zimasco turned to a new performance management system to get a better grip on current processes and future developments. The company introduced the BSC with the assistance of a US consulting firm. Employees initially accepted the BSC because they were promised that the BSC would help the company realise higher profits. This would make it possible to pay employees bonuses and dividends. However, several of the expected benefits of the BSC had not materialised. The employees therefore started to question the credibility of the BSC. Zimasco wants to reintroduce the BSC and therefore first has to regain trust in this performance management system among employees.

To identify the elements in the trust-building cycle that are of importance to rebuild employees' trust in the BSC, a questionnaire was constructed on the basis of the trust-building cycle and the underlying literature that had been consulted. This questionnaire was sent to ten employees at each of the four divisions of Zimasco; in total 40 questionnaires were completed and returned to the researchers. This high response rate (of 100 per cent) can be explained by the fact that a senior manager of the company personally chose potential respondents and distributed the survey to them. Simple and direct questions were formulated to make it possible to answer the questionnaire in 15 minutes. Open-ended questions were not used (except in the "background" section) because it was not possible for the researchers to be physically present to discuss any uncertainties in this type of question. The findings from the research are discussed per step of the trust-building cycle, after first giving the background information. (See the section "Building of trust" earlier in this chapter for a description of the cycle.)

Background information

The BSC was introduced in Zimasco in 2003. The reasons for implementing the new performance management system were:

- to translate company targets into local targets
- to align individual, team, and process performance to company targets
- to generate initiatives and coordinate work along the value chain in order to close performance gaps
- to create and sustain better business literacy and knowledge
- to communicate the reward structure and incentive pool and its relation to desired performance.

All respondents agreed that since the implementation of the BSC some of the expected benefits have materialised:

- Up-to-date information on the operations of the company is now available.
- Better discussion of the company's performance by teams and their leaders is possible.
- More accurate measurement of performance of each business unit against preset targets and identification of performance takes place.
- Better and more focused communication on initiatives needed to close performance gaps takes place.
- There is more often agreement on forecasts and resulting action plans for improving performance in the coming periods.

The respondents stated that, in principle, they had confidence in the BSC because they saw it as a strategic business tool to measure the performance of the business at particular points in time, and they acknowledged that it clearly defined the accountabilities of employees and all levels of management in relation to business performance. Also, both management and workforce had gained better knowledge about their performance successes and failures, because the BSC promoted an effective flow of information within the organisation.

Step 1: Appreciate the current situation

The majority of the respondents found it important that managers demonstrate that they understand the needs of their subordinates, that managers and employees share common goals, that managers want their employees to succeed, and that if employees do not feel valued they will not be inclined to help the managers meet their goals. These findings indicate that employees appreciate managers who feel with them as they struggle to cope with the changes that are happening in the company. The findings also reflect that employees trust managers who allow them to express their true feelings and who listen to their concerns.

Step 2: Formulate change objectives

The majority of the respondents agreed that Zimasco's management needed to develop challenging but achievable targets. At the same time, they stated that they themselves needed to be a part of the planning and target-setting processes so they could identify with the outcomes. In their opinion, one of the most crucial elements in achieving successful change was getting input from them. In this way, management could establish what employees consider important so that an environment of trust is created.

The respondents all stated that in their opinion it was important to keep the overall number of measures of the BSC low, recognising that it is easier to deal with a limited number of measures. They also agreed that one of the biggest challenges in Zimasco has been the culture change needed to achieve an environment where employees feel they should be, and are, accountable for results. Therefore, they considered it important that they become part of a performance measurement working group which would (re-)establish the performance measures in the company's BSC. These findings indicate that involving employees in the planning, target-setting, and measurement identification processes is an important success factor for the implementation of a BSC.

Step 3: Support employees

The majority of the respondents were of the opinion that managers could create trust through consistent behaviour:

- doing what they promised and what employees expect from them
- being candid with their subordinates
- showing compassion towards their subordinates
- demonstrating personal credibility and integrity
- being a role model in behaviour and work ethic
- being available to their subordinates
- communicating not only the bare facts and figures but also what they feel.

These findings indicate that trust develops when managers are available and willing to assist employees if necessary and in a credible and honest way.

Step 4: Identify communication media

The majority of the respondents stated that the input of employees contributed greatly to the success of a BSC implementation. For this, regular and effective communication is needed about the change process, and employees need to be given opportunity to review and comment on the BSC measures throughout the process. The findings indicate that trust is greatly fostered by constant and honest two-way communication, by sharing information and feedback, and by open dialogue between managers and employees.

Step 5: Formulate a resource budget and change targets

The majority of the respondents agreed that clear periodic targets were needed to focus activities and performance expectations, and that both managers and employees should be accountable for achieving targets. Then, managers and their subordinates have to agree on the resources needed to achieve these targets. This agreement will prevent any misunderstanding between managers and employees about the resources available. The findings indicate that managers should agree with their subordinates on both the targets and the resources needed to achieve these, in order to gain full support from the employees.

Step 6: Review progress

The majority of the respondents found it important that managers fulfil their promises of compensation made to employees for achieving the agreed targets, and that they are consistent in their treatment of employees. They agreed that progress reviews during the implementation of the BSC must be an ongoing process and not a one-off event. During reviews, managers' sincerity – admitting when they are wrong – will greatly increase trust. However, the respondents also stated that managers at Zimasco did not (fully) honour their commitments, and because of the detrimental effect of this on trust, they themselves did not necessarily fulfil their promises to the managers. They remarked it was better for managers to give definite promises at a time when they were certain it was feasible to honour them.

Conclusion

The employees from the mining company Zimasco are unanimous in their opinion that all stages of the trust-building cycle helped them regain trust in the BSC, indicating that the organisation's managers should work in a dedicated fashion on satisfying the requirements of the stages in the cycle. Employees are the medium through which managers and the organisation either succeed or fail. To help them perform at peak levels when implementing the BSC, the managers must therefore diligently work to establish trust with them.

10.6 CASE: PERFORMANCE-DRIVEN VALUES AT A TEMPING AGENCY IN THE NETHERLANDS

The core activities of the Temping Agency Netherlands (TAN) are dispatching and detaching temporary workers, recruitment and selection of personnel, and obtaining temporary work assignments. Two years ago, the company, which consists of several regional business units, had gone through a reorganisation during which a new structure, tasks, and responsibilities were introduced and a new performance management system was implemented. Since then, new KPIs and the BSC (Figure 10.4) have been used to evaluate the performance of employees. The scorecard contains, among others, indicators such as market share, client satisfaction, employee satisfaction, temp worker satisfaction, and fulfilment rate (i.e. have all the requests from the clients for temp workers been fulfilled?).

After all these changes, TAN's chief executive officer asked herself whether the new structure and performance management system resulted

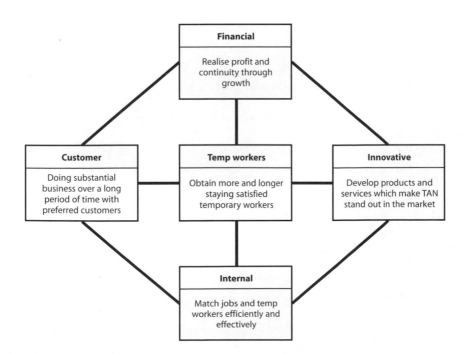

Figure 10.4 Set-up of TAN's balanced scorecard

in employees becoming more performance-driven, whether they felt enough responsibility for results and whether they were sufficiently action-oriented. Was the new structure clear enough and aligned enough with the responsibilities of individual people? The answers to these questions are very important under the current adverse economic conditions, in which temp agencies are confronted with increased competition and a resulting downward pressure on prices. The CEO decided to start a short investigation to obtain the answer to these questions. The investigation yielded many practical suggestions for improvement.

Among the recommendations there was one which proposed to establish the performance-driven values for TAN, so employees knew the code to live by. The CEO started a small project in which every business unit conducted a workshop in which, with the help of a facilitator, the performance-driven values for the unit were established. The management team of the company, consisting of the CEO, chief financial officer, chief human resource officer, and the directors of all business units also conducted a similar session. The box outlines the result of these efforts.

Working document: Overview of performance-driven values of TAN's MT and BUs

Management team
1. A deal is a deal.
2. Collectively sharing of results and successes: ALWAYS!
3. We are professionals.
4. We choose.

BU 1: Together
1. First choose what we do and don't do: and than we do it!
2. We are a role model.
3. Company interest has precedence over BU interest.

BU 2: This is us
1. We are proud winners.
2. Performance management is our foundation.
3. Quality is our choice.
4. We set the example.

BU 3
1. We make realistic choices.
2. We execute with discipline.
3. We develop a company focus.
4. We share mistakes and successes to improve ourselves.

BU 4: Stands for
1. We make choices!
2. We take our responsibility.
3. We help each other.
4. We are successful in the market.

BU 5: We are
1. Our motto is: plan – do – check – act.
2. We make choices, prioritise these and live accordingly.
3. We are a top team.
4. We have an exemplary function.

As the next step, all performance-driven values were collected and summarised in a matrix (Table 10.1).

Table 10.1 Performance-driven values of TAN

Unit	Values	Collective	Consistent	Focus	Pride	Professional	Quality	Role model	Transparent
MT	A deal is a deal			X					
	Collective sharing of results/successes	X							
	We are professionals					X			
	We choose			X					
1	Choose what we do and don't do			X					
	We are a role model							X	
	Company interest over BU interest	X							
2	We are proud winners				X				
	PM is our foundation					X			
	Quality is our choice						X		
	We set the example							X	
3	We make realistic choices			X					
	We execute with discipline		X						
	We develop a company focus	X							
	We share mistakes and successes								X
4	We make choices			X					
	We accept responsibility							X	
	We help each other	X							
	We are successful in the market					X			
5	Our motto is: plan - do - check - act					X			
	We make choices			X					
	We are a top team					X			
	We have an exemplary function							X	

Table 10.2 Performance-driven values of TAN, sorted by rate of occurrence

Values	Collective	Consistent	Focus	Pride	Professional	Quaity	Role model	Transparent
Collective sharing of results/successes.	X							
Company interest over BU interest	X							
We develop a company focus	X							
We help each other	X							
A deal is a deal		X						
We execute with discipline		X						
We choose			X					
Choose what we do and don't do			X					
We make realistic choices			X					
We make choices			X					
We make choices			X					
We are proud winners				X				
We are successful in the market				X				
We are a top team				X				
We are professionals					X			
PM is our foundation					X			
Our motto is: plan - do - check - act					X			
Quality is our choice						X		
We are a role model							X	
We set the example							X	
We accept responsibility							X	
We have an exemplary function							X	
We share mistakes and successes								X

Then the matrix was reorganised according to the frequency with which a performance-driven value was mentioned (Table 10.2).

Finally, based on the matrix in Table 10.2 the performance-driven values for TAN as an organisation were chosen:

1. We make clear choices.
2. We put company interest above our own interest.
3. We are professionals in everything we do.
4. We are proud of our company.
5. We are a role model, both internally and externally.

10.7 CASE STUDY: CREATING PASSION FOR PERFORMANCE MANAGEMENT

(This case is based on Ardon, 2003.)

> It's little over a year ago that we started with performance management. At that time, I warned everyone that the level of service to customers should increase dramatically, otherwise we would not survive in the long run. I assumed every employee in the company did his or her best, but that just wasn't enough. We had to focus on the matters that really add value to our customers, while at the same time keeping an eye on costs. We hired a consultancy firm to help us implement performance management. Everything has been done to the book: critical success factors, key performance indicators and the balanced scorecard have been introduced, as have new management reports and new information systems. But it did not bring us what I expected. I'm still missing enthusiasm and zest.

The chief executive officer of the research institute continues his story:

> We conducted information sessions for all personnel. Good communication is of vital importance. I myself gave a short presentation so they could see I find performance management important. All managers have been trained in working with performance management: analysing data, managing output, handling reporting techniques. On top of this, during all team meetings a consultant was present. A good guy, he certainly knew a lot. But still performance management is not in the bloodstream of people. You can still hear employees say things like "Performance management takes the heart out of our profession" and "We have come here to practise our profession, not to become number crunchers." Several senior researchers have let me know that they are not taken with the new performance management system. To be honest, I can see their point of view. When I used to be a researcher, I didn't like rules at all. But times have changed. The market has become more difficult. Because they have more choice, customers are more demanding and more particular. So performance management is no luxury, it is a necessity. Making clear agreements, measuring and performing, that's what it is all about these days.
>
> You know, I can increase the pressure on my people but I don't think that will win them over. After all, they do hand in their monthly reports with the results on their performance indicators, but the information is still rather "thin." It doesn't entice me to conduct a meeting about their business and results. I have the feeling they do it for me, not for themselves, not to help them monitor and improve their own business. Mind you, there are managers who have thrown themselves into performance management with heart and soul. They believe in it. But I see too many managers for whom the spark has not jumped over. They deliver their numbers but see this as an obligation. I have the feeling they will stop doing it as soon as I turn away. But in the meantime our position in the market has not improved. We need a club of entrepreneurs, but I'm stuck with a group of people whose main aim is to be excellent researchers. How can I create passion for performance management in this group? What do you think, what should I do?

Case question 1: What should the CEO do? How can he create passion for performance management in his organisation?

Case question 2: What are the organisational and cultural conditions needed to create this passion?

Key points

☑ Performance management can cause unintended and negative side-effects in organisations.

☑ If performance management is solely used for evaluating, rewarding, and punishing people on their results, and settling accounts, it will fail.

☑ Organisational members should themselves translate the organisational objectives and targets to objectives and targets for their own accountability areas, and independently achieve these themselves.

☑ Building trust in the workplace is crucial to successful change and organisational performance, therefore it is imperative to establish an organisational culture of trust. In this culture, managers not only give employees the responsibilities and the tools to achieve agreed-upon results, they also give them freedom to achieve these results in the manner that employees see fit.

☑ An organisation can help focus its employees on performance management by formulating a set of performance-driven values by which people in the organisation are going to live, in order to make performance management a success and thereby make themselves and the organisation successful.

REFERENCES

Albeda, H.D. (2002) *10 voor meten, 5 voor gebruik, over prestatiemeting en monitoring*. Rapportage Rekenschap, Stichting Rekenschap.

Andaleeb, S.S. and Charles, I. (1996) An experimental investigation of satisfaction and commitment in marketing channels: the role of trust and dependence. *Journal of Retailing*, 72 (1), 77–93.

Ardon, A. (2003) Creëer passie voor prestatiemanagement. *Consultant.*

Argyris, C. (1952) *The Impact of Budgets on People*. The Controllership Foundation, Cornell University.

Barrows Jr., E.A. (2004) Assessing your balanced scorecard's performance. *Balanced Scorecard Report*, May–June, 15.

Becerra, M. and Gupta, A.K. (2003), Perceived trustworthiness within the organisation: the moderating impact of communication frequency on trustor and trustee effects. *Organisation Science*, 14 (1), 32–44.

Beslin, R. and Reddin, C. (2004) How leaders communicate to build trust. *Ivey Business Journal*, November/December, 1–6.

Bourne, M. and Neely, A. (2000) Why measurement initiatives fail. *Quality Focus*, 4 (3).

Bourne, M., Mills, J., Wilcox, M., Neely, A. and Platts, K. (2000) Designing, implementing and updating performance measurement systems. *International Journal of Operations & Production Management*, 20 (7), 754–71.

Calabrese, R.L. (2002) *The Leadership Assignment: Creating change.* Boston, MA: Allyn and Bacon.

Canen, A.G. and Canen, A. (2004) Multicultural competence and trust: a new road for logistics management? *Cross Cultural Management*, 11 (3), 38–53.

Charlton, G. (2000) *Human Habits of Highly Effective Organisations.* Petoria: Van Schaik.

Child, J. and Rodrigues, S.B. (2004) Repairing the breach of trust in corporate governance. *Corporate Governance*, 12 (2), 143–52.

Costigan, R.D., Insinga, R.C., Kranas, G., Kureshov, V.A. and Hter, S.S. (2004) Predictors of employee trust of their CEO: a three-country study. *Journal of Managerial Issues*, 16 (2), 197–216.

Creelman, J. (1998) *Building and Implementing a Balanced Scorecard.* London: Business Intelligence.

Dwivedi, R.S. (1983) Management by trust: a conceptual model. *Group & Organisation Studies*, 8 (4), 375–401.

Eagleson, G.K. and Waldersee, R. (2000) Monitoring the strategically important: assessing and improving strategic tracking systems. In: A. Neely (ed.), *Performance Measurement: Past, present, and future.* Cranfield, UK: Centre for Business Performance, Cranfield University, 137–44.

Edis, M. (1995) *Performance Management and Appraisal in Health Services.* London: Kogan Page.

Erdem, F. and Ozen, J. (2003) Cognitive and affective dimensions of trust in developing team performance. *Team Performance Management*, 9 (5/6), 131–5.

Foster, S.F., Heling, G.W.J., Tideman, B. with Remme, J.H.M. (1996) *Teams in Intelligent Process Based Organisations.* Leiderdorp: Lansa Publishing.

Fukuyama, F. (1992) *Trust: The social values and the creation of prosperity.* New York: Free Press.

Galford, R. and Drapeau, A.S. (2004) *The Principles of Trusted Leadership: The trusted leader.* Minerva Solutions Inc.

Goodman, M.B. (2001) *Restoring Corporate Trust.* Fairleigh Dickinson University.

Herting, S.R. and Hamon, T.R. (2004) Dynamics of trust among entities in a mechanistic simulation model. *Public Performance and Management Review*, 28 (1), 30–52.

Holloway, J.A. (2000) Investigating the impact of performance measurement. Referred to in: A. Jaworski, Young, B.J. and Young, S.M. (1992) Dysfunctional behavior and management control: an empirical study of marketing managers. *Accounting Organisations and Society*, 17 (1).

Hope, T. and Hope, J. (1995) *Transforming the Bottom Line: Managing performance with the real numbers.* London: Nicholas Brealey.

Jaworski, B.J. and Young, S.M. (1992) Dysfunctional behavior and management control: an empirical study of marketing managers. *Accounting Organisations and Society*, 17 (1).

Johnson, H. T. and Kaplan, R.S. (1987) *Relevance Lost: The rise and fall of management accounting.* Boston, Mass.: Harvard Business School Press.

Jowett, P. and Rothwell, M. (1988) *Performance Indicators in the Public Sector.* Basingstoke: Macmillan.

Kim, W.C. and Mauborgne, R. (2003) Fair process: managing in the knowledge economy. *Harvard Business Review*, January: 127–36.

Koning, P., Canton, E., Cornet, M., Pomp, M., van de Ven, J., Venniker, R., Vollaard, B. and Webbink, D. (2004), Centrale doelen, decentrale uitvoering, over de do's and don'ts van prestatieprikkels voor semi-publieke instellingen, *Centraal Planbureau*, no. 45, January.

Korsgaard, M.A., Whitener, E.M. and Brodt, S.E. (2002) Trust in the face of conflict: the role of managerial trustworthy behaviour and organisational context. *Journal of Applied Psychology*, 87 (2), 312–19.

Lee, H.J. (2004) The role of competence-based trust and organisational identification in continuous improvement. *Journal of Managerial Psychology*, 19 (6), 623–39.

Long, C.P., Sitkin, S.B. and Cardinal, L.B. (2005) *Managerial Action to Build Control, Trust, and Fairness in Organisations: The effect of conflict*. Paper presented during the British Academy of Management conference, September.

Martins, N. (2002) A model for managing trust. *International Journal of Manpower*, 23 (8), 754–69.

Mayer, C.R., Davis, J.H. and Schoorman, F.D. (1993) An integrative model of organisational trust. *Academy of Management Review*, 20 (3), 709–34.

McEvily, B., Perrone, V. and Zaheer, H. (2003) Trust as an organizing principle. *Organisation Science*, 14 (1), 91–103.

Merchant, K.A. (1998) *Modern Management Control Systems: Text and cases*. Upper Saddle River, NJ: Prentice Hall.

Mishra, A.K. (1996) Organisational responses to crisis: the centrality of trust. In: R.M. Kramer and T.R. Tyler (eds), *Trust in Organisations: Frontiers of theory and research*. Thousand Oaks, Calif, Sage, 261–87.

Möllering, G., Bachmann, R. and Lee, S.H. (2004) Understanding organisational trust: foundations, constellations, and issues of operationalisation. *Journal of Managerial Psychology*, 19 (6) 556–70.

Morgan, R.M. and Hunt, S.D. (1994) The commitment-trust theory of realtionship marketing. *Journal of Marketing*, 58 (3), 20–38.

Morgan, D.E. and Zeffane, R. (2003) Employee involvement, organisational change and trust in management. *International Journal of Human Resource Management*, 14 (1), 55–75.

Neely, A. (1998) *Measuring Business Performance: Why, what and how*. London: Economist Books.

Neely, A. (ed.) (2000) *Performance Measurement: Past, present, and future*. Cranfield, UK: Centre for Business Performance, Cranfield University.

Nickols, F. (2003) *The Accountability Scorecard*. www.nickols.us

Ohloson, K. (1998), Leadership in an age of mistrust. *Industry Week*, February, 37–46.

Otley, D. (1994) Management control in contemporary organisations: towards a wider framework. *Management Accounting Research*, 5, 289–99.

Perry, R.W. and Mankin, L.D. (2004) Understanding employee trust in management: conceptual clarification and correlates. *Public Personnel Management*, 33 (3), 277–90.

Pfeffer, J. and Sutton, R.I. (2000) *The Knowing–Doing Gap: How smart companies turn knowledge into action*. Boston, MA: Harvard Business School Press.

Pidd, M. (2005) Perversity in public service performance measurement. *International Journal of Productivity and Performance Management*, 54 (5/6), 482–93.

Preston, J. and Hayward, T. (1999) Strategic information management and the balanced scorecard. In: M. Klasson, B. Loughridge and S. Loof (eds), *New Fields for Research in the 21st Century: Proceedings of the 3rd British-Nordic conference on library and information studies 12-14 April, 1999, Boras, Sweden,* Swedish School of Library and Information Studies, University College of Boras, 284–96.

Ramchurn, S.D., Jennings, N., Sierra, C. and Godo, L. (2004) Devising a trust model for multi-agent interactions using confidence and reputation. *Applied Artificial Intelligence,* 18 (9/10), 833–52.

Reina, D.S. and Reina, M.L. (1999) *Trust and Betrayal in the Workplace.* Berrett-Koehler.

Ridgway, V.F. (1956) Dysfunctional consequences of performance measurements. *Administration Science Quarterly,* 1 (2), 240–47.

Robinson, S. (1996) Trust and breach of the psychological contract. *Administrative Science Quarterly,* 41, 574–99.

Rousseau, D.M., Sitkin, S.B., Burt, R.S. and Camerer, C. (1998) Not so different after all: a cross-discipline view of trust. *Academy of Management Review,* 23 (3), 393–404.

Schneiderman, A.M. (1999) Why balanced scorecards fail. *Journal of Strategic Performance Measurement,* January.

Sharif, K.J., Kalafatis, S.P. and Samouel, P. (2005) Cognitive and behavioural determinants of trust in small and medium-sized enterprises. *Journal of Small Business and Enterprise Development,* 12 (3), 409–21.

Shaw, R.B. (1997) *Trust in the Balance.* San Francisco: Jossey-Bass.

Simon, H., Guetzkow, H., Kozmetsky, K. and Tyndall, G. (1954) *Centralization vs. Decentralization in Organizing the Controllers Department.* Paper, Controllership Foundation.

Smith, G. (2005) How to achieve organisational trust within an accounting department. *Managerial Auditing Journal,* 20 (5), 520–3.

Smith, P. (1995) On the unintended consequences of publishing performance data in the public sector. *International Journal of Public Administration,* 18 (2/3).

Stanley, T. (2005) Trust: a management essential. *Supervision,* 66 (2), 6–8.

Thiel, S. van and Leeuw, F.L. (2002) The performance paradox in the public sector. *Public Performance and Review,* 25 (3), 267–81.

Turner, C. (2002) *Lead to Succeed: Creating entrepreneurial organisations.* Texere.

Tzafir, S.S., Harel, G.H., Baruch, Y. and Dolan, S.L. (2004) The consequences of emerging HRM practices for employees' trust in their managers. *Personnel Review,* 33 (6), 628–47.

Vosselman, E.G.J. (1999a) *Innovaties in Management Accounting and Control en Financiering.* Focus Conference on Management Accounting & Control, 16 March.

Vosselman, E.G.J. (1999b) *Accounting en Gedrag: Zichtbare en onzichtbare effecten van management accounting.* Deventer: Kluwer.

Vroom, V. and Yetton, P. (1993) *Leadership and Decision Making.* Pittsburgh: University of Pittsburgh Press.

Waal, A.A. de (2002) *Quest for Balance: The human element in performance management systems.* New York: Wiley.

Waal, A.A. and Counet, H. (2006) *Lessons Learned from the Balanced Scorecard: Research into problems encountered and lessons learned from implementation and use of performance management systems.* Research report, Maastricht School of Management.

Waal, A.A. de and Nhemachena, W.Z. (2005) *Building Employee Trust in Performance Management: The case of a mining company in Zimbabwe.* Paper presented at the 20th Workshop on Strategic Human Resource Management, EIASM, Brussels, 28–30 April.

11

Individual performance-driven behaviour

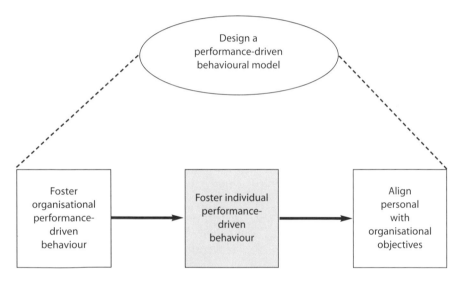

Figure 11.1 Fostering individual performance-driven behaviour

The definition of strategic performance management puts great emphasis on taking corrective actions on the basis of performance information about the execution of objectives (Figure 11.2).

If no action is taken, performance management has no consequences and this is basically of no use to an organisation. The main challenge for companies today therefore is not to have a good strategy but to make sure all organisational members work towards implementing this strategy. For an organisation to thrive, organisational members must be able to get things done, to deliver on commitments, to follow up on critical assignments, and to support and hold people accountable to their promises. Organisational members need to replace passive reporting performance measurement with

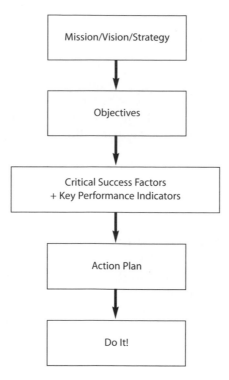

Figure 11.2 The performance management process in a nutshell

proactive, results-oriented performance management. For this, they need performance-driven behaviour. "Performance drive" is defined as a strong performance orientation of organisational members resulting in a drive for continuous improvement and better results.

In order to create an organisation with people who are passionate about performance-driven behaviour, several things must happen. Every individual needs to know "what is important" for him or her. What is the required performance expected and what actions are required to reach the goals? Individual responsibilities, targets, and incentives should be aligned with the strategic objectives of the organisation. Management should set the right example by "walking the talk," consistently delivering on what was promised. This walk the talk culture should be focused on actions and follow-up on these actions: Did they deliver the results we expected from them?

People should act on what was agreed and should display specific behaviour to make them regular users of performance management. Research shows that the combination of performance-driven behaviour and regular use of performance management leads to improved results (Lipe and Salterio, 2000; Martins, 2000; Ahn, 2001; Sandt et al., 2001; Waal, 2002). It is therefore important to establish which factors have a positive effect on performance-driven behaviour and regular use of performance management.

Chapter objectives

- ☑ To provide the reader with an insight into the behavioural aspects of performance management, and how to improve these.
- ☑ To teach the reader how to rate the performance drive of the organisation by applying the performance management analysis.
- ☑ To provide the reader with suggestions on how to foster the performance-driven behaviour of organisational members.

11.1 PERFORMANCE MANAGEMENT ANALYSIS

Special attention should be paid to the behavioural issues surrounding the use of a performance management system (Williams, 1998; Vosselman, 1999). Unfortunately, there are not many concrete examples in the literature of the importance of the human element to the use of a performance management system (Jones, 1999). A reason for this lack may be the influence of the widely adopted definition of management control by Anthony (1965). Although Anthony specifically suggested that the study of control should be broadly based in the behavioural sciences, his work showed little evidence of borrowing from behavioural sciences. Consequently, control has popularly taken on the connotation of accounting control, and the study of control systems has become overly narrow by remaining primarily focused on accounting control mechanisms (Otley, 1994; Kloot, 1997). Another reason could be that many organisations still operate using an oversimplified or incorrect model of human behaviour which has become institutionalised in certain types of measures and measurement systems.

These systems have become a signal of competent management and are so widely diffused that firms are reluctant not to follow them (Pfeffer and Sutton, 2000). Fortunately, in the recent literature many authors mention the importance of behavioural factors, and state that addressing these are crucial and beneficial for a successful implementation and use of a performance management system (Zairi, 1994; Holloway et al., 1995; Simons, 2000; Vagneur and Peiperl, 2000; Vodosek and Sutcliffe, 2000; McNamara and Mong, 2005).

Recent research identified 20 behavioural factors that have a positive influence on performance-driven behaviour (Waal, 2002). The term "behavioural factors" is used here in two senses: for activities of organisational members that can be observed, and for preconditions that allow organisational members to show certain behaviour.

The 20 behavioural factors are grouped into five categories, called "areas of attention." These are the areas to which an organisation needs to pay special attention in order to improve the use of performance management by organisational members, and foster and stimulate performance-driven behaviour (Table 11.1).

Table 11.1 Behavioural factors important for successful performance management

Areas of attention	Behavioural factors
Organisation members' understanding *Organisational members have a good understanding of the nature and goals of performance management*	1. Organisation members understand the meaning of KPIs, so they have an insight into the (possible) consequences that their actions have on the results of their KPIs. 2. Organisation members have insight into the relationship between business processes and CSFs/KPIs, so they understand that the results they achieve on their KPIs are important to the continuity of the organisation. 3. Organisation members' frames of reference contain similar KPIs, so they can compare their results with those of other members and obtain insight into how they are doing comparatively. 4. Organisation members agree on changes in the CSF/KPI set, so they keep on accepting their KPIs and keep on feeling responsible for the results they achieve on these.
Organisation members' attitude *Organisation members have a positive attitude to performance management*	5. Organisation members recognise and acknowledge the need for performance management, which makes them willing to cooperate during the implementation of performance management. 6. Organisation members agree on the starting time, which makes them willing to cooperate from the start of the implementation of performance management. 7. Organisation members have earlier positive experiences with performance management, so they can communicate the aim and goals of performance management to the organisation. 8. Organisation members realise the importance of CSFs/KPIs/BSC to their performance, so performance management becomes part of their daily activities. 9. Organisation members do not experience CSFs/KPIs/BSC as threatening, so they are not hesitant to use performance management.
Performance management alignment *Performance management matches the responsibilities of organisation members*	10. Organisation members' KPI sets are aligned with their responsibility areas, so they can be used for steering and control of those areas. 11. Organisation members can influence the KPIs assigned to them, so the acceptance and use of those KPIs is increased. 12. Organisation members prepare their own analyses, which increases acceptance of those analyses. 13. Organisation members find the quality of the analyses good, which increases the use of those analyses. 14. Organisation members can use their CSFs/KPIs/BSC for managing their employees, which increases regular use of performance management.

Table 11.1 *Continued*

Areas of attention	Behavioural factors
Organisational culture *The organisational culture is aimed at using performance management to continuously improve*	15. Organisation members' results on CSFs/KPIs/BSC are openly communicated, so everyone is aware of the status of the organisation and performance knowledge can be shared. 16. Organisation members are stimulated to improve their performance by using performance management, so they do not have to be afraid performance management will be used to punish lagging results. 17. Organisation members trust the performance information, which increases the acceptance of the information. 18. Organisation members clearly see (top) management using performance management, so they understand the importance of performance management to management and the organisation.
Performance management focus *Performance management has a clear internal management and control focus*	19. Organisation members find performance management relevant because it has a clear internal control purpose, and can therefore support their activities well. 20. Organisation members find performance management relevant because only those stakeholders' interests that are important to the organisation's success are incorporated, so performance management stays aimed at the continuity of the organisation.

A practical tool was developed on the basis of the behavioural factors mentioned in Table 11.1. This tool – performance management analysis® (PMA) – offers organisations a method to measure and evaluate their performance-driven attitude. PMA is based on the principle that the structural side and the behavioural side of an organisation need to be given equal attention to establish a performance-driven organisation. The nine dimensions of PMA (Table 11.2) have been derived from criteria mentioned in the literature as the being most important for successful performance management (Simons, 1995; Kaplan and Norton, 1996; Merchant, 1998; Neely, 1998; Lipe and Salterio, 2000; Malina and Selto, 2000; Marchand et al., 2000; Neely, 2000; Waal, 2001; Bauer et al., 2004). Dimensions of the structural side deal with the structure that needs to be implemented in order to use performance management. It usually includes CSFs, KPIs, and often a BSC. Dimensions of the behavioural side deal with organisational members and their use of the performance management system. The last column in Table 11.2 indicates where the behavioural factors mentioned in Table 11.1 fit in. Behavioural factor number 5 of Table 11.1 is not included because this factor is only relevant when it has to be decided when to commence inplementing performance management.

Appendix 1 contains the performance management analysis questionnaire, which organisations have to complete as part of the PMA. This questionnaire lists for each PMA dimension a number of criteria that managers of an organisation have to rate for their organisation on a scale of 1 to 10. "1" equates to

Table 11.2 The nine dimensions of the performance management analysis

Dimension	Side	Short description	Behavioural factors
Responsibility structure	Structural	A clear parenting style and tasks and responsibilities have been defined and these are applied consistently at all management levels.	-
Content	Structural	Organisational members use financial and nonfinancial performance information, which has a strategic focus through the use of critical success factors and key performance indicators.	-
Integrity	Structural	The performance information is reliable, timely, and consistent.	-
Manageability	Structural	Management reports and performance management systems are user-friendly, and more detailed performance information is easily accessible through information and communication technology systems.	-
Accountability	Behavioural	Organisation members feel responsible for the results of the key performance indicators of both their own responsibility areas and the whole organisation.	2, 4, 9, 10, 17, 18, 19, 20
Management style	Behavioural	Senior management is visibly involved and interested in the performance of organisation members and stimulates an improvement culture and proactive behaviour. At the same time it consistently confronts organisation members with lagging results.	8, 14, 15, 16
Action orientation	Behavioural	The performance information is integrated in the daily activities of organisation members in such a way that problems are immediately addressed and (corrective or preventive) actions are taken.	1, 7, 11
Communication	Behavioural	Communication about the results (top-down and bottom-up) takes place at regular intervals, as does the sharing of knowledge and performance information between organisational units.	3, 13
Alignment	-	Other management systems in the organisation, such as the human resources management system, are well aligned with performance management, so what is important to the organisation is regularly evaluated and rewarded.	6, 12

"very poor performance" and "10" to "very good performance." Managers have to rate each criteria twice: for the organisation's current performance and for the desired future performance of the organisation (the desired score in three years' time). After that, the average score for each dimension is calculated by dividing the total criteria scores by the number of criteria. When all respondents have completed the questionnaire, all scores are averaged for each dimension and the results are represented in a PMA radar diagram (Figure 11.3).

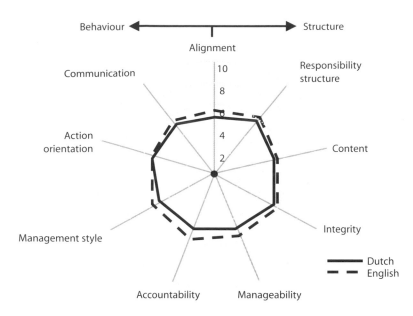

Figure 11.3 PMA radar diagram with the scores of 170 Dutch and 25 UK
organisations

The structural dimensions are shown on the right-hand side of the radar
diagram; the behavioural dimensions on the left. The radar diagram clearly
indicates which side of the diagram and thus which specific dimensions need
to be addressed to improve the organisation's performance drive (the
"dents" in the PMA diagram). It is up to the organisation to decide how
much it can and wants to improve, in order to pull up its performance to a
score of 10 (the desired score). In theory the more people fill in the questionnaire, the better the PMA diagram will reflect the actual performance
drive of the company. In practice the scores of between three to five respondents are enough to give quite an accurate picture. The PMA diagram for a
particular organisation can be compared with the diagrams in the PMA database, which contains scores for almost 600 organisations that have so far now
filled in the PMA. In this way, the performance drive of a company can be
benchmarked against that of other organisations.

Applying the PMA

The results of the first 195 organisations in the PMA database (170 Dutch
and 25 UK) have been analysed (Waal et al., 2004). The data was obtained
in the period 2002–05 from workshops organised with organisations (both
public seminars and in-house workshops) and from postgraduate students

in business administration and finance who submitted the questionnaire as part of their performance management assignment.

Statistical analysis shows that strong correlations exist between the scores on the PMA dimensions and the relative competitive performance for the organisations in the research sample. This means that a higher score on the PMA dimensions is related to better performance. It also shows that no PMA dimension is more important than any other: all dimensions have a strong relation with performance. The conclusion is that it is rewarding for an organisation not only to improve the PMA dimensions, but also to do this in a balanced way by paying equal attention to the structural and behavioural sides of performance management.

The PMA radar diagram that is based on the filled-in PMA questionnaires of both the UK and the Dutch organisations is shown in Figure 11.3.

As the radar diagram shows, UK organisations have better scores than Dutch organisations on all PMA dimensions. There could be several possible explanations for this difference in scores. First, the Dutch sample contains many more organisations than the UK sample, which can have a levelling effect on the result. Second, the majority of the UK questionnaires were completed by senior management/ director-level personnel (while the Dutch questionnaires were completed by people from all management levels), who generally score higher than people from lower management levels (Waal et al., 2004). Finally, UK organisations are known to adopt management techniques of US origin earlier and faster than other countries in Europe, leading to a longer period of experimentation and improvement, in this case with strategic performance management systems.

The research sample contained 153 private companies (144 Dutch, 9 UK) and 42 public sector and non-profit organisations (26 Dutch, 16 UK). The latter are defined as organisations that provide or support public services such as education, health, fire, police, and local and central government.

The analysis indicates that there is a significant difference between private and public organisations. Further analysis shows that this difference derives mostly from differences in the Dutch dataset.

Interestingly, the PMA scores in the UK are almost identical for private and public organisations, with the exception of the score on Alignment, where public organisations score significantly less. In the Netherlands, public organisations score significantly less on almost all dimensions than private organisations. A possible explanation for this difference between UK and Dutch public-sector organisations is that in the UK the drive for new public management over the past 20 years has lead to significant awareness of, and improvement in, strategic performance management systems. However, it could be argued that there has been a whole range of systems implemented (such as comprehensive performance assessment, the best value framework, performance assessment framework, charter mark, beacon scheme) which are basically not aligned, leading to the lower score on the Alignment dimension. However, the Dutch programme of implementing performance management in the public sector was relatively young at the time the PMA study started. The main focus of new public management in the Netherlands has been on improving the structure and content of the strategic performance management systems, but less on the management side of strategic performance management (Pollitt and Bouckaert, 2000; Radnor and McGuire, 2004; Waal and Kerklaan, 2004).

Discussion

There is a clear and strong relation between organisational performance and the attention given to performance management (in both the structural and behavioural dimensions). In the research sample, UK companies exhibit more performance-driven behaviour than Dutch companies. It is felt that this is because the UK has a longer history of implementing strategic performance management in the public sector than the Netherlands. Finally, for both UK and the Netherlands, private-sector companies have a greater alignment than public-sector companies. It could be argued that this is because the private sector has a longer history of implementing strategic performance management. Therefore companies have realised the importance of aligning all the performance management systems in the organisation, so what is critical to the organisation's success is regularly evaluated and rewarded. The study gives an interesting picture of the relation between organisational performance and performance management, and of the performance drive of Dutch and UK organisations, and consequently it can be assumed that the PMA is a good tool for organisations to self-test their performance drive.

11.2 BEHAVIOURAL IMPROVEMENTS

After an organisation has performed a PMA, it can start to make improvements. This section does not discuss how to go about strengthening the structural dimensions of performance management, because this is dealt with in the first two stages of the strategic performance management development cycle. Instead, it focuses on how the behavioural dimensions of an organisation's performance management system can be improved.

Behavioural dimension: accountability

The effectiveness of the performance management system is determined by the degree in which organisational members actually feel responsible for the results, and their willingness to use the system to obtain performance information which may help to improve the results. A noncommittal organisational climate is a real threat for the desired performance orientation of an organisation. The degree in which people feel responsible is expressly different from the degree to which they are made responsible. To stimulate feelings of responsibility, an organisation has to take two elements into consideration: *relevance of controls* and *freedom to act*.

The degree to which organisational members feel responsible for their results is connected to the relevance of the performance indicators that measure their responsibility area. The more relevant these indicators are in the opinion of the organisational members, the stronger the stimulus will be for them to get involved. For example, an operational manager will generally not be stimulated to take action when the results of the overall company are lagging. However, when it is made clear to him or her that the lagging results of his or her own unit are the cause of this, he or she will be strongly motivated to take responsibility and work on improving the results.

This shows that the defined CSFs and KPIs have to be evaluated regularly on their relevancy for control purposes, by asking the question, do they still give an accurate picture of the performance of a manager's responsibility area and its link with overall organisational performance? After all, there might have been many internal and external changes since the indicators were originally formulated, and the content of the performance information might thus no longer be representative.

Taking responsibility for results requires that organisational members are given a certain leeway so that they have the opportunity to influence their results favourably and the freedom to take action. This implies that people have to be authorised by their managers to independently and swiftly take action on problems without having to ask permission first. It also asks for the involvement of organisational members in defining the right KPIs for their responsibility areas.

Behavioural dimension: management style

A manager with an effective style is able to give an explicit steer on results while simultaneously giving support to employees to help them obtain the desired results. Steering entails making clear agreements, monitoring, discussing progress issues, and calling on the responsibility of employees. Support asks for a coaching management style that is aimed at enlarging people's insight into the possibilities for influencing their own results, and at stimulating their feelings of responsibility. When the management style is restricted to only steering, a directive style without much regard for the importance of individual responsibility will be the result. However, when the management style is limited to only supporting and coaching, decreased commitment and disorientation will be the result. The combination of result-oriented steering and coaching equals the style of "result-oriented coaching." To stimulate this management style, an organisation has to take three elements into consideration: *visible commitment, clear steering* and *support*.

Visible commitment entails that management uses the performance management system in such a way that it is clear and visible to the other members of the organisation. Visible commitment goes far beyond pronounced commitment. It is about visible behaviour and conduct with which a manager shows to employees that he or she is genuinely committed. In a formal context managers show commitment by using performance information during management team meetings and departmental meetings to discuss progress, problems, and improvements. Managers show commitment in an informal context by regularly expressing real interest in the advancements of employees and the progress of their improvement actions, and by investing time in visibly obtaining good results. The exemplary role model of management is essential. Only when management continuously shows it takes performance information seriously and bases its actions on it, will organisational members be enticed to also dedicate themselves to obtaining the desired results.

To focus the attention of organisational members completely on the desired performance, forceful steering by management is necessary. Forceful steering is characterised by setting clear goals, drafting clear improvement plans, monitoring progress in a disciplined way, and swiftly formulating additional corrective actions if necessary. To prevent a noncommittal attitude, the manager has to confront employees on lagging results and their accountability for this. In addition, managers should also notice and publicly acknowledge improvements made by their employees.

While steering is primarily focused on increasing accountability, support is aimed at stimulating the sense of individual responsibility of organisational members. Unilaterally imposing goals and targets and point-blank confronting people with lagging results will normally not stimulate and increase their sense of responsibility. The latter asks for a coaching style, aimed at letting organisational members think about their own opportunities for influencing results favourably. This entails, for instance, the involvement of members during the formulation of their goals and targets. It is of importance to entice members, during progress meetings, to think about which of their behaviours may have caused certain results and about how they themselves can improve these results. This requires questions to be phrased in a different way than the traditional rational one ('What is the reason for these bad results?") because that stimulates organisational members to look for excuses in the external environment or to shift the blame to others.

Behavioural dimension: action orientation

Action orientation is the degree in which performance information actually stimulates action to improve performance. Action orientation is a good predictor of the effectiveness with which performance management is being applied. After all, if performance information does not lead to action, the added value of this information will be nil. To stimulate action orientation, an organisation has to take three elements into consideration: *integration, corrective action management* and *preventative action management*.

Integration is the degree in which performance information is integrated into daily operational management. When there is good integration, performance information is regarded by organisational members as indispensable for their being able to do their "regular job" effectively. This means that information is the main basis for decision making. The management reporting set contains standard exception, analysis, and action reports, and is always discussed during management team meetings and departmental meetings.

Corrective action management entails organisational members taking immediate action on lagging results in order to influence these results favourably. This requires consistent and continuous transparency about how the organisation is performing, regular monitoring of progress, and a continuous analysis of how performance can be improved. In addition, it has to be clear to organisational members which corrective actions have to be taken and who is responsible for these actions. Finally, a consistent evaluation has to be made of the results of the corrective actions.

Preventative action management entails organisational members taking preventive action on an unfavourable prognosis in order to prevent problems from actually occurring. An important tool in this respect is the rolling forecast which looks four to six quarters ahead at expected results. As is the case with corrective action management, organisational members need clear insight into which preventive actions have to be taken and who is responsible for these actions. The results of the preventive actions must also be evaluated. By having a standard analysis and action reporting set at their disposal, organisational members are kept abreast of progress and the results of the preventive actions. Discussion of the rolling forecasts does not focus on the reasons for expected lagging results but on the quality of the prognosis and preventive actions and whether additional action is needed.

Behavioural dimension: communication

Effective performance management requires optimal communication about:

- the direction (strategy) of the organisation
- the boundaries between which organisational members are allowed to operate independently
- the results to be achieved
- the results that have been achieved
- the lessons learned.

Communication and alignment are needed for organisational members with the same frame of reference as for performance information, so that everybody in the organisation interprets this information in the same way. To stimulate communication, an organisation has to take three elements into consideration: *top-down communication, bottom-up communication,* and *horizontal information exchange*.

Top-down communication consists of two sub-elements: feedforward and feedback. During feedforward, top management sets a clear common direction for the company by communicating the strategy, organisational priorities, and results to be achieved. In this way, organisation members know which way the organisation is going and can experience a sense of belonging. During feedback, top management gives a clear picture to all organisational members about the overall consolidated results of the company and the results of the individual organisational units. As a result, organisation members know the status of their organisation and they can again feel committed to it.

Bottom-up communication also consists of the subelements of feedforward and feedback. During feedforward, lower organisational levels structurally provide top management with planning information, so management can base its strategy on a strong foundation. In addition, incorporating this lower-level information increases the support base for the strategy. During feedback, lower organisational levels structurally provide top management with information on the results achieved by them, so a clear picture of the company's status emerges. Both top-down and bottom-up communication requires a well-designed communication structure that is aligned with existing consultative bodies, so no inefficient overlaps occur. An important precondition for effective communication is a positive culture that is aimed not at punishing bad results but at continuous improvement. In such a culture, organisational members are most certainly confronted with their results, but in a positive way that is aimed at discussing how to improve these results.

The regular horizontal information exchange of performance information between organisational units leads to increased insight into the overall performance of the company and of the role of the unit in obtaining this result. A further exchange of information about problems, solutions, and lessons learned stimulates the overall quality of the company and fosters performance-driven behaviour. A culture is needed that not only stimulates information exchange but also rewards it.

There are several practical things that an organisation can do to foster the improvement of the behavioural factors during the implementation and use of performance management.

■ *Align communication.* Communication about performance management needs to be aligned with the values, culture, and experiences of organisation members in a specific industry or sector. For instance, in the health sector it has to be emphasised to organisation members that performance management is not a repressive tool which harshens the contact between a caregiver (doctor or nurse) and patient, but that it leads to higher-quality care. In essence, the (future) use of the performance management system is aligned with the type of organisation (lifecycle, sector, type of products and services, type of work processes, and so on) and the values of its members.

■ *Foster performance-driven thinking.* The management team is trained in how performance information can and should be used: how to interpret the data, how to analyse the results, how to develop action plans, how to monitor and evaluate actions, how to use performance information visibly in the organisation, how to safeguard the relation with the planning and control cycle, and how to create a performance management climate and etiquette within the management team. An atmosphere of "scoring off colleagues" is not conducive to an open discussion about performance information, while a climate in which making mistakes and experimenting is allowed is beneficial for obtaining improvements. In essence, the management learns to work in a different way with performance information.

■ *Foster performance-driven behaviour.* Managers discuss with organisational members how a system for result-oriented coaching can be designed: how to make result-oriented agreements, how to set targets for performance indicators, how to confront an employee with (lagging) results, how to coach, and how to strive for continuous improvement. A new way of asking questions is also discussed. What is the problem at hand? What have you done to try to solve this problem? How can I help you with this? This way managers learn to conduct a new type of performance review with their reports.

■ *Review relevance of information.* To assure that the performance management system supplies the right performance information, every organisational member is individually asked the following. What is the person responsible for? What work does the person perform? What are the most important processes in the person's responsibility areas? On whom is the person dependent in order to obtain good results? What authority does the person currently have? Do the current CSFs and KPIs measure the responsibility area adequately? Are there differences between the person's indicators and those of higher levels, and if not, is this is a problem?

  In addition, it is checked whether the organisation members have adequate resources and tools to react on the performance information. The link between objectives and resources is introduced explicitly during the making of result-oriented agreements. In essence, it is evaluated whether the current set of performance information is still relevant for managing the company, and whether its organisation members can actually steer on the basis of this information.

■ *Align all systems.* The aim is to ensure that what the organisation finds important, which is formulated in the strategy and the accompanying CSFs and KPIs, is mirrored in the educational programmes ("Are we teaching organisation members to work on those things that are important to us, and do we give them adequate support in doing this?") and the evaluation and reward systems ("Do we explicitly look at the results of the performance indicators and do these results determine – at least partly – the nature of the evaluation and the level of reward?"). In this way, all management systems within the company are aligned so that they support the organisation in reaching its goals optimally.

■ *Foster performance-driven values.* Organisation members discuss which values should apply within the organisation to make performance management a success. For example, mistakes are allowed; risks can be taken; there is complete transparency of results; there is a delegating management style which encourages self-management and taking responsibility; there is a duty for employees to report deviations to management as soon as possible; there is a focus on performance and continuous improvement; there is focus on knowledge transfer within the company. In essence, organisational members learn a new way of working and interacting with each other.

■ *Focus on sense-giving.* Because performance indicators, as the term already indicates, just give an indication of the performance without necessarily explaining the performance, and because KPIs are just a reflection of reality and nothing more, organisation members should not focus on the absolute outcomes of the KPIs. They need to concentrate on "the story behind the figures." In other words, the figures should always be accompanied by an interpretation of what they mean, or could mean. During performance reviews the discussion should be about this interpretation, and the actions that have to be taken when there is agreement on the interpretation. This prevents jumping to conclusions: the figures are merely the starting point of the discussion, not the end point.

■ *Limit the number of KPI functions.* The more functions a performance indicator has to fulfil, and the more interested parties there are who want to use this KPI, the greater the chance that perverse effects will occur. There is a serious risk of a KPI becoming more ambiguous because too much information has been crammed into it and because each stakeholder gives his or her own interpretation of the KPI result. KPIs might also be used for a goal that was not intended. Instead of being used for self-control they could be applied for justification to higher management levels or external stakeholders. There should be univocal agreement on the purpose of each individual KPI and on which interested party is supported by the KPI in question. These agreements cannot be changed without a consensus among all parties involved.

■ *Selection and limitation.* Striving for completeness in which all processes and products of the organisation are included in the performance management system, is not cost-effective and will inevitably lead to indicator overload and thereby information overload. This in turn will make it difficult for organisational members to discern between important and unimportant information, resulting in demotivation and abandonment of the system. Intelligent selection of KPIs, based on the real CSFs of the business, makes it possible to monitor organisational performance in a cost-effective and efficient way. Organisation members need to keep in mind that the selected set gives a less comprehensive view of the company than a complete set would, making the focus on sense-giving even more important.

11.3 CASE: PMA AT THE CITY OF GROW

(This case is based on Waal and Gerritsen-Medema, 2006.)

The city of GReater grOWth (GROW), a medium-sized municipality situated in the middle of the country, is a city on the move. Established three decades ago, it currently has over 100,000 inhabitants and 42,000 jobs. The city council has set itself two goals for 2010: 140,000 inhabitants and a total of 75,000 jobs. With this kind of growth there will be an increased demand on multiple facilities like housing construction, living environment, shopping facilities, infrastructure, and industrial estates. Council officials have therefore decided to concentrate on four themes:

- living, mobility, safety, health, and sustainability
- social independence
- a minimum standard of living
- multiform educational and cultural development.

GROW's civil service, employing 1000 people, consists of six sectors (City Works, City Development, Construction & Environment, Society, Social Affairs, and Business Support) and two staff departments (Communication and Corporate Staff). The directors of the sectors and the city manager constitute the management team, responsible for the execution of policies. Part of this responsibility consists of preparing and guiding the policy decision process through the city council. The city manager is chair of the municipal authority and therefore in charge of the local government officials. The sector directors are responsible for executing accepted policies in their own sectors.

In the current performance management system the emphasis is on financial data. There is little information on results and effects because the current system cannot provide this. The organisation has difficulty making accurate forecasts and confronting people with results. Bad performance and pessimistic forecasts do not automatically have consequences. All employees have an annual evaluation and performance interview. However, producing accountability for results achieved (achievement of policy goals and usage of resources) is a ponderous process. This is partly because most politicians tend to look to the future rather than to the past, so they generally take no real interest in whether results are being achieved or not.

Applying the PMA

The controller of corporate staff performed the PMA at the city of GROW, mainly within the Corporate Staff department. This department was established in 2000 with the aim of improving resource policy and management. It required a new way of managing and steering, consisting of collegiate management, integral management, and a strict focus on management control. Corporate Staff supported the city council especially in management control matters. Because the municipality was at the time undertaking two major improvement projects in the area of performance management, the organisation was interested in participating in the study to find out whether additional efforts were needed to improve its performance drive. The PMA was filled in by two management team members, the corporate controller, and five employees of the Corporate Staff department. The resulting PMA radar diagram and the averaged scores are given in Figure 11.4 and Table 11.3.

In Figure 11.4 the current and the desired scores both form almost perfect circles, which indicates that GROW divided its attention just about equally over the structural and behavioural dimensions of performance management. At the same time, the average score for all dimensions in the current situation is 3.5 which (on a scale of 1 to 10) indicates that the respondents regard the use of performance management in their city service as insufficient. It should be improved to an average of 7.5.

Looking at the standard deviations, it becomes apparent that especially for the current situation, the respondents differ in their opinion. An explanation

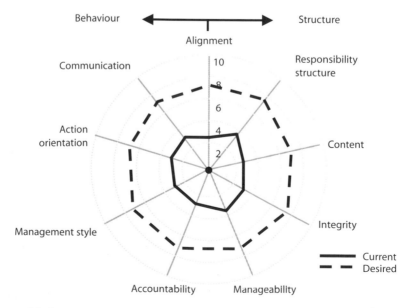

Figure 11.4 PMA radar diagram with the scores of the city of GROW

Table 11.3 PMA scores of the city of GROW (including standard deviations)

	Responsibility structure	Content	Integrity	Manageability	Accountability	Management style	Action orientation	Communication	Alignment	Average
Current	4.0	3.1	3.6	4.0	3.5	3.5	3.5	3.6	2.9	3.5
Std. dev.	1.5	0.8	1.0	1.0	0.8	1.2	0.9	1.2	1.1	
Desired	7.8	7.5	7.9	7.5	7.6	7.6	7.2	7.6	7.1	7.5
Std. dev.	0.7	1.1	0.8	0.8	0.7	1.1	0.7	0.7	1.0	

could be that because of the rapid growth of the municipality and the recent establishment of the Corporate Staff department, there has not been enough time for the managers to structurally discuss the quality of the current performance management system. The next four subsections discuss those dimensions of the GROW PMA radar diagram that have a current score substantially higher or lower than the average of 3.5. These dimensions are responsibility structure, content, manageability, and alignment.

Responsibility structure

The score on responsibility structure is higher than the average score. Shortly after the arrival of the new city manager in 2000, a programme called "Manifest Integral Management" was started. The focus of this programme was to make sector directors fully accountable for policy execution, required resources, and results. This was intended to increase the feeling of responsibility for the organisation's performance throughout the municipality. The programme was the start of a continuous improvement process which entailed a transition from a sector model with six directors to a director model with three directors. This effort was called "Leadership with Guts" and aimed to:

- improve integration between policy making and execution
- make tasks and responsibilities clearer
- increase accountability
- improve customer orientation
- increase the quality of management and employees
- improve communication across the organisation.

The improvement programmes have created renewed interest in and focus on the responsibility structure of GROW's civil service. Yet several managers who participated in the PMA mentioned that the right tools to fully implement integral management were still not available, and that the organisation showed a lack of "integral thinking." Many managers focused predominantly on the results of their own responsibility area ("functional thinking") instead of those of the organisation as a whole. In addition, the management team made too many ad hoc decisions, under the pressure of day-to-day operations.

Content

In the PMA, the city of GROW scored slightly below the average with respect to content. A possible explanation is the "functional thinking" mentioned earlier, which is prevalent in the organisation. In functional thinking, organisational performance is of secondary importance and as a consequence management reports usually include little strategic information. In addition, there is insufficient strategic alignment between the management reporting sets of the various organisational units. Another issue is that city council members were uncertain about their strategic priorities for the city, which made it difficult for the civil servants to anticipate developments and adapt the performance management system accordingly. As a result, GROW's management information had low added value.

Manageability

The municipality had a management information tool at its disposal that allowed financial analyses from different angles. The drill-down function of this tool helped to provide more detailed information quickly. Many civil servants, including financial specialists and general managers, have been trained in using this tool, so many people within the organisation were able to use it. This explains why the score for manageability is above the average current score.

Alignment

At GROW, performance information was hardly ever used for evaluating employees. There certainly was not a culture of "settling scores," and people were seldom "officially" held accountable for their performance. This basically is characteristic of the culture in many municipalities. It is reinforced by the fact that the reward structure of (local) government is often still based on the length of service and on earned rights, and not on achieved results. To improve its alignment, GROW had started, in one sector, a pilot called "Competences and Personal Development Plans" (PDP). This pilot focused on the career and development of individual employees. How was the employee to develop, which ambitions did he or she have, and what training was he or she interested in? The pilot's goal is to connect result-oriented agreements to employees' PDPs, so that agreements can be made with individual employees about the results they have to achieve in the next period. If this pilot turns out to be a success, GROW intends to implement PDPs across the entire organisation.

Improvement projects related to the PMA results

At the time of the PMA, the city of GROW had two major improvement projects up and running: "Leadership with Guts" and "Competences and Personal Development Plans." These were important because they addressed several of the areas that showed up as dimensions needing improvement in the PMA radar diagram (Table 11.4).

However, to balance the structural and behavioural sides of performance management, GROW has to make sure that additional projects are initiated for those dimensions of the PMA that are not covered by improvement projects. Consequently, a project is proposed called "GROW, Performance-Driven," which covers both the structural side of performance management and action orientation. The project goal is to introduce performance indicators that can help to actively monitor the municipal's programme budget. The introduction of the concept of dualisation several years ago, which separated execution of policies from control of execution, increased interest in the set-up and results of the programme budget. A programme budget is a coherent set of products, activities, and resources aimed at achieving specific, agreed-upon social outcomes. Questions in relation to the programme budget are:

- What do we want to achieve (which effects and results)?
- What do we need to do for that (which products and services)?
- What are the costs?

Table 11.4 Comparison of the PMA and GROW's running improvement projects

Type	PMA dimension	Improvement project
Structural	Responsibility structure	Leadership with Guts
	Content	
	Integrity	
	Manageability	
Behavioural	Accountability	Leadership with Guts
	Management style	Leadership with Guts
	Action orientation	
	Communication	Leadership with Guts
	Alignment	Competences and Personal Development Plans

Objective: Make GROW an attractive city to live in

Critical success factor: A clean city
Key performance indicator 1: Complaints of citizens about city cleanliness
Key performance indicator 2: Average number of sweeps per year

---

Figure 11.5 Example of a possible critical success factor for GROW, and its accompanying key performance indicators

- Have we achieved what we wanted to achieve?
- Have we done what we said we would do?
- Have the costs been what we thought they would be?

CSFs and KPIs are an effective tool to answer these questions. Figure 11.5 gives an example.

By converting the programme budget into concrete and tangible objectives and translating them at all organisational levels into CSFs and KPIs, GROW will increase the strategic relevance of its performance management system. If GROW additionally develops a method to obtain reliable data for measuring the KPIs, using the existing management information system, it will also improve the structural PMA dimensions of content, integrity, and manageability. To make sure that sectors and departments focus on executing policies effectively and efficiently, performance alignment is of crucial importance. It can be achieved by translating the municipality's strategic objectives, CSFs, and KPIs into sector and department objectives, CSFs, and KPIs (Figure 11.6). A clear focus by all organisational levels will have a positive influence on action orientation.

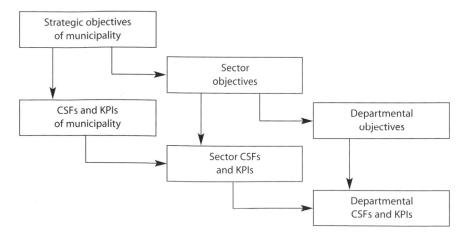

Figure 11.6 Strategic alignment in the municipality

Implementation and preconditions

To make sure that the "GROW, Performance-Driven" project will be executed in an efficient manner, the city of GROW formulated a high-level activities plan (Table 11.5).

There are several conditions that GROW has to fulfil to make the project a success. First, the city council has to commit itself to clearly formulating priorities and goals, including its expectations of the civil service, and to introducing and using performance management. Second, the management team of the municipality has to be totally committed to improving the PMA dimensions. The sector directors have to take the lead in developing and using CSFs and KPIs in their accountability areas, for instance by providing resources for the project, even if this means cutting other projects, and training people how to use the system. Management team members have to serve as the role model for others in the organisation: they have to visibly use the improved performance management system and give staff freedom in their use of performance management.

Table 11.5 Activities plan of the "GROW, Performance-Driven" project

Phase	Activities
1. Preparation	■ Set project goal ■ Formulate project plan ■ Establish project organisation/team
2. Analysis	■ Analyse current strategic documents (council programmes, programme budgets etc.) ■ Analyse current performance information (statistics, indicators, surveys, complaints etc.) ■ Formulate and streamline strategic objectives
3. MT workshop	■ Discuss results of the analysis ■ Prepare council workshop
4. First Council workshop	■ Discuss strategic objectives ■ Develop strategic CSFs and KPIs
5. Deepening	■ Translate strategic objectives into sector and department objectives, CSFs and KPIs ■ Formulate definitions for all developed KPIs
6. Second Council workshop	■ Agree on definitions ■ Determine targets for strategic KPIs ■ Determine targets for sector and department KPIs
7. Performance alignment	■ Update planning and control cycle ■ Draw up guidelines for review meetings on all levels ■ Draw up guidelines for performance-driven behaviour

The last few years have been hectic for the city of GROW as it has had many different projects running at the same time. This has forced the city council and council officials to review all projects and set priorities. It was decided to first finalise a limited number of programmes, as a result of which several projects were either combined or deleted. The PMA analysis confirmed that GROW was on the right track with some of its projects. In addition, it showed that GROW had to expand its activities to improve the performance management system in order to make optimal use of it. The results of the PMA analysis gave the municipality a clear indication of how to proceed, and consequently the "GROW, Performance-Driven" project has been scheduled for the following year.

11.4 CASE: PMA AT LABOUR REINTEGRATION COMPANY HOOS

Labour reintegration company Hands Out Of the Sleeves (HOOS) has two main tasks: to counsel employees who are in danger of dropping out or have already dropped out of the work process, to go back to their old workplace, or to a different workplace of their former employer or of a new employer; and to counsel employees with an unemployment allowance to help them get a regular job on the job market. The tools HOOS has at its disposal are job market planning schemes, to identify possible placements at the corporate clients; offering specialised reintegration training courses to employees; and supervision and coaching of these clients.

The labour reintegration market used to be a regulated market with a few specialised companies authorised by the government to offer reintegration services. A few years back, the reintegration market was privatised and a lot of competitors have appeared on the market lately. This increases the pressure on HOOS to become a performance-driven organisation.

HOOS has performed quite well over the past years. It has grown from one branch with 11 employees to a head office and ten branches with 125 employees. The branches are geographically dispersed across the country, and each is led by a branch manager. The management team consists of three people with the support of a staff bureau. The company is particularly good at acquiring new commissions, by offering a competitive price to its corporate clients, and in the coaching of employees joining new workplaces. However, it takes too long before a new client is taken on for the reintegration process. This is caused by unrealistic work planning for HOOS' employees, and unclear tasks and responsibilities in the organisation.

Because of the rapid growth of HOOS, its employees have not kept up with the new procedures and work processes that have been introduced to cope with this growth. They are also starting to lose touch with corporate clients because they are overworked. In addition, management does not receive the right performance information to base its decisions and actions on. The unbalanced PMA, filled in by the management team and several branch managers, depicts the problematic situation of HOOS (Figure 11.7).

Because of the strong internal growth and the changes in the external environment, HOOS has become an organisation in transition. This becomes apparent when looking at the mixed parenting style of the company (Table 11.6). The arrows in the table show the changes in the parenting style, which is going from strategic planning to strategic control. Because of this mixed parenting style, which can cause a lot of confusion in the company, HOOS scores very low on the PMA dimension "responsibility structure." Looking in more detail at this dimension, it turns out that management team members hardly issue strategic guidelines, so organisation members do not have a clue what they can and cannot do in their work. Most management team members have been working at HOOS from its inception, and have experienced the growth of the business without adapting their personal management style.

The management reports are mainly financial: nonfinancial information is missing or is provided in an ad hoc manner. There is a great need in the company for this type of information, but the current ICT systems are not designed to provide it. There is no exception reporting. Ironically, this does not cause such a problem because the branches get their own information anyway, but they do not see the results from the other branches or from HOOS in total. The execution of the strategy is hardly monitored on branch level because CSFs and KPIs have not been defined. The branches do not

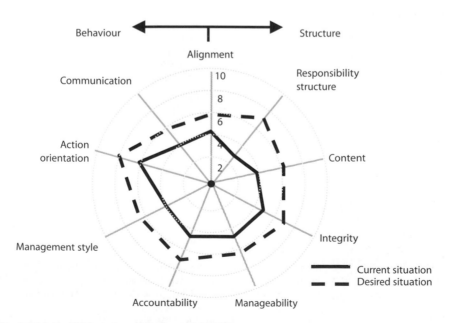

Figure 11.7 PMA radar diagram of HOOS

Table 11.6 HOOS' mixed parenting style

Definition		Strategic planning		Strategic control		Financial control
Type of industry	✓	Rapidly changing, fast-growing or ←— fiercely competitive industries	✓	Mature industries and stable competitive situations		Wide variety of industries
Parent role	✓	Closely involved with business unit in formulation of plans and decisions. Clear sense of direction. —→	✓	Planning decentralised to business units. Parent role is checking, assessing, and sponsoring.		Insists that all decisions are 'owned' by the business units themselves
Business role	✓	Seeks consensus with head-quarters and other units for business initiatives (in line with —→ strategic targets)	✓	Own responsibility for strategies, plans, and proposals		Independent entities, sometimes working together to achieve mutual benefits
Organisational structure	✓	Large or powerful functional staffs at centre. Shared service departments (marketing, R&D, etc.).		Decentralised with focus on individual business unit's performance. Headquarters operates as strategic controller.		Minimal staff at the headquarters level, focused on support and financial control.
Planning process		Resource allocation driven by requirements of long-term strategies. Planning influence of headquarters is high.	✓	Negotiation of financial and strategic performance targets. Planning influence of headquarters is medium.		No formal strategic planning, process focuses on business unit annual budget and financial targets. Planning influence of headquarters is low.
Control process	✓	Low priority on monitoring monthly financial results. Control by headquarters is flexible. —→	✓	Regular monitoring of actuals against planned, on financial and nonfinancial targets. Control by headquarters is strategic.	✓	Concentrates on financial targets and results (contracting). Control by headquarters is strictly financial.
Value creation focus	✓	Creation of new business units for long-term business development.		Long-term strategies and goals of the business units (facilitating + coordinating).		Operating improvements and financial control.

know how they can contribute to achieving the strategy, which is relatively unknown anyway. During budgeting a lot of negotiating takes place but in the end the management team forces targets onto the branches, which is demotivating for the branch managers because they feel they are stuck with an unrealistic budget.

The management reports are hardly used by both the management team and the branch managers for steering and decision making. Decisions are often taken on "gut feeling." Managers do not know, because of the unclear responsibility structure, for which (financial) indicators they are responsible. They do not feel truly accountable for the results of their branch, let alone the total HOOS result. In the organisation there is not a culture of "a deal is a deal." This is partly caused by the fact that managers are not held accountable when results are lagging. However, employees are held accountable in a rather harsh but inconsistent manner, and these employees do not get structural coaching and support. There is no real drive in the company for continuous improvement. Communication is one-way and there is no knowledge sharing between branches, or between branches and head office.

The management team of HOOS reacts in a shocked manner to the PMA results. It realises that the rapid growth of the company had caused more problems than managers were aware of, or had realised. It is clear to them that the quality of the management process has not received enough attention in the past years. The PMA radar diagram gives them the starting points to get into gear. In mutual deliberation with the branch managers it is decided to attack the most important dent in the diagram, that of "responsibility structure," and then to start working on improving the other dimensions. The following actions are decided:

■ Make a clear choice for an unambiguous parenting style, "strategic control." On the basis of this choice, the tasks, responsibilities, and authorities of both the management team and the branch managers are to be reviewed and redefined.

■ On the basis of the parenting style, the information needs of every management level are to be redefined. Nonfinancial information will become an important part of the new management reports. Communication structures and meetings will be centred around the new reports.

■ Performance-driven values will be defined for HOOS. Coaching and support of employees by managers will get a prominent place in these values.

Management of HOOS realises the company still has a long way to go before it will be in the desired situation, as depicted in HOOS' radar diagram. However, it also realises the company does not really have a choice: to survive in the increasingly competitive reintegration market HOOS has to become more performance-driven.

11.5 CASE STUDY: PMA AT A TEMPING AGENCY IN THE NETHERLANDS

As described in Chapter 10, two years ago Temping Agency Netherlands (TAN) went through a reorganisation during which new structures, tasks and responsibilities were introduced and a new performance management system was implemented. After the reorganisation, the chief executive officer asked herself whether the employees had indeed become more performance-driven. The answer was very important under the then current adverse economic conditions, in which temp agencies were confronted with increased competition and a resulting downward pressure on prices. The CEO decided to carry out a performance management analysis (PMA) to obtain the answer to her question.

A one-day workshop was organised during which all managers of TAN's business units filled in the PMA individually. The combined scores of all managers were averaged and included in a radar diagram, which was then discussed extensively by the participants. In addition, individual radar diagrams were drawn up for each business unit. Figure 11.8 shows the radar diagram for the North-East business unit. During the discussion, special attention was paid to possible improvements for the "dents" in the various diagrams, how these improvements could be implemented, and what the barriers were to implementation. Several concrete improvement projects were to originate from this discussion.

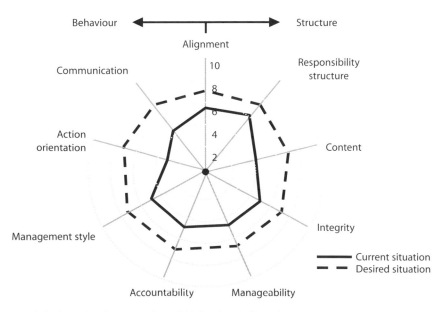

Figure 11.8 Result of the PMA at TAN's North-East business unit

Case question 1: What are the strong and weak dimensions of performance-driven behaviour at TAN's North-East business unit? How can the weak dimensions be improved (while maintaining the strong dimensions)? How will improving one dimension affect the other dimensions?

Case question 2: How should the improvement project be approached and executed? What are barriers the business unit manager could encounter during the project and how should he deal with these?

After a year, the CEO decided to organise another workshop with all business unit managers. She was anxious to know whether the various improvement projects, undertaken throughout the past year, had had any effect on the PMA scores.

A lot of time at the business units had been taken up by a particular Work Flow project. The goal of this project was to standardise the primary operational processes that took place in every business unit, such as registration of potential temporary workers, registration of potential clients (employers for the temp workers), payment of salaries to temp workers, invoicing to clients, client relationship management, and human resource activities at the unit. The North-East business unit had started several improvement projects to pep up the behavioural side of performance management, but these were basically stopped when the Workflow Project kicked into gear. Figure 11.9 shows the radar diagram for the North-East business unit that was composed during the second PMA workshop.

To the surprise of both the CEO and the North-East business unit manager, the radar diagram for the North-East unit only showed marginal

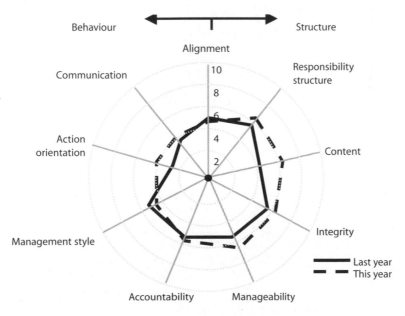

Figure 11.9 Result of the second PMA at TAN's North-East business unit

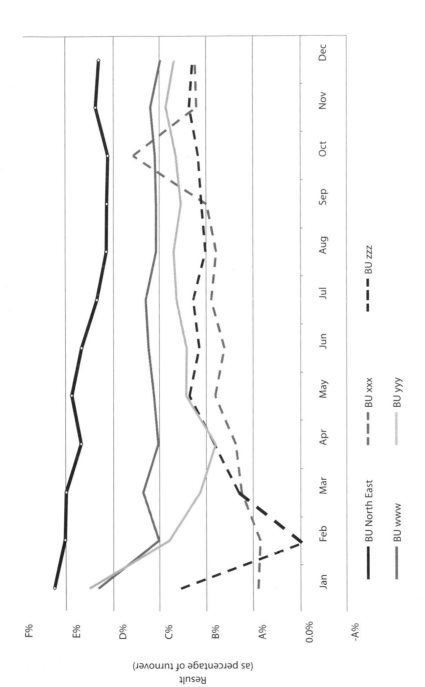

Figure 11.10 Financial results of TAN's business units during the past year

improvement on the behavioural side, more specifically for the PMA dimension action orientation, and much more improvement on the structural side, for all PMA dimensions. Their astonishment became even larger when they looked at the performance of the North-East business unit compared with the other business units during the previous year (Figure 11.10). Although North-East was still performing above the other business units, its results were steadily declining while the results of the other business units had improved to a certain level, after which they tailed off.

Case question 3: How can the second radar diagram and the declining results from the North-East business unit be explained? What should the business unit manager do this coming year?

11.6 CASE STUDY: UVD'S PERFORMANCE-DRIVEN BEHAVIOUR

UVD has now been working for almost two years with the new performance management system. Considerable progress has been made and results have steadily improved, but something is still bothering the Williams brothers. They have the feeling UVD could get more benefit from the new system, but they are not quite sure how to achieve the extra yield. Change the organisational structure? Focus more on behaviour? Do both? At long last they decide to call in Pete Fields to ask him to conduct a short investigation to come up with findings about the performance drive of UVD's employees.

Pete spends several days interviewing managers and employees, and accompanying various people during their shifts. After this, he writes a memo which concentrates on the issues that affect the performance-driven behaviour of the UVD organisation members.

Case question: After reviewing the findings of Pete Fields, what are the possibilities for improving the performance-driven behaviour of UVD's organisation members? Come up with practical suggestions.

Memo from Pete Fields

General observation
- All UVD's personnel demonstrate great commitment and dedication to the company. A lot of hard work has been put in to produce the best quality products possible. People are really worried when something does not go according to plan or expectation. Employees are very willing to "go the extra mile" and to put in overtime or to stand in for someone else. They also conscientiously fill in the data sheets needed for the calculation of the KPIs.

Management team

- The management team should by now have set the example by really using the CSFs and KPIs. However, it has been nice words and inconsistent behaviour. There are hardly any management team meetings to discuss results. The management team does not operate as a real team.
- Too many times good ideas from employees for improving the nonfinancial KPIs have been brushed aside by the CEO. People feel that "their heads are being chopped off" as soon as they dare to come up with an idea the management team does not like. This fosters an environment in which people always have an easy excuse: "John/Gary/Martin didn't want it."
- A rift is starting to appear in the management team, with Gary wanting to improve results by carrying out another restructuring, while Martin first wants to empower people more so they can improve their own results.
- John as CEO is still too much involved in day-to-day operations. The American part of the business in particular gets a lot of his attention. This seems to be demotivating for Jack Coopers, the general manager USA. John also seems to have already moved on to his next project, setting up a warehouse in the United States.
- John should be talking more about achieving the strategic objectives of UVD, but he keeps on discussing resources and absolute figures. Efficiency in the production process has become increasingly important for him. Other people are staring to worry that this will be detrimental to quality.
- People are still not held consistently accountable by the management team for their performance. At the same time, John wants to, as he puts it, "settle the score" with them at the end of the year. Martin keeps objecting that this is not possible when the management team have not sat down with managers, at least once a quarter, to discuss their performance and the expectations the management team has of them.
- A direct quote from an (unnamed) organisational member says it all: "If nothing changes within the management team, UVD will keep on drifting!"

Quality

- The KPIs for quality have not been implemented so the reports mainly consist of production indicators. The unique selling point of UVD, the quality of its products and processes, is coming under threat. In the continuous tension between efficiency and quality it seems quality comes off worst. It also seems that the management team takes quality less seriously.

Procurement

■ During an internal client satisfaction meeting, the Procurement Department received a grade of 4 on a scale of 1 to 10 from the Production Department. The head of procurement, John Smith, has still not reacted to this bad grade. When questioned about this, John said that he had asked the Production Department several times for a meeting but that they were too busy. After inquiry it turned out he had send the Production Department one e-mail.

Production

■ It is conspicuous that there are not many managers to be found on the production floor. The manufacturing manager Mick Jones and the warehouse manager Lee Brown, and their supervisors, excel in non-attendance. It seems much of their time is taken up with all kinds of meetings.

■ There are no billboards with the results of the production KPIs to be found on the shop floor, although this was agreed upon several months ago. People on the production lines do not know exactly how much they have to do, how they are doing, and how they did on the last shift.

Management style

■ Priorities are insufficiently set. The number of points on the "action to do list" has increased alarmingly. There are so many actions it is not possible to keep track of them all. As a result there are many actions "out there" without any kind of control.

■ Coaching is not a strong point of UVD's managers. If you start working at UVD, you get a short introduction and then you are basically left on your own to find your way around. People find what they can and cannot do by experience when they are criticized by their superiors.

■ The feedback loop is not closed at UVD. A lot is being measured and reported but hardly discussed. This starts at the top, but also at the various meetings on lower levels the CSFs and KPIs undoubtedly receive insufficient attention. Action points stay forever on the action lists. Nobody discusses what they have learned from certain actions. No knowledge is shared between the departments or between the organisational levels.

■ People have a tendency to tell others, especially their superiors, what they did and what they are going to do, but they do not say anything about what they have actually achieved. If they are questioned on this, which does not happen very often, the usual response is, "Everything is fine, nothing special to report." At the end of the quarter, however, it turns out that a lot of objectives and targets have not been achieved. It is then difficult to find out the causes for this and the people responsible, especially because responsibilities are still unclear in the company.

■ During meetings there is great relief when somebody owns up to having not done an agreed action. People are glad somebody else came up short so their own shortcomings are not that conspicuous.

■ Actions are being agreed upon but without 1) setting the priority, 2) deciding whether there is time to do the action, and 3) discussing what other action or activity has to be stopped in order to create room for this new action. Many planned actions therefore never happen.

Culture

■ People do not have the feeling they are running their own shop. Superiors, starting from the management team, are interfering so much with the day-to-day operations that people never get the feeling they are responsible for their own part of the company. They are also insufficiently involved in setting objectives and targets for their own responsibility area. As a result, when something goes wrong, there is a tendency of saying, "Let's wait to see what the management team wants us to do."

■ There are a lot of meetings which radiate a feeling of powerlessness. There is a lot of uttering phrases like "We should do something about that," "We should take a decision on that," "Let's first study it a bit more," "Let's set-up a task force," and so on. However, nothing really is being decided, so small problems tend to become serious issues.

Communication

■ Communication within UVD is not very efficient. A lot is communicated in a one-way manner, and there are many meetings where not enough dialogue takes place.

■ There is so much e-mail traffic that managers spend too much time behind their computer and not enough time in their department, managing their people. Also, important e-mails get lost in the heap because of the culture of putting everybody on the cc-list ("Just in case, now they can't say I didn't inform them"). There is no control by the sender whether the intended receiver actually did receive the message, let alone whether the receiver has the same understanding about the message as the sender has.

■ Much time during meetings is lost because the meaning of figures and graphs has to be explained every time. This has to do with: 1) people not being trained enough in the new reports, 2) not enough use of clear graphs, 3) no use of analyses and comparisons, and 4) no keys to the graphs in the reports.

Key points

☑ For an organisation to thrive, organisational members must be able to get things done, to deliver on commitments, to follow up on critical assignments, and to support and hold people accountable for their promises.

☑ Organisational members need to replace passive reporting performance *measurement* with proactive, results-oriented performance *management*. For this, they need performance-driven behaviour.

☑ "Performance drive" is defined as a strong performance orientation of organisational members resulting in a drive for continuous improvement and better results.

☑ The combination of performance-driven behaviour and regular use of performance management leads to improved organisational results.

☑ Special attention should be paid to improving the behavioural issues surrounding the use of a performance management system: accountability, management style, action orientation, and communication.

References

Ahn, H. (2001) Applying the balanced scorecard concept: an experience report. *Long Range Planning*, 34, 441–61.

Anthony, R.N. (1965) *Planning and Control Systems: A framework for analysis*. Boston, Mass.: Harvard Business School Press.

Bauer, J., Tanner, S.J. and Neely, A. (2004) Benchmarking performance measurement, a consortium benchmarking study. In: A. Neely, M. Kennerly and A. Waters (eds), *Performance Measurement and Management: Public and private*. Cranfield, UK: Centre for Business Performance, Cranfield University, 1021–28.

Holloway, J., Lewis, J. and Mallory, G. (eds) (1995) *Performance Measurement and Evaluation*. London: Sage.

Jones, N. (1999) *Performance Management in the Twenty-first Century: Solutions for business, education and family*. Boca Raton: St Lucie Press.

Kaplan, R.S. and Norton, D.P. (1996) *The Balanced Scorecard: Translating strategy into action*. Boston, Mass.: Harvard Business School Press.

Kloot, L. (1997) Organisational learning and management control systems: responding to environmental change. *Management Accounting Research*, 8, 47–73.

Lipe, M.G. and Salterio, S.E. (2000) The balanced scorecard: judgmental effects of common and unique performance measures. *Accounting Review*, 75 (3), 283–98.

Malina, M.A. and Selto, F.M. (2000) *Communicating and Controlling Strategy: An empirical study of the effectiveness of the balanced scorecard*. Paper presented at the AAA Annual Conference, Philadelphia, 13–16 August.

Marchand, D.A., Davenport, T.H. and Dickson, T. (2000) (ed) *Mastering Information*

Management: Complete MBA companion in information management. Harlow: Prentice Hall Financial Times.

Martins, R.A. (2000) Use of performance measurement systems: some thoughts towards a comprehensive approach. In: A. Neely (ed.), *Performance Measurement: Past, present, and future*. Cranfield, UK: Centre for Business Performance, Cranfield University, 363–70.

McNamara, C. and Mong, S. (2005) Performance measurement and management: some insights from practice. *Australian Accounting Review*, 15 (1), 14–15.

Merchant, K.A. (1998) *Modern Management Control Systems: Text and cases*. Upper Saddle River, NJ: Prentice Hall.

Neely, A. (1998) *Measuring Business Performance: Why, what and how*. London: Economist Books.

Neely, A. (2000) (ed) *Performance Measurement: Past, present, and future*. Cranfield, UK; Centre for Business Performance, Cranfield University.

Otley, D. (1994) Management control in contemporary organisations: towards a wider framework. *Management Accounting Research*, 5, 289–99.

Pfeffer, J. and Sutton, R.I. (2000) *The Knowing–Doing Gap: How smart companies turn knowledge into action*. Boston, Mass.: Harvard Business School Press.

Pollitt, C. and Bouckaert, G. (2000) *Public Management Reform: A comparative analysis*. Oxford: Oxford University Press.

Radnor, Z.J. and McGuire, M. (2004) Performance management in the public sector: fact or fiction? *International Journal of Productivity and Performance Management*, 3 (53).

Sandt, J., Schaeffer, U. and Weber, J. (2001) *Balanced Performance Measurement Systems and Manager Satisfaction*. Otto Beisheim Graduate School of Management.

Simons, R. (1995) *Levers of Control: How managers use innovative control systems to drive strategic renewal*. Boston, Mass.: Harvard Business School Press.

Simons, R. (2000) *Performance Measurement and Control Systems for Implementing Strategy: Text and cases*. Upper Saddle River, NJ: Prentice Hall.

Vagneur, K. and Peiperl, M. (2000) Reconsidering performance evaluative style. *Accounting, Organisations and Society*, 25, 511–25.

Vodosek, M. and Sutcliffe, K.M. (2000) Overemphasis on analysis: decision-making dilemmas in the age of speed. In: R.E. Quinn, R.M. O'Neill and L. St Clair (eds), *Pressing Problems in Modern Organisations (That Keep us up at Night)*. New York: Amacom.

Vosselman, E.G.J. (1999) *Accounting en gedrag: Zichtbare en onzichtbare effecten van management accounting*. Deventer: Kluwer.

Waal, A.A. de (2002) *Quest for Balance: The human element in performance management systems*. New York: Wiley.

Waal, A.A. de (2002) *The Role of Behavioural Factors in the Successful Implementation and use of Performance Management Systems*. PhD dissertation, Vrije Universiteit Amsterdam.

Waal, A.A. de (2001) *Power of Performance Management: How leading companies create sustained value*. New York: Wiley.

Waal, A.A. de and Gerritsen-Medema, G. (2006) Performance management analysis: a case study at a Dutch municipality. *International Journal of Productivity and Performance Management*.

Waal, A.A. de and Kerklaan, L.F.G.H. (2004) *De resultaatgerichte overheid*. The Hague: SDU.

Waal, A.A. de, Radnor, Z.J. and Akhmetova, D. (2004) Performance-driven behavior: a cross-country comparison. In: A. Neely, M. Kennerly and A. Waters (eds), *Performance Measurement and Management: Public and private*. Cranfield, UK: Centre for Business Performance, Cranfield University, 299–306.

Williams, R.S. (1998) *Performance Management: Perspectives on employee performance*. London: International Thomson Business Press.

Zairi, M. (1994) *Measuring Performance for Business Results*. London; Chapman and Hall.

12

Strategic alignment

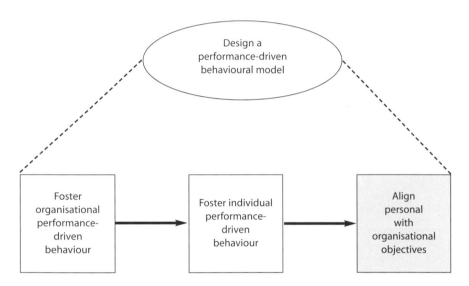

Figure 12.1 Aligning individual with organisational objectives

A sometimes confusing issue in the literature is the use of the term "performance management." In most US literature this term is used to describe the human resources management (HRM) process of setting individual expectations and goals, reviewing and evaluating individual performance, conducting performance appraisals, determining competencies, and deciding on monetary and nonmonetary consequences of individual performance. On the other hand, in much of the non-US literature, performance management is viewed as the process of setting and executing strategy, on all levels of the organisation. In recent literature it can be noticed that the two uses of the term performance management are moving toward each other. Those who look at performance management from the human resource perspective acknowledge that there has to be a direct link between personal objectives and organisational objectives, whereas those who look at it from the strategic perspective acknowledge that organisational strategies can only be achieved through the skills and commitment of individual organisation members.

Review the following typical statement regarding the goals of performance management as put forward by a human resources management scholar, who expressed the goals in question form (Walters, 1995):

- What are organisational objectives? What do we wish to achieve and in what time?
- How do we prioritise objectives? Do we expect prioritisation to change over time?
- What are our current strengths and weaknesses in relation to these objectives? What do we need to change or develop in order to achieve our goals?
- What specific contributions do we require from particular parts of the organisation?
- What kind of qualities are needed to deliver these objectives? What are the implications in terms of corporate skills and competencies, values, behaviours and working styles?

These questions largely coincide with the strategic perspective of performance management, except for the two questions in the last bullet point. These questions pose an important addition to the strategic perspective, as they explicitly involve the skills, experience, and competencies of individual organisational members.

People have been acknowledging for years that employee performance is the single most important characteristic that determines whether an organisation is successful (Gubman, 1998; Kouhy and Vedd, 1998). However, in practice the human resource perspective of performance management is often neglected (Ashton, 1997; Stephen and Roithmayr, 1998):

- Objectives for organisation members are defined in a vacuum, as a result of which they do not tie in with the strategic objectives of the organisation. In addition, these objectives are too often not (fully) representative of what organisation members do, which makes them difficult to accept and insufficiently motivating.
- Objectives of one organisational unit are insufficiently communicated to other organisational units, as a result of which there is a lack of understanding between units of each other's needs and activities, cooperation is difficult, and there is too much overlap in unit activities.
- There is often one-way communication (no feedback) between manager and employees, which frustrates employees because they do not have a say in matters. In addition, evaluating visible behaviour is emphasised while much of the good behaviour, like team work and creativity, is less visible. There is a tendency to hypocrisy because the

evaluator says there are official criteria that are used to judge performance, while in reality the evaluator uses his or her own private criteria.

▪ Maintenance of objectives, CSFs, and KPIs is insufficiently embedded in the planning and control cycle of the organisation, which causes an increasing discrepancy between the strategic objectives and the objectives of organisational units, teams, and individual organisation members.

These issues cause resentment and unmotivated organisation members, who are often late or absent, less concerned with customer satisfaction, and quit their jobs sooner. This poor work attitude results in lower productivity and lower organisational performance. Interestingly, this was noted by Professor Kerr in his famous 1975 article, 'On the folly of rewarding A, while hoping for B' (Kerr, 1975). Even more interesting is that in 1995 Dechant and Veiga observed that these issues were still posing problems for companies, 20 years after they were first described. These authors suggested that organisations still had an old-fashioned view of performance management and were unable to look at what causes good organisational results from a holistic point of view, and that management and shareholders were focused too much on short-term results.

If an organisation wants to make optimal use of the efforts of its organisational members, it has to meet four preconditions:

▪ The objectives of all management levels have to be aligned with the mission and strategy of the organisation.
▪ The objectives have to be translated into clear expectations regarding the performance of organisation members.
▪ Organisation members have to know how to realise the expectations and what kind of support they can expect from management.
▪ The set of human resource instruments (performance review, incentives, training, and development) has to be geared to realise the organisation's objectives.

To meet these preconditions, Cascio advocates the introduction of strategic human resources management, which he defines as:

> getting everybody, from the top of the organisation to the bottom, doing things to implement the business' strategy effectively. The idea is to use people most wisely with respect to the strategic needs of the organisation. That doesn't just happen on its own. An integrated framework that systematically links human resource activities with strategic business needs can help.
>
> (Cascio, 2000)

Such a framework is described in the next section.

Chapter objectives

☑ To give the reader insight into the importance of aligning all human management systems with performance management throughout the organisation.

☑ To describe the link between competency management and performance management.

☑ To teach the reader how to use the Performance Alignment Model to make sure that performance management is imbued on all organisational levels.

12.1 PERFORMANCE ALIGNMENT MODEL

In the performance alignment model (PAM) the preconditions described in the previous section are translated into a logical model (Waal, 2001). The goal of this model is to support the achievement of organisational objectives. For this it is required that every organisation member delivers output that is aligned with the mission and the strategy of the company. The intended output is made concrete and formalised in personal objectives. By applying the PAM, an excellent match is realised between the organisational and personal objectives. Performance alignment encompasses the complete performance management process, from developing strategy, CSFs, and KPIs to developing performance evaluation, reward, and training systems based on personal indicators. The added value of performance alignment lies in the fact that the evaluation criteria for performance-related pay (the KPIs) are directly derived from the strategic objectives of the organisation. The PAM consists of four steps, which are given in Figure 12.2.

Step 1

The starting point of the performance alignment process is the mission and strategy objectives of the organisation. These are formulated by answering the questions "What does the organisation want to achieve?" and "How does the organisation want to achieve this?" (1 in Figure 12.2). In order to make the strategy as tangible as possible, concrete strategic objectives are formulated. To measure whether these objectives are being realised, strategic CSFs and KPIs are defined (2A in Figure 12.2).

Organisational units can support the execution of the mission and strategy of the organisation by translating the strategic objectives into objectives for their own units, which is followed by trying to achieve these unit objectives. The success of the unit in doing this is measured by means of CSFs and KPIs, which are different for each organisational unit (2B in Figure 12.2).

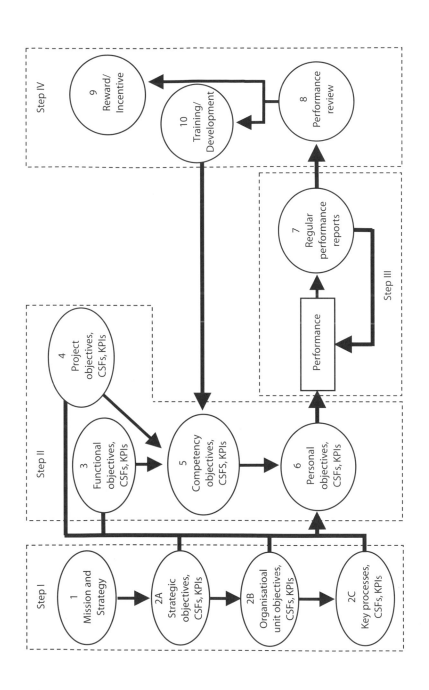

Figure 12.2 The steps in the performance alignment model

Finally, the key processes are identified, which are measured by means of process CSFs and process KPIs (2C in Figure 12.2). Step I is described in more detail in Chapter 6. Table 12.1 gives a summary of the activities which an organisation needs to perform in step I, including the input that is needed to execute the activities and the people who are involved in them.

Table 12.1 Activities in step I of the performance alignment model

Step	Activities	Inputs	Persons involved
I	1. Identify the characteristics of the industry/social sector.	Material on developments and trend in the industry/social sector.	Management team. Board of directors.
	2. Think about the future of the industry/social sector and formulate strategic scenarios.	Workshop.	Supervisory board.
	3. Define what the organisation wants to contribute to its industry and the society in the future and what its role should be in each scenario.		
	4. Formulate the strategy.		
2A	5. Make the strategy concrete by formulating strategic objectives.	Interviews with key personnel.	Management team.
	6. Define strategic result and effort CSFs.	Workshop.	Key personnel.
	7. Define for each CSF one or more KPIs.		
2B	8. Translate the strategic objectives into objectives for each organisational unit..	Interviews with key personnel.	Unit managers.
	9. Define result and effort CSFs for each organisational unit's objective.	Workshop.	
	10. Define one or more KPIs for each CSF.		
2C	11. Identify the key processes of each organisational unit.	Interviews with key personnel.	Unit managers.
	12. Define process CSFs for the key processes.	Workshop.	
	13. Define one or more KPIs for each CSF.		

Step II

The strategic and unit objectives and key processes are all used as input for the different functional objectives of the organisational units. Basically, these functional objectives are the requirements that people in a certain position or role should meet to be considered as adding value to the business. The functional objectives are translated in functional CSFs and functional KPIs (3 in Figure 12.2). Senior management's functional objectives are directly derived from the strategic objectives of the organisation. Organisational unit management's functional objectives come directly from the organisational unit objectives. The functional objectives of lower-level employees will mainly originate from the operational objectives.

Organisation members often participate on an ad hoc basis in special projects which take up a lot of time. To make sure these projects are also in line with the organisation's mission and strategy, project objectives are defined. In addition, project CSFs, project KPIs, and targets are defined (4 in Figure 12.2).

Eventually for every functional and project objective the competencies are identified that are required for achieving the objectives. "Achieving" means in this context achieving the target set for the KPI. The competencies are expressed in the knowledge and skills a person has and needs. If the person is lacking these competencies, they are translated into competency objectives (5 in Figure 12.2). Competency management is described in more detail in the next section.

Functional and project objectives become personal objectives once personal targets have been set for them (6 in Figure 12.2). When setting these targets, the current competencies of the person in question are taken into account. For instance, if an organisation member has just started to work in a particular function, the personal target will probably be set lower than is normal, to give the person some time to acclimatise. On the other hand, if an organisation member is very experienced and has worked for many years in this or a similar function, the personal target will presumably be set higher than the average for this function.

Personal objectives consist of general functional and project objectives with personal KPIs and targets, and personal competency objectives with KPIs and targets. Table 12.2 gives a summary of the activities an organisation needs to perform in step II, including the input that is needed to execute them and the people who are involved in them.

Step III

After the personal objectives and targets have been defined, the organisation member can start working at achieving these. Through regular, periodic performance reports (for instance in the shape of a personal balanced score-card), the person gets feedback on whether the achievement of the personal

Table 12.2 Activities in step II of the performance alignment model

Step	Activities	Inputs	Persons involved
3	1. Analyse the functions and roles in the operational unit. 2. Analyse the range of duties for each role and function. 3. Translate the duties into functional objectives for each role and function. 4. Define result and effort CSFs for each functional objective. 5. Define one or more KPIs for each CSF.	Diagram of the organisation and job descriptions. Interviews with key personnel of the unit and the HRM department. Strategic, unit, and operational objectives. Strategic, unit, and operational CSFs and KPIs. Workshop.	Unit managers. Key personnel. HRM personnel. Managers.
4	6. Define the objectives for each project. 7. Define result and effort CSFs for each project objective. 8. Define one or more KPIs for each CSF.	Interviews with project team members. Workshop.	Project team members. Steering committee members.
5	9. Identify "best performers" per function and project objective. 10. Collect examples of good behaviour of these "best performers." 11. Translate behavioural examples into competencies needed to demonstrate that behaviour (e.g. knowledge, skills, behaviour). 12. Determine current competency level of each organisation member. 13. Define the objectives for each lacking or insufficient competency. 14. Define result and effort CSFs for each competency objective. 15. Define one or more KPIs for each CSF.	Interview with managers. Interview with best performers. Core question is: "What do excellent employees more often do with more success in more situations than their average performing colleagues?" Workshop. Interview with organisation members. Interview with project team members.	Employees. Managers. If expedient: selected customers and suppliers. HRM personnel. Project team members.
6	16. Draft a "personal performance plan" with personal objectives composed of functional, project and competency objectives with their accompanying CSFs and KPIs. 17. Determine the target for each personal KPI, for all organisational members. 18. Evaluate yearly and, if necessary, adjust the personal objectives, CSFs, KPIs, and/or the targets. Adjust the personal performance plan.	Standard layout for the personal performance plan.	HRM personnel.

objectives is still on track (7 in Figure 12.2). If performance does not improve or is deteriorating, the organisation member can, together with his or her superior, define corrective and preventive actions. Table 12.3 gives a summary of the activities an organisation needs to perform in step III, including the input that is needed to execute them and the people who are involved in them.

Step IV

During the annual review, the performance of an organisation member is officially discussed (8 in Figure 12.2). On the basis of this review, an adjustment of the person's salary and bonus can be made. This adjustment depends on the reward structure of the organisation (9 in Figure 12.2). Also during the review, the personal objectives and targets for the following year are discussed and agreed upon by manager and employee.

The formal review gives important input for the personal development plan that is made for every organisation member (10 in Figure 12.2). This plan includes activities to improve the knowledge and skills of the organisation member, to improve performance in the current function, or to prepare the person for his or her next function. Table 12.4 gives a summary of the activities an organisation needs to perform in step IV, including the input that is needed to execute them and the people who are involved in them.

The chance of actually achieving the objectives of the organisation are considerably improved by using the PAM. This is because the objectives of all management levels are in line with each other, so all organisation members know what is important for the organisation and what is expected from them. Everybody works under the same clear-structured regime. The assessment and reward criteria are related to the strategic objectives of the organisation, which means that these human resource tools directly support

Table 12.3 Activities in step III of the performance alignment model

Step	Activities	Inputs	Persons involved
7	1. Draft a layout for the feedback between organisation members and managers.	Personal balanced scorecard layout.	HRM personnel. Finance personnel. IT personnel.
	2. Draft data delivery procedures needed to collect data for calculating the personal KPIs.		
	3. Calculate the scores on the personal KPIs.		
	4. Determine the reporting procedure for the personal BSC (frequency, delivery mode) and execute this procedure.	Personal balanced scorecard.	

Table 12.4 Activities in step IV of the performance alignment model

Step	Activities	Inputs	Persons involved
8	1. Analyse the current evaluation and assessment system.	Interviews with key HRM personnel. Workshop.	HRM personnel. Managers. Employees.
	2. Define the characteristics of the new evaluation and assessment system.	Personal balanced scorecard.	
	3. Define the evaluation procedure.		
	4. Conduct performance evaluation reviews.		
	5. Record evaluation in personal performance plan.		
9	6. Define the characteristics of the new reward system.	Interviews with management team members and key HRM personnel. Information from salary consultants. Workshop.	Management team members. HRM personnel. Managers.
	7. Determine the level of reward per performance level.		
	8. Draft reward structure and procedure.		
	9. Implement the new reward system.		
	10. Evaluate the reward system.		
10	11. Determine performance of organisation members. Identify areas of attention, on the basis of lagging results.	Personal balanced scorecard. Personal development plan. Training programmes.	Organisation members. Managers. HRM personnel.
	12. Identify causes of lagging performance and think of possible solutions/improvements.		
	13. Formulate learning goals of training programmes to remedy lagging performance.		
	15. Determine costs of training and other solutions.		
	16. Make choice for internal or external training.		

the achievement of the organisational strategy. In addition, the assessment criteria are clearly formulated and relevant, for both the organisation and organisation members, making them acceptable and motivating.

Research shows that the motivation of organisation members to perform well is improved if their goals are clear to them. An organisation member's ability to see the connection between his or her work and the organisation's strategic objectives is a driver of positive behaviour (Rucci et al., 1998; Bolger and Mulhern, 2005). This clarity is achieved by formulating and using personal objectives derived from the strategy. Uncertainty about the assessment criteria used for review and reward purposes also diminishes, because organisational members know beforehand which criteria will be used. The identification of functional objectives and competencies helps improve the quality of the development of function descriptions and competency profiles. This will eventually result in better qualified and skilled personnel in the right positions.

Finally, the implementation of personal objectives, personal targets, and clear assessment criteria, linked with a flexible reward structure, can lead to a culture change. The commitment of employees to achieve the objectives of the organisation increases. Standards of "what is good and what is wrong" are also increasingly clear and consistent with each other.

12.2 COMPETENCY MANAGEMENT

(This section has been prepared with the support of Julie Lindhorst, Laforte Consulting.)

Devising more effective ways of managing the performance of organisation members has become a cornerstone of organisational development in recent years. As part of this, identifying the competencies of individuals, in both their general contribution to the organisation and their specific contribution in the context of their function and role, has been key (Cheng et al., 2005).

In the performance alignment model, during step II (see Figure 12.2), objectives are formulated for the development of the competencies of an individual. A competency is defined as a cluster of related knowledge, skills, attitudes and behaviours that affects a major part of one's job (a role or responsibility), that correlates with performance on the job, that can be measured against well-accepted standards, and that can be improved through training and development (Lucia and Lepsinger, 1999). Competencies are functionally related, they progress from basic to advanced, and they reinforce one another as learning occurs.

A distinction can be made between basic and distinctive competencies. Basic competencies are the traits needed to be successful in a specific function or role. Distinctive competencies are exceptional traits that make an individual excel and achieve outstanding results. Since their inception in the late 1950s, competencies have been applied more and more by organisations throughout the world because they provide significant help with key problems such as:

- clarifying workforce standards and expectations
- aligning individuals, teams, and managers with the organisation's business strategies
- creating empowerment, accountability, and alignment of coach, team member, and employer in performance development
- developing equitable, focused appraisal and compensation decisions.

Competency models

Many organisations use a model to guide them in developing competencies. It is important to use a competency model because it provides information on the range of behaviours that lead to excellent performance. Competency models help teams and individuals to align their behaviour with organisational strategies; employee understanding of what behaviours and results are expected; and recruiters with the assessment and selection of employees. The process to develop a competency model is to identify excellent behaviour for each organisational unit and align the behaviours with the expected results (Figure 12.3).

Depending on the size of the organisation, it may be effective to use a standard database and link this database to standard HRM systems. Much research effort has gone into finding excellent behaviours for various job families. Therefore, model building generally starts with a standard

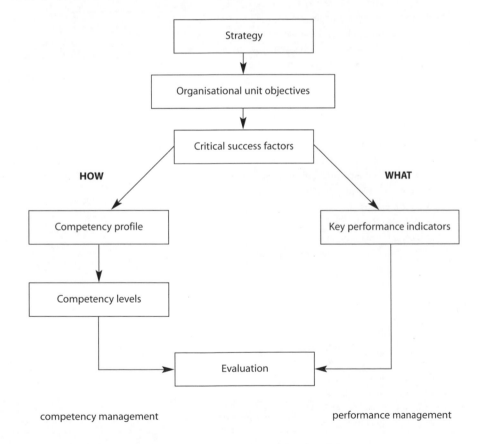

Figure 12.3 Relation between competency management and performance management

Source: based on an idea by Wim van Roomen, COKZ.

Competency: adaptability		Current Level	Level of Excellence
A.	Values need for adaptability		
B.	Demonstrates adaptability		
C.	Adapts approach		
D.	Adapts strategy		
Competency: client focus			
A.	Serves clients responsively		
B.	Maintains clear communication with clients		
C.	Takes personal responsibility		
D.	Establishes effective client relationships		
E.	Contributes to positive outcomes for the client		
F.	Meets long-term client needs		
G.	Advocates for client needs		
Competency: communication			
A.	Expresses self effectively		
B.	Listens effectively		
C.	Understands underlying issues		
D.	Adapts communication for the situation		
Competency: organisational awareness			
A.	Demonstrates understanding of formal structures in own work group		
B.	Demonstrates understanding of the informal structure within work group		
C.	Demonstrates understanding of the organisation beyond own work group		
D.	Demonstrates understanding of organisational realities		
E.	Demonstrates understanding of underlying organisational issues		
Competency: problem solving and judgment			
A.	Breaks down problems		
B.	Sees basic relationships		
C.	Sees multiple relationships		
D.	Makes complex plans or analyses		
Competency: result orientation			
A.	Meets job expectations		
B.	Improves performance beyond expectations of the role		
C.	Sets and works to meet challenging objectives		
D.	Improves performance in work unit		
E.	Sets challenging organisational goals and seizes opportunities		
Competency: teamwork			
A.	Cooperates		
B.	Actively participates in team		
C.	Involves other team members		
D.	Encourages others and facilitates effective outcomes		
E.	Builds a cohesive team		

Figure 12.4 Example of a competency worksheet
Source: based on the Competency Self-assessment Worksheet in the Competency Implementation Guide of the Government of Alberta.

library of validated competency profiles and competency levels which tie into the CSFs, and therefore by definition, to the strategy of the organisation. Examples of these competency profiles and levels can be found on the internet (Figure 12.4).

A competency model is developed through a process of clarifying the business strategy and determining how the model should be used (e.g. hiring and selection, assessment, performance management, training and development, and career development). Then data is gathered in structured interviews, and is subsequently analysed and used to develop "straw man" models of success criteria. Validation surveys are administered, and the model is refined based on the feedback. Finally, models are finalised and translated into appropriate end-user tools and applications (Schoonover, 2005). Key competencies that reinforce the goals and culture of the organisation in question are identified; critical HRM systems that support competency development are determined; integrated competency-based approaches for all evaluation systems, such as assessment, selection, development planning, succession/career planning, and pay-for-performance, are created; and results on KPIs are used in the evaluation process.

The competency model has to be placed in a larger perspective, to make sure it supports the achievement of an organisation's strategy. There are many models that aim to provide this perspective. One such model is the MACH model, originally developed for the health care sector, which makes a link between the organisational, competency-based and instructional theories that underpin workforce development and practice (Figure 12.5). The model represents a systematic process for identifying and meeting training needs. This is needed because approaching training in a consistent systematic fashion is the best assurance for creating a competent workforce.

The MACH model has the following components:

1. *Workforce competencies*. These are competencies that apply to the identification and design of work roles, responsibilities, and job descriptions. Workforce competencies generally do not outline the specific skills needed to handle responsibilities, but focus on the final set of expected outcomes. They are often used to define job descriptions.
2. *Defining elements*. These elements cover the who, what, where, and how of the workforce. They give the context in which organisational members are operating, and they give information about the characteristics of the workforce.
3. *Instructional competencies*. These are competencies that apply to the development of curricula and instructional materials to instruct workers in what is expected of them and how to do their job.
4. *Curriculum process*. This process give a structure for designing and conducting the training programmes that have been developed on the basis of the instructional competencies. The curriculum process encompasses the direct learning process of organisation members. It consists of five steps: assessment of organisation members' roles and

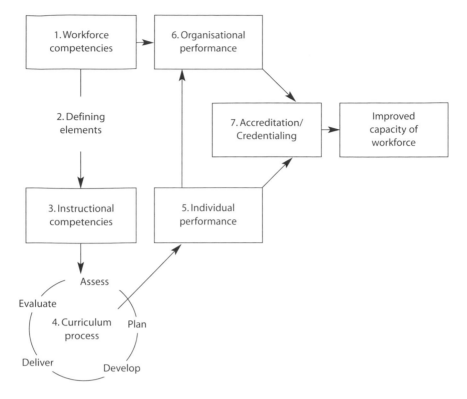

Figure 12.5 The MACH model
Source: Miner et al. (2005). Compared with the original MACH model, the component "intervening variables" has been removed.

responsibilities and individual levels of ability; planning to meet the educational requirements of the workforce by creating a blueprint for the training programme; development of training content and materials; delivery of the training; and evaluation of student performance and curriculum efficacy.

5. *Individual performance.* Individuals have to apply what they have learned during training in their work, and in that manner demonstrate their increased competency.

6. *Organisational performance.* Once enhanced individual performance is achieved, organisational performance is improved.

7. *Accreditation and credentialing.* In this component mechanisms are created that capture and assess organisational and individual performance according to relevant and consistent standards. Developing these mechanisms helps to evaluate whether organisations and individuals are competent, and to conduct benchmarking.

The MACH model starts from a set of assumptions:

- Expected organisational performance is defined.
- The contribution of organisational members to this organisational performance is defined as workforce competencies.
- Workforce competencies are defined.
- Instructional competencies are developed from workforce competencies to enable assessment of need and the development of relevant training.
- Relevant training and individual skills influence individual performance.
- Individual performance influences organisational performance.

Link between performance management and competency management

In practice, there exists a tension between competency management and performance management. All too often these management instruments are developed and implemented in isolation. Organisations find it difficult to give a short answer to the question, "Which is most important, results, behaviour, or development?" "We aim for the combination," is the general answer. It is not that simple, however. What needs to be done with the employee who does not meet work commitments but has made good progress in developing him/herself? Or the other way around? How much energy should an employee be allowed to put into his/her development at the cost of productivity? Who is put in a job: the most qualified employee, or should a less-qualified employee get the opportunity to grow into the job? These questions are hardly addressed during the implementation of performance management and competency management. The explanation for this phenomenon can be found in the initiative takers in the organisation.

Performance management is often initiated by the board or the Finance department: in other words, by people who in general are focused on concrete, quantifiable results. A performance management project often ends in setting targets at the department level, there is little follow-through to the employee level. In contrast, competency management is usually initiated by the HRM department with the goal of achieving employee development. Core competencies and competency profiles are derived from roles and positions, which are too often disengaged from the organisational strategy. The Finance and HRM departments still hardly ever work together, so they never fully realise that their performance management and competency management projects are directly related. When either of these two departments start its project, it should take the time to look at the bigger perspective and make sure there is a seamless connection between performance management and competency management, a connection that can be provided by using models such as the performance alignment model.

Criticism of competency management

In recent years, criticism has focused on the underlying assumptions of competency management:

- Those who excel in the same role all display the same behaviour.
- Each of these behaviours can be learned.
- Each of these behaviours should be learned because improving weaknesses leads to success.

However, research has found that these assumptions could be flawed, and that there are no truly general competencies, but only competencies that are context-specific (Buckingham and Coffman, 1999; Buckingham and Clifton, 2001; McKenna, 2002). Furthermore, these studies found that:

- Great managers who excel in the same role all create the same outcomes using different behaviours.
- Some behaviours can be learned while others may prove extraordinarily difficult to learn (i.e. the difference between skills and knowledge, which can be learned, and talent, which cannot).
- Weakness-fixing prevents failure but only strength-building leads to success.

Buckingham (2001) states that organisations should not focus in their competency management on fixing on the weaknesses of organisational members, but on building and on extending their strong points. He recommends the following approach to increase a person's performance, which seems to tie in very well with the principles of strategic performance management:

- Do not try to identify the competencies required for each role. Instead, identify the outcomes expected of each role.
- Do not try to select people based on whether they possess the required competencies. Instead, identify the natural talents that are common to the best in each key role, and design interviewing systems to select people who possess similar talents.
- Do not measure each person on the required competencies. Instead, measure each person on the required outcomes.
- Do not identify which competencies each person lacks. Instead, identify each person's areas of talent and non-talent.
- Do not encourage each person to improve in his/her areas of non-talent. Instead, encourage each person to strengthen his/her talents with skills and knowledge, then find ways to manage around his/her areas of non-talent.
- Do not label an employee's weaknesses as his/her "areas of improvement." Instead, apply this label to his/her areas of talent. A person's greatest opportunities lie in his/her talents, not his/her weaknesses.

- Do not rate people next year on whether they have improved on the required competencies. Instead, rate them on whether they have improved on the required outcomes.

12.3 CASE: PERFORMANCE ALIGNMENT AT UVD

During the sessions with consultant Pete Fields, the management team of UVD had defined a number of the strategic objectives (see Chapter 4). A selection of them is shown in Table 12.5, together with the strategic CSFs and KPIs that have been formulated after much deliberation. In this section, for a limited number of strategic objectives which have been defined (step I–2A in Figure 12.2), the performance alignment model is applied to selected departments of UVD (Table 12.5).

Step I (continued)

UVD's definition of strategic objectives, CSFs, and KPIs constitutes step I–2A of the performance alignment model. Three of UVD's departments – Marketing & Sales, Production and Finance – had formulated unit objectives based on the strategic objectives (step I–2B) and had defined unit CSFs and KPIs for them (Table 12.6). It has to be noted that the departments could not contribute to achieving all the strategic objectives.

UVD's key processes are fairly easily determined because they have just been described as part of a workflow project. For the marketing team of the

Table 12.5 Some of UVD's strategic objectives with corresponding CSFs and KPIs

Strategic objective	Strategic CSF	Strategic KPI
Be innovative	Innovative image	Image score (number of customers that judge UVD's products innovative vs. total number of interviewed customers)
	Innovative assortment	New products introduced
Produce high-quality products	Product quality as experienced by the customers	Product quality complaints
Create international coverage	Turnover new countries	Market share new countries
		Profitability new countries
Increase profitability	Profitability	Margin

Table 12.6 Some of UVD's unit objectives with corresponding CSFs and KPIs

Strategic objective	Unit objective, M&S department	Unit CSF	Unit KPI
Be innovative	Create an innovative image	Innovative image	Image score (number of customers that consider UVD's products innovative vs. total number of interviewed customers)
Produce high-quality products	Guard product innovativeness	Assortment lifecycle	Average product lifecycle in UVD's assortment
		Turnover share of new products	Turnover share of new products (new product turnover vs. total turnover)
	Predict sales chances and opportunities	Market saturation	Sales increase due to new products
			Repeat purchases (as percentage of total sales)
Create international coverage	Expand market share in new markets (countries)	Market share in new countries	Turnover in new country (as percentage of total market in the country)
			New country sales
			New country profitability
		Brand recognition in new countries	Brand recognition score for new countries (number of interviewees who know of UVD's products vs. total number of interviewees)
Strategic objective	Unit objective, Production department	Unit CSF	Unit KPI
Be innovative	Create new and efficient manufacturing processes	Flexibility of production processes	Average set-up time
			Average set-up costs
Produce high-quality products	Produce high-quality products	Quality of production processes	Rejects (number of rejected products vs. total number of manufactured products)
			Returns (number of products returned because of defects vs. total number of products sold)
Increase profitability	Have a safe manufacturing process	Safety of production processes	Industrial accidents (as percentage of total number of employees)
Strategic objective	Unit objective, Finance department	Unit CSF	Unit KPI
Increase profitability	Guard cost levels	Cost levels	Costs (per product, for all products in the assortment)
			Cost reduction (costs of current period vs. costs of last period)

Marketing and Sales department, the maintenance team of the Production department, and the accounting team of the Finance department, the key processes are determined (step I–2C in Figure 12.2) and corresponding process CSFs and KPIs are defined (Table 12.7).

Step II – Functional objectives

Martin Duvall is maintenance employee at UVD and is part of the maintenance team. He has worked for more than ten years with great enthusiasm at the company, and has gained a lot of technical expertise. Martin is responsible for the maintenance of the expensive D2 machine. Table 12.8 lists the functional objectives for Martin, which have been derived from the unit objectives and key processes of the maintenance team.

Step II – Project objectives

A project recently started at UVD has the goal to improve the work atmosphere, which has steadily deteriorated over the past few years. During several meetings of UVD's department heads, it came to light that employees had no respect for employees of other departments. Some examples were abusive language of warehouse employees toward production employees, and maintenance employees overreacting to requests and questions from production personnel. This bickering has seriously affected the overall productivity, so something has to be done about it. Several employees are chosen to work in a team to think up ideas to improve the atmosphere at UVD within a year. Martin Duvall is participating and he, just like his fellow team members, gets a project objective (Table 12.9).

Step II – Competency objectives

The competencies that Martin needs to achieve the function and project objectives are listed in Table 12.10. The first question is, which skills, knowledge, expertise and qualities does Martin need to achieve the personal targets for his personal objectives? The second question is, which competencies are lacking or are still underdeveloped in Martin? The lacking or underdeveloped competencies are translated into competency objectives. Martin's technical skills and experience are quite good: he has the highest possible score for his function. However, for client orientation his score is average, so he needs additional training in this area. His coaching skills are also slightly underdeveloped, so they also become a competency objective for Martin. Martin's competency objectives will also be made measurable with CSFs and KPIs.

Table 12.7 Some of UVD's key processes with corresponding CSFs and KPIs

Key processes of Marketing team	Process CSF	Process KPI
Evaluate effectiveness of promotional activities	Promotional effectiveness	Sales increase after promotional activity
Guard market positioning of UVD's products	Assortment of positionings	UVD's market share
		UVD's share of customers (number of UVD customers vs. total number of customers in the market)
Strengthen knowledge and skills of marketing team personnel	Training courses	Available training budget
		Courses attended (vs. total number of marketing personnel)
Key processes of Maintenance team	**Process CSF**	**Process KPI**
Maintain machinery	Usability of machines	Stoppage (hours that machines are not operating because of breakdowns vs. total available machine hours)
		Response time (average time needed to respond to breakdowns)
		Repair time (average time needed to repair machinery)
Use resources optimally	Capacity utilisation	Machinery-personnel mismatch (hours that machines are not operating because personnel are not available vs. total available machine hours)
Control maintenance cost	Maintenance cost	Average maintenance cost per machine
Maintain technical knowledge	Technical training courses	Available training budget
		Courses attended (vs. total number of maintenance personnel)
Key processes of Finance team	**Process CSF**	**Process KPI**
Guarantee optimal debtor payments	Debtor management	Open invoices (as percentage of total bills)
		Average payment period of debtors
Faultless processing of invoices	Invoice faults	Complaints about invoices
		Sent credit notes (as percentage of total number of sent invoices)
Provide high-quality management reports	Quality of management reports	Reports on time
		Complaints about management reports
Maintain financial knowledge	Financial training courses	Available training budget

Table 12.8 Martin's functional objectives with corresponding CSFs and KPIs

Key processes of Maintenance team	Functional objective for Martin Duvall	Functional CSF	Functional KPI
Maintain machinery	Effectively maintain the D2 machine	Uptime of D2 machine	Stoppage of D2 machine (hours that D2 machine is not operating because of breakdowns vs. total available D2 machine hours)
			Timely maintenance (number of overhauls carried out according to plan vs. total number of planned overhauls)
		Breakdown time of D2 machine	Response time (average time needed to respond to D2 breakdowns)
			Repair time (average time needed to repair D2 machine)
Use resources optimally	Coach new maintenance employees	Well-performing maintenance employees	Coaching time (hours spent on coaching new maintenance employees vs. total available working hours)
Maintain technical knowledge	Increase technical expertise	Technical expertise level	Attended advanced technical courses (vs. number of courses planned)
			Effectiveness of advanced technical courses (number of complex problems solved independently)

Table 12.9 Martin's project objective with corresponding CSF and KPIs

Project objective for Martin Duvall	Project CSF	Project KPI
Improve work atmosphere	Internal customer satisfaction	Complains about other departments
		Internal customer satisfaction score

Table 12.10 Martin's competency objectives

Functional and project objectives for Martin Duvall	Functional and project CSFs	Competency objectives
Coach new maintenance employees	Well-performing maintenance employees	Develop coaching skills
Improve work atmosphere	Internal customer satisfaction	Develop client orientation

Step II – Personal objectives

Because Martin's technical skills are well developed, the targets for the functional objectives can be set high. He scores average on client satisfaction but a person with his experience should be able to achieve a high target. For his coaching skills the target is set lower than before: Martin now gets three new employees to coach, where this used to be five employees. Together with his manager, Martin formulates the following personal objectives:

- Decrease stoppage time of the D2 machine next year by 10 per cent.
- Carry out all preventive maintenance according to plan.
- React to little breakdowns of the D2 machine, as of April 1 of next year, within half an hour and repair these within three hours.
- Coach three new employees next year.
- Help decrease the number of complaints about the maintenance team by 50 per cent at the end of next year.
- Help increase customer satisfaction of other departments with the maintenance team by 2 points (on a scale of 1 to 10) at the end of next year.
- Attend one customer orientation course and one advanced technical course next year.

CSFS, KPIs and targets are defined for all Martin's personal objectives,.

Step III – Execution

Martin's personal objectives and targets are now known to him, so he can start working on these. Halfway through the year Martin will have an evaluation meeting with his manager. This meeting will be centred on the interim performance reports that are send to Martin every quarter. Table 12.11 gives a performance interim report for Martin.

Table 12.11 Martin's interim performance report

Personal KPI	Results Q2	Explanation
Stoppage of D2 machine	Excellent	Machine stoppage, first measurement: 16 hours per month. Machine stoppage, second measurement: 13.9 hours per month. Target: reduce machine stoppage by 10%. Conclusion: machine stoppage has been reduced by 14.2% Martin performs well above target.
Timely maintenance	On target	Maintenance according to schedule: 100%. Target: 100%. Conclusion: Martin is exactly on schedule.
Response time	Almost on target	Response time, first measurement: 45 minutes. Response time, second measurement: 35 minutes. Target: 30 minutes. Conclusion: Martin has made good improvement but is not on target yet.
Repair time	Almost on target	Average repair time: 3.2 hours. Target: 3 hours. Conclusion: Martin is virtually on target.
Coaching time	Below target	Coaching time: 5%. Target: 10%. Conclusion: Martin does not spend enough time on coaching new employees. This is largely because there has been only one new employee joining his team this month.
Complaints about other departments	Below target	Complaints, first measurement: 12 complaints per month. Complaints, second measurement: 11 complaints per month. Target: reduction in complaints by 50%. Conclusion: Martin performs way below the target. Analysis is needed of why this is. It seems he spends so much time on his regular job that he has hardly any input into the project.
Internal customer satisfaction score	Below target	Internal customer satisfaction score first measurement: 4.0. Internal customer satisfaction score second measurement: 4.2. Target: increase in satisfaction of 2 points. Conclusion: Martin performs way below the norm. Analysis is needed of why this is. It seems he spends so much time on his regular job that he has hardly any input into the project.
Attended advanced technical courses	On target	Attended advanced technical courses this quarter: 1. Target this quarter: 1. Conclusion: Martin is right on target.
Effectiveness of advanced technical courses	On target	Effectiveness of advanced technical courses: seems to be good according to supervisor who states Martin is able to handle more difficult problems with the D2 machine without any help.
Attended customer orientation courses	Pending	Attended customer orientation courses this quarter: 0. Target this year: 1. Conclusion: Martin has not had time yet to attend this course, he is scheduled to attend in quarter 3.

Step IV

During the annual performance evaluation and review, the same report is used, this time of quarter 4 which contains the "end score." The results of the personal objectives and targets form the basis not only of the evaluation but also of a bonus award. UVD has a "pay for performance" schedule, where the achievement of, or surpassing of, a personal objective at the end of the year results in payment of €1000. Martin has, at the end of quarter 4, achieved six of his ten personal objectives, resulting in a payout of €6000.

During the annual performance review, the training requirements of employees is also reviewed. Martin continues to struggle with his coaching skills and customer orientation skills. It was decided that Martin should take priority in coaching new employees, which means the next two new employees will be his responsibility. With regard to the customer orientation, further analysis showed that the complete project team, which was supposed to think up ideas to improve the work atmosphere at UVD, was not functioning. This project has been stopped and for the time being no follow-up action is required for Martin.

12.4 CASE: PERFORMANCE ALIGNMENT AT SOCIAL HOUSING ASSOCIATION HET OOSTEN

(This case is a combination of the cases described in Waal (2001, 2002) and Hoff, 2002.)

In the past decade, the social housing association Het Oosten, much like other housing associations in the Netherlands, has had to change from being a public-sector organisation to a market-oriented organisation. In the old days, management of an association was based on policies and rules dictated by the government, and the finances of an association consisted of limited grants from that same government entity. In the new environment, an association must be managed in accordance with the development of the housing market. The association now also controls its own finances without grants. This change required a new management model for the associations. The need to become more market-oriented meant that management information had to meet different requirements than before. This case describes how the social housing association Het Oosten managed to change by aligning its strategy with functional and individual performance, using the performance alignment model.

Het Oosten is a prominent organisation in the public housing sector and ranks among the 20 largest Dutch public housing associations. It rents, manages, and sells houses in every price category throughout Amsterdam. The association also engages in new housing development, as well as the purchase and redevelopment of existing buildings. Het Oosten manages approximately 18,000 units: 16,000 for housing and 2000 for business accommodation and parking places in Amsterdam and surroundings. Large projects are usually undertaken in cooperation with property developers, private investors, and other housing associations.

Het Oosten consists of five business units:

1. *Project development*. This business unit develops new building projects and redevelops houses in the organisation's portfolio. Its projects range from urban renewal projects to the (re)construction of entire areas, including shopping centres and artists' studios.
2. *Real estate*. This business unit is responsible for portfolio management. Its main activities are the purchase and sale of properties.
3. *Renting*. This business unit develops and renders services to tenants and is responsible for communication between tenants and the association. Its tasks are to sign tenant contracts, to maintain communication with tenants, and to recover rent arrears. One of the business unit's departments is called Tenant Affairs.
4. *Maintenance and control*. This business unit takes care of the maintenance of houses and corporate buildings for both the association and third parties. Its activities include emergency repairs, planned maintenance, and the development and collection of technical housing information. One of the departments of this business unit is called Maintenance Advice Agency.
5. *Finance*. This business unit monitors the financial position of the association. Its main activity is to secure low-cost funding as well as solvency in the housing sector, which enables Het Oosten to continue its policy and investments.

The five business units are supported by the following departments: executive staff and secretary, product development, and information technology. The total workforce of Het Oosten amounts to 270 people.

To be able to change from a public sector to a market-oriented organisation, Het Oosten needed a new strategic performance management system that was accessible to all organisation members. This system would help the organisation to execute its strategy, initiate corrective actions, and encourage discussions about performance and quality. To guide it through the performance management development, Het Oosten chose the performance alignment model, which consists of the following steps (see Figure 12.2).

Step 1 – Mission, strategic objectives and strategic CSFs and KPIs

The first step in the development of the new strategic performance management system was to develop the mission statement and strategy of the association in more detail, and to create a framework to measure the execution of the strategy. The project began with an analysis of all relevant documentation, such as the annual report, discussion memoranda, and management conference reports. After the analysis, interviews were held with the supervisory board, the board of management, the management team, and a municipal representative (at that time, municipal authorities supervised housing associations). The interviews dealt with developments in the housing sector and questioned how Het Oosten was preparing for these developments. The mission and strategic objectives were further developed in a workshop and operationalised by means of strategic CSFs and KPIs. Both the management team and supervisory board participated in this workshop.

The mission of Het Oosten is "to guarantee good and affordable housing for various groups of people in an attractive and multicultural environment." To achieve its mission, Het Oosten developed the following strategic objectives:

- *To work in a customer-oriented fashion*. Customer orientation includes anticipating the housing needs of customers, being accessible to customers, involving tenants in housing policy and management, and facilitating housing choice by offering the possibility of customised housing.
- *To provide housing for those on low and moderate incomes*. The association wants to realise this by using the profit that is made in real estate for social housing purposes, by enabling tenants to move up the housing ladder (i.e. moving to higher-rent housing) and by creating and preserving affordable houses.
- *To invest in communities and neighbourhoods*. The association wants to play an active part in reducing urban decline. Het Oosten tries to do this by raising the quality of life in specific communities and neighbourhoods. This is important both to maintain property value and to get tenants involved in preserving the neighbourhood.
- *To build a strong internal organisation*. A strong internal organisation is essential to operate successfully in the commercial housing market. Such an organisation is built by promoting a professional, result-oriented culture, by improving associates' productivity and efficiency, and by striving for synergies between business units and departments.
- *To aim at a strong market position*. The association wants to achieve this by improving the price-to-quality ratio of its products and services and by entering into strategic alliances. Additionally, Het Oosten wants to improve its corporate identity on the housing market, to attract both tenants and buyers.
- *To improve the financial position*. In order to continue its operation as a housing association, Het Oosten needs a long-term stable financial position.

To monitor these strategic objectives, Het Oosten defined the strategic CSFs and KPIs shown in Table 12.12.

Table 12.12 Strategic objectives, CSFs and KPIs of Het Oosten

Strategic objective	Strategic CSF	Strategic KPI
To work in a customer-oriented fashion	Increase the range of housing products	Turnover of new housing products
To provide housing to low and moderate-income individuals	Appropriate supply of houses (existing and new)	Share of affordable houses in housing portfolio of Amsterdam
To invest in the community and neighbourhoods	Increase in housing value (financial) due to location	Degree of popularity with potential tenants
To build a strong internal organisation	Productivity	Cost price per productive hour
To aim at a strong market position	Demand for products and services of Het Oosten	Demand by potential tenants for a housing unit
To improve financial position	Improved financial position	Solvency

The KPI "degree of popularity with potential tenants" equals the difference in the number of housing requests made by potential tenants before and after the association invested in a specific neighbourhood. The KPI "cost price of productive hour" is measured by dividing the total salaries and allocated costs of a department by the total number of productive hours of that department. These hours can be gathered from the time reports that every employee of Het Oosten has to complete. The KPI "demand by potential tenants for a housing unit" is determined by comparing the average number of housing requests by potential tenants for a vacant Het Oosten unit with the average number of housing requests by potential tenants for a vacant unit (from any housing association) in Amsterdam.

Step I – Organisational unit objectives, CSFs and KPIs; and key processes, CSFs and KPIs

For the business units Het Oosten used basically the same approach as for developing strategic objectives and CSFs and KPIs. First, interviews were held with all business unit managers. This was followed by a customer survey, examining the demands and expectations of customers with regard to the services provided by each business unit. An analysis was made of the business unit's reporting set. The business unit objectives and key processes were then discussed in a number of workshops, and made measurable by means of business unit CSFs and KPIs and process CSFs and KPIs. All the business unit managers and some of the employees participated in these workshops. This section looks at the results of two business units, Maintenance and Control, and Renting.

As a result of the nature of the activities of the Maintenance and Control business unit, it can contribute to the following strategic objectives:

- ■ to work in a customer-oriented fashion
- ■ to provide housing to those on low and moderate incomes
- ■ to build a strong internal organisation
- ■ to aim at a strong market position.

Table 12.13 shows a selection of the CSFs and KPIs for this business unit.

The Renting business unit can contribute to all strategic objectives. Table 12.14 shows a number of the business unit objectives and indicators for this business unit.

Table 12.13 Objectives, CSFs, and KPIs of Maintenance and Control

Strategic objective	Business unit objective	Unit CSF	Unit KPI
To work in a customer-oriented fashion	Carry out housing management that meets customers' demands	Customer satisfaction with housing management	Maintenance response time
To provide housing to low and moderate-income individuals	Preserve and improve housing unit quality	Housing unit quality	Executed maintenance (corrective/ planned maintenance ratio)
To aim at a strong market position	Operate in accordance with the market	Price/performance ratio (performance = quantity and quality)	Cost price per product
Strategic objective	Key process	Process CSF	Process KPI
To work in a customer-oriented fashion	Execute high-quality maintenance planning	Quality of long-term maintenance plan	Unbudgeted costs for corrective maintenance
To provide housing to low and moderate-income individuals	Maintain budgetary control	Budgetary job control	Jobs executed within budget

Table 12.14 Objectives, CSFs and KPIs of Renting business unit

Strategic objective	Business unit objective	Business unit CSF	Business unit KPI
To provide housing to low and moderate - income individuals	Allocate units in accordance with municipal authorities rules	Right person in right unit	Number of appropriate unit allocations
To build a strong internal organisation	Professionalise the business unit	Productivity	Productive use of time
To aim at a strong market position	Efficient monitoring of price/quality ratio	Early signalling of unbalanced price/quality ratio	Level of acceptance by potential tenants

Step II – Functional and personal objectives, CSFs and KPIs

The objectives and indicators for the business units and their departments were developed in phases. The first phase consisted of drafting the procedures on how to develop functional and personal objectives and indicators. In the second phase the objectives and indicators were first developed for the business unit managers, and after that for the other employees of the business unit. For the business units, the first activity was an interview with the management team member who was responsible for that specific business unit. Some of the discussion topics were the activities that the business unit performed, possible factors for success or failure with respect to the business unit, and the content of the business unit's current reports. After the interview, the functional objectives were developed in a workshop in which business unit managers participated and so did the relevant management team member.

The functional objectives for the business unit managers were usually the same as the business unit objectives that had been developed in step I. After all managers had formulated their functional objectives, all other employees of the business unit did the same in the next workshop.

In a first workshop, employees had to formulate the functional objectives for themselves. As a starting point, they used the business unit objectives, the functional objectives of the managers, and job descriptions of the functions and positions within the business unit. Beforehand, the business unit managers were asked to indicate which objectives they considered important to their employees. The employees then discussed possible functional objectives. In a second workshop, they developed the objectives further into CSFs and KPIs. In a third workshop, they finalised the definitions for the KPIs, formulated personal objectives for each organisational member, and set targets for the KPIs.

The final output from the workshops was various sets of functional and personal objectives, functional CSFs and KPIs for each position in the business unit, and personal targets for the KPIs, which were then agreed upon by the employee and manager in question. The development of competency and project objectives, CSFs, and KPIs was postponed until the next year, because of time constraints.

The Maintenance Advice Agency, which is part of the Maintenance and Control business unit, consists of construction engineers, installation engineers, project managers, and tenant contact advisers. A project manager is responsible for the quality of houses and buildings, the quality of maintenance work, and budgetary control of projects. For a construction engineer, work quality is also important. However, the project manager is responsible for the quality of the entire project, whereas the construction engineer is only responsible for activities performed by him/herself. The project manager has to make sure that the work is done within budget, and employees have to watch the price/quality ratio of materials and services provided by contractors.

The tenant contact adviser is responsible for communication between tenants and Het Oosten. This includes both providing tenants with information on future maintenance work and informing the association about tenant wishes and complaints. Table 12.15 gives the functional objectives and corresponding CSFs and KPIs for the various functions of the Maintenance Advice Agency.

Tenant Affairs, which is part of the Renting business unit, consists of one senior staff member and a number of junior staff members. Most of the employees of this department have the same functional objectives. The reason for this is that Tenant Affairs operates as a team. Employees often have to step in for each other to deal with tenant contacts. This is why objectives are defined that apply to the team as a whole, such as supporting each other and sharing information (Table 12.16).

The personal objectives were derived from the functional objectives of Tenant Affairs. In practice, these two types of objectives were virtually the

Table 12.15 Functional objectives, CSFs and KPIs of the Maintenance Advice Agency

Project manager		
Functional objective	Functional CSF	Functional KPI
To create and maintain an acceptable technical quality of houses and buildings	Quality of housing unit	Housing units examined
To ensure good planning and supervision	Quality of planning and supervision	Activities executed within the time planned
	Complete and reliable documents on costs with regard to contracts	Discrepancies due to more or less work
To execute projects within budget	Budgetary control	Discrepancy compared to budget
Construction engineer		
Functional objective	Functional CSF	Functional KPI
To ensure good planning and supervision	Quality of planning and supervision	Activities executed to plan
To operate in accordance with the demands of the market	Price/quality ratio in accordance with market	Cost price of delivered products
Tenant contact adviser		
Functional objective	Functional CSF	Functional KPI
To inform customers sufficiently about maintenance projects	Customer satisfaction about information service	Tenant organisations' satisfaction with information service
To inform employees sufficiently about maintenance projects	Information on time	Advice provided on time
To incorporate tenant wishes into maintenance plans	Tenant wishes implemented	Tenant wishes implemented

Table 12.16 Functional objectives, CSFs and KPIs of Tenant Affairs

Senior staff member		
Functional objective	Functional CSF	Functional KPI
To carry out arrangements made with tenant organisations	Managers who are well informed about arrangements with tenant organisations	Managers who are satisfied with the information on arrangements with tenant organisations
Junior staff members		
Functional objective	Functional CSF	Functional KPI
To ensure good management of contacts with tenant organisations	Good contacts with tenant organisations	Satisfaction of tenant organisations about contacts
To be optimally accessible and recognizable for internal and external customers, in order to provide information that is timely, correct, and complete	Customer satisfaction about accessibility	Customer satisfaction about accessibility
	Sufficient number of employees on duty	Actual number of employees on duty (vs. planned number of employees on duty)
To find and contribute to solving problems relating to the quality of life and to propose improvements	Structural proposals to improve quality of life	Quality of proposals to improve quality of life
To deal in good time with objections to rent increases and rent disputes	Effective processing of rent increases	Reasonable rent increases
To cooperate optimally with other employees and support them	Prevent work backlogs	Reported backlogs

same. Targets differed when employees had less than average experience or worked part-time. In a number of cases, project objectives or competency objectives were added. Table 12.17 lists several examples of objectives for various positions.

The personal objectives and targets are discussed annually in an evaluation meeting between employee and manager. They discuss whether the results achieved on personal indicators have deviated from target in the past year, and possible causes for this.

The main aim of reviewing performance using personal indicators is not to judge the person but to improve his or her functioning. At the end of the

Table 12.17 Examples of personal objectives, CSFs and KPIs

Personal objective	Personal CSF	Personal KPI
To ensure quick and complete implementation of the new software system	Test plan	Timeliness of activities vs. test plan
To encourage commercial operation of Het Oosten vs. other housing associations	Insight into the commercial operation of Het Oosten	Delivery of a strengths-weaknesses analysis
To become all-round within own group	Growth with the organisation or group/knowledge transfer within projects	Days spent at other projects

meeting, the employee and manager need to complete a form for the next year. This form includes personal objectives, personal CSFs and KPIs, and personal targets for the coming year. For each objective it is indicated which resources or preconditions are needed to achieve it: for example special management information to be obtained from another department, a certain computer program, or extra time and resources. At the end of the meeting, it should be clear for both employee and manager what performance is expected the next year. A similar meeting is held between the manager and the management team member responsible for the business unit to discuss the manager's own personal objectives.

Because regular status reports are provided throughout the year, employees can follow whether they are performing at the expected level or not. They can, if necessary, talk to their managers and subsequently take action to improve their performance. Mid-year, there is an intermediate performance review in which progress and possible actions are discussed. These actions are then included in the report.

In the evaluation round that takes place several months after the performance review, the result of the performance reviews is just one element discussed in the evaluation. More important than the results on personal indicators are the actions that individuals have taken to improve the results on specific KPIs.

Lessons learned

During the project and particularly as a result of the discussions during the workshops, the following lessons were learned:

- *Involvement and support by management is crucial.* Managers played an important role in the success of the project. It turned out that if managers in business units or departments were not committed or were only partially committed to a project, employees showed little commitment as well. More than once, lack of time was given as a reason that managers and other staff had not achieved the personal objectives. It was found that other developments and activities in the organisation had absorbed much of the time and attention of employees. This is why it is important to determine in advance the priority level of the project compared with other projects, for instance by filling in the feasibility analysis (see Chapter 2).

■ *Be prepared for hidden problems.* The discussion about personal objectives, targets, and requirements to achieve those targets brought a number of problems to the surface. Some examples are decreased trust in managers, fear of continuously increasing targets, insufficient time and means to do the work properly, and discontent with having to share responsibility for results with colleagues who possibly work less efficiently. To gain support for the results of the project, it was important to open these problems to debate. To encourage employees to discuss problems during workshops, it was decided that managers should not participate in these workshops. In this way, employees felt free to address issues, especially if these concerned one of the managers.

■ *Safeguard the quality of the measurements.* The selection of the final set of KPIs was often done on the basis of how easy it was to measure them. This, however, endangers the quality of indicators as the final set does not provide a realistic picture of the current status of the organisation. In these cases, it may even have been better to leave out less relevant indicators entirely and choose indicators that are less specific but give an approximation of the actual result. After the workshops, it turned out that many KPI definitions had not been described in enough detail. It was often the case that if definitions were reviewed at a later stage, the exact meaning was unclear. For example, did "within a week" mean within five working days or within seven days? Or, did "as quickly as possible" mean within two weeks or within two months? Definitions with a high level of detail prevent confusion and ambiguity. Effort indicators, such as cooperation, atmosphere, effort, and customer friendliness often proved to be "soft" and difficult to measure. These indicators are, however, important input for performance reviews as they provide information on the competencies of individuals in their current work environment.

■ *Clarify and articulate instances of cross-departmental cooperation.* Since the complete organisation was involved in the project, overlaps and interrelations within and between departments came to the surface. This led to better insight into internal processes as well as improvement of them. This is why it was no surprise that during the workshops people more than once said that failure to achieve certain objectives was caused by other departments that had not fulfilled their commitments. To prevent the project from becoming an instrument to blame others for lagging results, it is important to focus on ways to improve the cooperation between departments and business units.

- *Develop a detailed vision of the relation between the new performance management system and the existing reward system.* Employees asked a lot of questions about the link between the new reporting system and the current evaluation and reward system of Het Oosten. During the project, the association had not yet developed a vision on how to link the two. One of the reasons for this was that working with personal objectives was completely new to Het Oosten. As a result it was difficult to prevent confusion among employees. By formulating a vision of how the new system would fit in an organisation's human resource architecture, management could significantly take away employee uncertainty.

After employees had worked for some time with the new system, they noticed that their responsibilities became clearer and that they could better align their work activities with these responsibilities. The staff departments in particular were positive about the fact that the project had made their work and consequently their contribution to the achievement of the association's objectives more visible and tangible. Employees who depended upon activities performed by others to meet their objectives suddenly wanted to have meetings to make agreements. As employees gained insight into each other's responsibilities and dependencies, there was an increase of clarity and consultation.

An important job for managers was to evaluate and complement the personal objectives formulated by their employees. In most of the cases, the quality of the objectives was sufficient and required little or no adjustment. As for the targets, management only had a monitoring role. One of the initial concerns of employees was that they would be judged on the basis of ever-increasing, unrealistic targets. But in practice it was management that adjusted the personal targets set by employees to more realistic levels.

Performance alignment made the control tasks of managers easier by improving the information supply. At any time of the year, both managers and employees could see and predict whether objectives and targets would be achieved. Additionally, performance measurement functioned as a means to make issues debatable. Employees usually first tried to improve their performance themselves, sometimes after consulting a colleague. Only if they did not succeed did they consult their managers to find the causes of lagging performance and to define actions to achieve better results in future.

Het Oosten: five years later

Het Oosten has been working with the new performance management system for five years now. In practice the organisation experienced some difficulties with the system. The strategic objectives were originally developed by the management team and the supervisory board. Because of this, almost automatically the objectives were of a high level of abstraction, which made them less recognisable for lower levels in the organisation. This made it harder for the business units to translate the strategic objectives into organisational unit objectives. It also became clear that the lower organisational levels felt a great need for "the story behind the objectives" in order to understand the strategic CSFs and KPIs better.

Because Het Oosten was functionally structured and the unit objectives had been developed for each business unit separately, a culture started to arise of "Don't look beyond your own department." Each organisational unit started to focus on achieving its own targets, especially because a bonus structure based on organisational units was introduced and fostered this focus. As a consequence, there was not much attention in the units on the overall organisational result. In fact the organisation was missing a lot of opportunities on achieving synergy. In addition, the objectives were not viewed as a coherent set. For example, people worked either on improving efficiency or on improving customer satisfaction. There is a natural tension between these two objectives so both have to be approached in a balanced way.

Because of these insights, Het Oosten decided to adapt its strategic objectives to make them more appealing. It also gave them a new name, "strategic principles," and made them less abstract and high-flown and more practical, and above all more comprehensible. As a consequence, some strategic principles were no longer formulated for a three to five-year period but for one year, which made them short-term priorities (Table 12.18). The general guideline when developing the principles became, "You have to be able to explain them to your grandmother!"

Reformulating the strategic objectives has resulted in a much better understanding of these objectives by the business units and employees, and

Table 12.18 Reformulated strategic objectives of Het Oosten

Old strategic objectives	New strategic principles
To work in a customer-oriented fashion	Better relations with customers
To provide housing to low and moderate-income individuals	To maintain the core inventory of affordable houses
To invest in the community and neighbourhoods	a. Create a liveable environment b. Support a vital city
To build a strong internal organisation	a. Foster more pleasure in the work b. Create a more professional organisation
To aim at a strong market position	a. Achieve a strong market position b. Create a better image for Het Oosten
To improve the financial position	Improve the financial position

more commitment by them to supporting the achievement of these objectives at their own level. Organisation members are willing to study the results, to analyse the real causes of lagging performance, to identify and execute improvements, and to ask for help from other organisational units. Many of these units now publish their own internal annual report, stating their goals and performance achieved. The initially separate objectives concerning customer satisfaction and efficiency have now been combined. For example, the newly named Market and City department jointly reports on these objectives.

In the old days, when a customer was called on for a short satisfaction survey, the only two questions asked were, "Has somebody from Maintenance and Control been to see you?" and "Did that person do a good job?" Now the department keeps on asking questions. "How was the contact with the maintenance person?" "Did you notice anything (both positive and negative) during the visit that you want to report?" "How long did the maintenance take?" "Do you have any questions yourself? Can we help you with anything else?" Through this approach, it is the customer who decides in which direction the conversation is going instead of the customer being pushed to a preset outcome. This provides valuable information to Het Oosten about bottlenecks in certain departments and business units, and the customer feels that he/she is being treated seriously.

The most striking answers from customers are recorded in the management reports. This way, information on both customer satisfaction and efficiency are simultaneously discussed in business unit meetings and management team meetings. As a result, a change in attitude has already taken place: as managers and employees now know that both objectives are equally important, they try to improve them simultaneously.

Preconditions for "living" performance management

Introducing strategic performance management is a process for the long haul. The culture change can take up to five years. This is because people cannot be changed overnight, they need to change their behaviour fundamentally themselves, which is a gradual process. An important condition to facilitate the change in attitude and to make performance management a "living instrument" in the organisation is that management is not overly worried about whether the new system is going to work. It should instead focus on fulfilling the following preconditions:

- Organisation members have to learn how to operate the new system. This requires a lot of training and experience because not everybody knows directly how to work with performance management.
- The right people have to occupy the right positions: only then can

good-quality analyses be expected. After all, people need to know their business, otherwise their analyses will stay shallow.

- Management has to visibly and continuously use performance management.
- Organisation members who refuse to work with performance management will eventually have to leave the organisation if they do not shape up.
- Management must keep investing in the system. A good way to do this is to have experienced users coach less experienced organisation members. This is an excellent way to introduce new employees to the system and its application. The new employees get an extensive introduction in the system in the first week they start working at Het Oosten.
- Only people who are comfortable in a performance management culture should be hired. In Het Oosten this is done by sending every applicant for a management position, after he or she has "survived" the first sift, a brochure on Het Oosten's performance management system and a management report. During the second round of interviews the system and its application is discussed extensively and the applicant is asked how he/she would handle several concrete issues which can be extracted from the report.

Looking back at the introduction of strategic performance management at Het Oosten, it can be concluded that the introduction required a lot of time and effort but that it was worthwhile. The investment was recovered during the first three years. This is because inefficiencies are discovered and resolved quicker than before, saving a lot of aggravation and costs. Because of the standardisation the CSFs and KPIs brought to the company, there is hardly any time wasted on discussions about differences in definitions and figures. In addition, the management reports, which were traditionally financially oriented and therefore hardly used by frontline people, are now much more "owned" by these people because they provide nonfinancial information. Mistakes are talked about openly and thereby resolved quicker than ever before. Also, management is aware of real issues and bottlenecks much earlier than was the case before. To sum up, it can be clearly stated that organisation members of Het Oosten are really empowered: they own the strategic performance management system and they use it for their self-management to their own and the organisation's benefit.

It is interesting to analyse to what extent Het Oosten has taken into account the behavioural factors discussed in Chapter 10. Table 12.19 shows that on the whole the organisation has given a lot of attention to the specific behavioural factors during the implementation and use of the strategic performance management system. Undoubtedly this has contributed considerably to the success of performance management at Het Oosten.

Table 12.19 The degree to which Het Oosten paid attention to behavioural factors

Areas of attention	Behavioural factors	Het Oosten
Organisation members' understanding *Organisation members have a good understanding of the nature and goals of performance management*	1. Organisation members understand the meaning of KPIs, so they have insight into the (possible) consequences of their actions on the results of their KPIs.	Much
	2. Organisation members have insight into the relationship between business processes and CSFs/KPIs, so they understand that the results they achieve on their KPIs are important to the continuity of the organisation.	Much
	3. Organisation members' frames of reference contain similar KPIs, so they can compare their results with those of other members and obtain insight in how they are doing comparatively.	Average
	4. Organisation members agree on changes in the CSF/KPI set, so they keep on accepting their KPIs and keep on feeling responsible for the results they achieve on these.	Much
Organisation members' attitude *Organisation members have a positive attitude to performance management*	5. Organisation members recognise and acknowledge the need for performance management, which makes them willing to cooperate during the implementation of performance management.	Much
	6. Organisation members agree on the starting time, which makes them willing to cooperate from the start of the implementation of performance management.	Much
	7. Organisation members have earlier positive experiences with performance management, so they can communicate the aim and goals of performance management to the organisation.	Little
	8. Organisation members realise the importance of CSFs/KPIs/BSC to their performance, so performance management becomes part of their daily activities.	Average
	9. Organisation members do not experience CSFs/KPIs/BSC as threatening, so they are not hesitant to use performance management.	Average
Performance management alignment *Performance management matches the responsibilities of organisation members*	10. Organisation members' KPI sets are aligned with their responsibility areas, so they can be used for steering and control of those areas.	Much
	11. Organisation members can influence the KPIs assigned to them, so the acceptance and use of those KPIs is increased.	Much
	12. Organisation members prepare their own analyses, which increases the acceptance of those analyses.	Much
	13. Organisation members find the quality of the analyses good, which increases the use of those analyses.	Much
	14. Organisation members can use their CSFs/KPIs/BSC for managing their employees, which increases regular use of performance management.	Much

Table 12.19 *Continued*

Areas of attention	Behavioural factors	Het Oosten
Organisational culture *The organisational culture is aimed at using performance management to continuously improve*	15. Organisation members' results on CSFs/KPIs/BSC are openly communicated, so everyone is aware of the status of the organisation and performance knowledge can be shared.	Average
	16. Organisation members are stimulated to improve their performance by using performance management, so they do not have to be afraid that performance management will be used to punish lagging results.	Average
	17. Organisation members trust the performance information, which increases the acceptance of the information.	Much
	18. Organisation members clearly see (top) management use performance management, so they understand the importance of performance management to management and the organisation.	Much
Performance management focus *Performance management has a clear internal management and control focus*	19. Organisation members find performance management relevant because it has a clear internal control purpose, and can therefore support their activities well.	Much
	20. Organisation members find performance management relevant because only those stakeholders' interests that are important to the organisation's success are incorporated, so performance management stays aimed at the continuity of the organisation.	Little

12.5 CASE: COMPETENCY-BASED PERFORMANCE MANAGEMENT AT BOUWFONDS

Bouwfonds is one of the largest property companies in the Netherlands. The company is also active abroad. It operates in the private and commercial markets and has a banking licence. Bouwfonds is a wholly owned subsidiary of ABN AMRO, with an annual turnover of €4 billion and net profits of over €280 million. The company built close to 10,000 houses in 2004 and employs around 1800 people, of which 300 are located outside the Netherlands. Bouwfonds is currently active in France, Germany, Belgium, Scandinavia, Spain, the Czech Republic, and Slovakia, and outside Europe in North America and Canada.

Bouwfonds has several business units which operate in different markets. Bouwfonds Property Development (BPD) and Hopman Interheem Groep conduct property development activities. In November 2004, BPD took over the developer MAB. In the Netherlands, the combined company operates under the name Bouwfonds MAB Ontwikkeling. Following the takeover, BPD is now one of Europe's largest developers of owner-occupied homes and commercial property.

BPD is headquartered in the Netherlands. Bouwfonds Hypotheken is one of the larger specialist residential mortgage providers in the Netherlands, with a market share of almost 6 per cent. The majority of the mortgages are sold through independent intermediaries. Bouwfonds also offers its customers a comprehensive package of housing insurance policies.

In addition to its own mortgage products, Bouwfonds develops and sells mortgages marketed by third parties under their own name (private labels). Rijnlandse Bank provides mortgage loans and focuses on small commercial property. Its mortgage products are sold both directly and via intermediaries. The activities of Bouwfonds Property Finance include property financing, investment financing, leasing arrangements and risk-bearing equity holdings. Its strength is in the combination of tailor-made financial solutions and many years of knowledge and experience in property. International projects account for around 25 per cent of the portfolio.

Bouwfonds Asset Management focuses on the development, structuring and management of property portfolios. These are unlisted funds for both private and institutional investors in the Netherlands and abroad. The investment funds comprise both residential and commercial property.

Bouwfonds Asset Management develops structured, very specific, tailor-made investment products. Through its fund management activities, Bouwfonds applies its expertise to finding solutions to social issues relating to spatial planning in the broadest sense. In this context, Bouwfonds manages a number of funds in the areas of public housing and spatial planning. The policy of these funds is determined by independent executive boards.

Bouwfonds' ambition is to be a leading European property development, financing, and asset management company by 2010. Bouwfonds selected six main areas where it wants to grow in the coming years: the Netherlands, Belgium, France, Germany, Scandinavia and Spain. In these countries Bouwfonds wants to achieve a top five position in property development, financing, and asset management.

Introduction of performance management and competency management

Bouwfonds' board of directors has opted for ambitious growth objectives in its strategic plan. This ambition can only be achieved if special efforts are made in the coming years to improve result-focused management and to foster the positive development of staff. "To do this, we have opted for performance and competency management (PCM)," according to the internal project leader, Tjark van Heijningen. PCM is an instrument that allows the activities of Bouwfonds and its employees to be monitored.

Performance management aims at control on the basis of financial and nonfinancial parameters. The financial parameters are measured with indicators relating to customers and markets, internal working procedures, and the development of people and products. These KPIs are represented in a BSC. Competency management aims at control of the components of experience, knowledge, skills, attitudes, and behaviours of organisational members. The requisite combination of these components is set out in a competency profile.

Van Heijningen clarifies:

> Before we start looking at improving results, we must first know what results we want. And we must also know what kind of performance is expected from Bouwfonds as a whole and from divisional, departmental, sectional and individual levels. The performance levels must be derived from Bouwfonds' mission and strategic objectives, from business and department plans, and from individual function descriptions. Then, a decision needs to be taken on the essential competencies that are required by Bouwfonds, the divisions, the departments, the sections, and the individual section leaders to achieve the required performance levels. Once both the required levels of performance and the needed competencies have been identified, Bouwfonds' managers are in a position to lead their staff effectively.

Bouwfonds uses an annual cycle of agreements, coaching, and assessment. In November/December, management agrees with organisational members on the necessary competency development and the required performance levels. In April/May a progress meeting takes place, to evaluate how matters are progressing and if further agreements are necessary. In September/October there is an appraisal meeting, to discuss whether targets have been reached and whether the required improvements in competencies have been achieved.

The important instruments in the cycle are the BSC and the competency profiles. The competency profile is intended to represent the knowledge, skills, and attitude that are necessary for a particular function. Because each competency is clearly defined and explained, using practical examples, organisation members are better able to understand what is expected of them. Using the BSC, strategic objectives can be converted directly into BSCs for lower organisational levels and for individual organisational members. Van Heijningen stresses, "This is how we can be sure that every organisational member is absolutely clear as to what part he or she has to play in the attainment of Bouwfonds' ambitions and goals."

Alignment

Bouwfonds made a clear choice of a system of control in which competencies and performance levels are interlinked. "It is really a discussion between managers and organisational members, during which clear agreements have to be made on what is expected of the employee and what help he needs in this respect," explains Van Heijningen:

And it is also a matter of people having a clear idea of where their sections, their departments, and Bouwfonds as a whole are heading. Unfortunately, they do not always have this clear picture. When you walk around the site and ask any 15 people what Bouwfonds' strategic objectives are, you will get diffuse answers. This seems very surprising because these are the people that have to achieve the objectives in their day-to-day job. What you actually find is that people tend to set their own objectives on the basis of their own perceptions and realities, and these they pursue with enthusiasm. Putting this into context, we do not believe that this attitude is peculiar to Bouwfonds but that it can be found in most companies.

Because of this discrepancy, much effort was put by Bouwfonds into integrally setting up the BSC and the competency profiles. Pilots were conducted in the Property Development and Mortgages divisions. On the basis of the pilot results, Bouwfonds took the decision to introduce PCM. To prevent the introduction running out of steam, Bouwfonds' approach was very considered and consistent. All managers were heavily trained in PCM during the implementation, and they can now follow optional PCM2 and PCM3 training courses which go deeper into how to arrive at agreements with staff and how to conduct appraisals. The external consultancy firm that was involved in the implementation was impressed with the commitment shown by Bouwfonds management. One of the consultants commented:

> It's not always like this. Competency management is often taken up enthusiastically by the HRM department. They do their utmost best to produce competency profiles, but as soon as these have been finalised, management turns round and asks: "Competency profiles, what are they? And why do we need these? Are they important?" And when they then learn that the board of directors is not really involved in the project, they will not give it any priority. Then you know for sure that the implementation is not going to be a success. At Bouwfonds, the chairman of the board of directors was part of the steering committee. He stated repeatedly the reasons he considered the system to be so important and that he expected everyone to do their bit. This involvement has been crucial to the success of PCM.

It is important for PCM to be internalised and integrated into regular procedures. The BSCs of the company's departments have been incorporated in the quarterly reports. This means that they now appear on the agendas at management team meetings and are used during discussions between heads of department and individual members of staff. In order to prevent enthusiasm for PCM ebbing away, one of the project leaders emphasises that the board of directors must continue to monitor the project: "Employees must have the feeling that it is on the agenda, that it is considered important and that help is offered when required. People need to be held accountable if they are not attaching the proper importance to the process."

Key points

- ☑ In practice the human resource perspective of performance management is often neglected, resulting in unmotivated organisation members.
- ☑ The set of human resource instruments (performance review, incentives, training, and development) should be aligned with performance management in order to support the realisation of the organisation's objectives.
- ☑ The performance alignment model requires that every organisation member delivers output that is aligned with the mission and the strategy of the company. The intended output is made concrete and formalised in personal objectives.
- ☑ A competency is defined as a cluster of related knowledge, skills, attitudes and behaviours that affects a major part of a job (a role or responsibility), that correlates with performance on the job, that can be measured against well-accepted standards, and that can be improved via training and development. Competency management should be aligned to performance management.

References

Ashton, C. (1997) *Strategic Performance Measurement: Transforming corporate performance by measuring and managing the drivers of business success.* London: Business Intelligence.

Bolger, B. and Mulhern, F. (2005) People performance management: the science that supports soft metrics. *Business Performance Management,* June.

Buckingham, M. (2001) Don't waste time and money. Competency programs are well-intended, but ineffective. Here's a better alternative. *Gallup Management Journal*, 3 December.

Buckingham, M. and Clifton, D.O. (2001) *Now, Discover Your Strengths.* New York: Free Press.

Buckingham, M. and Coffman, C. (1999) *First, Break All the Rules.* New York: Simon and Schuster.

Cascio, W.F. (2000) *Costing Human Resources: The financial impact of behavior in organisations*, 4th edn. South-Western College Publishing.

Cheng, M.I., Dainty, A.R.J. and Moore, D.R. (2005) Towards a multidimensional competency-based managerial performance framework: a hybrid approach. *Journal of Managerial Psychology*, 20 (5), 380–96.

Dechant, K. and Veiga, J. (1995) More on the folly. *Academy of Management Executive*, 9 (1).

Gubman, E.L. (1998) *The Talent Solution.* New York: McGraw-Hill.

Hoff, J. (2002) Hoe gaat prestatiemanagement 'leven' in de organisatie? Empowerment door prestatiemanagement bij woningbouwvereniging Het Oosten. *Bedrijfskunde*, 74 (4).

Kerr, S. (1975) On the folly of rewarding A, while hoping for B. *Academy of Management Journal*, 18.

Kouhy, R. and Vedd, R. (1998) Performance measurement in strategic human resource management. *International Journal of Business Performance Management*, 2 (1/2/3).

Lucia, A.D. and Lepsinger, R. (1999) *The Art and Science of Competency Models*. San Francisco: Jossey-Bass.

McKenna, S. (2002) Can knowledge of the characteristics of "high performers" be generalised? *Journal of Management Development*, 21 (9), 680–701.

Miner, K.R., Childers, W.K., Alperin, M., Cioffi, J. and Hunt, N. (2005) The MACH model: from competencies to instruction and performance of the public health workforce. *Public Health Reports*, 120, supplement 1, 9–15.

Rucci, A.J., Kirn, S.P. and Quinn, R.T. (1998) The employee – customer – profit chain at Sears. *Harvard Business Review*, January–February.

Schoonover, S. (2005) www.schoonover.com.

Stephen, A. and Roithmayr, T. (1998) Escaping the performance management trap. In: M. Butteriss (ed.), *Reinventing HR: Changing roles to create the high-performing organisation*. New York: Wiley.

Waal, A.A. de (2001) *Power of Performance Management: How leading companies create sustained value*. New York: Wiley.

Waal, A.A. de (2002) *Presteren is mensenwerk*. Deventer: Kluwer.

Walters, M. (1995) *The Performance Management Handbook*. London: Institute of Personnel and Development.

Part 3

Implementing Strategic Performance Management

Part 3 deals with implementing strategic performance management. Topics discussed are:

- how to keep the strategic performance management system simple yet effective
- the implementation plan
- barriers encountered during the implementation
- dos and don'ts
- change management issues.

13

Implementation

Using the experiences of organisations that have implemented strategic performance management successfully, this chapter discusses a number of useful guidelines, a project approach, dos and don'ts, and change management issues with regard to performance management.

Chapter objectives

- ☑ To provide the reader with a structured approach for the implementation of strategic performance management.
- ☑ To discuss the dos, don'ts, and pitfalls the reader can encounter during the implementation.
- ☑ To discuss the change management aspects of a performance management implementation.

13.1 KEEP IT SIMPLE

In many organisations there is a tendency to make the strategic performance management process too complicated. This is quite natural because there are many conflicting challenges that have to be addressed, all at the same time. The long-term focus has to be balanced with the short term, financial information has to be supplemented with nonfinancial information, strategy has to be linked with operations, personal objectives have to be aligned with organisational objectives, and a clear parenting style and parenting structure have to be defined. It is not easy to devise a clear, simple, practical, and concise strategic performance management system that works. But it can be done through organising the process around the CSFs and KPIs of the organisation (Figure 13.1).

The strategic performance management process provides a powerful tool for aligning the organisation. By linking the strategy, budgeting/target setting, execution/forecasting, performance measurement, performance

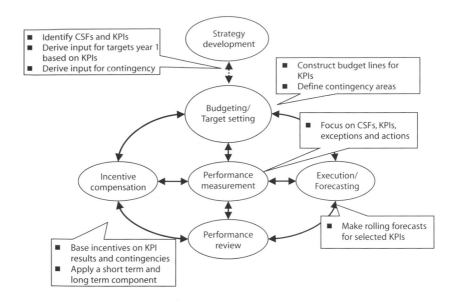

Figure 13.1 Keep the strategic performance management process simple

review, and incentive compensation subprocesses into one integrated process, an organisation not only achieves excellence in each subprocess, but also aligns the information flows and activities between the subprocesses. If every part of the strategic performance management process refers to the same value drivers then the potential for confusion, misunderstanding, and error is minimised. This consistency also supports the organisation's need for simplicity and speed.

The key concept is that a limited number of CSFs and KPIs provide the link between the stages in the strategic performance management process. These measures are identified during the strategy development process as being the most important critical items on which the organisation has to focus to achieve success and create value. The strategic action plans are centred around these CSFs and KPIs. The strategic plan becomes less complicated, because it only focuses on the key items. For each KPI, targets are set for all the years in the strategic horizon. The financial budget is made only for the limited number of KPIs. A complete, detailed budget for the profit and loss statement and the balance sheet is not needed. The financial targets for year one of the strategic plan make up the budget for the coming year. For each KPI the contingency areas are defined, based on the sensitivity analysis made during the strategy development process.

With the targets defined in the strategic plan for the coming year, and the contingency areas, the budget lines and intervention areas can be constructed. Contingency areas (which stipulate when higher management levels should consider intervening) only need to be established for the KPIs. The lines and areas determine what kind of information has to be reported when and to whom. Management only needs information about results and forecasts for the CSFs and KPIs, and can, therefore, strictly focus on exceptional results (positive or negative). When the results wind up in one of the intervention areas, exception reports are delivered to higher management levels (push). These management levels can obtain, if needed, additional information by surfing around on the management web (pull). Corrective and preventive actions are formulated for the exceptions.

Organisational members are rewarded on the results they obtained for the CSFs and KPIs. Because these contain both lagging financial and leading nonfinancial indicators, managers are evaluated on the short-term (lagging financial) and long-term (leading nonfinancial) components of organisational performance. The deviation of the actual results from the targets on the budget lines stipulates the amount of bonus and compensation.

13.2 IMPLEMENTATION APPROACH

Implementing strategic performance management process is not achieved overnight. It is a gradual process in which organisational members need to be convinced of the merits of performance management and then get used to the new way of managing. It therefore requires a structured project approach. Figure 13.2 shows the main steps of the approach for implementing the strategic performance management development cycle.

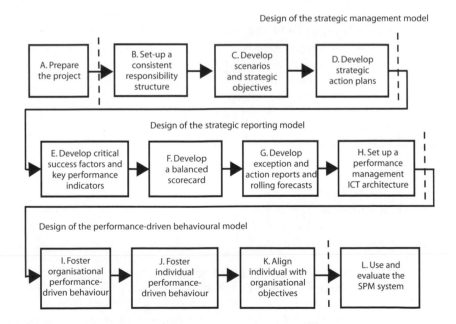

Figure 13.2 Project plan for strategic performance management

Step A: Prepare the project

The purpose of the first step is to inform and prepare the organisation about the planned strategic performance management development project. Information meetings are organised and information memos are distributed. In this phase a project team is established, consisting of people from all the organisational areas that are relevant to the project. A detailed implementation plan and a communication plan are also drawn up.

Step B: Set up a consistent responsibility structure

In this step, a consistent responsibility structure is set up in the organisation by choosing an unambiguous parenting style and parenting structure. The roles and responsibilities of each management level are made clear, and mechanisms are put in place that make sure the chosen management style is applied consistently. Managers and employees need to know what they are held accountable for.

Step C: Develop scenarios and strategic objectives

In this step, the organisation formulates or reformulates its strategic objectives based on possible scenarios. These scenarios depict possible external and internal trends and developments that could have consequences for the organisation. When developing strategic objectives, management should reach consensus in order to be able to develop a coherent set of CSFs and KPIs that is sufficiently supported by the organisation. In addition to strategic objectives, objectives are formulated for each organisational unit. It is essential that the unit and strategic objectives are aligned so the whole organisation works towards the same goals.

Step D: Develop strategic action plans

During step D, the long-term orientation of the strategy is translated into realistic and workable short-term yearly actions. These actions are recorded in a strategic action plan, which is a document that describes the activities that need to be executed in order to achieve strategic objectives and reach measurable performance improvement.

Step E: Develop CSFs and KPIs

In this step, strategic CSFs and KPIs are developed based on the strategic objectives and the key processes of the organisation. This is done in a series of workshops, in which all management team members partake in order to create support in the organisation and to prevent the "not invented here" syndrome. In a similar manner CSFs and KPIs are developed for all organisational units. The workshops result in a "brainstorming list" of CSFs and KPIs. Therefore, also during step E, the list is reduced until a manageable set of measures remains. This is necessary because otherwise managers would get an overload of information and lose control. During additional workshops, managers decide with which CSFs and KPIs they want to start working. These will be included in the organisation's management reports.

After prioritising the CSFs and KPIs, detailed definitions are made for the KPIs. In addition, reporting procedures are drafted, managers are appointed who are going to be responsible for specific indicators, and targets are determined for each KPI. These are all put in what is known as a "KPI definition document" (Figure 13.3).

Step F: Develop a BSC

In this step, a reporting layout for the performance information is made based on the BSC.

Step G: Develop exception and action reports and rolling forecasts

During step G, the chosen reporting layout is refined so organisational members can focus on the most critical business issues and take swift action on these. Exception and action reporting are set up so users' attention is directed: to exceptional events and figures; on a focus on analysing financial and nonfinancial results; on drafting and executing corrective action plans; and on the impact of those action plans. Proactive behaviour of organisational members is fostered by using rolling forecasts.

Step H: Set up a performance management ICT architecture

In this step, a performance management ICT architecture is installed that can provide organisation members with the required performance management information in an efficient way.

Before the organisation starts with this, two questions have to be answered: can the organisation use simple spreadsheets to provide performance information, or is a full-blown application needed? When deciding to implement a new software system, does this have to be done in parallel with the development of CSFs and KPIs, or does it have to be done after all the new measures have been

KEY PERFORMANCE INDICATOR – TRAINING DAYS

Belongs to CSF: Quality of personnel

Definition of KPI: Total number of training days attended by employees in the department since January 1, divided by total number of training days that have been planned as of January 1.

- Attended training days: the days on which an employee attended training. The attended training should have been conducted by a qualified trainer (internal or external) and should be relevant to the function of the employee.
- Personnel: all persons that are employed on a permanent basis (temporary employees are not included).

Reporting procedure – Activities to be performed	Data file	By
Make a training plan for all employees and register the planned training days for them.	'Training'	Business unit manager
Register in the file the attended training and the number of training days attended by the employee. The updated information must be approved by the business unit manager.	'Training'	Business unit manager
Count all the attended training days of all employees in the department in the last quarter (= X).	'Training'	Business unit manager
Count all the planned training days of all employees in the department for this quarter (= Y).	'Training'	Business unit manager
Calculate X/Y * 100 percent	'Training'	Business unit manager
Enter the resulting percentages in the report.	Report	Business unit manager

Target: The target for 20xx is that 100 per cent of the planned training days have been attended before year-end. Expected is a linear increase of 25 percent each quarter. The number of planned training days for 20xx is ten per employee.

Explanation of the KPI: If the result of the key performance indicator is below target at the end of one of the first three quarters, a corrective action is needed to make sure that employees can attend the planned training days in the next quarter(s). If this does not happen, the employee will not be sufficiently trained to function in his or her (new) position. If in a certain quarter the result turns out higher than the target (perhaps more training was attended than planned), corrective actions are only necessary if it is expected that at the end of the year the number of attended training days will be higher than the number of planned training days (increasing the risk of exceeding the training budget).

Figure 13.3 Example of a KPI definition document

DATA FILE

CSF:	Quality of personnel
KPI:	Training days
KPI def:	Total number of training days that have been attended by employees in the department since January, 1 divided by the total number of training days that have been planned as of January, 1.

Quarter	Target	Attended training days
I	25%	22%
II	50%	44%
III	75%	74%
IV	100%	80%

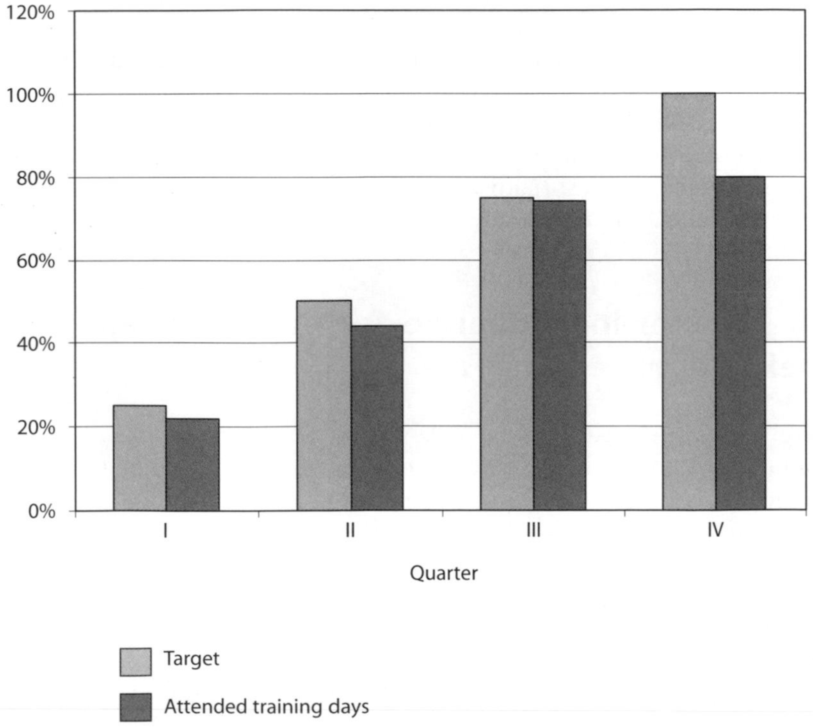

Figure 13.3 *Continued*

defined? (Waal and Geelen, 2002). The answer to the first question depends on the size of the organisation (the larger the organisation, the greater the need for a software application like CPM), the complexity of the new performance management system (the more complex, the greater the need for a software application), and the complexity of the current ICT architecture (the more complex, the greater the need for a software application on top of the current architecture). The answer to the second question depends again on the complexity of the organisation and the dynamics of the industry it operates in. Generally speaking, the more complex and dynamic the organisation, the greater the need for an efficient support of the performance management process by ICT. This entails a parallel implementation of a software application during the implementation of strategic performance management.

Step I: Foster organisational performance-driven behaviour

In step I, the organisation decides on the manner in which performance management is going to be used throughout the company. Clear agreements are made on how management levels are going to use performance information in their dealings with lower management levels. It is clearly established that performance management is not going to be used for accountability purposes but for continuous improvement. Also, management works on establishing trust in the organisation in the new technique, and develops clear performance-driven values.

Step J: Foster individual performance-driven behaviour

During step J, the organisation works on fostering an attitude in organisational members to get things done, to deliver on commitments, to follow up on critical assignments, to support and hold each other accountable for promises, to be proactive, and to be performance driven. Management sets the right example by "walking the talk", focusing on actions, and following up on these actions. Organisational members are coached to start acting on what was agreed and on displaying specific behaviours that make them regular users of performance management.

Step K: Align individual with organisational objectives

In this step, individual responsibilities, targets and incentives are aligned with the strategic objectives of the organisation in order to make sure that every organisational member delivers output that is aligned with the mission and the strategy of the company. The intended output is made concrete and formalised in personal objectives.

Step L: Use and evaluate the SPM system

The final step consists of actually using the new strategic performance management system by applying the new CSFs and KPIs, using and discussing the new management reports and the BSC, and taking action on these. After the system has been used for a period, an evaluation of the system, the CSFs, KPIs and BSC, and their use is made. This may well lead to adjustments of the CSF/KPI set, the reports, the accountability structure, the reporting procedure, or the targets. The evaluation takes place periodically, at least once a year, preferably during the annual strategic development process.

13.3 IMPLEMENTATION DOS, DON'TS, AND PITFALLS

Forewarned is forearmed. Now that it is clear how the performance management process in an organisation can be improved, it is time to get to work. In practice, the implementation of the ideas may turn out to be not quite as easy as expected or hoped. When starting the implementation of the strategic performance management development cycle, the following issues should be taken into account.

- Clearly analyse beforehand what the bottlenecks are in the current performance management process. If this is not done, there is a real risk that the new strategic performance management process will not deal with these bottlenecks in a satisfactory manner. The consequence will be that people are not motivated to really implement the new system and carry on in the same old way.
- To successfully implement strategic performance management, the involvement and commitment of top management and organisational members is needed right from the start. When the implementation has too low a priority for them, it is doomed to failure. It is important to continuously communicate the advantages of the new system to the people, and to also show them the practical benefits. In addition, the implementation has to be as efficient as possible and should not take up too much of organisation members' time.
- A structured approach for the implementation is important for the acceptance of strategic performance management by organisation members. Such an approach, which has been used successfully before at other organisations, can save an organisation a lot of unnecessary problems and hiccups. In addition to that, a proven approach makes it possible to see the expected end result beforehand, which not only

motivates people but also makes it possible to monitor the progress towards this end result.

■ One of the biggest changes that results from implementing an improved performance management system is that people's performance becomes much clearer and more transparent. This can make the system threatening to organisation members. If there is a culture of severe repercussions in an organisation, people will try to delay the implementation and manipulate the result of the KPIs ("How to lie with statistics"). Therefore, do not use information from the performance management system for settling scores, but for self-control and continuous improvement. If at the time of the implementation sufficient attention is paid to changing the management style from punishing to coaching and focusing on improvement, strategic performance management will be less threatening and people will more easily accept it. This change in management style appears to be one of the most difficult elements of an implementation.

■ During the implementation, ICT systems play a crucial role in collecting and reporting the data that is required to calculate the new measures. If it turns out that organisational members have to produce most data manually, they will see this as an additional task on top of their normal work. The willingness to make this extra effort every month or quarter will quickly diminish. It is, therefore, important to schedule enough time for research, adjustment, and improvement of the ICT architecture within the organisation. In practice, creating a strategic performance management portal can turn out to be one of the most delaying factors in the implementation process, when it is not started in time.

■ By making strategic performance management part of the daily operation, there is a better chance that it will continue to be used in the future by organisational members. The daily work of an organisation member consists primarily of acting on information that he/she has received. This means there is a lot of focus on future and action orientation. Or, in the words of a CEO the author once interviewed, "Do not give me overviews, but issues. I want to know what is happening, what we are going to do about it, and what is going to happen next." This quote indicates that it is not sufficient to include only future-oriented indicators in the strategic performance management system: actions and forecasts on the expected results of the actions taken also need to be incorporated. This will help to diminish the noncommittal attitude that is present in many organisations with regard to taking action, and will turn performance management into a "living" instrument.

■ The internal aspects of the organisation such as key processes are at least as important as the external aspects ("What do customers and shareholders think of us?") and should therefore constantly be included in decisions. For example, a customer might think that 100 per cent on-time delivery is important, but the organisation does not necessarily have to comply with that. It could choose not to serve this customer because 100 per cent on-time delivery is too costly and therefore not one of the organisation's objectives. Whether the organisation is going to meet a certain customer need or not should always be a conscious decision, taking both external and internal factors into consideration. By letting managers partake in such decisions, there will be more support in the organisation for the strategic objectives and thereby the strategic performance management system.

■ A successful implementation of strategic performance management will be severely harmed by:
   - not making sure there is a support base for performance management in the organisation
   - making too many changes in the new system
   - not enough commitment from top management
   - not enough involvement of organisational members
   - not the right combination of skills in the implementation team
   - too many projects in the organisation at the same time
   - unclear responsibilities for implementation tasks
   - not enough insight into and clarity of the strategy
   - not enough control of primary processes
   - not enough training of organisational members
   - not paying enough attention to organisational members' fear of performance management being used by managers to settle scores
   - going too fast!

■ Watch out for the repetitive change syndrome, which occurs when successive levels of change bring about so much stress in the organisation that change slows down, becomes more expensive, and is much more likely to fail than if the pace of change had been more reasonable (Abrahamson, 2004). There are three symptoms of the syndrome:
   - initiative overload: more change initiatives are launched than any organisation can ever reasonably handle
   - change-related chaos: there are so many waves of initiatives that hardly anyone knows which change is being implemented or why
   - employee cynicism/burn-out: people begin to fake participation in the change while at the same time displaying "gallows humour" and circulating Dilbert cartoons.

■ Every implementation in which behavioural changes are involved is difficult, and there are many obstacles on the way to continuous improvement. The matrix depicted in Figure 13.4 may help to identify the status of the organisation and possible remaining barriers during the implementation of strategic performance management. If one of the components mentioned in the matrix is missing, an organisation cannot proceed with the implementation. Only if all components are in the right place can an organisation successfully implement performance management.

Pressure to change	+ Involvement	+ Communication	+ Training	+ Support structure and process	+ Reward/ recognition	=	Continuous change
X	✓	✓	✓	✓	✓	=	No action
✓	X	✓	✓	✓	✓	=	No emotional tie
✓	✓	X	✓	✓	✓	=	Quick start; quick ending
✓	✓	✓	X	✓	✓	=	Concern and frustration
✓	✓	✓	✓	X	✓	=	Fight symptoms instead of causes
✓	✓	✓	✓	✓	X	=	No long-term change
✓	✓	✓	✓	✓	✓	=	Continuous change

Figure 13.4 Components of successful change

13.4 PERFORMANCE MANAGEMENT AND CHANGE MANAGEMENT

Implementing strategic performance management is a big change for an organisation. It is to be expected that such a change will create resistance in the company. Therefore, change management has to be taken very seriously in order to increase the chances of a successful implementation. This section describes a structured approach to incorporating change management activities into the implementation of strategic performance management. It incorporates many tips and dos and don'ts that have been discussed earlier in this book.

The activities have been subdivided into four categories: activities performed at the start, before the actual implementation of strategic performance management starts; activities performed during the preparation for implementation; activities performed during the implementation; and activities performed at the end of the implementation.

Activities at the start

■ *Create awareness of the need for strategic performance management.* The need for the intended change to strategic performance management is conveyed to everyone in the organisation by defining and articulating a succinct and compelling reason for change. This reason is based on a sense of urgency or on a desire or aspiration. The most obvious case is a "burning platform" (caused by severe problems) or a compelling event (for example a change in strategy or a change in the execution of the current strategy), when there is no alternative but to change. However, even if there is a sense of complacency in the organisation, urgencies and chances for improvement can and will exist. The reasons for change can be:
  - showing how other organisations (preferably competitors) have made successful turnarounds, using benchmark figures to show the comparative performance of these organisations
  - showing the negative difference in performance that exists between the organisation and its main competitors
  - talking about current bottlenecks and failed projects and what the costs of these are to the organisation
  - discussing how the urge "to be the best" requires the transition
  - indicating the organisation is not ready (enough) for the increasing dynamics of the economy and the environment.
  The gap between performance in the current state and performance in the desired state is quantified in monetary terms, to show the potential and opportunity that exist within the organisation. However, do not focus only on the negative things. A positive way to create awareness is

to appeal to the ambition of people in the organisation. Aspiration – the desire to become a better person – is a great motivational force, and strategic performance management will certainly appeal to this desire.

■ *Paint an appealing picture of the future.* Creating a positive and inspiring picture of the future organisation makes people enthusiastic and believe in the change. This picture should describe the purpose of the change, the reasons it is worth the effort, and the differences between the current and the desired state. In addition, the organisation may decide to make an appeal to people's emotions to convince them of the need to change: for example by emphasising the negative consequences of failure, using emotive language, or using metaphors to stimulate people's imagination. The message can be made enlivened by using an imaginative name, images, pictures, slogans, music, colours, and humour, to create a good feeling about strategic performance management. Active language is used to convey the dynamics of the change. When delivering the message, managers should show some emotion, to carry across warmth and sincere commitment. Fears about the change are reduced by emphasising the opportunities that strategic performance management brings. People can "smell" and almost "touch" the new improved organisation. They can start the journey with an image of the end goal in their mind.

■ *Translate strategic performance management to each organisational level.* The consequences of what strategic performance management means are made tangible and concrete for every level of the organisation, by discussing in a positive way the practical implications for the structure, processes, and people of those levels. Make clear what is and what is not going to change for them, and emphasise that good things will remain. Management has to anticipate conflicting interests and resolve these in a swift and clear manner. The role of every level and individual in the transition to strategic performance management is discussed. A clear strategy, with short-term and long-term objectives, is set for the change so that the transition is guided steadfastly. People can picture what strategic performance management will bring for them, how they will personally benefit from it ("What's in it for me?"), and how they can contribute to it. They might not understand all the ins and outs of strategic performance management and its implications, but they can certainly believe in it.

■ *Choose the priorities and make resources available for these.* As strategic performance management is going to improve the value drivers of the organisation and the organisation's performance, this should be the most important priority for the coming years. Therefore, top management has to make a clear choice by designating the three most important things to achieve over this period. These should address the value drivers and high-priority issues of the organisation, of which strategic performance management is one. Potential and running projects are evaluated for their contribution to the new course. Projects that have added value to strategic performance management need to be incorporated, and other projects either not commenced or not continued, to free up the organisation's time and resources. Enough resources should be made available on a continuous basis to fund the transition to strategic performance management. The implementation should preferably be started in good times, when enough funds are available and the attention of the organisation is not on "just surviving" but on building for the future. Strategic performance management means innovation, it takes time and should therefore be started from a position of strength.

■ *Appoint one or more sponsors for strategic performance management.* A sponsor from top management is appointed to supervise the implementation of strategic performance management and to take responsibility for a successful process. This person has to be acceptable to the organisation based on his or her experience, seniority, credibility, likeability, and objectivity. If the sponsor is not accepted by the organisation, this individual will not be able to influence the implementation activities enough to make sure the end result can be reached successfully. If the sponsor has been accepted, he/she must make sure to spend enough time on the implementation. Then the organisation will see that the promoter (and therefore the management team) takes strategic performance management seriously.

Because the implementation takes a lot of the organisation's effort, active and visible support by top management, and budget made available by them for the transition, it is essential to convey the importance of strategic performance management to the organisation. The sponsor regularly communicates progress and results to the organisation. For instance, this can be done by regularly scheduling meetings to discuss implementation results. Top management clearly drives the transformation, and helps people to make this transition by creating the conditions that make it possible for them to make the change and excel. Top management (and especially the sponsor) leads by example, it expresses its belief in strategic performance management not only in formal communications but continuously and explicitly in all its actions.

■ *Seek sponsors for strategic performance management throughout the organisation.* On every management level and in every part of the organisation, there should be people who believe in strategic performance management. They function as ambassadors of the new system, and are kept informed at all times about the status of the transition, its difficulties, and its progress. The sponsors appeal to the pride of people in their work, and stimulate a mentality and a drive to increase the quality of processes, products, and services. Sponsors create a feeling of unity and a winning spirit among the people in the organisation: "We are all going for it!" After all, everybody wants to belong to an excellent company.

Activities during preparation

- *Assemble the right team of people willing and capable of implementing strategic performance management.* The core competencies (with accompanying patterns of behaviour) have to be identified that are required to implement strategic performance management. These competencies relate not only to skills and intelligence but also to mentality and attitude. People inside the organisation should be selected and new people hired, based on the match between their characteristics and these competencies. This might mean that the organisation has to part from people who lack the needed capacities and who probably cannot learn these (fast enough), or who lack the willingness to make the transition.

  A core team that guides the transition is put together from good, strong people who are supported by personal coaches. This should be a cross-functional team consisting of people with different backgrounds, genders, cultures, ages, experiences, and organisational functions, to get a good mix of ideas, flexibility of thought, and different opinions. The "booster" of strategic performance management is the CEO, who appoints a process manager to manage the day-to-day activities. This process manager is preferably an expert in implementation, and knows how to deal with the pitfalls and opportunities of this type of transition. This person can become the chief performance officer (CPO). People from the marketing (for the communication side) and human resources (for the people side) departments should be part of the team.

- *Apply a mix of the experience-based and readiness-based approach.* The transition approach is chosen based on the experience that the organisation has with similar change processes and the level of acceptance that exists in the organisation for strategic performance management. What management knows about managing what has to be done, and how far others are open to it, decides the mix between the experience-based and the readiness-based approach (Hickson et al., 2003).

  In the experience-based approach, management knows enough to assess correctly what the aims of the transition to strategic performance management are, specifies accurately what has to be done to implement strategic performance management, and resources these activities in the right manner (planned option). This creates acceptance for strategic performance management by all concerned. In the readiness-based approach, the climate in the organisation for implementing strategic performance management is receptive but experience with this type of transition is relatively lacking. Management moves forward by making sure there are no structural obstacles (like departmental structures and authority structures) that prevent people from working on strategic performance management activities. Management also ensures priority for the implementation so that other issues do not intrude too much and managerial attention is focused on the process (prioritised option). This way, the organisation chooses to "go ahead and learn by doing."

Because strategic performance management is new for many organisations, the prioritised option is the most obvious choice. However, by identifying people in the organisation that have previous experience with similar types of change processes (for example at previous employers) and giving these people a leading role during the journey, a combination of both approaches can be used. This is the best choice: the planned option gives stability to the process while the prioritised option makes the organisation open to new experiences and learning.

- *Make a flexible and adaptive implementation plan.* Set implementation goals and a timeline for these, to build momentum and to show progress from day one. Do not schedule giant leaps but small steps (preferably with a maximum time span of one year) to keep the activities manageable and adaptive to changing circumstances. Take time to implement strategic performance management, build in some slack so unexpected setbacks or delays can be dealt with without having to change the complete schedule, but do not falter in getting to the end result, which is fixed. Take current performance management activities into account and use these as a starting point for the plan. Do not only deal with changes in the current organisation (with its current processes) but also anticipate (fundamental) changes in the environment which might affect (the transition to) strategic performance management.

  Involve people in deciding how to implement strategic performance management, the set-up of the implementation plan, and the starting time for the journey. Mobilise the collective knowledge of the organisation in this way, and increase its brainpower and thereby its self-confidence. Obtain employees' ideas to increase the quality of the plan and to gain their support for the plan. Give everybody in the organisation a role in the transition.

- *Continuously train the organisation.* Introduce "change-eager management" training sessions to help people make the transition to strategic performance management. People start to understand what strategic performance management means for their activities, results, and behaviours. They start speaking the same language and believe in the same performance-driven values. Set up a strategy to deal with "the noise" in the organisation: the political games that are played and the egos that come into play during a change process. Accentuate the start of the implementation by celebrating the past before departing from it ("Look at what we have achieved") and then introduce stimulating content ("And now we are going to become even better").

- *Establish and execute a tailored communication strategy.* Establish a communication strategy to create shared expectations and to report progress. Tailor the communication to the type of the organisation: use words, images, and symbols that are aligned with the organisation's current culture and that resonate with people. Convey the message that strategic performance management is definitely coming and that it is not just a toy of management, and emphasise that it will make the organisation the frontrunner in its industry.

Stress that the implementation is a joint voyage of discovery. Make sure the communication has the shape of a real dialogue: people really listing to each other and speaking with each other. Identify who is losing what and make sure the communication addresses this. Set up a dedicated intranet site with a forum where employees can actively discuss strategic performance management with executives.

▪ Establish "the tone at the top." In every change, the role model of management is crucial for its success. By guarding the tone at the top there is always alignment between the pronouncements, statements, and declarations of top management and its actual deeds and behaviour. When management walks its talk, does what it says, shows the organisation that strategic performance management is really important by paying continuous attention to it, and also gets "dirty hands" by involving itself in some of the day-to-day transition activities, then the organisation will follow suit.

Define a key set of transition principles at the outset of the transition. These principles stipulate for example that management always treats people in the organisation with respect and in a fair and honest way during the transition to the new system, that people can raise objections to, and criticise certain parts of, the new system or the route towards it, that management will sympathise with people's needs, that managers will always hold each other and employees accountable in a constructive way for results, and that everybody will persevere with strategic performance management.

Activities during the execution

▪ *Create a culture of dialogue and cooperation.* During the execution, individuals and groups have, and take, the opportunity to question, challenge, interpret, and ultimately clarify the goals of the different activities that need to be performed to implement strategic performance management. They regularly engage in a dialogue to monitor behaviour and ensure it is aligned with the goals of strategic performance management and with the transition principles. This is real two-way communication.

Top management takes the lead to instigate the dialogue and to guard the transition principles, and at the same time it is willing to be addressed by employees on its own behaviour. There are regular discussions, for example during management team meetings, in which progress of the journey is openly discussed, including the wrong turns that have been taken, and where suggestions for adaptations of the transition approach can be made.

Top management also makes sure it creates a temporary evaluation and reward system for the implementation, so the implementation team can be evaluated and rewarded for its effort and progress during the change, and the organisational members can be assessed and remunerated for their support during the implementation. For this to be possible, performance indicators are used that monitor the transition process itself.

■ *Regularly measure the "rate of change."* "Organisational change speedometers" are regularly used, in which small samples of the employees and managers are surveyed to measure the current rate of organisational change, degree of organisational stability, interference of the transition process with daily routine operations, time spent on the initiative, and possible damage of excessive change and changes going too fast. Appropriate follow-up action is taken to either slow down or speed up the process. Continued delivery of service is balanced with implementation activities, making sure that delivery of regular services is not disrupted by the transformation activities. Clients need to be serviced no matter what internal things are going on, so the organisation has to stay externally oriented.

The different steps in the implementation are acknowledged by celebrating that the organisation completed a step successfully, reviewing the way forward, and reviewing the required team competencies for the next step. After completing a step, it is maintained and its quality is guarded while the other steps are implemented.

■ *Create a training environment.* Create an environment in which people can safely practise strategic performance management and train together with colleagues. They learn how to perform old processes (like budgeting and forecasting) in new ways, to read and use new types of reports, to act in new ways (by using role plays), and to speak the same "performance management language." Implementing strategic performance management is not just about transferring knowledge on new processes and techniques but also about practising and incorporating these new ideas and the accompanying behaviour (proficiency training). This practice environment increases the self-confidence of people and creates the trust that they are capable of meeting the new demands put upon them by strategic performance management. The ultimate goal is of course to bring what you have learned into practice as soon as possible.

■ *Balance coaching with resolution and firmness.* Management treats people with respect by:
   – listening to them with an open mind (management does not know everything) and actively involving them in the implementation activities
   – giving them room to plot their own way (within boundaries set by management)
   – not immediately nagging about each and every detail that goes wrong

- reserving enough time for progress reviews
- actively coaching people during the implementation.

Management sets the example and is a role model by being interested in people's results, continuously improving its own performance during the process, and consistently reacting to people and fellow managers about their performance in a positive critical manner. This might mean management team members themselves use a personal coach, for an extended period of time, to help them change and adapt to their new role and to regularly reflect on themselves.

Management keeps its eyes firmly on the destination of the journey and maintains discipline. Management does not ignore information but faces the facts, especially negative ones, and bites the bullet to immediately deal with the consequences of negative information. Management monitors the transition team closely and makes personnel changes (in a dignified way) when necessary, without delay. Negative obstructionists are bought off quickly so they do not take up more management time than necessary. If needed, extra or more tailored communication is deployed. Management is consistent in its vision, execution, and application of the "expect and inspect" principle (expect a lot of your people but make sure you inspect results regularly).

Activities at the end

- *Update the evaluation and reward system.* To secure the new strategic performance management system, a new or updated evaluation and reward system is installed that is aligned with the changed culture and new organisational goals. In this system, people who are willing to take (calculated) risks and who want to be creative, are visibly rewarded. The temporary evaluation and reward system established for the implementation can be the basis for the new or updated system.
- *After celebration, set new goals and targets.* When strategic performance management has been implemented, the organisation takes time out to celebrate its achievements, to recuperate, and to enjoy its success. After the celebration, management takes stock and sets its sight on new objectives. In the spirit of continuous improvement, the new goals and targets are higher and more difficult than the old ones. Management starts to think of new objectives and starts preparing the organisation for these.

Key points

- ☑ In organisations there is a tendency to make the strategic performance management process too complicated. It can be made be simple by organising the process around the CSFs and KPIs of the organisation.
- ☑ Implementing strategic performance management process is not easy and it therefore requires a structured project approach.
- ☑ There are some specific dos, don'ts, and pitfalls an organisation should take into account during the implementation of strategic performance management. In particular, change management has to be taken very seriously in order to increase the chances of a successful implementation.

References

Abrahamson, E. (2004) Avoiding repetitive change syndrome. *MIT Sloan Management Review*, Winter 2004, 45 (2).

Hickson, D.J., Miller, S.J. and Wilson, D.C. (2003) Planned or prioritised? Two options in managing the implementation of strategic decisions. *Journal of Management Studies*, 40 (7), November.

Waal, A.A. de, and Geelen, P. (2002) Prestatiemanagement en informatietechnologie: een perfect paar? *FSR Forum*, 5.

Part 4

Specials

Part 4 deals with two special topics in the area of strategic performance management which each have their own particularities: implementing strategic performance management in the nonprofit sector, specifically the government, and implementing strategic performance management in emerging countries.

14

Performance management in the public sector

In the past decade, several attempts have been made to improve performance management in the public sector. Making the results of public agencies more transparent allows for better prioritisation of programmes and choices of where to apply resources. In addition, it allows for better management of the agencies themselves because performance on nonfinancial objectives becomes verifiable.

While it was originally developed in the private sector, there are indications that performance management, and in particular the BSC, is gaining ground in public-sector organisations (Modell, 2004). These organisations, with a culture that is outcome-oriented and mission-driven, appear to have higher levels of performance than organisations lacking performance management (Grindle and Hildebrand, 1995; National Partnership for Reinventing Government, 1999; United States General Accounting Office, 1999; Executive Session on Public Sector Performance Management, 2001; Moriarty and Kennedy, 2002; Mihm, 2003).

One of the most important attempts is called new public management (Hood, 1991, 1995), which started in the United States and the United Kingdom (Wilson, 1998; Bovaird, 2002; DeMaio, 2002; Weinstock, 2002; Breul, 2003; Kingsbury, 2003; Pollitt, 2003; Neely and Micheli, 2005). However, practice has revealed that implementing strategic performance management in the public sector is more difficult than it is in the private sector (Pidd, 2005). This chapter discusses areas of special attention for applications in public-sector organisations, and in particular the differences between performance management in the public and the private sectors, and the role of politics in the use of performance management information (Waal and Kerklaan, 2004).

Chapter objectives

☑ To provide the reader with an insight into the differences of implementing performance management in the public sector, compared with the private sector.

☑ To discuss the various types of indicators in use in public sector organisations.

☑ To provide the reader with a structured approach for the implementation of strategic performance management in public sector organisations.

14.1 DIFFERENCES BETWEEN PUBLIC AND PRIVATE PERFORMANCE MANAGEMENT

It used to be common practice to adopt in the public sector management methods and techniques that were developed in the private sector. However, there are some important differences between the two sectors that can greatly influence the implementation of performance management in the public sector (Ittner and Larcker, 1998; Dewatripont et al., 1999; Andersen and Lawrie, 2002; Thiel and Leeuw, 2002). These differences are:

- *Responsibility structure*. In a private organisation, the responsibility structure is relatively simple, with a management team and a board of directors. In a public organisation, on the other hand, there is political leadership, which is responsible for developing the strategy, and executive leadership, which is responsible for executing the strategy. This division in leadership and responsibilities causes many conflicts, for example regarding the focus of performance management.

- *Strategy and added value creation*. Again this is relatively simple for private organisations, in which value (ROI) has to be created for the company's shareholders. For public organisations, added value is defined by the supervisory agency. This is not one party but rather several ones that often have conflicting interests, for example citizens who do not want to pay more tax as opposed to social security recipients who would like to receive more benefits. Because these interests are often politically motivated, they are subject to change during election times as a result of lobbying.

- *Clients and customer satisfaction*. It is more difficult for public organisations than it is for private organisations to aim at increasing customer satisfaction, because they may be forced to act against the immediate interest of their clients. For instance, increasing public security may limit people's freedom of movement. In addition, it is not always clear who exactly are the clients of a public agency. In private-sector organisations, customers pay for and receive products or services. In public-sector organisations, citizens pay tax without directly benefiting from it. It is also often difficult to define precisely the goals of a public agency, and consequently measure its results.

■ *Resources.* Both public and private organisations have at their disposal material assets (e.g. capital) and immaterial assets (e.g. employees). Yet public organisations have another important asset which private organisations do not have: political power, resulting from the activities they perform (e.g. tax collection, law enforcement, environmental legislation). This means that performance management in the public sector should monitor misuse of this particular resource.

In summary, it can be concluded that both private and public-sector organisations operate in a dynamic environment which expects them to show added value. Performance management can help organisations in both sectors to achieve this. Thus it can be used in the public sector as long as the specific features of this sector are taken into account.

14.2 ROLE OF POLITICS

Politics can have both a stimulating and a discouraging role during the implementation of public strategic performance management. The attitude of politicians towards performance management and performance information is of the utmost importance for the acceptance of this type of management technique by public servants. There is often no concrete mechanism available for monitoring the relationship between politics and public agencies. However, only if one knows what is being asked is it possible to define tangible goals and start steering on these. Therefore, politicians who want public agencies to start using performance management should use it themselves and start defining concrete (long-term) goals.

Currently politicians mostly react to incidents, and public officers who deploy performance management become the object of quickly shifting moods and focuses. As a result, many public servants have an understandable fear of becoming the victim in the political "blame game." If politicians start using performance information to make public officers their scapegoats in order to benefit their own career and interest, these public officers will immediately show "strategic behaviour." They will try to distort performance results in such a way that official reports include only the results desired by politicians, while in reality this might not be the case. Consequently, performance information becomes unreliable as it does not necessarily reflect the actual situation. In this game, the interests of citizens are completely ignored (Koning et al., 2004).

In order to remedy, or rather prevent, this situation, tangible agreements about outputs should be at the centre of attention of both parties (politicians and public agencies). These agreements can be set down in a performance management contract, such as a covenant. Public officers will focus on achieving the desired outputs, and politicians will use the covenant as the basis for evaluating this output. Such a covenant can work well if the following conditions are met:

- The desired output can only be accurately defined if both parties have the same level of knowledge and information. When one of the parties does not have the required knowledge, the other party has a moral obligation to help remove the information gap.
- Both parties should agree not only on the desired outputs but also on the desired positive effects of these outputs (the outcome).
- Politicians should evaluate public agencies based on information provided by public servants, not on articles in the press. Public agencies are required to deliver high-quality performance information.
- Public organisations should measure both output and outcome. If it turns out that the output has an insufficient positive effect on the outcome, politicians should set new priorities. Public servants have to cooperate in this and allow for the covenant to be changed. At the same time, politicians should realise that public officers can not be held fully accountable for achieving the desired outcomes.
- Public servants should be allowed if necessary to change the direction and strategy of their agency, without being punished for this by politicians.
- Public agencies should be flexible and adapt to change every time elections are being held: new politicians will have new agendas. Of course public officers can then adjust the conditions for the covenant.

14.3 PUBLIC SECTOR CRITICAL SUCCESS FACTORS, KEY PERFORMANCE INDICATORS, AND BALANCED SCORECARD

In the public sector there are different types of performance indicators than there are in the private sector (Figure 14.1).

Input CSFs and KPIs provide information on the resources, such as people and the financial budget, that are available to execute the processes to deliver public products and services. Activity CSFs and KPIs provide information on the status of internal processes and activities that are executed to deliver the products and services. These types of indicators are also called "throughput indicators." Output CSFs and KPIs indicate what the public organisation produces. Outcome CSFs and KPIs indicate the effects the products and services of the public organisation have on society. They are a yardstick of the success of the policies of the public organisation.

While the results of input, activity, and output CSFs and KPIs are within the responsibility sphere of the public organisations, outcome CSFs and

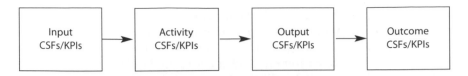

Figure 14.1 The four types of public sector CSFs and KPIs

KPIs are not. The effects of policies and regulations in society are influenced by many factors outside the control of the public organisations. Also they are often only noticeable after a lengthy period of time, and they are often interpreted in a political way. Nevertheless, these types of indicators still provide a lot of information to the public organisation: if the outcomes are not as intended, this may mean that the policies of the organisation were not good or not good enough, or that circumstances have changed so much in the meantime that additional or new policies are required.

Related types of indicators are environmental factors and indicators. These provide information on the environment in which the public organisation operates and on the developments that are relevant to the organisation (Figure 14.2). A public organisation only has limited influence on these indicators but they can certainly influence its performance. Therefore, while setting targets for the other types of indicators, and especially the output and outcome indicators, the public organisation has to take the environmental factors and indicators into account.

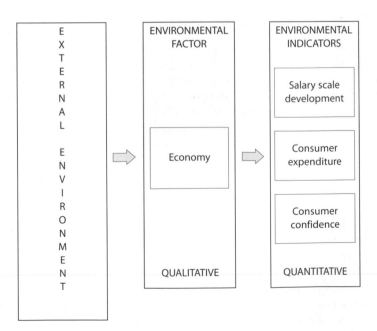

Figure 14.2 Example of an environmental factor and accompanying environmental indicators

To most organisations, the development of the economy is of crucial importance. This is therefore an important environmental factor which can be measured with environmental indicators such as salary scale development, expenditures of customers, and consumer confidence. In the private sector, these environmental indicators give an indication of expected sales: if the indicators go up, a higher turnover may be expected. For a public organisation the same indicators are important: if they go down this may indicate that consumers are spending less because unemployment is rising and therefore it can be expected that social benefits and unemployment allowances will increase.

The output and outcome CSFs and KPIs indicate whether the public organisation realises its strategic objectives. In this sense, they are result CSFs and KPIs. The output CSFs can be determined by answering the following questions, "What is the result when we achieve the objective successfully?" and "What is the result when we execute the key process successfully?" To determine the outcome CSFs, the following question has to be answered: "What are the effects on our customers and society when we achieve the desired outputs successfully?"

The input and activity CSFs and KPIs monitor the critical resources and efforts needed in order for the public organisation to successfully achieve its objectives, outputs, and outcomes. In this sense, they are effort CSFs and KPIs. There are many efforts that may lead to achieving the desired output and outcome, but only those that are most critical need to be monitored. A "critical effort" is that effort that is most likely to lead to achieving the desired result. The input CSFs can be determined by answering the following question: "What do I absolutely need to achieve the objective and its outputs and outcomes successfully?" To determine the activity CSFs, the following question has to be answered: "What do I absolutely need to do to achieve the objective and its outputs and outcomes successfully?"

After the CSFs have been identified, we need to answer the following questions to identify the KPIs for each CSF: "How do I measure the critical success factor?" and "How can I see the result of the critical success factor?" A KPI is usually defined as a ratio or a percentage (the numerator and the denominator).

Figure 14.3 gives an example of the four types of CSFs and KPIs for the public sector.

In Figure 14.3, the organisation has as one of its strategic objectives to foster development of its personnel. The outcome CSF for this objective is better treatment of customers (members of the public or companies) by the organisation's personnel than was the case in the past. Whether this is the case can be monitored by measuring the number of customers who state that they are satisfied with the way they were treated, and by measuring the time it takes to serve customers (because the employees have become more efficient because of their training).

To achieve this outcome, the quality of the employees has to be improved. This output CSF can be measured by the average education level of staff,

Strategic objective:
Foster development of public sector personnel

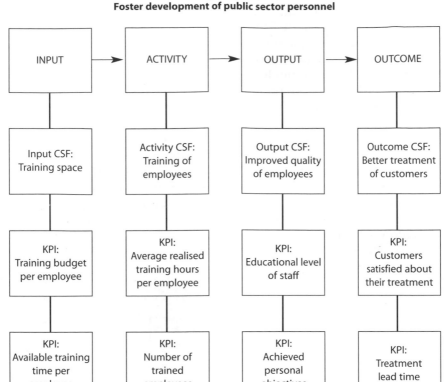

Figure 14.3 Example of the four types of public sector CSFs and KPIs

which should be higher than it was the previous year. In addition, employees should be better able to achieve their personal objectives because they are better equipped to do so. One of the crucial requirements to achieve this output is to train employees. This activity CSF is assessed by the number of training hours that an employee has received on average, and the number of employees that have participated in training. To make training possible in the first place, space has to be created for it in the organisation. This input CSF is monitored by the budget that is available to train employees, and the hours that employees have available to follow training.

With the BSC, a public organisation can assess its performance from four different angles, which together give management the possibility of monitoring the organisation's results in a balanced way:

- level of innovation in products, services, processes, and personnel
- efficiency and effectiveness of internal processes
- customer perception
- financial results.

In the traditional BSC, which was developed for profit organisations, the financial perspective is placed above the other perspectives. However, in nonprofit organisations the financial aspect is less important and the customer perspective is placed on top. After all, nonprofit organisations are not there to maximise profits for their shareholders, but to maximise their added value to their stakeholders. These stakeholders – citizens, companies, and other groups in society at large – are often called "target groups" (Figure 14.4) (Maholland and Muetz, 2002; Niven, 2003).

- *The innovative perspective* measures how often a public organisation introduces new products and services. In this way, the public organisation makes sure it does not become complacent but continuously renews itself. Sometimes organisations include people aspects in this perspective, which are used to measure the well-being, commitment, and competence of people in the organisation. People aspects measure cultural qualities, such as internal partnership, teamwork, and knowledge sharing, and aggregate individual qualities such as leadership, competency, and use of technology.

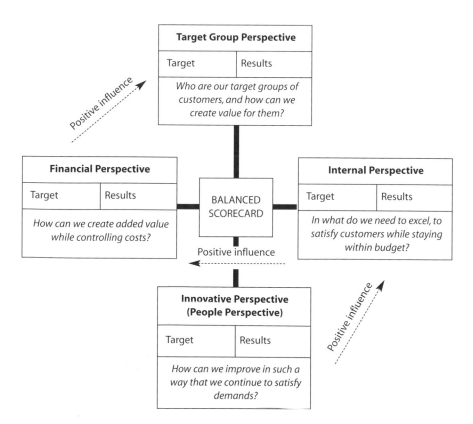

Figure 14.4 The set-up of the public BSC

- *The internal (or process) perspective* measures the efficiency and effectiveness of the processes by which the public organisation creates value. It comes after the innovative perspective because innovation and people influence the ability of the public organisation to create value by implementing and managing effective processes.
- *The financial perspective* measures the depletion of the budget and developments in costs. This perspective covers the financial space in which good, committed, and qualified employees get to apply efficient processes in order to add value for the chosen customer target groups.
- *The target group perspective* measures performance in terms of how the customers in the chosen target groups experience the value created for them by the public organisation.

14.4 IMPLEMENTING PUBLIC-SECTOR PERFORMANCE MANAGEMENT

When implementing strategic performance management in the public sector, there are a number of elements that public agencies have to take into consideration (Boorsma, 2001; Wye, 2002; Waal and Kerklaan, 2004).

- *Keep it simple.* Performance management should not aim at monitoring all possible performance indicators. It should concentrate on specific areas of attention regarding policy objectives and on specific areas of risks regarding the execution of this policy. These have to be monitored closely.
- *Be selective with information that is distributed outside the organisation.* A public agency does not have to be 100 per cent transparent and open about its efforts in order to be sufficiently accountable for achieving the desired outputs. By producing separate reports for external and internal performance information, an organisation can protect itself against misuse of performance figures by politicians or journalists.
- *Present only a limited number of lagging indicators.* For several policy areas, only a limited number of crucial longer-term objectives is presented. The short-term goals (leading indicators) should only be known "inside" the organisation as they are only intended to give public officers early warning signals.
- *Hold public officers accountable for output, not for outcome.* Public performance management has to focus on outcomes – the desired effects. However, public servants cannot be held fully accountable for these. The outcomes of public organisations are after all influenced by a great number of factors which cannot always be directly influenced and controlled by public officers.
- *Accept that politicians have a constantly shifting focus.* The way to deal with this shifting focus is for the management of a public organisation to set its own distinct and well-defined course aimed at increasing public

satisfaction with the organisation. Doing this makes its performance less politically sensitive, because the long-term interests and influence of the public at large have become more important.

■ *Encourage politicians to set a clear focus.* Public agencies should take the initiative to produce policy proposals, describing their outcomes and (budgetary) consequences, on which politicians can comment. Once results to be achieved are agreed upon, a covenant should be drafted which stipulates not only the required performance but also the conditions and required resources.

■ *Align personal objectives with organisational objectives.* Organisational objectives can only be achieved if everyone in the organisation understands what he/she is expected to do individually. Abstract policy objectives therefore have to be specified for individuals so that commitment and performance drive can be increased.

■ *Keep a focus on the behavioural side of performance management.* This can be done in many ways. Results can be shown in charts. Training can be organised on how to deal with performance information (e.g. how to interpret and discuss it). Managers have to be coached in achieving quality improvements and in recognising and acknowledging the results of their efforts.

14.5 CASE: PUBLIC PERFORMANCE MANAGEMENT AT THE DEPARTMENT OF TRADE AND INDUSTRY

(This case originates from Waal and Kerklaan (2004). The ministry is a fictitious one and only used for illustrative purposes.)

The Department of Trade and Industry (DTI) is responsible for laws and regulations regarding commercial intercourse. DTI consist of three directorates which each have an area for special attention: Industry, Small and Medium-sized Enterprises (SME), and Transport (Figure 14.5). The Directorate of SME consist of three units:

■ Policy, responsible for designing policies and strategies to foster the position of SMEs.
■ Execution, responsible for executing the strategies set by the Policy unit.
■ Support, responsible for providing the other two units with sufficient people and other resources.

The Execution unit consists of four departments:

■ Application, responsible for receiving, checking, and processing requests for subsidies.
■ Disposition, responsible for deciding on the subsidy requests.

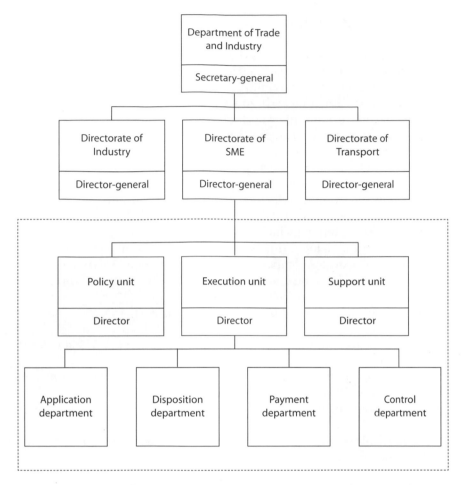

Figure 14.5 Simplified organisational diagram of the Department of Trade and Industry

- Payment, responsible for providing advances on approved requests and for the settling of payments.
- Control, responsible for carrying out random checks on whether the execution of the subsidy scheme is done legitimately and lawfully, and whether subsidised companies receive subsidy justifiably.

The mission of the Directorate of SME is "Fostering the competitive position of small and medium-sized enterprises." The Directorate wants to achieve its mission through this strategy:

Designing policies aimed at improving the competitive position of small and medium-sized enterprises though stimulating cost control, knowledge expansion, and quality improvement; and executing these policies efficiently and effectively.

The RIW regulation

An important stimulation policy is the "Returner in the Workplace" (RIW) regulation. This regulation establishes a scheme aimed at people who have not participated in the labour market for a while (such as mothers, early retirees and the long-term unemployed) and was introduced shortly after the law governing the hours of trading was changed. This change made it possible for shops to stay open longer at night, from the earlier regular closing time of 18.00 to a new one of 22.00.

It turned out that chain stores in particular profited from the longer opening hours. Many smaller retailers had to hire additional staff to keep their shops open in the evening, which cost them more than the proceeds of the extra sales. Therefore, many retailers decided to return to closing at the regular time of 18.00, something which had a dismal effect on the competitive position of SMEs because a lot of the extra turnover now went to the chains. The RIW regulation provides compensation for the increased salary costs and at the same time stimulates the employment of relatively experienced returners, which improves the unemployment figures.

The main characteristics of the RIW scheme are:

- Returners are employed for four to five days a week, especially for the period between 18.00 and 22.00.
- Returners are employed for at least one year at the minimum wage, increased with an evening allowance.
- The regulation fully compensates employers for paying the evening allowance, for a period of one year.
- Only retailers with less than five employees are eligible to partake in the scheme.

The activities that the units of the Directorate of SME have to perform in connection with the RIW regulation are as follows. The Policy unit drafts the RIW regulation, evaluates the regulation for content effectiveness and financial implications, proposes improvements to the regulation, checks the improvement proposals with the Execution unit, formalises the adapted regulation, and communicates the adaptations to the other units.

The Execution unit advises the Policy unit, drafts a budget for the costs of executing the regulation (both subsidy costs and the costs of unit personnel involved in the execution), gives information and advice on the regulation to retailers, and executes the regulation. The execution of the regulation consists of several activities:

- receiving the application form
- evaluating the application
- entering a decision to grant the application (or not) in the information system
- payment of an advance (often 76 per cent of the total subsidy)

- receiving a certificate from the retailer's auditor on the correct use of the subsidy
- checking the certificate
- drafting the final order
- paying the remainder of the subsidy.

In addition, the Execution unit checks the process randomly to identify possible improvements in the execution and to make sure that the execution is just and lawful.

The Support unit takes care of the administration of the regulation by providing management information reports on the regulation, and is responsible for control. The unit is also responsible for human resources, and maintains the information systems.

Need for new performance information

The management of the Directorate of SME is not satisfied with the current management reporting. In addition, the DTI demands a higher quality of management information than the Directorate currently provides to the secretary-general. The director-general decides to start a project to improve information for the internal use of the Directorate and information for use by DTI, by applying CSFs and KPIs. As a first step in the improvement project, the outcome CSFs and KPIs are derived from the strategic objectives of the Directorate (Tables 14.1 and 14.2).

The main activity of the Directorate of SME is executing efficacious policies. By applying the right mix of policies the competitive position of SMEs can be improved. This can be measured by assessing the market share of SMEs in the retail sector and their contribution to the gross national product. The results on these KPIs cannot fully be controlled by the Directorate because there are

Table 14.1 The outcome CSFs of the Directorate of SME

Strategic objectives of the Directorate of SME	Outcome CSFs
Execute efficacious policies	■ Market share of SMEs ■ Contribution of SMEs to GNP ■ Policy efficiency
Stimulate cost control at SMEs	■ Cost levels of SMEs ■ Cost consciousness at SMEs
Stimulate knowledge expansion at SMEs	■ Levels of education of SME personnel
Stimulate quality improvement at SMEs	■ Quality as experienced by SME customers ■ Image of SMEs on labour market

Table 14.2 The outcome KPIs of the Directorate of SME

Outcome CSF	Outcome KPI	KPI definition	Data source
Market share of SMEs	Market share of SMEs	Turnover of SMEs versus turnover of retail branch	Branch statistics, SME statistics
Contribution of SMEs to GNP	Contribution of SMEs to GNP	Contribution of SMEs as percentage of the gross national product	Country statistics, SME statistics
	Policy effectiveness	Contribution of the policies to improving the competitive position of the SMEs in a specific period, as experienced by the SMEs	Ratings given by SMEs during satisfaction survey
Policy efficiency	Directorate costs	Costs of policies and the Directorate itself	Financial system
Cost levels of SMEs	Operating expenses of subsidy receivers	Operating expenses as percentage of gross turnover averaged over all subsidy receivers, versus average operating cost percentage of the retail branch	Survey of subsidy receivers, Branch statistics
	Cost trends of subsidy receivers	Cost levels of subsidy receivers of this year versus last year	Survey of subsidy receivers
Cost-consciousness at SMEs	Cost reducing measures	Number of cost-reducing measures implemented by subsidy receivers versus average number of cost-reducing measures implemented by nonsubsidised SMEs	Survey of subsidy receivers, Branch statistics
Levels of education of SME personnel	Education level	Average number of employees with a relevant education at subsidy receivers versus average number of employees with a relevant education at nonsubsidised SMEs	Branch survey
	Vacancies	Average number of vacancies filled by employees with an inadequate education level at subsidy receivers versus average number of vacancies filled by employees with an inadequate education level at nonsubsidised SMEs	Branch survey
	Training costs	Average budget spent on training employees at subsidy receivers versus average budget spent on training employees at nonsubsidised SMEs	Branch survey
Quality as experienced by SME customers	Customer responses	Average number of positive responses from customers at subsidy receivers about the service versus average number of positive responses at nonsubsidised SMEs	Consumer survey
	Complaints	Average number of complaints at subsidy receivers versus average number of complains at non-subsidised SMEs	Consumer survey, Complaint registration of SMEs
Image of SMEs on labour market	Graduate employees	Number of graduate employees at subsidy receivers versus average number of graduates at non-subsidised SMEs	Branch survey
	Perception	Number of responses on job ads from subsidy receivers versus average number of responses at nonsubsidy SMEs	Branch survey

many other determining factors. They do however give a lot of information on the effects of the Directorate's policies on the competitive position of SMEs.

If, despite all the efforts of the Directorate of SME, the competitive position of SMEs has not been significantly improved, this could be because the policies of the Directorate are either ineffective or inadequate. This would suggest a need to change or supplement the policies, or replace them with new ones. It could also be that in itself the Directorate's policies are good but circumstances have changed in such a way that they hinder an improvement in SMEs' competitive position, so additional policies are needed. In addition, the costs of designing and implementing the policies have to be closely watched because the Directorate does not have a limitless budget.

The effects of stimulating cost control can be measured by comparing the current cost levels of SMEs with those of last year. In addition, an increased awareness of cost control at SMEs is important for overall cost control. This can be measured by a number of cost control measures that SMEs have taken. Whether knowledge expansion has taken place at SMEs can be assessed by comparing the average level of education of SME staff of this year with that of last year.

Monitoring the effects of stimulating quality improvement at SMEs has two aspects. The quality of service at SMEs as experienced by their customers should increase. At the same time, this quality improvement should have increased the image of SMEs so they become more attractive as employers. Table 14.2 gives in detail the KPIs with which the outcome CSFs can be tracked, the definition of the KPIs, and the data source containing the information needed to calculate the KPIs.

Unit CSFs

The unit CSFs and KPIs are derived from the unit objectives, which are themselves derived from the strategic objectives of the organisation. In this case, we concentrate on the objectives, CSFs, and KPIs that concern the RIW regulation (Table 14.3).

The Policy unit helps the Directorate of SME to achieve its objective of executing efficacious policies by designing and maintaining regulations

Table 14.3 The output CSFs for the Policy and Execution units

Strategic objective of the Directorate of SME	Objectives of Policy unit	Output CSFs
Execute efficacious policies	Design and maintain a high-quality RIW regulation	■ Effectivity of RIW regulation ■ Efficiency of RIW regulation
	Objectives of Execution unit	Output CSFs
	Execute the RIW regulation well	■ Lawful execution of RIW regulation

which are of a high quality. This high quality is expressed in the effectiveness of the regulation: in this case the number of stores that stay open at night, at the same operating costs as apply in the daytime, because the owners have requested and received a subsidy. Another output is that the RIW regulation should increase the knowledge level in the stores because experienced returners are hired.

The quality of the regulation can also be assessed on its efficiency: as many subsidy applications as is possible within the available budget have to be granted. The Execution unit helps the Directorate of SME to achieve its objective of executing efficacious policies by executing the RIW regulation in a uniform way: that is, all subsidy applications are processed in the same manner so the process is lawful. The Support unit simply executes the process on behalf of the other two units. These processes always have to be performed well, irrespective of the policy or regulation. Therefore the Support unit does not have unit objectives, but only key processes.

Table 14.4 gives in detail the KPIs with which the output CSFs can be

Table 14.4 The output KPIs for the Policy and Execution units

Output CSF	Output KPI	KPI definition	Data source
Policy unit			
Effectiveness of RIW regulation	Stores with RIW subsidy	Number of stores with RIW subsidy versus total number of stores qualified for RIW subsidy	SME statistics
	Stores open with RIW subsidy	Number of stores with RIW subsidy that are open in the evening versus the number of stores with RIW subsidy which would have been closed in the evening without the subsidy	Branch survey
	Experience level of staff	Average number of staff with more than three years of retail experience in stores with RIW subsidy versus average number of staff with more than three years of retail experience in all stores	RIW regulation tracking system
	Change in cost level	Average difference in operating costs (in %) of SMEs with subsidy, before and after the introduction of the evening opening	Survey of subsidy receivers
Efficiency of RIW regulation	Total RIW subsidy receivers	Number of SMEs that receive RIW subsidy versus the total number of RIW subsidy receivers possible in the given budget	Financial system, RIW regulation tracking system
Execution unit			
Lawful execution of RIW regulation	Lawfully executed subsidy allowances	Number of subsidy applications that have been processed in a lawful way versus the total number of subsidy applications processed	RIW regulation tracking system, Random checks

tracked, the definition of the KPIs, and the data source containing the
information to calculate the KPIs.

Accountability report

As discussed in Chapter 10, the CSFs and KPIs can be used not only for self-
control and self-management but also to provide accountability information
to a higher management level, as long as this is done carefully and deliberately (see Section 10.2). In addition to the regular financial information, the
Directorate of SME regularly sends an accountability report summary to the
DTI. This report consists of a subset of CSFs and KPIs that are relevant to
the DTI, and is aimed at informing the Department about the status of the
Directorate. It is not intended as a mechanism to evaluate and assess
performance (Figure 14.6)

Accountability report summary of Directorate of SME Period: 2nd quarter 20xx				
Output CSFs	Output KPIs	Target	Actual	Clarification
Contribution of SMEs to GNP	Contribution of SMEs to GNP Policy effectiveness	10 % 25 %	9.5 % 23 %	The share which our policies had in improving the competitive position of the SMEs, in the opinion of SME owners, is after two disappointing quarters almost back on budget. This has also had positive effects on the contribution of the SMEs to the gross national product. We expect that policy effectiveness will be completely on budget in the next quarter.
Policy efficiency	Directorate costs	100 %	116 %	Because policy effectiveness was not on target the last two quarters, the Directorate has put in extra effort in the form of an unplanned public rela-tions campaign for the RIW regulation. This has caused unbudgeted costs which will lower overall efficiency of the Directorate at least for another quarter. We aim at reducing costs in some other subsidies to get back on budget.

Figure 14.6 A part of the accountability report summary of the Directorate of SME

Key points

☑ Public-sector organisations that have a culture that is outcome-oriented and mission-driven achieve higher levels of performance than organisations that lack performance management.

☑ Practice has proved that implementing strategic performance management in the public sector is more difficult than in the private sector because the results in the public sector are harder to define, and because of the role of politics in the use of performance management information.

☑ In the public sector, there are different types of performance indicators than there are in the private sector. Input indicators provide information on the resources that are available to execute the processes to deliver public products and services; activity indicators provide information on the status of internal processes and activities to deliver the products and services; output indicators indicate what the public organisation produces, and outcome indicators indicate the effects the products and services of the public-sector organisation have on society.

References

Andersen, H.V. and Lawrie, G. (2002) Examining opportunities for improving public sector governance through better strategic management. In: A. Neely, A. Walters and R. Austin (eds), *Performance Measurement and Management: Research and action*. Cranfield, UK: Cranfield School of Management.

Boorsma, P.B. (2001) *Modern Public Management in Theory and Practice with Special Reference to the Netherlands*. Twente University, Department for Public Administration.

Bovaird, T. (2002) From corporate governance to community governance: citizen-driven community score-cards for UK local service providers?. In: A. Neely, A. Walters and R. Austin (eds), *Performance Measurement and Management: Research and action*. Cranfield, UK: Cranfield School of Management.

Breul, J.D. (2003) The government performance and results act: 10 years later. *Journal of Government Financial Management*, 52 (1), Spring.

DeMaio, C.D. (2002) Pioneering performance. *Government Executive*, 34 (9), July.

Dewatripont, M., Jewitt, I. and Tirole, J. (1999) The economics of career concern, part II: application to missions and accountability of government agencies. *Review of Economic Studies*, 66, 199–217.

Executive Session on Public Sector Performance Management (2001) Get results through performance management: an open memorandum to government executives. In: *Visions of Governance in the 21st Century*. Cambridge, Mass.: John F. Kennedy School of Government, Harvard University.

Grindle, M.S. and Hildebrand, M.E. (1995) Building sustainable capacity in the public sector: what can be done? *Public Administration and Development*, 15 (5), 441–63.

Hood, C. (1991) A public management for all seasons? *Public Administration*.

Hood, C. (1995) The new public management: variations on a theme? *Accounting Organisations and Society*.

Ittner, C.D. and Larcker, D.F. (1998) Innovations in performance measurement: trends and research implications. *Journal of Management Accounting Research*, 10, 205–38.

Kingsbury, N. (2003) *An Evaluation Culture and Collaborative Partnerships Help Build Agency Capacity*. FDCH Government Account Reports, 2 May.

Koning, P., Canton, E., Cornet, M., Pomp, M., van de Ven, J., Venniker, R., Vollaard, B. and Webbink, D. (2004) Centrale doelen, decentrale uitvoering, over de dos and don'ts van prestatieprikkels voor semi-publieke instellingen. *Centraal Planbureau*, 45, January.

Maholland, L. and Muetz, P. (2002) A balanced scorecard approach to performance measurement. *Government Finance Review*, 18 (2), April.

Mihm, J.C. (2003) *Creating a Clear Linkage between Individual Performance and Organisational Success*. FDCH Government Account Reports, 14 April.

Modell, S. (2004) Performance measurement myths in the public sector: a research note. *Financial Accountability and Management*, 20 (1), 39–55.

Moriarty, P. and Kennedy, D. (2002) Performance measurement in public sector services: problems and potential. In: A. Neely, A. Walters and R. Austin (eds), *Performance Measurement and Management: Research and action*. Cranfield, UK: Cranfield School of Management.

National Partnership for Reinventing Government (1999) *Balancing Measures: Best Practices in Performance Management*. www.npr.gov/library/papers/bkgrd/balmeasure.html, August.

Neely, A. and Micheli, P. (2005) *Performance Measurement in the UK's Public Sector: Searching for the golden thread*. Paper presented during the British Academy of Management conference, September

Niven, P.R. (2003) *Balanced Scorecard Step-by-Step for Government and Nonprofit Agencies*. New York: Wiley.

Pidd, M. (2005) Perversity in public service performance measurement. *International Journal of Productivity and Performance Management*, 54 (5/6), 482–93.

Pollitt, C. (2003) *The Essential Public Manager*. Manchester: Open University Press.

Thiel, S. van and Leeuw, F.L. (2002) The performance paradox in the public sector. *Public Performance and Review*, 25 (3), 267–81.

United States General Accounting Office (1999) *Managing for Results: Opportunities for continued improvements in agency's performance plans*. GAO/GGD/AIMD-99-215, July.

Waal, A.A. de and Kerklaan, L.A.F.M. (2004a) Performance management in the Dutch public sector: an overview and latest developments. In: A. Neely, M. Kennerly and A. Waters (eds), *Performance Measurement and Management: Public and private*. Cranfield, UK: Centre for Business Performance, Cranfield University.

Waal, A.A. de and Kerklaan, L.A.F.M. (2004b) *De resultaatgerichte overheid, op weg naar de prestatiegedreven overheidsorganisatie*. The Hague: SDU.

Weinstock, M. (2002) Perfecting performance. *Government Executive*, 34 (6), May.

Wilson, J. (ed.) (1998) *Financial Management for Public Services*. Buckingham: Open University Press.

Wye, C. (2002) *Performance Management: A "start where you are, use what you have" guide*. Managing for Results Series, IBM Endowment for The Business of Government.

15

Performance management in developing countries

Historically, countries have been clustered based on their economic condition as measured by indicators such as gross national product (GNP) and gross domestic product (GDP), with "developed" and "developing" as the two main clusters (Farashahi and Molz, 2004).

The developing countries comprise 156 nations with approximately 80 per cent of the world's population, almost 5 billion people (Akbar and Samii, 2005). They form some of the potentially most important growth opportunities for companies from both the developing and the developed world. It is therefore remarkable that a recent systematic review of the last 20 years of empirical research grounded in institutional theory found that most studies focused on developed countries (95 per cent) and that only a small portion (5 per cent) of the studies tried to test institutional theory in developing countries (Farashahi et al., 2005). As a result, there has been little structural research on institutional effect and change in emerging countries (Hofstede, 2001). This is surprising because many of these countries offer a highly dynamic environment which is a good testing ground for new theory, techniques, and concepts of business and management (Pacek and Thorniley, 2004).

It has to be noted that quite a few scholars doubt whether existing Western management practices can and will work in emerging markets, and it has long been recognised that culture is a major source of differences in measurement and reporting standards and methods (Daniels et al., 2004; Piercy et al., 2004). At the same time, interest in this type of research is increasing as countries start to realise that the study results can be important input in the development of policies to reduce poverty (Hopper et al., 2003; Pacek and Thorniley, 2004). Performance management can in this respect be regarded as one of those institutional theories whose validity needs to be tested in an emerging country context, as this context can be more dynamic and completely different from a developed country context.

In this chapter a short overview is given of the characteristics of developing countries and the status of strategic performance management in several developing countries. After this, prescriptive empirical research, in the shape of a case study, is used to test whether strategic performance management is a useful tool for organisations in emerging markets.

Chapter objectives

☑ To discuss the difficulties of implementing performance management in developing countries and emerging markets.
☑ To give the reader an overview of the status of performance management in various developing countries.
☑ To discuss the applicability of performance management in developing countries.

15.1 CHARACTERISTICS OF DEVELOPING COUNTRIES

The sheer size of the developing world already indicates that developing countries are not as homogeneous as developed countries. The developing world covers a range from small island states to subcontinents, from communism to kingdoms to democracies, many ethnic groups, and all religions. However, despite their obvious differences developing countries also have many characteristics in common that set them apart from the developed world (Aycan, 2002; Hopper et al., 2003; Farashahi and Molz, 2004; Pacek and Thorniley, 2004):

■ *High unpredictability*. High degrees of environmental uncertainty and turbulence, and political instability and uncertainty of policies constrain private investments and create budget deficits. Governments are often unstable, switching from multi-party democracies to military dictatorships, and formal institutions are less stable, causing informal institutions to become more powerful and of importance for the behaviour of organisations. At the same time, developing countries have a high population growth and a young workforce, which creates even more pressure and unpredictability. The uncertainty creates a low sense of control and low self-efficacy in people, causing feelings of helplessness and fatalism. (People with low "self-efficacy" have a tendency to attribute things that happen to them to external reasons. This can be used to deny responsibility and as a reason for not meeting deadlines or goals.) As a result, people are not proactive and do not take the initiative because this increases risks and creates even more uncertainty.
■ *Economic problems and poverty*. More than 1.3 billion people in the developing world live on less than $1 a day (Akbar and Samii, 2005).

The disparities between rich and poor have grown considerably, while in general the majority of African, South Asian, and Latin American countries have suffered economic decline during the past 30 years. This has caused huge debts, as developing countries have gone on a "foreign borrowing binge" to counteract their economic decline. The biggest part of the debt is now public debt or publicly guaranteed debt.

The way to deal with the high unpredictability mentioned above and the risk it brings is to have a diversified project portfolio and to purchase financial mechanisms to offset risks. However, this is difficult for businesses in developing countries which are under-financed because of economic problems. Poverty also ensures that people in developing countries have limited access to social services such as good education and health care. As a consequence there are low literacy and numeracy rates.

- *Dominant public sector.* A public sector that plays a dominant role as the provider of basic commercial goods and services, and as the creator of public infrastructure facilities. Commercial enterprises are less central to economic activity than in the developed countries. Governments actively participate in the public and private sectors of the economy. They impose controls on elected products, promote industrial development in export products through special tax incentive programmes, and have large shares in public and private enterprises.

- *Prominent role of powerful groups.* Powerful groups, like families, political groups, religious groups, and business groups, play a vital role in economic and social activities. Examples of these groups are royal families in Middle Eastern and African countries, religious leaders in Iran, authoritarian regimes in Central Asia, and business groups such as the *chebol* in South Korea, *grupos economicos* in Latin America, and family businesses in Indonesia, Taiwan, and Pakistan. These powerful groups impose and institutionalise social and economic norms. They have significant social and economic power, which is often translated into political and capital power. Institutional regimes "bend" to the wishes of these powerful groups. Political and economical powers in the hands of a class or particular group in society are thus institutionalised in developing countries. Loyalty and trust are key elements of the groups.

- *Dominant family and relationship orientation.* A strong relationship and family orientation that is replicated in political and economic life, in which people defer to the leaders of their country. Interdependence in a trusting relationship serves to reduce uncertainties and maximise benefits when resources are scarce. Harmony within the group is preserved at all costs. The relationships supersede rules and procedures in every aspect of social, political, and economic life. Family has priority over all else. Work is perceived as a duty to the family. Those who are close to the group in power (like family members) get the benefits, while those who are not in the group are left out. Loyalty and trust are key elements of the relationships. In organisational settings, the family orientation is replicated such that the employer takes care of the employees, getting loyalty and compliance in return. Superiors treat their employees like their children ("paternalism"). Job performance does not matter as much as good interpersonal relationships. The intention to do well is as important as achieving results.

■ *High authority orientation.* Respect, loyalty, and deference towards superiors are extremely important. People respect authority more than rules, and authority is rarely challenged and questioned. Obedience to authority is a prescribed norm in many of the religions predominant in developing countries. Leaders like to exercise power while maintaining a good relationship with their subordinates at the same time, which creates conflicts. Decisions are taken centrally and unilaterally. Subordinates expect the leader to be decisive. Quite naturally, communication is usually downwards, especially in organisations. At the same time, it is indirect, non-assertive, and non-confrontational. Negative feedback is seen as destructive and is often taken personally. It implies losing face to the superior and is considered to be harmful to group integrity and harmony. Subordinates do not give performance feedback to their superiors. There is much room for subjective interpretation of the meaning of messages between the various parties. It is common for leaders to use their authority and power for personal benefit.

■ *Weak capital markets.* The focus on privatisation – the sale of state-owned enterprises to private investors – in many developing countries has left little time for improving regulation, corporate governance, and market processes. This has created a lack of developed financial service institutions, such as stock markets and investment banking, and a weak legal system. The lack of transparency and political influences during privatisation, combined with the small and weak capital market, have given rise to malpractices. Stock market rules in these markets do not work because of compliance failures, poor enforcement, and share-price rigging. Inadequate regulation results in deficient external reporting, and inadequate protection for minority shareholders, creditors, and employees.

Quite a few of these characteristics have to do with the cultures prevalent in developing countries. Culture is defined as: "the collective programming of the mind that distinguishes one group or category of people from another" (Hofstede, 2001). National culture seems to be a major source of differences between developed and developing countries (Farashahi and Molz, 2004). To distinguish between national cultures, Hofstede formulated four dimensions or distinguishing characteristics (Hofstede et al., 2002). He later added a fifth dimension, but there has been so much criticism of it that as a result the number of studies that include this dimension is limited. Therefore in this chapter only the first four dimensions are used:

1. *Uncertainty avoidance*. The extent to which people in a society feel comfortable with ambiguity and uncertainty. In cultures with high uncertainty avoidance, people tend to show their "fear" of the unknown through expressive behaviour. In cultures with low uncertainty avoidance, people tend to be less expressive: they do not show their emotions or aggression easily. The core value associated with high uncertainty avoidance is certainty. Rules and clarity are highly appreciated, whereas things that are different or not "normal" are seen as dangerous.

2. *Individualism versus collectivism*. The extent to which one's identity is derived from the self as opposed to the group of which the individual is a member. A society is individualistic if the mutual ties between individuals are loose. Everybody is expected to take care of him or herself and his or her next of kin. In a collectivist society, individuals are institutionalised in strong, tight groups that offer the individual lifelong protection in return for unconditional loyalty to the group.

3. *Power distance*. The extent to which members of a society accept that institutional power is distributed unequally. In a country where a large power distance prevails, few think that people are or should be created equal. Respect for status and power are core values, and "subordinates" expect to be given orders or directions rather than act on their own. In contrast, in low power distance societies equality between people is stressed. Subordinates expect to be consulted: their opinions matter.

4. *Masculinity versus femininity*. A society is masculine if social gender roles are clearly separated: men are expected to be assertive and hard, aiming at material success; women are supposed to be modest and tender, aiming at quality of life. In contrast, in a feminine society social gender roles are blurred: men as well as women are supposed to be modest, aiming at quality of life. The core value in strongly masculine societies is winning. In strongly feminine societies caring for others, most notably the weak, is the core value.

Using these dimensions, Kanungo and Jaeger (1990) have characterised the culture of developing countries as in general being:

▪ relatively high on uncertainty avoidance, which ties in with the characteristic of high unpredictability
▪ high on power distance, which ties in with the characteristic of high authority orientation
▪ low on individualism, which ties in with characteristics of prominent role of powerful groups, and dominant family and relationship orientation
▪ low on masculinity, which ties in with the characteristic of dominant family and relationship orientation.

An additional dimension for developing countries, "abstractive versus associative thinking," is proposed by Kedia and Bhagat (1988). In abstractive societies, cause–effect relationships and rational types of thinking are predominant (context-free thinking), while in associative societies people make associations between events that may not have a very logical basis (context-sensitive thinking). Developing countries are found to be relatively high on associative thinking and low on abstractive thinking. In many of these nations, traditional beliefs stipulate that causality and control of outcomes are external to the individual (Farashahi and Molz, 2004).

A change of culture in developing countries can be brought about by employees becoming better educated, and as a result seeking more influence in the decision-making process of their organisations. This will require different leadership traits from managers in organisations in these countries. Based on research, the ideal leader profile for developing countries is empowering, participative and at the same time decisive, trustworthy, knowledgeable, skilful, administratively competent, paternalistic, performance-oriented, fair and just, diplomatic, conscious of status differences, modest and humble, and a team integrator (Hartog et al., 1999; Aycan, 2002).

15.2 STATUS OF PERFORMANCE MANAGEMENT IN DEVELOPING COUNTRIES

There is a growing body of literature on the modernisation of management control and information systems in developing countries, with an emphasis on management accounting practice (Anderson and Lanen, 1999; Joshi, 2001; Waweru et al., 2004) and the development of new public management (Polidano, 1999; Mwita, 2000; Schacter, 2002; McCourt, 2002). However, the scientific and professional literature specifically on implementing performance management in developing countries is scarce (Abdel Aziz et al., 2005). The popularity of the BSC is gradually changing this, mainly in Asian countries, but it is still a relatively new concept for developing countries (Anand et al., 2005; Creelman and Makhijani, 2005; Pandey, 2005).

This section provides an overview of the development in developing countries of management control and information systems, and their transformation into strategic performance management systems. This development is closely tied to historical developments in these countries. The emphasis is on public organisations because these, as argued before, play a main role in the economy of most developing countries. In addition, many private companies have been modelled, at least initially, on public organisations.

In countries that gained their independence in the past decades, a "new feeling of citizenship" emerged as well as a sense of identification with the new state (Monteiro, 2002). As a result, people started to expect too much of the public administration, feeling that the new state had limitless capacity to fulfil their needs. However, the state was not even able to cover basic needs, because of the dire financial situation, and many able public servants left to work for the private sector. Unfortunately, there was not yet a sufficiently large private sector to take over part of the service delivery. In addition, the administrative structure that was inherited from the colonial period was basically minimal because it was only aimed at domination and exploitation, without concern for the welfare of the people. This kind of structure was totally unprepared for the upsurge of demand from the people after the beginning of independence.

As a reaction, many developing countries pursued modernisation through central state planning and government control of large enterprises. Many new state services were created, and even today the trend is still to create a new public institution for every identified need. Central management control and information systems were expected to provide performance information for decision making at both state and enterprise levels, and had a focus on budgeting and monitoring. However, in practice the performance information from these systems often proved unreliable and therefore marginal to decision making.

In the second part of the twentieth century, developing countries started to suffer from increasing tension and conflicting demands (Polidano, 1999; Monteiro, 2002). There was a growing demand for services while at the same time the capacity of public organisations to deliver these services was weakening. The increased demand put even more pressure on the fiscal balance of the country, which hindered pursuit of a healthy financial situation. This commendable aspiration was further thwarted by a tax collection system which could not get a grip on the growing "informal economy" in many countries, where people tended to abandon the formal economy with its rules and taxes to which they did not see the need to contribute.

In addition, there was increased pressure for a growing regulatory role by the state, which put even more strain on the diminished public administration capacity. Complicating this is the fact that the regulatory role is more complex, and requires more expertise and knowledge, than the direct management of organisations. Setting rules, devising regulatory frameworks, and exercising control through indirect mechanisms such as legislation and taxation, require different skills, including more flexibility and improvisation. Not only had developing countries to deal with both traditional and modern functions, there also came completely new functions like combating new types of crime which are transnational and for which a efficient system of international cooperation is needed.

Developing countries were not able to make a good link between the modern public administration, which is based on formal rules, and the traditional forms of society, which are based on informal rules, relationships, and patronage. The informal realm is predominant, which means that the rules of behaviour that people actually follow can be very different from those that are written down. Contractual mechanisms of accountability are simply ignored and disregarded. This is aggravated because many countries opted for administrative frameworks and techniques from the Western world which did not match local conditions and culture. This mismatch caused increased resistance from people and organisations rooted in tradition.

Many developing countries inherited a strong centralised administration from the colonial period and continued to use this set-up, while increased globalisation and different local conditions required decentralisation and devolution. It was difficult to carry through many reforms because of their long-term nature. Reforms require a long-term perspective and may not always be popular, making them at odds with the political cycle which in many developing countries often is rather short because of the unstable political situation. To make matters worse, the management of public organisations is afflicted by corruption and nepotism, which also blocks many improvement efforts. Central controls and procedures are seen as the only safeguard against further proliferation of such practices, increasing the tendency for centralisation.

Globalisation also put pressure on states to introduce and start using new technologies, especially in the area of information and communication technology. Often new tools and systems were purchased and installed without a proper maintenance and training programme, resulting in unused and broken-down systems. The lack of expertise and the unreliability of information systems often made it unviable to develop complex structures such as sophisticated performance management systems. Developing countries therefore concentrated more on introducing and copying tools and systems from the Western world, which were not always the best suited to local circumstances. At the same time, public organisations established mechanisms of central control over functions such as finance to try to guarantee better quality of these functions.

It gradually became clear that central state planning could not cope sufficiently with the conflicting demands put on the government and was not able to sustain, let alone increase, the standard of service provision and standard of living. At the same time, developing countries had become increasingly dependent on foreign aid and on increasing the supply of money to pay for services. The latter could only be sustained through borrowing huge amounts from external parties, thereby increasing the international debt to record highs.

At the end of the second half of the twentieth century, many developing countries decided to change over to market-based development. This change was also fostered by external donors, like the World Bank, which exerted pressure on governments by making their financing conditional on structural economic adjustment such as free trade, competition, privatisation, and limited state intervention (Schacter, 2002; Hopper et al., 2003).

The shift to a market-based economy required modernisation of accounting practices and new management control and information systems, a trend that is known as "public sector reform." This was sorely needed because research at the time showed that there was a significant positive correlation between public sector effectiveness and increased per capita income, increased adult literacy and reduced infant mortality (Kaufmann, 1999).

Developing countries started to introduce new public management (NPM), which has several core elements:

- Devolve authority and provide flexibility.
- Develop competition and choice.
- Provide a responsive service.
- Be performance-oriented.
- Be customer driven.
- Focus on efficiency.

In practice, many developing countries have only adopted elements of the NPM model, notably privatisation and downsizing. At the same time, there are a lot of reform initiatives going on that are unrelated or even contrary to NPM, making NPM just one of a number of current reforms in developing countries.

Many countries have also experimented with performance management initiatives, but most of these were limited to the introduction of performance-oriented staff appraisal systems. These have not been very successful because in these systems promotions are linked to performance, while in many developing countries promotion is still linked to seniority or to relatives. Attempts to use performance targets have produced mixed results. This element of NPM is the hardest to implement as it significantly changes the structure of accountability and the steering of public organisations, therefore inciting much resistance (Polidano, 1999).

The fact that NPM is not a resounding success in the developing world is no surprise considering the preconditions that have to be fulfilled in order to successfully implement NPM (Monteiro, 2002):

- NPM is based on contracts that require a developed judicial system, something that is often not present yet in developing countries.
- NPM is based on responsibility, while in many developing countries the work ethic is low, employee skills are underdeveloped, and people's loyalties are to their families and not to their employer.
- NPM requires a clear distinction between policy formulation (politicians), policy implementation (public servants) and policy support (service providers), while these relations in developing countries are often missing or unclear and muddled.

This raises the question whether Western techniques like NPM, and as a derivative strategic performance management, are suitable for developing countries. There is no question that in theory adopting management practices that have proven to be effective is a better alternative for an organisation than investing limited and scarce resources in efforts that do not amount to much more than "reinventing the wheel." Also, the poor management practices, bureaucratic inefficiencies, and low productivity levels in many developing countries organisations create considerable pressure for managers to adopt speedy, ready-to-implement strategies. The state-of-the-art techniques and practices currently in operation in Western organisations can undoubtedly be of great benefit to organisations in developing countries. However, these techniques and practices have evolved in the Western context and it cannot be expected that they can be transplanted "just like that" to the different sociocultural environment of developing countries.

Looking specifically at management control and information systems, the following issues can be noticed (Mendonca and Kanungo, 1996; Hopper et al., 2003; Farashahi and Molz, 2004; Pacek and Thorniley, 2004):

- The conventional management control and information systems approach to managing uncertainty is to design and implement flexible and decentralised systems, which are also able to monitor environmental factors. But implementing these complicated and expensive systems and having enough multiskilled employees to use these systems might be beyond the reach of many organisations in developing countries.
- The phenomenon of patronage is at odds with formal management control and information systems. Politicians and civil servants often have to respond to supporters' expectations of patronage based on family, village, caste, religious, regional, or ethnic ties. Consequently, management control and information systems may appear to be used in a strict manner while at the same time in reality being circumvented for illicit purposes.
- Inadequate regulation results in deficient management control and information systems, which result in deficient external reporting.
- In many developing countries employees' loyalties may be primarily to their family, village, ethnic, or religious group, rather than to their employer. This presents serious problems for managers because they must align management control and information systems with employee values that are inconsistent with those underpinning the formal design of the systems.
- The sociocultural environment in developing countries seems to be incompatible with the attitudes, values, and behavioural norms necessary for effective performance management practices: a good work ethic, an "internal locus of control" (basically the opposite of low self-efficacy: people with an internal locus of control feel they can determine their own faith), religion which causes individuals to work for betterment of their own and other people's lives, and loyalty to the employer while at the same time being critical in order to achieve continuous improvement.

The issues discussed above make it difficult to introduce and use effectively management control and information systems, and specifically strategic performance management systems, in developing countries. However, organisations in these countries do not need to force employees to give up their cultural backgrounds in order to satisfy the requirements of modern performance management. It is more practical and effective to build on those cultural characteristics that have the potential to enhance the effectiveness of performance management. This means that organisations have to tailor not only their performance management systems but also the management style of their managers in the following ways (Mendonca and Kanungo, 1996):

- The relatively high uncertainty avoidance of people in developing countries can be dealt with by involving organisational members in setting their targets. Initially these targets are set within fairly easy reach of employees' competency level to get them to feel more comfortable and self-assured. Gradually, the targets can be increased to a challenging level. In addition, organisational members should receive sufficient training and coaching, and managers should work diligently to remove organisational obstacles that can hinder reaching the targets.
- The relatively low individualism implies that individual accomplishments are disregarded in favour of group concerns. The emphasis for organisational members is not on "a job well done" but on "a job well recognised." In an ongoing dialogue between manager and employee it should be stressed that the well-being of the organisation coincides with the well-being of the group the individual belongs to. After all, if the organisation does well because of the efforts of the employee, that employee will be rewarded for this and is therefore better able to care for his/her group. Rewards should be visible so the group sees the individual is recognised for his or her contribution.
- The relatively high power distance implies that both supervisor and subordinate operate from fixed positions in the organisational hierarchy, with a clear and almost insurmountable gap between them. To overcome this, the manager has to act as a clear, honest, interested, and sympathetic coach and mentor to his or her subordinates. This makes the relationship between them more personal and supportive. This creates trust and encourages subordinates to view performance feedback by the manager as a means to improve their work deficiencies, which can be overcome with the help of the manager, and not be viewed as a personal attack. The manager has to explicitly ask for feedback from the subordinates, react in a professional manner to this feedback, and use it to visibly improve his or her own way of working.
- The relatively low masculinity means that satisfying an employee's affiliates takes precedence over his or her individual job satisfaction, and that the needs of these affiliates take precedence over the job needs. The way to overcome this is to formulate the objectives and targets with the employee. These should focus on meeting the needs of the user of the product or service to which the employee's job contributes, and meeting the needs of the organisational unit and the organisation, so as to benefit the community and the group the employee belongs to. In this manner, the job becomes a means to satisfy the relationship orientation of people.

- The high associative thinking of people means that they continuously interpret what is happening in the context of that moment, effectively making them live in the present. And since the present is always changing, they are also always changing because of changing interpretations, making them unpredictable with regard to uniform execution of a job. Setting specific time targets and forecasting expected results is not within their frame of reference. The way to overcome this is still to set clear targets, but to stress during the target-setting process the possible negative effects on the employee's colleagues, work team, and organisation of not achieving the targets. The targets should be accompanied by clear time frames, action plans, and behaviours to be displayed, so the employee knows what is expected of him or her. During performance reviews, managers should pay explicit attention to the time frame in which the targets have been achieved and the behaviour of the employee while striving for these targets.

Fundamental to the success of strategic performance management systems are the adoption of real empowerment, in the sense that employees are actively involved in setting targets and working with performance management, and a coaching management style of managers which is aimed at achieving results and improving service to the public (Schacter, 2002). This is no different from the "recipe" for successful performance management in developed countries!

The introduction of modern management techniques like strategic performance management is also helped by the recent theory that management accounting practices and methods and leadership styles seem to be converging. This especially happens within multinationals that operate in developing countries. The national cultures of the countries in which these conglomerates operate do indeed influence the use of the strategic performance management system, but this influence is considerably less than the effect of formal procedures and processes (as prescribed by the corporation) on the system. Because multinationals play an important role in the economic life of developing countries, this "convergence phenomenon" may well foster the implementation and use of modern strategic performance management systems in developing countries (Stede, 2003; Trompenaars and Woolliams, 2003; Zagersek et al., 2004; Waal, 2005).

The increased interest in performance management, and specifically the BSC, may be an indication that this is one of the concepts that is, with some tailoring, suitable for both public and private organisations in developing countries. It is however important to remember that organisations in the developing world are trying to implement strategic performance management in the space of a few years, while organisations in the developed world have been doing it for decades. For the advancement of emerging countries it is essential that organisations in the developing world take advantage of experiences of organisations in the developed world. Therefore, organisations should be prepared to share their performance management experiences and transfer knowledge worldwide.

15.3 STATUS IN INDIVIDUAL COUNTRIES

This section provides an overview of the status of strategic performance management in various countries in Asia and Africa (at the time of writing, not enough information was available to give a comprehensive overview of the status of performance management in South America). It is by no means a complete outline because, as stated before, the literature on performance management in the developing world is not very extensive.

Asia

In general, many Asian organisations still have underdeveloped strategic development processes. Many companies have no formal strategic planning group and often only a limited annual strategic development process. As this area is maturing, organisations will increasingly turn to the leading tool in this area: performance management and specifically the BSC. A study in southeast Asia found that already 36 per cent of the surveyed companies are using the BSC, with another 18 per cent planning on using the scorecard in the near future (Creelman and Makhijani, 2005).

Another study of the BSC in India found the adoption rate of the scorecard in corporate India to be 45 per cent, with the financial perspective still being the most important. Most surveyed companies claim that the implementation of the BSC has resulted in identification of cost-reduction opportunities and in improvements of the bottom line. The most critical issues in Indian BSC implementations were difficulty in assigning weights to the different perspectives, and difficulty in establishing cause-and-effect linkages between the perspectives (Anand et al., 2005).

It is expected that in the near future the scorecard will be used more in Asia, and that it will spread in popularity from its early strongholds in Singapore and Hong Kong to other emerging countries. This is promising for the success of performance management because in Asian organisations, unlike Western organisations, once a new management tool or technique is accepted it tends to remain. It might take longer than in the Western world for performance management to become part of Asian management, but when it does it will be there to stay.

One reason that strategic performance management might work well in Asia is that Asian organisations are more willing to take a long-term view than Western companies. In addition, management in Asian countries is more based on trust and relational management than it is in the Western world, a feature which contributes greatly to the acceptance and therefore success of performance management (Akbar and Samii, 2005).

However, the implementation of performance management in Asian countries will not be without its difficulties. Anand (2005) lists various challenges, which tie in with the issues of strategic performance management systems in developing countries described in the previous sections:

- Many Asian companies do not have a complete strategy. This gives rise to a lot of initiatives and projects in the company without clear ownership, clear timelines, and tangible business value. All these initiatives have to be approved by the chief executive officer (CEO), which takes too much time and takes away ownership from lower levels.
- Nine out of ten Asian organisations that do have a strategy cannot implement it successfully, partly because the strategic development process is underdeveloped. The process takes a long time and nobody in the organisation actually owns it.
- People confuse the BSC with other techniques such as total quality management (TQM) and economic value added (EVA™), causing organisational members to think the scorecard is mainly used for improving operational processes.
- CEOs tend to be easily distracted by new, "promising" tools, offering them new opportunities to improve, which results in a loss of focus of running improvement projects. In addition, they tend to react slowly to low performance. Many CEOs would rather tamper with the scorecard to hide problems than confront people with disappointing results or admit failure in public.
- Many companies are family owned, with family members tending to be involved in all details of the operation. These companies have a hard time moving from family owned/family managed to family owned/professionally managed and spending more time on strategic issues.
- Performance measurement is still seen as a threatening process which does not motivate organisational members to participate. The primary motto for many people is "the less information the better." Annual performance reviews are not linked to quantifiable performance so the system does not have much value added for both manager and employee. It is risky for organisational members to share their views and opinions openly in a meeting. Lagging performance is blamed on external causes, and a much-heard phrase is "It won't work" to cover oneself in advance against failure.
- There is a lack of historical performance data, which makes it difficult to perform trend analyses and learn from the past. There are not enough ICT systems to collect the data structurally, while at the same time there is unwillingness to manually collect and report historical and current data needed for the KPIs. If data is collected, there is a tendency to strive for almost 100 per cent accuracy. There is an aspiration to define the perfect measure and to choose too many indicators. Unfortunately it is difficult to reach consensus on a subset of limited, not-so-perfect KPIs, so many organisations suffer from "indicator overload."

In China, the effort of setting up, implementing, and perfecting a strategic performance management system has become an urgent task for many CEOs of both private-sector and state-owned enterprises. Until recently, state-owned enterprises regarded reconstruction and system reform as the focal points. However, reconstruction, reform, and implementing a well-thought-out company structure did not automatically improve the results of enterprises. In fact, many state-owned enterprises that have finished their reconstruction and system reform have not experienced significant performance improvement. Managements of these organisations believe strategic performance management should be the new focus, after the reconstruction and system reform.

The private business sector in China has developed prosperously since the mid-1980s. With the booming 1990s, many companies made good use of newly opened markets. Using marketing as their main tool, they experienced growth of up to 80 per cent. With the maturity of the market and intensifying competition, doing business and achieving good performance have become more difficult. In order to compete better, the private companies also turned to strategic performance management. In practice, those implementing performance management in China experience various difficulties (Xiaoming, 2005):

- *Confusion in the organisation about performance management.* When implementing performance management, management does not pay enough attention to the role of the employees. As a consequence, employees are not clear about the core ideas and goals of performance management, resulting in confusion and misunderstandings. In the worse case, they question the function and effectiveness of the system.
- *Difficulty with making the performance management system an institutionalised tool.* This is a very common and serious problem in Chinese enterprises. Many companies have a performance management system in place, but employees consider it to be a bureaucratic tool and treat it as a formality. They are not serious about analysis, management, and maintenance of the system.
- *Lack of qualified people to use the performance management system.* Many enterprises with a good performance management system in place have no qualified people to analyse the data in the system. Therefore the system does not provide adequate feedback on performance.
- *Misuse of performance management.* In some enterprises, the performance management system produces a lot of valuable information. However, management does not use this information for decision making, but "puts it on the shelf," which basically makes the system useless. Another misuse is management applying the results to control and punish employees instead of encouraging and helping them to improve. Some enterprises do not want to communicate the results to employees because they might want to use them as a "secret weapon" to manipulate other employees.
- *Resistance to the performance management system.* It has been a long Chinese tradition to use management systems to compare employees. The process of selecting only a few of the best frustrated many people. So many employees in private companies try to cover up the true results of

their work because they worry that evaluators will not review their results in a fair way, which is even more damaging when they are also going to be compared with their colleagues. In many state-owned enterprises, performance management often does not have any link with employees' training and promotion, so the performance management system is most of the time considered irrelevant.

Africa

Although performance management is relatively unknown in many African countries, the interest in such an improvement tool is growing among African organisations. For instance, there seems to be a real need for the BSC in Burkina Faso's state-owned companies. As it will help these companies to improve their performance and then contribute to the country's growth, both management and government want to work diligently on a successful implementation of performance management (Waal and Augustin, 2005).

In Egypt, there is a trend in many manufacturing organisations to combine financial and nonfinancial measures because there is growing awareness that sole reliance on financial data is no longer effective for an organisation. Despite this growing awareness, performance management systems are not widespread yet in Egypt, and many Egyptian organisations are still using traditional financial measures like return on investment and return on assets (Abdel Aziz et al., 2005).

In Zimbabwe, all government departments, local government institutions, and most private companies are using zero-based budgeting systems. However, since the success of the BSC has been noticed, Zimbabwe is trying its best to catch up with the rest of the world in the area of leading-edge performance management systems. The country has the advantage that it hosts many transnational companies which are already applying the latest performance management systems. These companies can serve as an example for Zimbabwean organisations (Nhemachena, 2004).

In South Africa, the term "performance management" is relatively new in the field of management. However, there are many pressures on South African organisations, enticing them to investigate the concept of strategic performance management. Competition has increased dramatically over the past decade because of many multinational companies investing in South Africa. The battle against nepotism and corruption has intensified. In addition, many South African companies have to take the development of employee skills, knowledge, and experience seriously in order to deal with today's rapidly changing workplace. However, many companies have difficulty competing well in the current business environment as a result of traditional organisational cultures which are rigid and bureaucratic, and because of the lack of technological resources.

There is growing acknowledgement that for a South African organisation to

remain competitive and to retain its reputation for excellence, its employees
need to:

- have up-to-date performance information
- have the ability to use new technologies
- be able to adapt to organisational change
- work in flatter organisations in which cross-functional skills and
  knowledge are required
- work effectively in teams and other forms of collaboration.

For this, these organisations are increasingly turning to strategic performance
management (Motswiane, 2004).

In Kenya, performance management was traditionally defined as the
process of financial control, in which the mission and strategy are translated
into budgets, and subsequently results are compared with budgets.
Budgeting is done by adding 5 per cent on the actuals of last year to arrive
at forecasts for the next year. This process is more of a financial exercise
than a process of value creation. However, as many Kenyan companies are
trying to qualify for the ISO standard, they are turning more and more to
performance management, especially the BSC. Some organisations have
already implemented the scorecard, particularly if they are part of a multinational that is using the BSC. Those organisations that have done so show
much better performance than their "scorecardless" competitors. However,
there are various issues that impede a full-scale adoption of strategic
performance management in Kenya (Malinga, 2004):

- The Certified Public Accountants' syllabus does not include performance management as a subject, which means many financial people are
  not aware of this technique.
- CEOs of most public corporations are political appointees whose main
  interest is to please the government of the day. As a consequence, they
  are not very interested in long-term management improvement tools.
- Budgets are not driven by performance but by getting support and
  favours from influential people. Therefore they are not very effective
  in management organisations.
- ICT and internet infrastructure lag behind those of neighbouring
  countries.
- Kenya has not as many scholars as other developing countries.
- Kenyans need a lot of training, especially where updates of profession
  knowledge and short courses are concerned. However, many training
  facilities use outdated books and equipment.
- It is hard to get people to work as a team, because of ethnic conflicts
  and government policies of divide and rule.
- Corruption is unfortunately still a problem in Kenya. Corrupt people
  do not want the transparency that performance management brings.
- Most companies still use traditional management control techniques
  and are not willing to abandon these.

In Ethiopia, the performance management systems of organisations are characterised by:

- a lack of nonfinancial data
- lack of computer-based support
- no regular meetings to discuss performance
- no regular use of the system
- little knowledge about new performance management techniques.

However, there are some developments for the benefit of performance management. More and more Ethiopian enterprises are expressing a strong interest in the BSC, their managers are starting to acknowledge the importance of regular formal and informal performance review meetings, communication about results is being improved by applying modern means of communication like the intranet, people are willing to train in the use of performance management, and government is fostering the improvement of performance (Tessema, 2005).

Conclusion

It is difficult to treat developing countries as a homogeneous group. They have poverty in common but its degree and distribution may fluctuate greatly. Varied colonial and cultural histories have given rise to diverse ethnic, religious, and cultural relations, and economic and political systems. Many researchers argue that organisations in developing countries need different performance management systems from those used in developed countries. There is however no obvious evidence that large organisations in developing countries currently use different systems than their counterparts in the developed world (Hopper et al., 2003). A reason for this could be that organisations in developing countries do not have enough resources to create new or tailored performance management systems that fit better with the indigenous culture. It may be more effective for them to adopt existing methods and techniques (transfer of technology). Another reason may be, as mentioned before, that Western management techniques seem to spreading over the world.

This short overview of the history of performance management in the developing world, and the examples of various developing countries, clearly show that there is a need for and interest in strategic performance management. It remains to be seen whether organisations in the developing countries can assimilate the whole performance management "package" from the Western world. That this is not inconceivable is illustrated by the following two cases of Burkina Faso and Tanzania.

The benefit of transfer of performance management knowledge is that organisations in developing countries can learn from the experiences and mistakes of organisations in the developed world that have preceded them.

This may have the advantage that strategic performance management can be implemented more quickly in the developing world than in the developed world, and possibly with less difficulty.

15.4 CASE: THE NEED FOR PERFORMANCE MANAGEMENT IN BURKINA FASO

(This case originates from Waal and Augustin, 2005.)

Burkina Faso is a country of 274,000 km^2 located in the heart of Western Africa, approximately 600 miles from the Atlantic Ocean. Ouagadougou, the capital city, has about one million inhabitants. The country borders Benin, Côte d'Ivoire, Ghana, Mali, Niger, and Togo.

Like other Sahelian countries, Burkina Faso suffers from drought and desertification, overgrazing, soil degradation, deforestation, and an uneven population distribution (large areas of the country are almost deserted). With 11.9 million inhabitants, belonging to 60 ethnic groups, Burkina Faso is one of the most densely populated states in Africa.

Burkina Faso is a constitutional state. The constitution, adopted by referendum in 1991, secures a democratic and civil state. It recognises inherent freedom of expression and free association of all citizens. Members of parliament are elected for a five-year term. Burkina Faso has good relations with international financial institutions like the World Bank and the International Monetary Fund, and is a member of the International Organisation for Intellectual Property and the African Organisation for Intellectual Property. Burkina Faso is also a member of the West African Economic and Monetary Union, of which it hosts the headquarters, and of the Economic Community of West African States.

The currency, the CFA franc (FCFA), is currently fixed at a rate of €1 to FCFA 655.957. The annual rate of population growth is 2.3 per cent and the average life expectancy is 42.9 years. The GDP per capita is €240 with a growth of 7.9 per cent in 2003. Agriculture accounts for 60 per cent of export revenues, with the main agricultural export products being cotton, sesame, fruits, vegetables, and tobacco. Livestock breeding remains a pillar of the economy, accounting for 12 per cent of GDP. The industrial sector, which remains relatively small at about 20 per cent of GDP, is mostly made up of mining and manufacturing activities. Burkina Faso has important mining potential, which consists of gold and base metals including magnesium, zinc, and phosphates. Trading activities and transport constitute an important component of the services sector, roughly 42 per cent of GDP.

Burkina Faso offers the private investor access to a market of 11 million consumers, a stable democratic political system, a reliable legal system, standardised business laws, and diversified economic potential. Free enterprise is the main characteristic of the investment environment in the country. Reforms made by the government have given the private sector the driving role in economic development. These reforms include the government's withdrawal from competitive sectors and the restructuring of support institutions for the private sector, such as the Chamber of Commerce and the Office of Foreign Trade.

The state-owned companies of Burkina Faso are an important source of revenue for the government through the payment of taxes and dividends. They are classified into four major groups:

- services, such as electricity, telephone, water, postal services, gambling, IT services, the hotel industry, and mortgages
- trade in oil, gold, and precious metals
- manufacturing, especially pharmaceuticals and agricultural equipment
- corporations with specific missions, such as pension funds and food security stocks.

Most of these state-owned companies are undergoing restructuring programmes that will end with a privatisation, a liquidation, or maintenance of state-ownership status. This is reflected in the total number of the state-owned enterprises, which was 23 in 2002 and 17 in 2003. The companies are governed by the State-owned Companies' Board, which consists of members of the government, and can be extended with chairpersons and CEOs of companies and with governmental auditors. The state-owned companies contribute considerably to the economy of the country. In 2003, the tax and dividend contribution was FCFA 26.6 billion, up from FCFA 20 billion in 2002. The results of the individual state-owned companies during the last four years show that some are doing well, others are unstable in their performance, while the remainder actually show a poorer performance. Because of the importance of these companies for Burkina Faso's economy, the government is looking for ways to ensure that the state-owned companies continue or start to consistently contribute to the country's growth. One of the management techniques looked at in this respect is performance management.

Research in Burkina Faso

To evaluate whether performance management, and in particular the BSC, is a viable opportunity to improve the results of state-owned companies in Burkina Faso, a survey was conducted. This survey assessed the existing status of performance management in the state-owned enterprises, and identified preconditions and best approaches to implement a multidimensional performance management system, such as the BSC, in these companies. The survey targeted the state-owned companies in the service, trade, and manufacturing sectors. It discarded organisations with specific missions and manufacturing companies that were under liquidation and were going to be written off from the list of state-owned companies. The survey was conducted over a period of three months, May 2004 to July 2004. It targeted

14 state-owned companies, all located in the capital city, of which nine responded. The data collection procedure consisted of formulation of a questionnaire, distribution of the questionnaire to the participating state-owned companies, and collection of the survey data.

The respondents were asked to answer questions by selecting from among the possible answers the most appropriate to their situation. In each company, two to four people responded: at least one senior manager and one employee (usually from the human resources department). Their answers were averaged to represent the results per company. The questionnaire was divided into four parts: general company information, inventory of existing tools, need for the BSC, and corporate social responsibility (to ascertain the viability of a fifth BSC perspective which focuses on the social responsibility of a company). The complete questionnaire is available from the author on request.

Status of performance management

Looking at the actual status of performance management at the state-owned companies yields a varied picture. All the companies examined use traditional management systems for accounting, finance, budgeting, cash management, and human resources, which they refer to as performance measurement tools. These systems are used for the purpose of decision making, control of budget items and cash monitoring, and financial reporting. They are generally computer-based systems but in most of the cases they are insufficiently integrated. There are however no formal multidimensional performance management systems that integrate the four BSC perspectives, finance, customer, internal process, and innovation and learning.

The current systems focus mainly on the financial perspective (88.9 per cent) and on internal processes (especially cost reduction, 55.6 per cent). The innovation (22.2 per cent) and customer (22.2 per cent) perspectives get considerably less attention. All companies have monthly management reporting and management team meetings for monitoring activities and communicating the results to management. The general time frame for publishing full financial performance information is annually, to comply with the boards' requirements. Both management and employees are willing to improve the company's performance and to give support to improving the existing systems. Employee appraisal is mostly linked to individual performance, but the people generally do not have a clear understanding of performance objectives and targets. The State-owned Companies' Board makes recommendations to all the companies with regard to reducing costs, recovering outstanding debts, and making annual financial reports available.

With the current performance management system, 44.4 per cent of the companies achieve a positive financial trend while the other 55.6 per cent have negative results. Figure 15.1 shows the performance orientation of the nine state-owned companies by comparing the characteristics and use of their current performance management systems. The higher the score in the table, the higher the performance orientation of the company. Companies with a score above 10 are considered performance oriented. Based on this evaluation, three of the state-owned companies can be designated as performance-oriented: C, E, and J.

Figure 15.2 shows the financial performance of the state-owned companies, in terms of earnings before interest and taxes (EBIT), over a period of four years (2000–03). There seems to be a relation between the companies' performance orientation as given in Figure 15.1 (companies that qualify as performance-oriented are C, E, and J) and their financial results as given in Figure 15.2 (companies with good financial results in the last four years are C, E, and J). Companies A and D also achieved positive financial results but these organisations did not respond to the questionnaire and it therefore cannot be related to their performance orientation. In addition, these companies, despite still having positive financial results, suffered a decline in their EBIT in the last two years.

It can be stated that in three of the examined state-owned companies, improving the performance orientation of the company resulted in better financial performance (an effect that has been already discussed in Chapter 2). Therefore it appears to be rewarding for the state-owned companies to foster their performance orientation by improving their performance management systems, for instance by implementing the BSC. The survey results also show that only a small number of the state-owned companies examined are performance oriented (three out of nine), and that too many of them achieve insufficient financial results (six out of nine). In a developing country like Burkina Faso, constant performance improvement of the state-owned companies is important for the improvement of the country's economy and for setting a good example for other profit and nonprofit organisations in the country.

Aspect	A	B	C	D	E	F	G	H	I	J	K	L	M	N
Evaluation of current PMS			3		3	3	3	3		3		3	3	3
Coverage of current PMS			2		1	2	1	1		1		1	1	2
Monitoring with current PMS			2		2	2	2	3		2		2	2	2
Effective use of current PMS			2		2	3	2	3		2		1	1	2
Contribution of current PMS			3		3	0	0	0		3		3	0	0
SCORE			**12**		**11**	**10**	**8**	**10**		**11**		**10**	**7**	**9**

Figure 15.1 Performance orientation of Burkina Faso's state-owned companies
Companies A, B, D, I, and K did not participate in the research

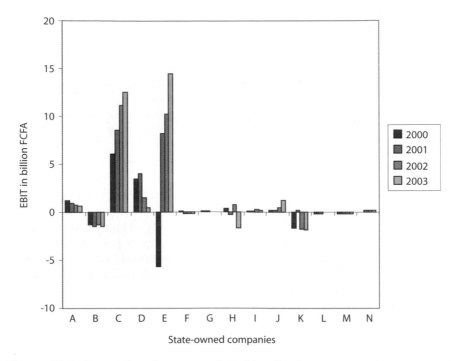

Figure 15.2 Financial performance of Burkina Faso's state-owned companies in the years 2000-03

Interest in the balanced scorecard

An analysis of the answers to the questions regarding the need for the BSC reveals the following. Most of the respondents had no information on the BSC or knowledge of it. At the same time, once the concept was explained there was a real interest in the BSC, and the majority of management expressed a willingness to give full support to the BSC (while the majority of employees are expected to give it moderate support).

In addition, there is great willingness in the companies to create open vertical and horizontal communication of performance information. The BSC is a management tool that is very new to Burkina Faso's managers. Nevertheless, many seem to recognise the advantages that it can bring to their companies, and are ready to adopt it.

However, implementing the BSC means change. The questionnaire addressed the preconditions for a successful implementation of the BSC in Burkina Faso's state-owned companies. The respondents' answers indicate that during the implementation special attention has to be paid to the following:

■ The prevailing culture in state-owned enterprises is strongly influenced by the public administration's culture, which in general experiences many difficulties in the performance (management) area. Most of the state-owned companies used to be monopolistic organisations in their industry. Nowadays, even with the competitive environment they start finding themselves in, employees of state-owned enterprises continue to exhibit the negative habits of the old days. Adopting the BSC successfully is only possible if it is supported by a performance-driven culture. However, most respondents think that people will tend to stick to their old habits of underachievement, and that existing systems will prove to be barriers to change.

■ In Burkina Faso, state properties are generally considered as impersonal and not something to care about. The mentalities of employees of state-owned companies are influenced by this negative attitude, and therefore employees tend not to strive for the best performance. The majority of respondents think that an attempt to change the situation will be difficult and will meet with resistance from people.

■ Issues relating to transparency and communication of results are strictly controlled within Burkina Faso's organisations. If top management is not really committed to the BSC and the increased transparency it brings, the performance of a company can suffer from distorting effects such as lack of transparency and unreliability of performance data. Management has to make sure that it uses the BSC to honestly measure performance and results to incite people to take corrective action, and not to blame and punish employees.

■ Most of the state-owned companies are experiencing financial difficulties and cannot afford the high costs involved in acquiring ICT systems and using expensive consultants for the BSC implementation, which can seriously hamper implementation of the scorecard. Therefore the respondents are hoping that a practical implementation formula can be found to make the BSC affordable to them.

■ Corporate social responsibility – the responsibility of companies to the social community and their direct involvement in the improvement of people's standards of living – is increasingly becoming a subject of concern for Burkina Faso's society. Organisations are increasingly expected to protect and take care of the environment in which they operate, promote human rights by ensuring a good working environment for people, improve the social climate, implement security policies to ensure safety in the neighbourhood, and provide support to improve social and educational activities and local developments (Pacek and Thorniley, 2004). These requirements are expected from foreign companies, national private companies, and state-owned enterprises. Corporate social responsibility is regarded as so important that respondents are of the opinion that it must be included in companies' strategies and monitored through the BSC. A fifth dimension referring to the corporate social responsibility therefore has to be integrated in the BSC.

There seems to be a real need for the BSC in Burkina Faso's state-owned companies. As it will help companies to improve their performance and then contribute to the country's growth, both the state-owned enterprises and the State-owned Companies' Board should work diligently on successful implementation, in which they both have an important role to play. The management of the state-owned companies should involve, inform, and stimulate people to adopt the BSC and develop a performance-driven culture in their companies. The State-owned Companies' Board should:

- modify the current reporting design of the nine state-owned companies examined to incorporate the BSC perspectives
- adopt this reporting design for all state-owned companies and take legal measures for the institutional use of multidimensional performance management systems (such as the BSC) in state-owned companies
- extend the role of the board secretary to a supervisory board, to supervise further performance management development and improvement in the state-owned companies
- initiate a closer follow-up of the companies' performance on a regular basis
- consider the introduction of a multidimensional performance management system in other public and administrative sector organisations, like universities, hospitals and development projects.

These new arrangements should be incorporated in what is known as a "shareholder performance agreement" (Khoza and Adam, 2005).

15.5 CASE: STRATEGIC PERFORMANCE MANAGEMENT AT THE TANZANIAN COLLEGE OF BUSINESS EDUCATION

The history of the College of Business Education (CBE) is closely linked to the history of Tanzania. Soon after the independence of the former British colony, Tanzania found itself in dire need of sufficiently trained personnel for running commercial and industrial companies. As a result, after first offering several short courses from 1963 onwards, in January 1965 the then President Nyerere officially opened the new College of Business Administration in Tanzania's capital Dar es Salaam. Over the years, CBE has grown from initially one campus with 28 male students and one programme, to two campuses (Dar es Salaam and Dodoma) with 3000 male and female students and six programmes. The main activities of the college are:

- to provide facilities for study, training and research mainly in the fields of business administration, accountancy, purchasing and supplies management, marketing management, legal, industrial and general metrology, and computer and information technology

- to award certificates, diplomas, advanced diplomas, and postgraduate diplomas in these fields
- to provide consultancy, counselling, arbitration, and business advisory services to the Tanzanian business community.

The college has several hostels on both campuses which together can accommodate up to 500 students. CBE's vision reads as follows:

> To be a centre of excellence that is dynamic, well-equipped, known and respected in the provision of training, research and advisory services in the fields of account-ancy, procurement and supplies management, business administration, entrepre-neurship, marketing management, legal, industrial and scientific metrology information and communication technology (ICT) and other related disciplines.

CBE falls under the Ministry of Industry and Trade and has a governing body which puts policies in place for running the activities of the college. The principal, who is the chief executive of the college, reports to the governing body. CBE's management is made up of the principal and vice-principals, the registrar, the director of human resources and administra-tion, and the heads of the academic departments. Figure 15.3 shows the organisational structure of the CBE.

CBE's strategic plan

During 2000 CBE's vision, mission, and strategic objectives were developed in a structured way for the first time, under the guidance of the newly appointed principal, and documented in a strategic corporate plan for the period 2000–05. This plan had 21 strategic objectives to be accomplished. In the five years that the plan covered, student enrolment increased from 600 to 3000, which put a lot of strain on the organisation. In addition new programmes were introduced, physical facilities were improved, such as drilling a reliable water-hole at the Dodoma campus and upgrading the water system at the Dar es Salaam campus, more than 100 personal computers were procured, the hostels were refurbished, and tutors received much additional training. At the same time, many objectives were not achieved and the social, economic, political, and business environments changed considerably.

A SWOT analysis, performed in 2005, showed that CBE has considerable strengths and opportunities but at the same time needed to work on several weaknesses and deal with specific threats. The college has much experience with teaching and has two accessible locations to do this from. It has forged many strategic alliances and built strong national and international networks. CBE has provisional accreditation from the National Council for Technical Education (NACTE), a good library and ICT sources, and acts as an information centre for academia in Tanzania. At the same time, the college suffers from a shortage of teaching facilities, many ageing tutors who

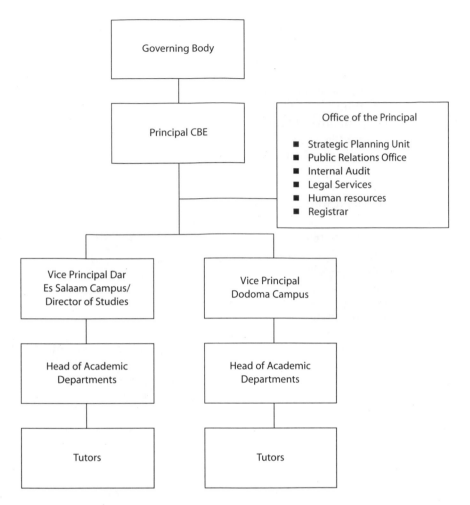

Figure 15.3 Simplified organisational structure of CBE

are about to retire while replacements are not readily available, expensive communication lines between the two campuses, and an insufficient number of administrative and support staff.

Opportunities are abundant:

- a large pool of school leavers who are potential "clients" of CBE
- increased demand for professional training in Tanzania
- a large network of CBE alumni in the country who are good for relations and marketing and are also potential candidates for advanced degrees
- the positive attitude of sponsors towards the college
- much potential for enlarging the current network and alliances and creating new ones.

However, specific threats are looming such as:

- low income levels of Tanzanian citizens who consequently are not able to pay the tuition fees, thereby impacting CBE's financial stability
- increased competition from universities and emerging institutions for higher learning
- high labour turnover because competitors are offering more attractive remuneration packages
- a lack of employment for CBE's graduates partly because of the freezing of governmental jobs
- the potential reversal of the government's decision to move its seat to Dodoma, which will have a negative impact on the Dodoma campus
- the possibility that full NACTE accreditation will not be obtained, which would make certain courses either impossible to run or restricted
(CBE, 2000, 2003, 2005).

To deal with the outcomes of the SWOT, a second five-year corporate strategic plan was made. This plan states an ambition to:

- increase the student capacity of the college to 5000 students and 4200 graduates in the academic year 2009–10
- increase both tutor quality (by hiring more tutors holding master degrees and PhDs) and staff quality (e.g. by additional training and improving the incentive package)
- offer more new (postgraduate) diploma programmes and expand existing programmes, modernise teaching and learning facilities
- ascertain the financial sustainability of the college.

As a first consequence of these ambitions, the mission and strategic objectives of the college were revised. The updated mission of the college is:

To train highly competent and practice-oriented professionals in business administration, metrology (weights and measures), accountancy, procurement and supplies management and related fields at certificate, diploma, higher diploma, postgraduate diploma and professional degree levels; to undertake relevant basic and applied research and to provide consultancy and advisory services to the public.

A total of 26 strategic objectives were formulated, consisting partly of "old" objectives from the previous strategic plan and partly of new ones. In order to make these rather abstract objectives more tangible and measurable, a workshop was organised with the complete management team of CBE, under the guidance of the author of this book. It took place in Morogoro, a town 200 kilometres and a two and a half hour drive west of Dar es Salaam, halfway to Dodoma.

CBE's performance management analysis

The three-day workshop at CBE started by conducting a performance management analysis (PMA). In total 24 participants, including all of CBE's management team including the principal and the two vice-principals, individually filled in the PMA questionnaire. With the PMA, the strengths and improvement opportunities of the current performance management system and the performance drive of CBE were evaluated. The resulting PMA radar diagram and the averaged scores are given in Figures 15.4 and 15.5.

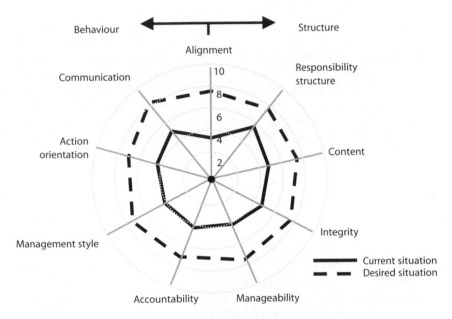

Figure 15.4 PMA radar diagram with the scores of CBE

	Responsibility structure	Content	Integrity	Manageability	Accountability	Management style	Action	Communication	Alignment orientation	Competitive performance
Current	5.7	4.9	4.9	4.5	4.6	4.6	4.6	5.1	3.9	5.8
Std. dev.	1.9	1.7	1.9	1.8	1.9	2.0	1.7	2.2	1.8	1.5
Desired	8.0	7.8	7.8	7.7	7.5	7.9	7.6	8.3	7.9	
Std. dev.	1.2	1.5	1.1	1.3	1.2	1.1	1.2	1.1	1.4	

Figure 15.5 PMA scores of CBE (including standard deviations)

The PMA scores showed CBE's management team was not satisfied with the current performance management system and with the performance drive of the organisation. The average scores for the structural aspects were 5.0 and for the behavioural aspects 4.6, while the desired average was 7.9. In addition, the management team was clearly aware that a competitive score of 5.8 did not fit an organisation which has in its vision "to be a centre of excellence," so it wanted to improve the PMA scores considerably in the next five years. Splitting the scores into subscores for first, the principal and vice-principals, and second, the remaining managers, showed no significant difference between the two, so CBE's management seemed to be united in its ambition to grow and become a better managed unity.

When the PMA scores were discussed, the relative high score for the aspect "responsibility structure" was put into perspective: CBE had indeed defined the daily tasks and responsibilities of the various management levels, but it had not defined the more strategic ones. For the managers, in particular, it was not clear how much room they had to make strategic decisions in their own responsibility areas. Although guidelines were regularly communicated through memos from one of the vice-principals, in practice these were either unclear or did not receive enough attention. The absence of concrete and tangible CSFs and KPIs was reflected in the low score for "content," while the lack of good ICT systems showed up in the "integrity" and "manageability" scores.

The behavioural side of performance management had not received enough attention in recent years; CBE had focused its improvement efforts on the structural side by appointing a new principal and developing corporate strategic plans. Managers did feel accountable for their own department but not necessarily for CBE as a whole. Training in a modern management style had not been promoted under the previous leadership. It was suggested that the low score on "action orientation" was caused by the management being composed of mainly academics who, in contrast to practitioners, tend to think things through for too long a period before acting.

It seemed surprising that the score for "communication" was relatively high, as the two campuses were so far apart. However, the principal and vice principals had taken special care to visit the campuses regularly and to conduct meetings and discussions with local managers. Finally, the major problem area for CBE proved to be "alignment." The lack of alignment was basically caused by the facts that the current incentive structure was outdated and that government regulations did not give the organisation much room to manoeuvre in this respect.

The standard deviation for the scores (see Figure 15.5), which indicates how much the respondents agree (low deviation) or disagree (high deviation), was relatively high. This is caused by the fact that CBE's management had not spent much time talking about performance management. In fact, the joint workshop in Morogoro was one of the first plenary meetings in which both Dar es Salaam and Dodoma managers participated, and in which the desired performance-driven behaviour was discussed.

It was interesting to see that respondents from different campuses had different scores (Figure 15.6).

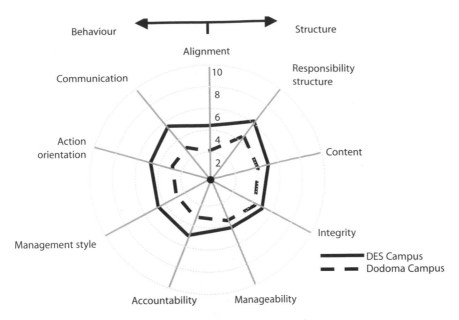

Figure 15.6 PMA radar diagram with the scores of both CBE campuses shown separately

Although the shape of the radar diagram was roughly the same, the scores for the Dodoma campus were considerably lower than those of the Dar es Salaam campus. The Dodoma-based managers commented that they often felt marginalised because many of the important, strategic decisions were made at Dar es Salaam without consulting them. Because both the principal and one of the vice-principals were based in the capital, as was the governing body, the centre of the college's power was clearly far from Dodoma. The Dodoma respondents stated that they were more than willing to improve the current situation, and that they were well aware that a lot needed to be done. The meeting concluded that the improvement effort was not just a Dodoma affair but the responsibility of the entire college, and therefore of managers from both campuses.

Developing CBE's strategic performance management system

During the three-day workshop, several alternatives were discussed to improve CBE's current situation and to get the college on the road to being a performance-driven organisation. It was decided to review the possibility of turning the departments into cost centres with clearly defined tasks, responsibilities, and a cost budget. This would increase clarity about who was responsible for what.

The management team also resolved that future communications within the college, and especially between the two campuses, between principal and vice-principals and the rest of the management team, and between management team members in general, would be characterised by a continuous dialogue. This should ensure two-way communication instead of one-way, and that both sides will listen to each other and have a right of input. This would result in a better quality of information exchange and knowledge transfer.

The management team determined to repeat the exercise of filling in the PMA regularly, to get a frequent update on the performance drive of the CBE. The PMA aspects were to be referred to from then as "the nine CBE commandments," focusing the complete organisation on what is important to the college.

Although the CBE had scored higher on the structural aspects than on the behavioural aspects, it was nevertheless agreed to first start improving the college's structural performance information. The reason was that the performance information should better match the responsibility structure, so managers could base their management style, action, and communication on it. The performance management needed to contain performance indicators that monitor the execution of the strategic objectives on all levels in the organisation, so managers could feel more accountable for the results of CBE.

The first activity to improve CBE's performance information was to review the 26 strategic objectives included in the strategic corporate plan. It was decided to take not all the objectives but the ten that were included in the budget for the coming year and therefore had the highest priority. They were formulated as follows:

1. CBE made more accessible to its customers through establishment of centres in other geographical zones/regions in Tanzania.
2. ICT institutionalised, and training strengthened.
3. Impact of CBE current curricula and programmes on the market assessed, improvements made, and new programmes and courses identified and designed.
4. Teaching and learning improved.
5. Status of the college upgraded.
6. Financial management and resources rationalised, and sustainability of the college maintained and continuously improved.
7. New skills in project proposal write-up for academic staff developed.
8. Communication with the market, between campuses and public relations strengthened and enhanced.
9. Dodoma campus strengthened, promoted, and made more financially sustainable.
10. Culture for training, research, and consultancy on entrepreneurship and small business management promoted.

The participants of the workshop agreed that these ten objectives in general were not SMART enough: that is, they were not specific, measurable, acceptable, realistic, and timely enough. The managers were consequently divided into four groups and each group discussed five to six objectives. After a few hours, the groups reconvened to reach consensus on the newly formulated strategic objectives, with the following result:

1. *Make CBE more accessible to its customers by establishing at least two centres in other geographical zones/regions in Tanzania by June 2010.* In order to fulfil CBE's vision and mission to make its services better available to Tanzania's population, greater coverage has to be achieved. This will be done by establishing at least two, and preferably three, new campuses in the country in the next five years. The locations of these campuses still have to be decided upon, but likely candidates are the north and the south, as students from those territories do not yet have easy access to CBE's facilities.

2. *Srengthen ICT programmes by setting up a fully fledged department by June 2006.* Information and communication technology is seen as an important tool to make the college's programmes more affordable to a greater number of students, and to increase CBE's reputation as a frontrunner in education.

3. *Assess the impact of CBE curricula and programmes on the market every six months, identify and make improvement to existing programmes and courses, and offer new programmes and courses.* In order to keep CBE's services relevant to Tanzanian students, current programmes have to be regularly assessed on the support they give CBE's graduates in getting a job. If CBE's graduates get jobs sooner than graduates from other colleges or universities, the relevancy of CBE's curricula and programmes for Tanzanian businesses is considered to be good. On the basis of the assessment, current programmes can be improved and new programmes can be developed and offered to students.

4. *Improve teaching and learning continuously.* By continuously improving the quality of the tutors and the teaching and learning facilities (such as classrooms and the library), the added value students receive from CBE will constantly increase.

5. *Upgrade the status of the college by meeting NACTE accreditation criteria by 2006 and achieve NCA level 9 within five years.* As the NACTE accreditation is provisional, it is crucial for CBE to obtain full and permanent accreditation in order to be able to continue offering and developing certain programmes. After the accreditation, higher quality levels have to be obtained, which fits in with the continuous effort to display the college as a centre of excellence.

6. *Sustain and continuously improve the financial position of the college.* A constant threat in Tanzania is the lack of funds to continue operating and improving. The financial situation of the college therefore requires management's dedicated attention.

7. *Rationalise and maintain all college resources.* Because of the rapid growth in student enrolment, the college's resources have become fragmented

and unevenly divided over the two campuses. The resources therefore need to be identified, redivided and monitored.

8. *Develop new skills in project proposal write-up for 80 per cent of academic staff within five years.* Funds for each new training or programme have to be authorised by the Ministry of Trade or attracted from sponsors, and consequently have to be backed up by a clear and convincing project proposal.

9. *Strengthen and enhance inter-campus communication.* Because of the great physical distance between the two current campuses, and future campuses (see objective 1), and because of unreliable internet facilities, dedicated attention has to be paid to increasing the quality of communication. This is important to create a sense of belonging to CBE, to solicit ideas, and increase the sharing of knowledge in order to improve the quality of operations of the college as a whole.

10. *Increase student enrolment through strengthening and enhancing marketing and public relations.* As competition from other institutions of higher learning and of universities is increasing, the quality and offerings of CBE have to be marketed to potential students and sponsors in an efficient and effective manner.

11. *Strengthen and promote Dodoma campus and make it more financially accountable.* The growth of the Dodoma location has not been as rapid as people expected, though the potential is certainly present in the market. Therefore the facilities of the Dodoma campus have to be better promoted in order to ensue that the location is viable.

12. *Promote training, research, and consultancy on entrepreneurship and small business management.* The growing needs of Tanzanian small and medium-sized businesses and the many start-up companies increase the demand for dedicated programmes.

The second activity to improve CBE's performance information consisted of developing tangible CSFs and KPIs for the strategic objectives, in order to make it possible for the management team to monitor the execution of the objectives. Again the four groups of managers set to work: they took a subset of the strategic objectives and developed measurements for these, which were subsequently presented during a plenary meeting to reach consensus. Further details of two of these strategic objectives are given below.

Objective 3: Assess impact of CBE curricula and programmes on the market every six months, identify and make improvement to existing programmes and courses, and offer new programmes and courses.

Result-CSF$_A$: Graduate attractiveness
KPI$_1$: Graduate employability
KPI$_2$: Graduate admission in higher learning and professional exams
Result-CSF$_B$: Good fit curricula – labour market
KPI$_1$: Positive responses from stakeholders (employers and students)

KPI_2: Student enrolment
Result-CSF_C: Enhanced college image
KPI_1: Positive responses to college image

This objective has several results. First of all, relevant programmes which match the needs of the Tanzanian market will increase the attractiveness of CBE's graduates for Tanzanian employers and higher learning institutions. The "absorption" of these graduates in the job market and the admission to higher learning programmes will be swifter and more complete than that of graduates of other institutions. It is important that both employers and potential students acknowledge the good fit between CBE's programmes and labour market demands and that CBE is actually seen in the country as a high-quality college that is a frontrunner in the education field. This will result in increased student enrolment.

Effort-CSF_D: Improved programmes offered
KPI_1: Increased enrolment in improved programmes
Effort-CSF_E: New programmes offered
KPI_1: Enrolment in new programmes
Effort-CSF_F: Mobilised financial, human and physical resources
KPI_1: Budgetary space for new and improved programmes
KPI_2: Student/tutor ratio
KPI_3: Number of classrooms available

As a result of the six-monthly assessment, current programmes may have to be improved to create a better match with labour market and educational demands and new programmes may have to be offered to CBE's students. In order to successfully adapt CBE's offerings, the facilities and budgetary space have to be present and put into effective use, for instance by reducing the student/tutor ratio (so students will receive more personal attention from the teacher).

Objective 4: Teaching and learning continuously improved.

Result-CSF_A: Increased efficiency and effectiveness of teaching
KPI_1: Increased competitive edge
KPI_2: Student enrolment
KPI_3: College image
Result-CSF_B: Improved student performance
KPI_1: Student pass rate

This objective has two results: better teaching and better learning. A better absorption of CBE's graduates in the job market is a good indication that CBE's students have received higher-quality teaching and are therefore more knowledgeable and qualified. This enhances the image and reputation of CBE, which subsequently results in increased student enrolment. A good indication that the learning capabilities of the students has improved is noticeable in their improved performance, which manifests itself in a higher pass rate on exams.

Effort-CSF$_C$: Improved tutor quality
KPI$_1$: Student satisfaction with tutors
KPI$_2$: Tutor quality evaluation
KPI$_3$: Academic staff competence level

In order to improve the quality of teaching, the quality of CBE's tutors has to be increased. This can be measured by asking the students their opinion about the quality of their teachers, and by making an objective evaluation (e.g. requiring the teachers to obtain higher qualifications and diplomas) and a subjective evaluation (e.g. by letting other teachers sit in during classes for evaluation purposes) of the tutors' competence.

Effort-CSF$_D$: Improved quality of teaching facilities
KPI$_1$: Student complaints about facilities
Effort-CSF$_E$: Improved teaching and learning environment
KPI$_1$: Use of teaching and learning facilities and tools

Another important effort is to improve the teaching facilities by, for instance, offering better equipment and learning tools and monitoring their use. This should reduce students' complaints with regard to the quality of these facilities.

Through the development of the second strategic corporate plan and the performance management workshop, CBE has set its first promising steps on the way to a strategic performance management system. Additional steps have to be taken in the form of:

- finalising the development of the CSFs and KPIs
- choosing the indicators with which the college wants to start working in the coming year
- translating these to lower levels in the organisation
- making sure the indicators are measured and reported monthly
- regularly discussing them to base action on them.

Additionally, several follow-on activities were identified during the workshop, such as discussing and determining the responsibility structure of the college, which includes a discussion on whether individual managers merely represent their department in the management team meetings or are accountable for the overall result of CBE; and identifying better communication structures, which includes discussing the nature of a continuous dialogue.

The recent history of improvements in Tanzania's public sector has shown mixed results. There have been many steps forward but overall reform progress seems to be slow. A possible explanation for this is that Tanzania's public sector has been cautious and gradual in implementing reform, and has not dealt with all the blind spots and difficulties in the reform process (Clarke and Wood, 2001; Ronsholt and Andrews, 2005). CBE's management team is confident that through performance management the reform at the college will be pushed forward considerably, and that the organisation is ready for the challenges ahead.

Key points

☑ Developing countries are starting to realise that performance management can be important for improving the execution of development policies that aim to reduce poverty.

☑ Developing countries are not as homogeneous as developed countries, and therefore a technique such as performance management should be tailored to local circumstances, and should be particularly tailored to local culture.

☑ The increased interest in performance management, and specifically the balanced scorecard, is an indication that this is one of the concepts that is suitable for both public and private organisations in developing countries.

☑ For the advancement of emerging countries it is essential that organisations in the developing world take advantage of experiences of organisations in the developed world with performance management.

References

Abdel Aziz, A.E., Dixon, R. and Ragheb, M.A. (2005) *The Contemporary Performance Measurement Techniques in Egypt: A contingency approach.* Paper presented during the EDHEC conference, Nice, September.

Akbar, Y.H. and Samii, M. (2005) Emerging markets and international business: a research agenda. *Thunderbird International Business Review*, 47 (4), 389–96.

Anand, S. (2005) *Challenges in Implementing the Balanced Scorecard in India/Asia.* Presentation on www.cedar.com

Anand, M., Sahay, B.S. and Saha, S. (2005) Balanced scorecard in Indian companies. *Journal of Decision Makers*, 30 (2), 11–25.

Anderson, S.W. and Lanen, W.N. (1999) Economic transition, strategy and the evolution of management accounting practices: the case of India. *Accounting, Organisations and Society*, 24 (5&6), 379–412.

Aycan, Z. (2002) Leadership and teamwork in developing countries: challenges and opportunities. In: W.J. Lonner, D.L. Dinnel, S.A. Hayes and D.N. Sattler (eds), *Online Readings in Psychology and Culture*, unit 5, chapter 8. Bellingham: Washington Center for cross-cultural research, Western Washington University.

CBE (2000) *Strategic Corporate Plan 2000/01–2004/05*. Dar Es Salaam: College of Business Administration.

CBE (2003) *Facts and Figures*. Dar Es Salaam: College of Business Administration, October.

CBE (2005) *CBE Strategic Corporate Plan for 2005/06–2009/10*. Dar Es Salaam: College of Business Administration.

Clarke, J. and Wood, D. (2001) New public management and development: the case of public service reform in Tanzania and Uganda. In: W. McCourt and M. Minogue (eds), *The Internationalization of Public Management: Reinventing the third world state*. Cheltenham: Edward Elgar.

Creelman, J. and Makhijani, N. (2005) *Mastering Business in Asia: Succeeding with the balanced scorecard*. Singapore: Wiley Asia.

Daniels, J.D., Radebaugh, L.H. and Sullivan, D.P. (2004) *International Business*, 10th edn. Upper Saddle River, NJ: Pearson Education.

Farashahi, M. and Molz, R. (2004) A framework for multilevel organisational analysis in developing countries. *International Journal of Commerce and Management*, 14 (1), 59–78.

Farashahi, M., Hafso, T. and Molz, R. (2005) Institutionalized norms of conducting research and social realities: a research synthesis of empirical works from 1983 to 2002. *International Journal of Management Review*, 7 (1), 1–24.

Hartog, D.N., House, R.J. and Hanges, P.J. (1999) Culture specific and cross culturally generalizable implicit leadership theories: are attributes of charismatic/transformational leadership universally endorsed? *Leadership Quarterly*, 10 (2), 219–56.

Hofstede, G. (2001) *Culture's Consequences: Comparing values, behaviors, institutions and organisations across nations*, 2nd edn. Thousand Oaks, Calif.: Sage.

Hofstede, G.J., Pedersen, P. and Hofstede, G. (2002) *Exploring Culture: Exercises, stories and synthetic cultures*. Yarmouth, Maine: Intercultural Press.

Hopper, T., Wickramasinghe, D., Tsamenyi, M. and Uddin, S. (2003) The state they're in, *Financial Management*, June, 16–19.

Joshi, P.L. (2001) The international diffusion of new management accounting practices: the case of India. *Journal of International Accounting, Auditing and Taxation*, 10 (1), 85–109.

Kaufmann, D. (1999) *Governance Matters*. Policy research working paper 2196, Washington DC: World Bank.

Kanungo, R.N. and Jaeger, A.M. (eds) (1990) *Managing in Developing Countries*. London: Routledge.

Kedia, B.L. and Bhagat, R.S. (1988) Cultural constraints on transfer of technology across nations: implications for research in international and comparative management. *Academy of Management Review*, 3 (4), 559–71.

Khoza, R.J. and Adam, M. (2005) *The Power of Governance: Enhancing the performance of state-owned enterprises*. Hyde Park/Rivonia: Pan Macmillan and Business in Africa.

Malinga, G. (2004) *Current State and Future Developments of Performance Management in Kenya*. Paper, Maastricht School of Management.

McCourt, W. (2002) New public management in developing countries. In: K. McLaughlin, S. Osborne and E. Ferlie (eds), *New Public Management: Current trends and future prospects*. London: Routledge.

Mendonca, M. and Kanungo, R.N. (1996) Impact of culture on performance management in developing countries. *International Journal of Manpower*, 17 (4/5), 65–75.

Monteiro, J.O. (2002) *Public Administration and Management Innovation in Developing Countries: Institutional and organisational restructuring of the civil service in developing countries*. Working paper, Maputo.

Motswiane, M. (2004) *Current State and Future Developments of Performance Management in South Africa*. Paper, Maastricht School of Management.

Mwita, J.I. (2000) Performance management model, a systems-based approach to public service quality. *International Journal of Public Sector Management*, 13 (1), 19–37.

National Geographic (2005). *Africa In Fact: A continent's numbers tell its story*, September.

Nhemachena, W.Z. (2004) *Current State and Future Developments of Performance Management in Zimbabwe*. Paper, Maastricht School of Management.

Pacek, N. and Thorniley, D. (2004) *Emerging Markets: Lessons for business success and the outlook for different markets*. London: Economist Publications.

Pandey, I.M. (2005) Balanced scorecard: myth and reality, *Vikalpa*, 30, 1, 51–66

Piercy, N.F., Low, G.S. and Cravens, D.W. (2004) Examining the effectiveness of sales management control practices in developing countries. *Journal of World Business*, 39, 255–67.

Polidano, C. (1999) *The New Public Management in Developing Countries*. IDPM Public Policy and Management working paper no. 13, November.

Ronsholt, F.E. and M. Andrews (2005) Getting it together ... or not: An analysis of the early period of Tanzania's move towards adopting performance management systems. *International Journal of Public Administration*, 28, 313–36.

Schacter, M. (2002) *Public Sector Reform in Developing Countries: Issues, lessons and future directions*. Ottawa: Institute on Governance, www.iog.ca.

Stede, W.A. van der (2003) The effect of national culture on management control and incentive system design in multi-business firms: evidence of intracorporate isomorphism. *European Accounting Review*, 12 (2), 263–85.

Tessema, A.M. (2005) *Performance Management Tools: Is the balanced scorecard applicable in public enterprises in Ethiopia?* Thesis, Maastricht School of Management.

Trompenaars, F. and Woolliams, P. (2003) *Business Across Cultures*. Chichester: Capstone.

Waal, A.A. de (2006) The Role of Behavioural Factors and National Cultures in Creating Effective Performance Management Systems. *Systemic Practice and Action*, 19, 1.

Waal, A.A. de and Augustin, B. (2005) *Is the Balanced Scorecard Applicable in Burkina Faso's State-Owned Companies?* Paper for EDHEC conference, Nice, September.

Waweru, N.M., Hoque, Z. and Uliana, E. (2004) Management accounting change in South Africa, case studies from retail services. *Accounting, Auditing and Accountability Journal*, 17 (5), 675–704.

Xiaoming, L. (2005) *Performance Management in China*. Paper, Maastricht School of Management.

Zagersek, H., Jaklic, M. and Stough, M.J. (2004) Comparing leadership practices between the United States, Nigeria, and Slovenia: does culture matter? *International Journal of Cross Cultural Management*, 11 (2), 16–34.

Appendix

Performance management analysis questionnaire

This appendix lists the criteria of the performance management analysis for each dimension. For research purposes, the detailed PMA questionnaire can be obtained from the author (www.andredewaal.nl).

Structural dimension: Responsibility structure of the organisation		
Criteria	Unclear and inconsistent (1 - 5)	Clear and consistent (6 - 10)
Parenting style	Not clear	Clear
Tasks and responsibilities	Not clear	Clear
Guidelines for planning and targets	None	Strategic
Application of parenting style	Inconsistent	Consistent

Structural dimension: Content of the performance information		
Criteria	Low-quality information (1 - 5)	High-quality information (6 - 10)
Balance of information	Financial	Financial and non-financial
Strategic focus through CSFs and KPIs	Lacking	In place
Strategic alignment in the company	Hardly	Structured
Targets	Incremental and fixed	Ambitious and relative
Ranking between organisational units	Not applied	Applied

Structural dimension: Integrity of the performance information		
Criteria	Low-quality information (1 - 5)	High-quality information (6 - 10)
Reliability of information	Low	High
Inventory of user needs	Ad hoc	Regularly
Information on time	No	Yes
Consistency between data elements	Low	High
Standardisation of data elements	Limited or not	For relevant elements

Structural dimension: Manageability of the performance information		
Criteria	Difficult to access (1 - 5)	User-friendly (6 - 10)
User-friendliness of information	Low	High
Volume of information	Large	Limited
Exception reporting	Not used	Used
Accessibility of underlying data	Low	High
Tools for information presentation	Stand-alone	Integrated

Behavioural dimension: Accountability		
Criteria	Discouraged (1 - 5)	Fostered and stimulated (6 - 10)
Relevance of information to users	Low	High
Managers usage of KPIs	Limited	Continuously
Influence on KPI results	Low	High
Commitment to results	Low	High
User involvement in changing KPIs	No involvement	High involvement

Behavioural dimension: Management style		
Criteria	Distant (1 - 5)	Committed (6 - 10)
Commitment to results	Not visible	Very visible
Managers' interest in employees' results	Limited	Continuously
Type of organisational culture	Settling accounts	Continuous improvement
Coaching by management	Limited	Frequent
Consistency in management behaviour	Low	High

Behavioural dimension: Action-orientation of the organisation		
Criteria	Inactive (1 - 5)	Pro-active (6 - 10)
Analysis of results	Limited	Frequent
Daily use of performance information	Limited	Continuously
Corrective action taken	Limited	Always
Prognosis made	Limited	Frequent
Decision-making based on information	Limited	Always

Behavioural dimension: Communication about performance		
Criteria	Ad hoc (1 - 5)	Open and continuously (6 - 10)
Top-down communication about results	Limited	Frequent
Bottom-up communication about results	Limited	Frequent
Communication structure in place	Closed	Open
Knowledge sharing between units	Limited	Frequent
Strategy formulation together with units	Limited	Always

Alignment		
Criteria	Stand-alone systems (1 - 5)	Aligned systems (6 - 10)
Evaluation system linked with PMS	No	Yes
Reward system linked with PMS	No	Yes
Training system linked with PMS	No	Yes
Improved results through the PMS	No	Yes
Attitude of people towards performance management	Negative	Positive

Index

THE AUTHOR

André ... de ... ...
management ... Ma... ...nd
guest lecturer ... management ... ... courses
of the University of Amsterdam and Erasmus University Rotterdam, and the
masters course at Free University Amsterdam. In addition, he works as an
independent consultant. André holds a MSc in chemistry from Leiden
University, a MBA from Northeastern University, Boston (USA) and a PhD
in economics from Vrije Universiteit Amsterdam. His PhD thesis was on the
topic of the role of behavioural aspects in the successful implementation and
use of performance management systems. André was selected by
www.managementboek.nl as one of the ten 'Hollandse Meesters in
Management': Dutch experts who have influenced Dutch management
thinking the most in the last decade.

André has been a consultant and partner with Arthur Andersen and
Holland Consulting Group for 17 years, before becoming an independent
consultant in 2002. As such, he focuses on performance management projects,
on improving production, logistic, financial and management reporting
processes, and on performing benchmark studies.

André has published over 140 articles and 19 books, including *Power of
Performance Management: How leading companies create sustained value* (Wiley,
2001), *Presteren is Mensenwerk* (Kluwer, 2001), *Minder is Meer: Competitief
voordeel door beyond budgeting* (Holland Business Press, 2002), *Quest for
Balance: The human element in performance management systems* (Wiley, 2002),
Management Rages: 35 managementconcepten ontrafeld (Kluwer, 2002), *Ontwikkelingen en Trends in de Financiële Functie* (Kluwer, 2003), *Prestatiegericht
Gedrag* (Kluwer, 2003), *Beyond Budgeting, het praktische alternatief voor budgetteren* (Kluwer, 2004), *De resultaatgerichte overheid* (SDU, 2004), and *Van
budgetteren naar sturen* (Bohn Stafleu van Loghum, 2005).

André can be reached via www.andredewaal.nl

Praise for de Waal: *Strategic Performance Management*

'The insights, examples, and evidence offered in *Strategic Performance Management* are invaluable for managers who are struggling to help their companies compete in this era of extreme competition. In this text, de Waal has integrated relevant technical and behavioural materials and presented them in an easily accessible way.' – Dr Kenneth A. Merchant, Deloitte & Touche LLP Chair of Accountancy, Marshall School of Business, University of Southern California, USA

'A worthy addition to our knowledge of strategy approaches. This new work by de Waal combines traditional approaches such as the formality of the planning cycle along with the more current focus on individual performance and its contribution to organisational success. All of this is suitably set within an operational environment that includes both the public and private sectors.' – Bill Ryan, Lecturer in Accounting and Deputy Director, Distance Learning MBA, School of Management, Royal Holloway, University of London, UK

'This is a well researched yet accessible text that connects strategy formulation with the tools of strategy reporting, issues of organisational behaviour, and key questions of implementation. I liked the clear presentation and the use of case studies and exercises for reflective learning throughout.' – Professor Thomas Ahrens, Professor of Accounting, Warwick Business School, UK

'The author has managed to adopt an innovative approach which helps to enrich the arguments and the reasoning, and he has brought up a good and extensive academic literature on strategy and planning issues to support the development of his models and enhance the discussion. The book is very well supported with many charts, diagrams, appendices and case studies to support the discussion and the argument. The inclusion of the developing countries in this topic area of strategy and planning is very interesting.' – Professor Kadim Al-Shaghana, TQM & Excellence, Faculty of Organisation & Management, Sheffield Hallam University, UK

'This new book on strategic performance management fills in a void in the literature. Contemporary commercial and non-profit organizations are increasingly searching for ways in which they can improve their performance. In practice, most attention is normally given to the introduction of new "systems hardware", like IT-solutions, advanced performance indicators and accounting systems. André de Waal combines the systems hardware with the "social software" of people in organizations. This combination gives the reader a better understanding of under what conditions strategic performance management systems may become successful. Although this book is based on the academic literature, it is in no way "theoretical": de Waal has been very successful in translating theoretical concepts into practical solutions, bringing the reader back to the common business themes like planning, forecasting, budgeting and the use of information technology.' – Prof Dr Tom L.C.M. Groot, Professor of Economics and Chairman in Accounting Department, Vrije Universiteit, the Netherlands